CONSUMER BEHAVIOUR

CONSUMER BEHAVIOUR

Munish Vohra

ANMOL PUBLICATIONS PVT. LTD.
NEW DELHI - 110 002 (INDIA)

ANMOL PUBLICATIONS PVT. LTD.
H.O.: 4374/4B, Ansari Road, Darya Ganj,
New Delhi-110 002 (India)
Ph.: 23278000, 23261597

B.O.: No. 1015, Ist Main Road, BSK IIIrd Stage
IIIrd Phase, IIIrd Block,
Bangalore - 560 085 (India)
Visit us at: www.anmolpublications.com

Consumer Behaviour

First Published, 2006

ISBN 81-261-2871-2

[Responsibility for the facts stated, opinions expressed, conclusions reached and plagiarism, if any, in this book is entirely that of the Author. The Publishers bear no responsibility for them, whatsoever.]

PRINTED IN INDIA

Printed at Mehra Offset Press, Delhi.

Contents

Preface

"Consumer Behaviour" as a paper is being taught at M.B.A., B.B.A. and other Management Courses at various universities and institutions. This book is designed as an introductory text to the above paper, encompassing vital information on all pertinent aspects. Thus the material presented here would be of interest as well as of great use to the students, teachers and professionals of Management Courses This book will provide complete knowledge of consumer behaviour, marketing strategy, information search strategy, market segmentation, advertising, consumer motivation, consumer choice, perception and information process, communication strategy, consumer attitudes, buying behaviour, diffusion of innovation, leadership, family decision making, consumer protection and other behaviour studies in India, etc. to the students.

The major topics dealt in this book are—Introduction to Consumer Behaviour; Consumer Behaviour and Marketing Strategy; Consumer Involvement and Decision Making; Information Search Strategy and Market Segmentation; Consumer Behaviour and Advertising; Consumer Motivation; Problems of Advertising and Consumer Choice; Consumer Perception and Information Processing; Communication Strategy; Consumer Attitudes and Attitude Change; Personality and Buying Behaviour; Diffusion of Innovation; Opinion Leadership; Family Decision Making; Consumer Attitudes and Purchasing Behaviour; Consumer Protection; Consumer Behaviour Studies in India; Consumer Orientation etc.

It is hoped that all those will benefit from the contents of this book for whom it is meant. The author will feel amply rewarded, if motive is achieved.

Editor

1

Introduction to Consumer Behaviour

The term consumer behaviour refers to the behaviour that consumers display in searching for purchasing, using, evaluating and disposing of products and services that they expect will satisfy their needs. The study of consumer behaviour is the study of how individuals make decisions to spend their available resources on consumption related items. It includes the study of what they buy, why they buy it, from when they buy it, how often they buy it, where they buy it, and how often they use it. Take a simple product toothpaste. What types of toothpastes do consumers buy (gel, regular, stripped in a tube, with a pump); what brand (national brand, private brand, generic); why do they buy it (to prevent cavities, to remove stains, to brighten or whiten teeth, as a mouthwash to attract romance); where do they buy it (supermarket, drugstore, convenience store); how often do they use it (when they wake up, after each meal, when they go to bed, or any combination thereof); how often do they buy it (weekly, biweekly, monthly)? Or, consider a more durable product, the fax machine. What kinds of consumers buy fax machines for home use? What features do they look for? What benefits do they seek? What lines of documents do they fax? For what reasons? How likely are they to replace their old models when new models with added features become available? The answers to these questions can be found through consumer research and provide Fax manufacturers with important input for product scheduling design modification and promotional strategy.

How and why consumers make decisions to buy good services, consumer behaviour research goes far beyond these facets of consumer behaviour and considers the uses consumers make of the goods they buy and their subsequent evaluations. For example, a couple may experience disssatisfaction with their choice of an automobile, perhaps because of continuing service problems. They may communicate their dissatisfaction to friends, and in turn influence their friends' future automobile purchases. Or, they may vow never to buy the same make or model again, prescribing their own future selection decisions. Each of these possible consequences of consumer post purchase dissatisfaction has significant ramifications for automobile marketeers; who have to build post purchase strategies into their promotional campaigns.

In addition to studying consumers uses and postpurchases evaluations of the products they buy, consumer researchers also are interested in how individuals dispose of their once new purchases. For example, after consumers have used a product do they store it, throw it or give it away, sell it, rent it or lend it out? The answers of these questions are important to marketeers because they must match their production to the frequency with which consumers buy replacements. But it is also important to society as a whole because solid waste disposal has become a major environmental problem that marketeers, must address in their development of new products and packaging.

Personal Consumers Versus Organisational Consumer

The term consumer is often used to describe two different kinds of consuming entitie the personal consumer and the organizational consumer. The personal consumer buys goods and services for his or her own use *e.g.*, shaving cream or shampoo, for the use of the household (a VCR) or as a gift for a friend (a book). In each of these contexts the goods are bought for final use by individuals, who are referred to as "end users" or "ultimate consumers."

The second category of consumer, the organizational consumer, encompasses for profit and non-profit business, government agencies (local, state and national), and institutions (*e.g.*, schools, hospital prisons) all of which must buy products, equipments, and services in order to run their organizations. Manufacturing companies must buy the raw materials and other components needed to manufacture and sell their own products; service companies must buy the equipments necessary to render the services they sell, government agencies must buy the office products needed to operate their agencies, and institutions must buy the materials they need to maintain themselves and their populations.

Despite the importance of both categories of consumers—individuals and organizations—this book in focus on the individual consumers, who purchases for his other own personal use or for household use. End use consumption is perhaps the most pervasive of all types of consumers behaviour, for it involves every individual of every age background, in the role of either buyer, or user or both.

Why we study 'Consumer Behaviour'?

Just as consumers and marketeers are diverse, the reasons why people study consumer behaviour are also diverse. The field of consumer behaviour holds great interest for us as consumers, as marketeers, and as scholars of human, behaviour. As consumers, we benefit for insights into our own consumption related decisions. What we buy, why we buy, how we buy, and the promotional influences that persuade us to buy. The study of consumer behaviour enables us to become better—that is wiser consumers.

As marketeers and future marketeers, it is important for us to recognize why and how individuals make their consumption decisions so that we can have better strategic marketing decisions. If marketeers understand consumer behaviour, they are able to predict how consumers are likely to react to various informational and environmental uses and are able to shape their marketing strategies accordingly. Without doubt, marketeers who understand consumer behaviour have great competitive advantage in the market place.

As scholars of human behaviour, we are concerned with understanding consumer behaviour, with gaining insights into why individuals act in a certain consumption-related ways and with learning what internal and external influences impel them to act as they do. Indeed, the desire for understanding consumption-related human behaviour has led to a diversity of theoretical approaches to its study.

Consumer behaviour was a relatively new field of study in the mid to late 1960s. With no history or body of research of its own, the new discipline borrowed heavily from concepts developed in other scientific disciplines, such as psychology (the study of the individual), sociology (the study of groups), social psychology (the study of how an individual operates in groups), anthropology (the influence of society on the individual and economies). Many early-theories concerning consumer behaviour were based on economic theory on the motion that individuals act rationally to maximize their benefits (satisfaction) in the purchase of goods and services.

The initial thrust of consumers research was from a managerial perspective; marketing managers wanted to know the specific causes of consumers behaviour. They also wanted to knowhow people receive, store and use consumption-related information, so that they could design marketing strategies to influence consumption decisions. They regarded the consumer behaviour discipline as an applied marketing science; if they could predict consumer behaviour, they could influence it. This approach has come to be known as positivism, and consumer researchers primarily concerned with predicting consumers behaviour are known positivists.

Given the interdisciplinary background in which the consumer behaviour discipline is rooted, it is not surprising that academicians from a variety of contributing disciplincs, including marketing itself, give become interested in the study of consumer behaviour, not necessarily from a managerial or applied perspective, but simply to understand the consumer better. The study of consumer behaviour from the point of view of understanding consumption behaviour and the meanings behind such behaviour is called interpretivism. (sometimes reforced to as post modernism). Interpretivists have expanded the boundries of study to include many subjective aspects of consumer behaviour, such as the effects of moods and emotions and types of situations on consumer behaviour, the role of fantasy, of play, of rituals, even the sensory pleasures that certain products and services provide. Many interpretivists consider each purchase experience unique because of the diverse set of variables, at play at that one particular moment in time. Because of its focus on the consumption experience, the interpretive approach is also known as experientialism. Despite the apparent diversity of these two major approaches to the study of consumer behaviour, each can be seen to complement the other.

Bristle-Mysers Company hoped to reverse its very mixed trade record in new product introduction with 'Small Miracle'. Its clairoil hair care line was stipping, and it was hoped that this new conditioner would dominate a $ 640 million market., Small Miracle was launched with one of the heaviest advertising barrages in the company's history only to achieve a sales volume that was 30 per cent of expectations, Consumer just did not seem to respond to the product benefit of once or twice weekly hair, conditioning that would last through daily shampooing one after another advertising campaign was rolled out with no apparent impact in persuading the consumer to embrace a Miracle.

From the cited example it is obvious that the understanding of consumer motivation and Behaviour is not an opinion—it is an absolute necessity for competitive survival.

BUYERS AND USERS

The person who makes a product purchase is not always the user, or the only user of the product in question. Nor is the purchaser necessarily the person who makes the product decision. A mother may buy toys for her children (who are the users); she may buy food for dinner (and be one of the users); she may buy a handbag (and be only user). She may buy a magazine that one of her teenagers requested, or rent a video that her husband requested, or she and her husband together may buy a station wagon that they both selected. Clearly, buyers are not always the users, or the only users of the products they buy nor are they necessarily the persons who make the product selection decisions.

Marketeers must decide at whom to direct their promotional efforts; the buyer or the user. For some products, they must identify the person who is most likely to influence the decision. For example, as people live longer, they often depend more and more upon the advice and counsel of their children or other care givers. Should retirement community advertise to the elderly or to their middle-aged children? Should an, emergency response system be targeted to elderly people or to their concerned relatives? Some, marketeers believe, that the buyer of the product is the best prospect, others, believe it is the user of the product, while still others play it safe by directing their promotional efforts to both buyers and users.

Why the Field of Consumer Behaviour Developed?

There are a number of reasons why the study of consumer behaviour developed as a separate marketing discipline. Marketeers had long noted that consumers did not always or react as marketing theory would suggest. The size of the consumer market in this country was vast and constantly, expanding. Billions of dollars were being spent on goods and services by tens of millions of people. Consumer preferences were changing and becoming highly diversified. Even in industrial markets, where needs for goods and services were always more homogeneous than in consumer markets, buyers were exhibiting diversified preferences and less predictable purchase behaviour.

As marketing researchers began to study the buying behaviour of consumers, they soon realized that despite a sometimes, "me too" approach to fads and fashions, many consumers rebelled at using the identical products everyone else used. Instead they preferred differentiated products that they felt reflected their own special needs, personalities and lifestyles.

To better meet the needs of specific growth of consumers, most marketeers adopted a policy of market segmentation, which called for the division of their total potential markets into smaller, homogeneous segments for which they could design specific products and/or, promotional campaigns.

They also used promotional techniques to vary the image of their products so that they would be perceived as better fulfilling the specific needs of certain targets segments—a process now known as positioning. Other reasons for the developing interest in consumer behaviour included the rate of new product development, growth of the consumer movement, public included the rate or new product development, growth of the consumer movement, public policy concerns, environmental concerns and the growth of both non-profit marketing and international marketing.

The swift pace of technological advancement after World War II resulted in the rapid introduction of new products at an ever increasing rate. Many products some experts estimate over 80 per centproved to be marketing disasters: To try to improve the new product success ratetry to ensure consumer acceptance—marketeers made a determined effort to learn everything they could about their prospective consumers (*e.g.* their needs preferences; changing lifestyles). Research into consumer behaviour provided them with the necessary insights to develop new products and services and to design persuasive promotional strategies.

In addition to the fast pace of new product introduction, other factors, contributed to the development of consumer behaviour as a marketing discipline. The growth of the consumer movement created an urgent need to understand how consumers make consumption decisions, *e.g.*, in order to identify sources of consumer confusion and deception consumer advocates, sought to discover how consumers perceive and interpret various marketing and promotional information (*e.g.*, promotional appeals, package, labels, warranties).

Increased public concern regarding the environment made both marketeers and public policy makers aware of the potentially negative impact of such products as aerosol sptays and plastic bottles.

Consumer research revealed a large segment of socially concerned consumers who favour products that have been modified to meet environmental concerns and many marketeers have responded with what has come, to be known as 'green marketing'.

Organizations in the public and private non-profit sectors began to recognize the need to use marketing strategies to bring their services to attention of their relevant publics. To develope persuasive promotional programmes, they realized it was essential to understand their various publics.

Most large companies have long recognized the need to market globally to achieve major economies of scale. In an effort to correct the balance of trade deficit, the Federal government encourages small and mid-sized companies to sell their products abroad. A major stumbling black to many international marketing efforts has been the general lack of familiarity with the needs, preferences and consumption habits of consumers in foregin markets. Marketeers now use cross cultural consumer research studies as the basis for product development and promotional strategies to meet the needs of targeted foreign consumers.

MODEL OF CONSUMER BEHAVIOUR

In earlier times marketeers could understand consumers through the daily experience of selling to them. But the growth in the size of companies and markets has moved many marketing managers from direct contact with the customers. Increasingly, managers have had to rely on consumer research. For answers to the following key questions about any market.

—Who constitutes the market?	Occupants
—What does the market buy?	Objects
—Why does the market buy?	Objectives
—Who participates in the buying?	Organizations
—When does the market buy?	Occasions
—Where does the market buy?	Outlets.

MODEL OF BUYER BEHAVIOUR

Marketing Stimuli

(a) Product

(b) Price

(c) Place

(d) Promotion

Other Stimuli

(a) Economic

(b) Technological

(c) Political

(d) Cultural

Buyer's Characteristics

—Cultural

—Social

—Personal

—Psychological,

Buyer's Decision Process

1. Problem Recognition

2. Information Search

3. Evaluation

4. Decision

5. Post Purchase Behaviour

Buyers decisions

—Product Choice

—Brand Choice

—Dealer Choice

—Purchase Timing

—Purchase Amount

MAJOR FACTORS INFLUENCING BUYING BEHAVIOUR

1. Cultural Factors

(a) Culture

(b Sub-culture includes, nationality, religions, racial groups and geographical regions.

(c) Social class.

2. Social Factors

I. Reference Groups

2. Family

3. Roles and Statutes

Consumer Buying Roles. The marketeer needs to know that what people are involved in the buying decision and what role each person plays.

People might play any of several roles in a buying decision:

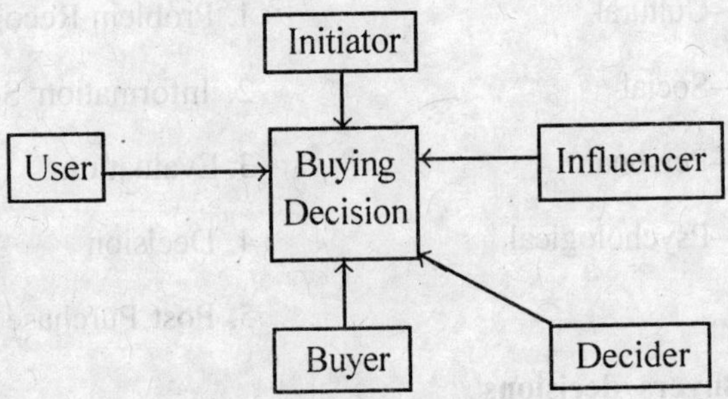

Initiator. The person who first suggests or thinks of the idea of buying a particular product.

Influencer. A person who views or advices influences the buying decision.

Decider. The person who ultimately makes a buying decision.

Buyer. The person who makes actual purchase.

User. The person who consumes or uses a product or service.

TYPES OF BUYING BEHAVIOUR

Complex Buying Behaviour. Consumers undertake complex buying behaviour when they are highly involved in a purchases and perceive significant differences among brands.

Consumer may be highly involved when the product is expensive, risky, purchased infrequently and highly self-expressive.

Dissonance. Reducing Buying Behaviour. It occurs when consumers are highly involved with an expensive or risky purchase, but see little difference among brands.

Habitual Buying Behaviour. It occurs under conditions of low consumer involvement and little significant brand difference. For example—salt.

Complex Buying Behaviour. In this situation the consumer does not know much about the product category and has much to learn. In other words the consumer or buyer will pass through a learning process. This process has been characterised by fast developing beliefs about the product, then attributes, and then making a thoughtful purchase choice.

The marketeer of a high involvement product must understand the information gathering and evaluation behaviour of high involvement consumers. Thus he needs to develop strategies that help the buyer in learning about the attributes of the product class, their relative importance and the high standing of the company's brand on the more important attributes. Under this situation when the buyer faces complex buying behaviour. A marketeer should try to distinguish the brands features and describe the benefits of the brand. In this way the marketeer can influence the buyers in the final brand choice.

Dissonance-Reducing Buying Behaviour. In this case the buyer may respond primarily to a good price or to purchase at convenience. For example, carpet buying is highly involvement decision because it is expensive and self-expressive.

After the purchase, the consumer might experience dissonance that arises from noticing certain disquiting features of the carpet or hearing favourable thin'gs about other carpets.

To counter such dissonance, the marketeers after sale communication should provide evidence and support to help consumers feel good after their brand choice.

Habitual Buying Behaviour. Under this situation, a marketeer should repeat advertisement of such product to create brand familiarity rather than brand conviction, consumers do not form a strong attitude towards a brand but select it because it is familiar. Thus according to Shitip Hofler, after purchase they may not even evaluate the choice because they are not highly, involved with the product. So the buying process is brand beliefs formed by passive learning, followed by purchase behaviour which may be followed by evaluation.

Therefore, marketeers of such product should use instrument like price and sales promotions to stimulate product trial as the buyer are not highly involved or committed to any brand.

Further, it is suggested that marketeers can try to convert the low involvement product into one of higher involvement product. This can be done in two ways. First they should link the product to some involving issues. For example, toothpaste avoiding cavities and secondly by linking the product to some involving personal situation.

Consumer Behaviour Principles and Marketing Strategy

To operate successfully, marketing firms must have a thorough understanding—explicit rather than implicit—of what makes consumers buy. They have to know why they buy, what needs they are trying to fulfill, and what outside influences affect their product choices in order to design marketing strategies that will favourably influence related consumer decisions.

The field of consumer behaviour is rooted in the marketing concept, a marketing strategy that evolved after World War II. When the war was over, marketers found they could sell almost any goods they could produce to consumers who had done without while the nation's manufacturing facilities were dedicated to the production of war materiel. The marketing objective implicit in this production orientation was cheap, efficient production and intensive distribution. A production orientation is a feasible marketing strategy when demand exceeds supply, and when consumers are more interested in obtaining the product than in its specific features. For example, when World War II was over, automobile-hungry consumers sometimes waited six to twelve months for delivery of a new car. When the dealer notified a consumer that a new car was available, the consumer grabbed it, regardless of style, colour, or accessories.

After consumer production had been resumed for a number of years, competition intensified and marketers moved from a production orientation to a product orientation. The assumption underlying the product orientation is that consumers will buy the product which offers them the highest quality, the best performance, and the most features. A product orientation leads the company to constantly strive to improve the quality of its product, with a result often referred to as marketing myopia (that is, a focus on the product rather than on the consumer need it presumes to satisfy). A marketer "in love" with its own product may improve it far beyond its worth to the consumer, passing the cost of unneeded quality or features through to the public. For example, an office equipment manufacturer can make a file cabinet so strong that it will remain intact when dropped from a fourth story window. Its durability may be noteworthy, but the likelihood of having to withstand a four-story drop is not high. On the other hand, given the rough treatment that suitcases receive from airline baggage handling facilities, crash-resistant strength in luggage may realistically fulfill consumer needs.

When the public's appetite for consumer goods had become somewhat stated and consumers began to exercise discrimination in their selection of products, many companies switched to a selling orientation; that is, they changed their primary focus from improving the product to selling the product. During this period, companies exerted a tremendous "hard sell" on consumers in order to move the goods they had unilaterally decided to produce. The implicit assumption in the selling orientation is that consumers are unlikely to buy a product unless they are actively and aggressively persuaded to do so. The problem with the selling orientation is that it does not take consumer satisfactions into account. If a consumer is induced to buy a product that he doesn't want or doesn't need, his unhappiness is likely to be communicated through negative word-of-mouth that is likely to dissuade other potential consumers. The only kinds of goods and services that are possible candidates for a selling orientation are unsought goods, such as life insurance and encyclopedias, and non-profit marketing activities like funa-raising and political campaigns. However, even in these cases, if the product (or service or political candidate) does not fulfill a consumer need, it is unlikely that a repeat purchase (or donation or vote) will be forthcoming.

In the mid-1950s, many marketers began to realize they could sell more goods, more easily, if they produced only those goods they had predetermined that consumers would buy. Instead of trying to persuade customers to buy what the firm had already produced, marketing-oriented firms endeavoured to produce only what they had predetermined consumers were willing to buy. Consumer needs became the firm's primary focus. This consumer-oriented marketing philosophy came to be known as the marketing concept. The key assumption underlying the marketing concept is that to be successful, a company must determine the needs and wants of specific target markets and deliver the desired satisfactions better than the competition.

Product-Oriented Vs Market-Oriented (Definitions of the Firm's Business)

A company that defines itself according to the needs of the market it serves is likely to remain in business long after the product-oriented company has perished. For example, if buggy whip manufacturers had defined their business as fulfilling consumer transportation needs, chances are they would still be in business even if space shuttles were the prevailing mode. They would simply have had to adapt their product lines to the evolving needs of transportation consumers. Companies that focus on need satisfaction rather than product manufacture are likely to survice over the long term, since generic needs tend to remain; only the products needed to satisfy them change. Another example: If Atari had viewed itself as a supplier of family entertainment rather than as a producer of video games, it might still be around today. As it turned out, however, when the video game fad was over, the company went under.

Market Segmentation, Targeting, and Product Positioning

The marketing concept is a philosophy which is reflected in a marketing strategy based on market segmentation, targeting, and product positioning.

Market Segmentation

Market segmentation is the first step in the development of a successful marketing strategy. Consumer behaviour research enable the marketer to identify consumers' needs in relation to the product category, and to group consumers according to these needs or some other relevant characteristic. The resulting market division provides a "map" of the market broken into consume segments.

Selecting Target Markets

After considering the size and potential of each of the segments identified, and further considering the firm's own expertise and objectives, the marketer selects one or more segments as its target market(s). Companies generally do not have the capability to target all potential segments, nor do all segments have the same profit potential.

Product Positioning

The marketer must persuade the selected target markets that its product will satisfy their needs better than competitive products. To do so, the marketer attempts to develop a special image for its product in the consumer's mind relative to competitive products; that is, it tries to position its product as filling a special niche in the marketplace. For example, AT&T, since its breakup, has tried to position itself as far superior to competing phone companies with the line, "The more you hear, the better we sound." Similarly, to reflect consumer interests in natural foods, the Thomas J. Lipton Company has positioned its dry soup mixes as healthy soups "made with no artificial ingredients."

Marketing Strategy Reflects Positioning Strategy

The marketer uses the marketing variables under its control-product, price, promotion, and distribution (*i.e.*, the marketing mix)—

to operationalize its marketing strategy. Thus research into consumer needs enables marketers to segment their markets, to target profitable market segments, and to position their products as a unique way to fulfill identified consumer needs.

FIGURE 1. Knowledge of Consumer Behaviour Facilitates Development of Successful Marketing Strategies.

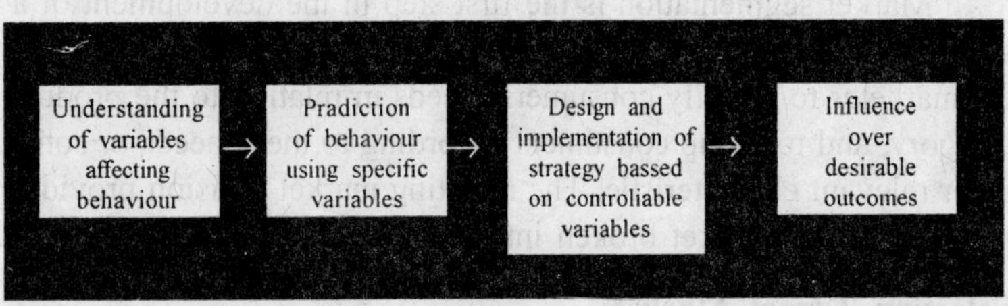

Knowledge and understanding of consumer behaviour principles enables marketers to design effective marketing mixes to operationalize their positioning strategies. As depicted in Figure 1, understanding (and this is true of any human phenomenon) leads to prediction, which in turn leads to the development of strategies designed to achieve favourable outcomes.

ROLE OF CONSUMER BEHAVIOUR IN STRATEGIC PLANNING

Strategic planning is a management approach that stresses organizational adaptability—the adjustment of the firm's objectives, its use of resources, and its operations—to the changing environment. The purpose of strategic planning is to develop a long-range game plan to ensure the company's survival, its profitability, its growth, and its perpetuity. By means of strategic planning, a company can be one that makes things happen (*e.g.*, IBM or Kodak), rather than a company that watches things happen or worse, one that wonders what happened.

A recent survey of chief executive officers and other top executives found that companies are adopting a strategic marketing approach by integrating marketing plans into their firms' overall strategic plans. As the following discussion indicates, consumer behaviour principles are applicable to each step of the strategic market planning process.

Step 1. Define the Firms's Business Domain. Here, consumer behaviour and the marketing concept dictate that definitions of the firm's business domain must be market-oriented (*i.e.*, satisfying consumer needs) rather than product or sales-oriented (satisfying the firm's needs).

Step 2. Environmental Scanning (Opportunites and Threats Analysis). If diagnosed in time, most environmental "threats" can be turned into marketing opportunities. In consumer behaviour terms, a company that closely monitors evolving lifestyles and trends can anticipate changing consumer needs and respond promptly with new or revised products or promotional programms to meet those needs.

Step 3. Establish Goals and Objectives. Company objectives should be realistic in terms of its resources—technological, financial, and human. The company should establish objectives consistent with its image in the marketplace. For example, a sales penetration objective to be achieved through a relaxation of quality and a decrease in price would be inappropriate for a company which enjoys a high quality image (*e.g.*, Hewlett-Packard).

Step 4. Analyze the Companys Existing Product Portfolio. Management should determine through sales analyses and consumer research which products still satisfy consumer needs and which are on their way out (*i.e.*, where each product stands in terms of its product life cycle).

Step 5. Develop a New Business Plan. In consumer behaviour terms, management should develop plans for new product concepts that correspond to changing lifestyles and emerging consumer needs, and should consider modifying or repositioning existing products to better fit changing needs. It should evaluate and select market segments with good profitability and growth potential. Table 1 gives examples of products developed or adapted to meet consumer needs.

Step 6. Develop a Marketing Strategy Congruent with the Firms's Strategic Plan. In consumer behaviour terms, the company should develop a positioning strategy congruent with its objectives and operationalize it through its marketing mix.

Step 7. Measuring Markeing Performance. The company should closely monitor actual consumer behaviour in the marketplace to measure the success or failure of its marketing strategy and modify or change the marketing plan as needed.

As an input to the strategic planning process, consumer behaviour affects marketing strategy; as a measure of marketing performance, consumer behaviour reflects marketing strategy and signals the need for timely adjustment or change.

TABLE 1. Products Developed or Adapted to Meet Consumer Needs

* Medical home test kits meet the needs of the educated, health-oriented consumer.
* Disposable diapers and pre-mixed baby formulas in sterlized, disposable bottles take the drudgery out of infant care.
* Microwave ovens with a browning device bring food to the "color" preferred by users of conventional ovens.
* A phone answering machine with a built-in telephone and radio consumer with minimal bedside table space.
* Television sets with built-in video-cassette recorders save space for apartment dwellers.
* Cordless telephone sets provide convenience for people who wish to speak beyond the confines set by the length of a telephone wire.

❐

2

Consumer Behaviour and Marketing Strategy

The consumer behaviour is a psychological process leading to decision making. The consumer behaviour in decision making is governed by:

(i) Sources of information.

(ii) Role of family members (neighbours friends).

(iii) The role of retailers in the purchase process.

(iv) The price and quality of products.

The role of rural markets for many product is increasing if one looks to the data these are as 75 per cent bicycles and portable radios are sold in rural markets, 60 per cent of table fans, sewing machines and wrist watches were brought in rural India, 72 per cent washing cake (soap) share is of rural markets.

Items	*Year* 1989 to 1992-93	*Percentage*
Black and White T. V.		44% to 47%
CTV's		19% to 31%
Cassette Recorders		42% to 49%
VCP and VCR		5% to 8%
Cold and Vanishing Cream		24% to 26%
Tooth Paste		30% to 38%
Washing Powder		48% to 52%
Edible Oil		65% to 68%
Washing Powder		48% to 52%
Biscuits		46% to 49%
Tea		54% to 5%
Electric Tubes and Bulbs		34% to 39%

APPROACH ROCEDURE FOR CONSUMER BEHAVIOUR

Sample Design. In a research a sample of 2,000 consumers were selected, one thousand each from urban and rural consumers, these were taken from different levels of income groups. Consumer satisfaction is the soul of each producer, every producer should know the consumer requirements. On the basis of consumers wants the manufacturer prepares its strategy, a producer who takes into account its valued consumers preference in mind are in general more successful. Marketing is described as engineering customer satisfaction.

"Marketing concept is a philosophy of business that states that customers want satisfaction, that is, the economic and social justification for a firm's existence. Consequently, all company activities must be devoted to finding out what the customers want and then satisfying those wants while still making a profit over the long run." (Stanton J. William, 1984). The executives must think in terms of what benefits they market—what needs (wants) they are satisfying.

The understanding of consumers has to come invariably from the consumer. The information relating to consumer behaviour has to be necessarily based on an enquity into his purchase process. Each decision made by a consumer to buy a product or brand involves the problem solving process. Through the purchase, a consumer attempts reducing the drives. In the process, the consumer tries to reach maximum satisfaction.

Factors "for Purchasing. "The purchase act by a consumer is governed by various factors such as *(1)* economic, *(2)* social and *(3)* psychological. Consumers are inherently concerned with meeting their needs, with living their lives witil all that implies in. terms of cultural socio-economic and psychological influences." Since the purchase is a process, it is necessary for a marketer to analyse the factors involved in the process. The act of purchasing a product can be very complex. The consumer not only must collect information and determine the selection criteria, but also must make many decisions concerning style, size, colour, retail agent, and the like. "Buyers act like rational people, decide after applying themselves thoughtfully to problems. Only a few decisions are made as a matter of habit and generally buyers have an interest in the social as well as personal effects of their choices."

Sources of Information. In general consumers are not always sure of their preferences, availability of product more often these are based on persuasion. Marketing communication can help shape wants and beliefs. In general marketing analysis the consumer is termed a central processing unit (CPU) as in a computer, which receives, stores, process and delivers the output. In a sense, a consumer is exposed to the information created and transmitted by the marketers into the environment. The transmission (delivery) may be through different media available, such as radio, television, print, fillp, and outdoor. Though there are different media, it is possible that consumers may be receiving information only through one or some of the media, depending on the accessibility to media. It would, therefore, be of interest to study the source from which consumers gather the information relating to product offerings.

A consumer before buying needs information for the following purposes:

(a) Product Awareness. The consumer must be aware of a product before he can buy it. He needs information about the existence or availability of a product or brand, *i.e.* awareness.

(b) Interest in Product. On the assumption that interest is a necessary precondition, considering the fact that consumer needs — information which will give him a reason to become interested in a product. The consumer has three basic types of information sources to which he can turn in order to satisfy his information needs. Firstly, the marketer-dominated sources, which are under the direct control of the marketer, such as the product itself, packaging, promotion through different medical distribution, etc. Secondly, the consumer-dominated sources, *i.e.,* all interpersonal sources of information (family, friends and neighbours). Thirdly, neutral information sources, such as reports and magazines, and newspaper articles about products. (Birmill, 1966). It was revealed in one of the recent studies that "information to the poor generally passes through a zig-zag and a horizontal fashion. Most of our mass media, like television the press/ print/ad., messages, transfer information in a vertical fashion to the rural and urban slums. This moves in a horizontal and non-linear fashion. The information transfer among the poor households takes place through indirect mechanisms like gossip among men in tea and bidi shops and gossip sessions of women when they gather around the village well, pond, bathing ghat or temple.

Findings. The following are the findings of the study:

(i) Variation in Sources of Information has maximum reach in terms of providing information to rural consumers. For urban consumers, the most important source of information is television. Friends and dealers in rural areas and friends and radio in urban areas are the next important sources of information. Comparatively fewer consumers in urban areas gather information from retailers, compared to those in rural areas. It may be due to the exposure an urban consumer has through more media. Another revealing finding of the study is that about one-third of the rural consumers did not draw information from any of the sources listed. They are from lower and middle income groups, while tb,ere is no such case in urban areas. The one similarity between rural and urban consumers, as regards the sources of information, is that a majority of them draw information from friends. This explains the social dimension of consumer behaviour.

(ii) Income-wise Source of Information. An income-wise analysis reveals that for lower income rural consumers, the most important source is the retailer followed by friends, whereas for the same category in urban areas, the important source of information is radio and films. For both middle and higher income groups, in rural areas, radio is the most important source, whereas for those in urban areas television and print are the most important sources. The study thus highlights further differences within different income groups in rural and urban markets.

(iii) Selection of Source of Information. Consumers vary in the types and number of sources of information they consult when they need information for reaching a purchase decision. The nature of information sources, consumers seldom find it necessary to consult the mass media. Often they find it necessary to supplement mass media information with information from sources they consider more complete, or more trustworthy. One of the most important published studies (Katz and Lazarafeld, 1955) in consumer behaviour showed that intetpersonal communication among friends plays a major role in a great many consumer decisions, and thus some consumers,—the "Opinion Leaders"—have a more central role in this process than others. It is well accepted by marketing scholars and managers that non-marketing dominated sources of information are given substantial weight by consumers in forming opinions and making product decisions.

The study enquired about the source which was used most (the source acting as a great influencer) for the putpose of decision making by the consumer. Interestingly, friends and retailers are the major sources of information, in both rural and urban areas, and the consumer relied more on personal sources of information compared to market-dominated sources. The retailer, comparatively, has a greater role to play in rural markets, particularly for convenience products.

Role of Advertisement. It is of importance to study the impact of advertisements released by marketers through mass media. The analysis is not made product-wise. The question asked was whether the consumers had taken the messages from advertisements into consideration in their purchasing process. The responses broadly indicate the perceptions of the consumers towards the reliability of the advertisements. Surprisingly, very few consumers felt that advertisement through mass media have made any impact. Though the primary objective of an advertisement is to increase awareness, it should also induce action on the part of consumers. Then only can the advertisement be said to be truly effective. The study shows that advertisements have been mainly playing the role of increasing awareness, but for the decision-making, consumers appear to have been dependent mostly on their peer groups.

Inter-Personal and Social Influences. No consumer is an island. It implies the consumer's constant and frequent interaction with his immediate neighbours. Consumer behaviour cannot be fully understood unless consideration is given to the effects of inter-personal influence on development of attitudes, norms, values, aspirations and purchase behaviour. Consumer susceptibility to inter-personal influence is defined as the need to identify or enhance one's image with significant others through acquisition and use of products and brands, the will ingness to conform to the expectations of others regarding purchase decision and/or the tendency to warn about products and services by observing others or seeking information from others. One's family is also an inter-personal determinant of consumer behaviour. The influence of household members is often significant iu the purchase decision process.

The selection process of a brand may be primarily decided within the family. Roughly more than fifty per cent of the cases, family members (husband, wife, son and daughter) would select the brand in both rural. and urban areas. Rural consumers are influenced by neighbours in the selection of a brand, which is not that much cited social prestige. It is clear from the data that even in rural areas, higher income consumers are conscious of social prestige. It may thus be inferred that consumers associate brand use with social prestige, a factor to be reckoned with by marketers. This observation would be highly useful in the development of positioning strategies for various brands.

An interesting phenomenon was observed regarding the use of brand. It was found that 70 per cent of the rural consumers used the same brand used by their neighbours, whereas only 20 per cent of the urban consumers did so.

Price Consideration in Buying Process. On an average, for both rural and urban consumers, price is relatively more important in the use of durable products, and less important for non-durables. In one of the studies, it was found that price is the most important economic factor which affects the behavioural pattern of the textile consumer. (Sainin D.R. 1986) In the mral market, price is the most important element in the purchase decision. About 90 per cent of consumers in rural markets have the attitude that price is always important in case of consumer durables. The corresponding figure for the urban market is marginally low at about 80 per cent.

Price-Quality Relationship. There is much evidence that a relationship exists between a product's price and its perceived quality. Strong relationship for perceived product quality and price leads to the propensity to buy generic products. It was reported in a study that, "The findings, in conjunction with those of earlier studies strongly suggest that consumers rely heavily on price as a predictor of quality when there is a substantial degree of uncertainty involved in the purchase decision. (Boring and Gonsior 1964) However, no study has evidence that the price-quality relationship can be generalised to various products with varying prices and consumer purchasing patterns.

Consumers generally perceive a product to be of inferior quality when it is priced low. On the other hand, when a product is priced high, it is observed that the quality of the product is perceived to be very high. There are no meal, urban and income-wise variations found regarding this perception.

Price Increase and Change of Brand. It would be of interest to marketers to find the general attitude of consumers relating to the change of brand on account of price increase. A marketer would be able to analyse and set the pricing strategies for his product. A study on price theory showed during 1970 that "consumers do have ranges of acceptable prices for products they want to purchase. Anything above or below the range is considered unacceptable." Another study revealed that there was no relationship between price consciousness of consumers and income level. The study, however, found an inverse relationship between education and brand loyalty.

The number of consumers changing the brand on account of price increase from the higher income group is low. It implies higher Income consumers are, by and large, less price sensitive. The study fmds that a majority of the higher income consumers in both rural and urban markets are fairly brand loyal. This conclusion is based on the fact that about 50 per cent of consumers in both the markets stated that they never chimged their brand due to price increase. But, in case of durables, it may be emphatically stated that the second purchase may be only to replace the product. That being the case, change of brand, as given by the consumers in the study, may not be a valid result.

Place of Buying. It is equally necessary for a marketer to find out the place where consumers buy their products. The place of buying has important implications to the marketers for designing the distribution network. The type of distribution network varies across products. In a country of the size of India, with a majority of the population living in a large number of wedely dispersed settlements, distribution has a crucial role in meeting the needs of the masses by making goods available in every part of the country. It often provides the key to the development of potentially large markets for various products. The reach of distributive trade varies from product to product. The widest coverage is for soap, tea, foodgrains and edible oil, which are carried by 63 per cent to 81 per cent of all the outlets. In rural India, a much larger proportion of outlets carry items of daily necessity than in urban India, for lack of specialisation in rural areas. However, the reach in urban India is better due to the larger number of retailers (per lakh population) that exist there.

CHANGE IN CONSUMER BEHAVIOUR

The market structure in India is dichotomous comprising rural and urban markets. In spite of the same needs, aspirations, beliefs and attitudes, certain specific characteristic features of rural consumer behaviour call for unique marketing strategies to be distinctively developed.

The sea change one finds in India is that material and multinational companies have started concentrating on rural markets to sell their products with multiple marketing inputs. The rural market's contribution to the total market has gone up from 28 per cent in 1985 to 40 per cent in 1991.

Pressure in the urban market are forcing many to move into rural areas because of some reasons like demand for heavy promotional expenditure due to tough competition, decrease in product life cycle, increase in the awareness level of consumers, etc.

As a result, the rural markets are becoming green pastures for marketers. They are growing faster than the urban markets. The potentialities of the rural market are like a "woken up sleeping giant", and to tap these potentialities or opportunities, marketeers need to have challenging marketing strategies.

However, for exploitation of this market its scattered nature and the changing behavioural patterns of consumers must be recognised and analysed, so that a better platform for the exploitation of the opportunities can be created.

Changing Behaviour of Rural Consumers. The life-style and purchasing patterns of rural consumers are undergoing significant changes. Widespread availability of consumer products in village during the last decade is changing the line and attitude of rural consumers. Exposure of TV and radio has made consumer more aware, which result in composite effect of change in the purchasing patterns and habits of rurual consumers. This change has created a latent opportunity and demand calling for a unique developmental marketing.

The basic changes in the consumer behaviour can be highlighted as:

1. Better Quality of Life. Increase in income and improved awareness level have made villagers seek a better quality of life. This desire has led to significant changes in the market size of consumer products. Rural consumption now covers a variety of items from food to electronic items.

2. Desire for New Products and Fashion Consciousness. The rural consumers are willing to experiment with new products and a variety of brands without any hesitation. TIus makes it easier to get higher trial rates when new products are launched in the villages.

Increase in awareness of new fashions stimulates the demand for textile goods, readymade garments and cosmetics. The market for these products in the rural areas is growing at a much faster pace as compared to other products.

3. No Desire to Save. A new tendency is noticed among rural consumers, they are willing to spend money instead of keeping it. Today, they spend their surplus income on several products like clothes, entertaimnent items, insurance policies, etc.

4. Brand Awareness. Now rural consumers do not ask for just tooth paste or soap, but for specific brand such as 'Close-Up' 'Lux' or other brands. Sharpened brand awareness demands creative advertising and promotional strategies to create brand loyalty.

5. Influence Through Demonstration. Rural consumers have greater faith in a product if they actually see it in use. It is therefore usefid to conduct demonstrations with a new product to strengthen creditability. This type of promotional campaigning hastens consumer adoption.

6. Role of the Retailers. The rural consumer has always relied strongly on the recommendation of rural retailers. This factor can have an impact on the distribution network. The retailer can become a very useful link between the marketer and the rural consumer.

7. Re-designing Product Front. Increased disposable incomes, raised aspirations and improved levels of general awareness have made consumers more demanding. They except value for money. Their aspirations are, in a way, comparable to those of urban consumers. While quality and packaging appeal to him, it will not influence his paying if the product is not perceived to be offering satisfaction at an affordable price.

8. Selection of Target Market for Proper Penetration and Profit. Marketers, necessarily, will have to tap the rural market rigorously in the future. It will be necessary to segment the rural market in a structured manner. Here, identification of clusters must be made on a scientific bases.

Each segment of the rural market has to be judiciously evaluated for its total sales and contribution, after estimating the receptivity of the villagers to a new product, their level of satisfaction with existing products, current level of competition, and possible reactions of competitors.

9. Pricing Strategies. Pricing strategies must be framed keeping in mind the estimated rural market size, perceived value of consumers, target share of the market, and margin expected by retailers and distributors. In spite of the decreasing the role of pricing, as compared to other tools of the marketing mix, it becomes a critical determinant of the fate of the product, its sales volume, and the market of the company.

10. Distribution Strategies. Considering the vastness of the rural market, the main problem is essentially that of distribution. The distribution cost of serving the rural market, tends to be high due to several factors, *viz.* poor communication facilities, less offtake, and high scattered distribution of outlets. Further, in spite of increasing awareness, there is a tendency among rural consumers to buy those products, which are readily available at convenient retail outlets.

In farming distribution strategies, the importance of the retailer and the local staff should be considered. Being local, the dealer can feel the pulse of the market much better.

11. Promotional Measures. The right communication of promotional strategies make the difference between success and failure. Consumer education forms an essential part of brand promotion.

Technological advancement in the field of television has made it a powerful medium to expose products to rural people. In addition to formal organised media, a variety of non-formal media like mobile audio-visual publicity, public meetings, etc., have to be developed to meet the specific requirements of these areas.

Both the media and the advertising messages should be tailored to appeal to rural audiences. Urban aesthetic cannot always strike the right chord with rural consumers. To market a product effectively, we have to get off our high horses and understand rural ways.

In short, unique promotional strategies depend on correct identification of opportunities. Creating vehicles of conunùnication for the local environment and experimenting with new media are essential steps towards reaching out to the unreached rural audience. Some other strategies like proper packaging can also work. In sales management, the company should take the help of local staff to handle the specialised market successfully. Understanding the coonsumer's needs properly is vital.

MARKETING STRATEGY

Sometimes an expert marketeer fails in marketing their product because he commits certain mistakes which are as follows:

Pro.luct Problem

International marketeers frequently neglect to modify their products to meet local customs and tastes. American mark teers, selling food products in Japan, learned the novel way (through poor sales performance) that they must after traditional product characteristics. For example, when Oreos were introduced in Japan, Nabisco reduced the amount of sugar in the cookie better (the box promoted them as having a "bitter twist") to meet Japanese tastes. But some Japanese still considered them too sweet and told the company that they "just wanted to eat the base" without the cream.

Nabisco belatedly introduced new Petit Oreo Non-cream Cookies that consisted of single wafers without the cream. To avoid such problems, marketeers must ascertain in advance whether the 'physical characteristics of their products will be acceptable to the new market.

Colour is also a critical variable in international marketing, because the same colour has different meanings in different cultures. For example consider the colour blue. In Holland, it stands for warmth; in Iran, it represents death; in Sweden, it connotes coldness; in India, it means purity. Or take yellow, which represents warmth in the United States but connotes in fidelity in France. Pepsodent erred when it tried to sell its toothpaste in Sutheast Asia by promising white teeth. In that part of the world, chewing betel nuts is considered an elite habit, and consequently, brownish-red teeth are viewed as a status symbol. Thus Pepsodent's slogan "you'll wonder where the yellow went," did not help to sell the product. It is critical that the colours of products and packages convey the proper meaning in the countries in which they are marketed.

Promotional Problems

When communicating with consumers in different parts of the world, the promotional message must be consistent with the language and customs of the particular society. International marketeers have faced various problems in communicating with widely different customer groups. For example, the Seven-Up Company's highly successful "uncola" theme, developed for the

United States market, was considered inappropriate for many foreign markets because it did not translate well into other languages. Procter & Gamble ran a Camay soap commercial that shaved a Japanese husband in the room while his wife was bathing,. an invasion of privacy that Japanese consumers found distasteful. Sales improved when P & G switched to a more abstract commercial. Product names and promotional phrases can also cause considerable problems for international marketeers. The Chevrolet Nova did not sell well in Latin America because in Spanish the word "nova" means "it does'nt run". GM also blundered with its "body by Fisher" tag line, which in Flemish ranslates into "Corpse by Fisher". Another mistake was Pepsi's come alive with Pepsi "Campaign" which in German literally means "come alive out of the grave."

International direct marketing has increased in recent years. For example, the famed British retailer Harrods invited consumers to participate in a transatlantic shoping spree by means of advertisement in Sunday New York Times that included a toll free 800 number, American direct marketeers who now enter overseas markets are likely to have a computer edge over those who follow in future years,

These firms however, must be aware of the differences in doing business in other countries. For instance, in Japan,direct mail customers not only expect the same liberal return policies as American customers, but also expect the delivery company to arrange a pickup time at their home should they such to return merchandise.

Not every country has the same array of media available to advertisers. Some nations, for example do not permit commercials on their government controlled TV stations. The table given below presents the result of a survey designed to determine the allocations of advertising budget by media for a number of countries, Notice that Denmark and Sweden make-up for the lack of commercials on their broadcast media (because of government regulation) with heavy advertising in maggazines. Finally, to illustrate, the diversity of coding worldwide advertisers.

Table

Allocation of Advertising Budget by Media

Advertising Media	*Frequency of Use*	*Standard Deviation*	*Major Differences*	
			Lowest Percentage	*Highest Percentage*
Television	44%	38	Denmark (0%)	Australia (72%)
			Sweden (0%)	Great Bretain (68%)
			Israel (1%)	US (68%)
Newspaper	19%	26	United States (3%)	Sweden (43%)
			Brazil (4%)	Singapore (41%)
			Denmark (40%)	
Magazine	19%	25	Australia (5%)	Germany (45%)
			Argentina (7%)	Denmark (43%)
			Singapore (6%)	Sweden (38%)
Radio	6%	13	Denmark (0%)	Mexico (17%)
			Sweden (0%)	
			Finland (0%)	

Billboard	5%	10		Israel (18%)
Cinema	1%	5		Israel (11%)
Transit	1%	5		
Other	6%	16	Germany (0%)	Mexico (14%)
			Australia (1%)	Denmark (12%)

Pricing and Distribution Problems. International marketeers must 'adjust their pricing and distributing policies to meet local economic conditions and customs. For instance in many developing nations, small-sized product packages often are a necessity because consumers cannot afford the cash outlay required for the larger sizes popular in the United States and other affiuent countries. Given in developed nations, important differences do exist. For example, supermarkets are very popular in Switzerland, but in France which is just' across the border, consumers prefer smaller and more intimate stores for grocery shopping. Thus marketeers must vary their distribution channels by nation.

List of Top ten ranked non-United States advertisers (*i.e.* in terms of advertising expenditure) and the countries in which they advertise.

Table. Ten Top Ranked Non-United States Advertisers

Rank	Advertiser	Country of Headquarters	Reported Ad Expenditures In
1.	Unilever NV	Holland Great Britain	Argentina, Australia, Austria, Brazil, Britain, Canada, Denmark, France; Germany, Greece, India, Italy, Japan, Malaysia Mexico, Netherlands, Pan Arabıa, Portugal, Puerto, Rico, SA, Spain, Switzerland, Taiwan, Thailand, Turkey, US.
2.	Procter & Gamble	United States	Australia, Austria, Britain, Canada, France, Germany, Greece; India, Italy, Japan,

			Malaysia, Mexico, Netherlands, Pan Arabia, Puerto Rico, Taiwan, Thailand, US.
3.	Nestle SA	Switzerland	Argentina, Australia, Brazil, Britain; France, Germany, India, Japan; Malaysia, Mexico, Netherlands, Pan Arabia, Thailand.
4.	Renault Sa	France	Argentina, Austria, Britain, France, Germany, Italy, Netherlands, Pan Arabia, portugal, Spain, Switzerland, Taiwan, Thailand, US.
5.	Phillip Morris	US	Brazil, Britain, Denmark, Argentina, Denmark, France, Hongkong, Japan.
6.	Fiat SPA	Italy	Brazil, Britain, Denmark, France.
7.	Matsushita Electric Industrial Company	Japan	Brazil; Britain, Hongkong, Japan, Malaysia, pan Arabia, Taiwan, Thailand, US.
8.	PSA Peugot-Criteon SA	France	Argentina, Austria, Britain, Denmark, France, Germany, Netherlands, Pan Arabia, Portgal, Spain, Switzerland, Thailand, US.
9.	Nissan Motor companies	Japan	Australia, Britain, Germany, Japan, Mexico, Pani Arabia, Switzerland, Thailand, US.
10.	Volkwagan AG	Germany	Brazil, Britain, France, Germany, Mexico, SA, Spain, Sweden, Switzerland, Thailand, US.

Source: "UnileverRanked No. 1 in Non-US. Advertising," Advertising Age (Nov. 19, 1990) 94, Reprinted with permission from the November 15, 1990 issue of Advertising Age, Gynzht Crain Communication Inc. 1990.

Gifting Behaviour of a Consumer

In terms of both dollars spent each year and how they make givers and receivers feel, gifts are a particularly interesting part of consumer behaviour. Products and services chosen as gifts represent more than ordinary "everyday" purchase. Because of their symbolic meaning, they are associated with such important events as Mother's day, births and birthdays, engagements, weddings, graduations and many other accomplishments and milestones.

Gifting behaviour has been defined as the process of gift exchange that takes place between voluntarily (*e.g.* "just to let you know I'm thinking of you"), as well gifts that are an obligation (*e.g.* "I had to get home gift"). It includes gifts given to (and received from) others and gifts to oneself, *i.e.*, self gifts.

Still further gifting is an act of symbolic communication,. with explicit and implicit meanings ranging from congratulations, love and regret to obligation and dominance. The nature of the relationship between gift given and gift receivers is an important consideration in choosing a gift.

Five Giver-Receiver Gifting Sub-divisions

	RECEIVERS		
	"OTHER"		
GIVERS	INDIVIDUAL	GROUP	SELF*
Individual	Interpersonal gifting	Intercategory gifting	Intrapersonal gifting
Group	Intercategory gifting	Intergroup gifting	Intergroup gifting

This 'SELF' is either singular self ("me") or plural ("US")

Source: Based on DEBOROH cy COHN, and LEON G. SLHH MAN, "Gifting: A taxomony of Private Realm Giver and Recipient Relationship." Working Paper, City University of New York, Branch College, 1996,2-7.

The above table presents a model of the relationships between various combinations of gift givers and gift receivers in the consumer gifting process. The model reveals the following five gifting sub-divisions: *(1)* Intergroup gifting, *(2)* Intercategory gifting, *(3)* Intragroup gifting, *(4)* Interpersonal gifting; and *(5)* Intrapersonal gifting.

Intergroup gifting behaviour occurs whenever one group exchanges gift with another group (*e.g.* one family and another). Gifts given to families will be different than those given to individual family members. For example, a "common" wedding gift for a bride and a groom may include products for setting up a hausehold, rather than a gift that would personally be used by either the bride or the groom. When it comes to intercategory gifting either an individual is giving a gift to a group (*e.g.* a single friend is giving a couple an anniversary gift) or a group is giving an individual a gift' (*e.g,* friends chip in and give another friend a joint birthday giftf The gift selection strategies "Buy for joint recipients" or "Buy with someone" (creating intercategory gifting) are especially useful when it comes to a difficult recipient-situation (*e.g.* "Nothing seems to satisfy her)". These strategies can also be applied to reduce some of the time pressure associated with shopping for the great many gifts exchanged during the American Christmas season gift-giving ritual. For example, a gifts consumer may choose to purchase five intercategory gifts for five aunts and uncles (intercategory gifting), instead of buying ten personal gifts for five aunts and five uncles interpersonal gifting). In this way, less time, a money, and effort may be expended.

An Intragroup gift can be characterised by the sentiment "we gave this to ourselves", that is, a group gives a gift to itself or its members. For example, a dual income couple and wife. Therefore, an anniversary gift ("to use") of a "gateway weekend" would be an example of Intragroup gift.

It would also remedy the couple's problem of not spending enough time together. In contrast, interpersonal gifting occurs between just two individuals, a gift given and gift receiver. By their very nature, Interpersonal gifts are "Intimate" because they provide an opportunity for a gift-giver to reveal what he/she thinks of the gift receiver. Successful gifts are those which communicate that the giver knows and understands the receiver, and their relationship. For example, a sweater given to a friend in just the right colour and size can be viewed as "She really knows me." In contrast, a clock radio given as a Valentine's Day gift, when the recipient is expecting a more "intimate" gift can mean a detereoration of relationship. Still further, researchers that have explored the gender of gift-givers and their feeling about same sex gifting (*i.e.* female to female or male to male) and opposite sex gifting (*i.e.* mate to female or female to male) have found that both male and female gift givers feel more comfortable in giving gifts to the same sex. However, they also reported that they felt more intense feeling with respect to gifts given to members of the opposite sex. Knowledge of such gender differences are useful for marketeers to know, because they imply that additional support might be appreciated at the print of purchase (*e.g.* while in a store) when a consumer is considering a gift for an opposite sex recipient.

Intrapersonal gifting or a self-gift (also called "monadic giving") occurs when the giver and the receiver are the same individual. To some extent a self gift is a "state of mind". If a consumer sees a purchase as the "buying of something I need," then it is simply a purchase. On the other hand, if the same consumer sees the same purchase as a "self-gift", then it is something special, with special meaning. Consumers may "treat" themselves to self-gifts that are products (*e.g.* clothing, compact, discs, or jewellery), services (*e.g.* hair styling, restaurant meals, spa membership), or experiences (*e.g.* socializing with friends). Such Intrapersonal gifts have their own special range of meaning and context. The Table illustrates specific circumstances and motivations that might lead a consumer to engage in self-gift behaviour. Research focusing on college students self-gifting behaviour found that when they had the money to spend and when they either felt good or wished to cheer themselves up, they were particularly likely to purchase self gifts.

Table

Reported Circumstances, and Motivations for Self-Gift Behaviour

CIRCUMSTANCES	MOTIVATIONS
Personal accomplishment	To reward oneself
Feeling down	To be nice to oneself
Holiday	To Cheer up oneself

Feeling stressed	To fulfil a need
Have some extra money	To Celebrate
Need	To relieve stress
Had not bought for self in a while	To maintain a good feeling
Attainment of a desired goal	To provide an incentive towards a goal
Others	Others

Finally the table given below summerizes the five gifting behaviour sub-divisions explored above.

Gifting Relationship Categories: Definition and Examples

Gifting Relationship	Definition	Example
Intergroup	A group giving a gift to another group	A christmas gift from one family to another family.
Intercategory	An individual giving a gift to a group or a group giving a gift to an individual.	A group of friends chips in to buy a new mother a baby gift.
Intragroup	A group giving a gift to itself or its members	A family buys a VCR for itself as Christmas gift.
Intrapersonal	An Individual giving a gift to another individual.	Valentine's Day Chocolates presented from a boy friend to a girl friend.
Intrapersonal	Self gift	A woman buys herself jewellery to cheer herself up.

Importance of Public Image

A firm's reputation or public image tends to be taken for granted until something untoward occurs and an organization is brought to painful awareness that an image problem exists. The public image for the most part is controllable. It can and should be protected, but it can also provide powerful strategic thrust. It deserves to be considered as one of the elements of the marketing mix an active tool, not a passive appendage.

The Four "P's" of the Marketing Mix. Marketing strategy has been viewed as manipulating the "four P's" the elements of the so-called marketing mix, in such a way as to best appeal to those customers the firm seeks *i.e.* the target market. Subject to certain constraints of customer acceptance, of competition, of company resources, of governmental regulations, for example the marketeer has been seen as able to control or direct only four variables the product, its quality level, and particular features; the price to be charged; how it would be promoted; and how it would be distributed or placed in the market.

The four P's are interdependent. Decisions regarding one of the P's will impact on the others. For example, if a product is to the distributed as a prestige item, the pricing must reflect this s should also the distribution structure and the promotional efforts.

Many alternatives are possible for each of the P's, and they may be mixed or blended in endless combinations. But if the strategy is to be effective, the P's should be tailored, compatible, and coordinated, as described in the following guidelines:

1. A mix should be specially tailored to a product or campaign, keeping in mind particular target markets the firm most-wishes to attract.

2. The various elements of the mix must be screened for compatibility. If the firm, for example, wants to appeal to those consumers interested in economy its choice of dealers, prices promotional efforts, and of course the product itself should be geared to this objective. In this instance, distributing an attractively priced product through discount stores with sufficient advertising to pre-sell customers might seem indicated.

3. Decisions regarding the P's should be coordinated and the complete marketing mix strategy made at one time. Some trade of may be desirable. For example, a decision might be made trend to spend more money on advertising and reduce the sales force because the advertising should make the product easier to sell. If the price is made low enough and if distribution is through discount stores then sales personnel may also be reduced because these customers hare central buying for the entire chain concentrated at their headquarters.

In order to meet these guidelines, the marketing strategy is generally best selected by one person or group, rather than having each element decided independently. Most firms accomplish this by placing authority for all dements of the marketing mix under the control of a marketing manager or marketing Vice President.

The Fifth "P". An additional "P" a fifth "P", deserves consideration as another element of the marketing mix. This is the firm's public image that is, its reputation, how it and its output (products and or services) are perceived. Figure given below depicts the idea of the public image being added to the other P's and interrelating with them.

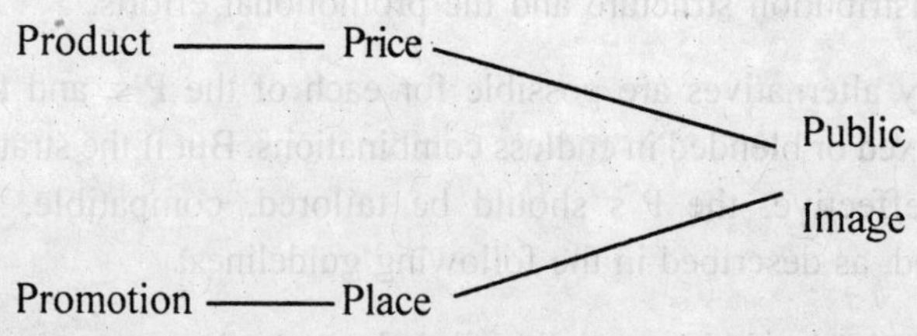

A Firm's Marketing Mix. A public image is a composite of how an organization is viewed by its various publics: its customers, suppliers, employees, stockholders, the financial institutions, the communities in which it dwells, and the various governments, both local and federal. And to these groups must be added the press, which cannot always be relied upon to deliner on objective and unbiased reporting, but is influenced by the firm's reputations.

Two other terms, publicity and public relations, one related to public image development. Publicity is communication about the firm, sometimes, but not always, initiated by it which is disseminated by the media without change and with little control by the firm.

Public relations involve a broad set of planned communications about the company, including publicity releases, designed to promote goodwill and a favourable image.

Publicity then is part of public relations when it is initiated by the firm. However, it can also come about through no planned efforts of the firm; in such cases it can be adverse and bring notoriety because of some controversial action or happening. Since public relations involve communications with stockholders, financial analysts, government officials, and other non-customer groups, it is usually placed outside the marketing function, perhaps as a staff department or outside consultant reporting to top management

Types of Images. The general impressions of a firm or organizations and of its output, be this product, services, or even future expectations, can range from strongly positive to neutral to strongly negative. The degree or intensity of positive or negative feelings towards it can be depicted on a scale or centinuum as shown in the figure.

Worst	–		+	Best
	Bad	Neutral	Superior	
		Blend		
		Unciistinctive		

Intensity of Public Image Perception of an Organization

Following are some representatives images or perceptions that can be categorised as negative, as neutral and as positive:

Negative Perceptions of Image

A Polluter	I just don't like their attitude
Unfriendly	I don't trust them
Junky	Not a sharp operation

Low quality	Inefficient
Poor servicing	Not on top of things
Not a good neighbour	Fading in their industry
Could't care less	Too demanding
Stodgy	Bound up in red tape
Always understaffed	Second rate
Instituting advertising	
A dirty store	
Distant	

Neutral and Undistinctive Perceptions or Images

Haven't heard of them	Who ?
Just another	OK, I guess
Boring ads	An unknown quantity
They haven't proven themselves	

Positive Perceptions of Image

A good neighbour	An etfrcient operation
A good place to work	I trust them
Maker of quality products	In the front of the industry
Provides good value	Honest, dependable services
Has the customer's interest in mind	They care
Friendly	Courteous and helpful employees
Interesting and entertaining advertising	A "fun" place

The public image may not necessarily be valid. For example, a firm may be viewed as a polluter despite strenuous and effective efforts to remedy the problem.

Furthermore, not all will have the same opjnion of an organization and of its output. Perceptions of the firm by its own executives may differ considerably from how its employees, customers and the general public see it. But even among one group, such as customers some will be more favourable; others more negative. But if an unfavourable opinion is common, this is serious problem and needs drastic corrective action. Even if only a few people are negatively inclined, this should not be ignored. Such people are likely to switch to competitors soon if they, have not already done so and their negative attitudes tend to become contagious as they spread bad word-of-mouth publicity.

How Controllable is the Public Image? Within certain limits, image is controllable just as the original four P's. (Of course, when a disaster occurs, such as that at Union Carbide's Bhopal, some would maintain that the resulting poor image is for the most part uncontrollable.) Now skeptics would argue that the public image cannot be changed by efforts and prices. A firm's reputation, after all, would seem rather durable. Therefore, how can image be considered part of the marketing strategy ?

Joel Hyatt, in his TV commercials featuring himself as the founder, has conveyed a warm, helpful, and concerned image for his Hyatt legal clinics. That this is so different from the general public's impressions of law firms and lawyers has enabled the firm, first established in 1978, to grow to the largest law firm in the U.S.

Importance of the Public Image. A firm's public image plays a vital role in the attractiveness of the firm and its products to employees, customers, and to such outsiders as stockholders, suppliers, creditors, government officials, the new media, as well as diverse special groups. In some situations it is impossible to satisfy all the diverse publics. For example a new highly automated plant may meet the approval of creditors and stockholders, but it will undoubtedly find resistance from employees who see jobs threatened.

On the other hand, high quality products and service standards should bring almost complete approval and pride of association-given that operating costs are competitiv while shoddy products and false claims would be widely decried.

A firm's public image, if it is good, should be cherished and protected. It is a valuable asset that usually is built up cover a long and satisfying relationships of a firm with its various publics. If a firm has developed a quality image, this is a not easily countered or imitated by competitors. Such an image may enable a firm to change higher prices, to woo the best distributors and dealers to attract the best employees, and to expect the most favourable creditor relationships and the lowest borrowing costs. It should also enable a firm's stock to command a higher price-earnings ratio than other firms in the same industry not having such a good reputation and public image. All these can give a competitive advantage.

Consequences of a Negative Image. A bad hurts a firm with all the different publics with which it deals. All can turn critical and even litigious depending on the source and extent of the bad image. At best, present and potential customers may simply seek alternative sources for goods and services and switch to competitors wherever possible.

At the worst the Bhopal disaster, or Love Canal and Agent Orange, or the MGM Grand Hotel fire in Las Vegas major liability suits can cost hundreds the costs of liability insurance, and even spread a badly tarnished image to other firms in the industry. Years may be required to mute the negative perceptions and millions of dollars of advertising may be committed to try to improve public impressions. For example, after Love Canal Agent orange triggered a wave of adverse publicity, the chemical industry launched an advertising campaign to try to allay the image. Monsanto alone spent millions on a campaign with the theme, "without chemicals, life of itself would be impossible."

The consequences, of course, of a bad image translate directly to the bottom line, to reduced profits, or worse.

EFFECT OF FACILITIES ON PUBLIC IMAGE

The total combination of facilities and the visible accouterments of the firm can create an impression that ranges from positive to neutral to negative. Facilities include trucks, plants, stores, office buildings, the company logo and signs and any other publicity visible aspects of the firm.

Factories can be eyesores, unpleasant places to work in, as well as they can be neighbours. They can have a bad environmental impact and can create air and/or water pollution and worse or they can be neatly landscaped, pleasing to the eye and have strict pollution control. Of course, type of industry plays a major role: Steel mills, paper mills, oil refineries, chemical plants, by their very nature are dirtier, less desirable neighbours than electronics factories or, indeed, factories of most other industries. In any industry, the firm with an old plant may not be able to invest millions to modern he and improve the appearance. But even in heavy industry a firm can pave a good reputation or a bad one, can be a good citizen and neighbour to the community, or a disgrace. For example:

"Some years ago a paper mill, in attempting to improve its public image, had an advertising campaign showing the clear waters of a river supposedly down-stream from its plant. It fell into disgrace when some diligent investigative reporter found that the idyllic scene in the commercials was upstream from the plant."

Where a firm is a dominant employer in a community, the posibility of real public image problems looms very important where layoffs are necessary, whether temporary or permanent. The layoffs of some no-longer competitive steel mills in the Mahoning Valley of northeastern ohio devastated the cities involved, of which the largest was youngstown. Regardless of the necessity, the bad publicity emanating from such closings blackened the public image of the entire steel industry. Perhaps one of the worst closing in recent years was that of the insulite division of Boise Cascade Corporation in International Falls, Minnesota, a community of 6000 people on the. Canadian border.

If a firm uses its own trucks, this can impact on the image. Retail firms in particular often have their own delivery system and this can add prestige and advertising for the store, especially if it is well maintained and if the drivers are uniformed. As we noted before, the choice of dealers their reputations and facilities will also rub off on the manufacturer's image and vice-versa.

Many major firms, especially those that have widely diversified in to unrelated areas, have undertaken corporate identity programmes to improve their images through new logos, new signs and distinctive business forms. However, face-lifting alone, without more fandamental changes where there is a problem, is seldom enough to change an image in a positive fashion.

Effect of Company Employees. Contacts of employees with outsiders, be they customers, suppliers, or others, convey positive impression of the firm. Even the way the telephone is answered casts an impression. Smart firms devote attention to this aspects of the image special employees training may be needed, special policies established and some type of follow-up used to ensure that the company's image efforts do not deteriorate. The bill telephone company was one of the pinoeers in emphasizing this aspect of the public image.

Servicemen were imbued with the need to leave customers' premises neat and courtesy was stressed. Telephone operators were trained with the objective, "voice with it smile". Company representatives in business offices learned the technicalities of handling many different kinds of customer contacts through role playing and they were judged on the quality of their speech, their understanding, explanations and interested and helpful manner. Periodic retaining was used to ensure continuous high quality.

Product Quality and Dependability. The product, its level of quality compared with competition brands and particularly its dependability or freedom from defects, is another aspects of the marketing programme that can strongly affect the image. The American auto industry has long been plagued with product defects and although concerted efforts have been made to try to lessen defects in new cars, these have not been wholly successful, as most of us know from personal experience.

In the interests of improving products dependability and freedom from defects, quality control may have to be improved. Most firms use statistical quality control which accepts a predictable number of defective units with only every *nth* item checked. This is far less expensive than complete quality control that accepts zero defects. But the latter perhaps ought to be considered for some items in which serious servicing problems cannot otherwise be eased. Multiple inspections of critical parts are rejected by most firms as too costly, but compared to the costs of customer brand switching and costly callback programmes, improved quality control might sometimes offset the increased costs. It would certainly favourably affect the public image.

The intrisive nature of the products or type of business that a firm handles will also affect the image. For example, cbnsider these extreme examples: diamonds versus prunes; a garbage collection versus air express; a salvage store versus a department store. For certain lines of business, the public image will be more negative than for others, not because of the efforts of the personnel involved but because of the nature of the business and of the products or services.

The Price Components Inputs		Outputs perceptions and attitudes of
Physical facilities		Customers/consumers
Employees		Employees
Dealers		Dealers
Products	Public	Suppliers
Prices	Image	Creditors
Customer services	Mix	Investors
Advertising		Media
Public relations efforts		Government
Publicity		General public
Miscellaneous		

As shown in the figure that price has a two-way arrow. This reflects that prices of a firm's products relative to competing brands tend to be a rather powerful conveyor of image, particularly as to whether the firm is a maker of high-quality or low-quality products, or something in between. A higher price than other brands usually connotes higher quality of course, if there is a serious discrepancy between a high price and the realized quality of a product, image is affected adversely.

The perceived image of a firm also helps determine the prices that it can realize for its products. With a favourable image, especially regarding product dependability and customer service, relatively higher prices will be accepted by customers.

Importance of Customers Service. Viewed in the broadest sense, customer service includes all, offerings to a firm's customers beyond the product itself. Repair and warranty service usually receives the most attention (and complaints), but customer services include such diverse things as return-goods privileges extended by retail stores and conveniences such as delivery, telephone ordering, customer parking, credit and so on.

The effect of a firm's reputation for good services in attracting potential customers and preventing the loss of existing customers is obvious. It results in customer satisfaction, in loyal customers and repeat business and in word-of-mouth influence, which is potent, if not easily measured less obvious is the protection from price competition that a good reputation for service can provide. Although some customers are swayed by a better price, many place a higher value on a firm's' reputation, for dependable service. Some services such as extended warranties, are easily imitated. Others, such as prompt and dependable delivery and high caliber maintenance and repair facilities, are less easily matched and their effective performance slowly builds reputations.

Indirect benefits can come from a customer service programme as a major part of the public image mix. A firm's good reputation for service can make customers easier to sell to. Recruiting salespeople tends to be easier and higher morale and lower personnel turnover often-result from the harmonious customer relations that good service engenders.

Rather than giving customer service the attention it deserves, in many firms executive time is directed elesewhere. Operational crises and problems claim attention, for example, making a decision on promotioal scheduling that cannot be delayed breaking in a salesperson in a new territory, devoting immediate attention to several territories in which planned sales were not reached. And the customers who are antagonized, who quietly fade away, never to return-all these are over-looked in the pressure of "more important" matters.

A good part of the reason. that many firms neglect the customer relations aspect of their business is a lack of awareness of how serious such problems might be. The extent of customer dissatisfaction often cannot be detected by sales and profit figures, at least not until such problems may have assumed major proportions. Moreover, because only a small proportion of total complaints ever reach the ears of responsible executives expressed dissatisfactions tend to be viewed as involving only a few customers with mostly unjustified complaints.

PUBLIC IMAGE FOR NON-PROFIT ORGANIZATIONS

Not only should product oriented firms be concerned and protective of their public image; so too should non-profit organizations such as schools, charitable drives, police departments, hospitals, even politicians. Let us consider here the importance of public image and how it might be improved or built by several no product organizations and persons.

Large city police departments of frequently have a poor image among important segments of the population. The need to improve this image is hardly less important than for a manufacture faced with a deteriorating brand image. A police department can develop a "marketing" campaign to win friends; examples of possible activities aimed at creating a better image are promoting tours and open houses of police stations, crime laboratories, police lineups, cells and so forth; speaking at schools; and sponsoring recreation projects such as a day at the ballpark for youngsters.

Public schools systems, faced with taxpayers' revolts towards mounting costs of education and with image damage due to teacher strikes need conscious effort to improve the image in order to obtain more public support and funds.

Many.non-business organizations and institutions, such as hospitals, schools, governmental bodies, even labour unions, have grown self-serving, with a bureaucratic mentality dominating, so that perfunctory and callous treatment is the rule and the image is in the pits. Improving the image can only come through a greater ephasis on satisfying customers' or the public's needs.

Building images of political candidates represent the most extensive use of marketing techniques in non-business areas. Two marketing tools are commonly employed public opinion research and mass media, especially television, advertising. Using these tools and especially the latter, to win elections almost precludes the candidate without much money from effectively competing. With money, a candidate may bypass political party organizations, challenge entrenched incumbents, in fact manufacture an instant public image.

Types of Image Problems. Image problems can be categorized as: *1.* overcoming a dull image; *2.* trying to upgrade an image; *3.* combating a fading image; and *4.* overcoming a bad image.

Certainly a dull or innocuous image is a lodestone for any firm and a major competitive drawback. The only thing worse is to have a decidedly negative image. Image is not an easy thing for a firm to improve or change. But efforts certainly need to be made by such a firm. Sometimes a firm wants to upgrade its image. Perhaps it had originally formulated its niche as a low-price, bargain operation and now wants to attain more a quality image. But upgrading an image is not easily done, as described in the korvette case. Some firms that attempt this fail because they expect results too quickly. But other firms might be better advised to change their name-start a fresh, perhaps with a new division-rather than try to upgrade a long-establihsed name and image.

Even mighty sears, in 1974, 1975, attempted to upgrade its image and its profit margins with higher-price goods and higher-fashion women's apparel. Its earnings tumbled 28 per cent as its traditional price-conscious customer became disillusioned by the emphasis on higher prices. Sears soon abandoned the attempt to change its image, but the damage had been done and sales and profits were slow in recovering.

Combating a fading image would seem easier than upgrading a longe stablished one. However, aggressive and effective efforts need to be ta,ken to reverse the fading trend, as, Coors found out. Reversing an established trend is not easily done, and may never succeed in recouping all the lost ground. Overcoming a bad image normally is the most difficult problem. This is the extreme position of image illness and it could even be the death knill. It is far worse than a dull image an image of low quality, or a formerly good image that is now fading.

A bad image may be formed slowly by a history of questionable practices that have become widely publicized; for example, unsafe products, deceptive advertising, illegal payoffs, callousness towards community relations and employees, and so on.

Occasionally something catastrophic will bring down an image. The calamity of Union Carbide has, of course, been widely publicized. But firms have been known to be more directly involved in their own violent image destruction.

Errors in Handling the Public Image. Firms can do a great injustice to their image. They may:

1. Blantantly ignore matters that have a probability of affecting it adversely.
2. Abdicate their image-building and image-maintaining efforts to public retations.

3. Disregard the constraining consequences of their image.
4. Not coordinate all aspects of the operation that can affect the image.

Ignoring Possible Negative Image Consequences. The Nestle case, also illustrates unseemly myopia regarding public image.

Why do firms ignore their image, or at least greatly underestimate the consequences of their actions on it ? Several factors usually account for this. First, a firm's public image generally makes a non-specific impact on company performance. The cause and effect relationship of a poor or deteriorating image is virtually impossible to assess, at least until and unless image problems worsen. The inability to be able to point the blame directly to the intangible image results in other areas of performance being given the closer scrutiny and the efforts at corrective action.

Second, an organization's image-how it is perceived by the various publics is not easily and definitively measured. While some tools are available for tracking public opinion, they tend to be imprecise and of uncertain validity. Consequently image studies are often ignored or given short-shrift relative to more quantitative measures of performance.

Third, it is difficult to determine the effectiveness of image-building advertising, measures of the effectiveness of such expenditures are inexact and also of questionable validity. For example, a survey may be taken of attitudes of a group of people before and after the image-building campaign is run. Presumably if a few more people profess to be favourably, disposed towards the company after the campaign than before, this is an indication of its success. But an executive can question how much this really translates into sales and profits.

Disregarding Constraints. A firm's present image ought to be considered and recognized as a factor affecting strategy options. Public image is a resource, just as much so as manpower, facilities and finances. But it is also a constraint. Most firms do not have unlimited resources, so their planned strategies must be geared to what is realistic and practical. So it is with the image. To expect a Korvette, or a K mart, to be on the same status level as a Neiman Mascus in a few years is unreasonable. As is the expectation that a Volkswagon can soon achieve the status of a Mercedes Benz."

Two generalizations can be made about the constraining influences of firm's public image:

(1) A dull, a negative, or a low-quality image is extremely difficult to upgrade. Massive advertising efforts and years of persistence may be necessary to overcome such an image.

(2) A favourable image can be quickly turn down if a firm is careless with its product quality, service, or other aspects subject to public scrutiny.

Abdicating Image Efforts. In many firms a public relations department, either in-house, or through an advertising 'agency or other outside consultant is responsible for all image related matters. This supposedly places public relations in expert hands as well as under the control of those who can have the detached objectivity that supposedly no operating executive can have.

Some firms are beginning to move in the direction of greater participation by marketeers. This is hardly meeting with the approval of all concerned. Public relations practitioners tend to view such a move as "encroachment", and the marketeers as' "carpet baggers";'. "Marketing people are making inroads. They are like 'carpet baggers' who move into an organization, then pull out and let PR pick up the pieces."

Yet we know that many other aspects of a firm's operation affect the public image-public relations pronouncements and publicity releases are just one of the factors. A firm that recognize the importance of its public image, not only as something to be protected but also as a valuable tool for opening up new opportunities and guiding the marketing strategy would to well not to totally abdicate this important resources to a staff department.

Non Co-ordinating Internal Image Inputs. From the public image mix we know that a good many aspects of a firm's operation have at least the potential of offecting the firm's public image, for good or for bad. To protect or to build an image, all the various contributors should be in close communication and working with coordination. For example, a sales department's effictiveness in sure to be undermined if servicing of orders or quality control is deficient.

Kotter puts it in its way: "Marketeers typically think of their jobs as manipulating the 4 P's.....This is the outside job of the marketeer. But marketeers also have an inside job to do. That is, they have to make other company departments marketing and consumer-oriented."

❑

3

Consumer Involvemen and Decision Making

Involvement theory developed from a stream of research called hemispheral lateralization or split-brain theory. The basic premise of the split-brain theory is that the right and left hemispheres of the brain "specialize" in the kinds of information they process. The left hemisphere is primarily responsible for cognitive activities such as reading and speaking. Individuals who are exposed to verbal information cognitively analyze the information through left-brain processing and form mental images. Unlike the left hemisphere, the right hemisphere of the brain is concerned with non-verbal, timeless, and pictorial information. Put another way, the left side of the brain is supposed to be rational, active, realistic; the right side is emotional, metaphoric, impulsive, and intuitive.

High and Low Involvement Media

Building on the notion of hemispheral lateralization, a pioneer consumer researcher theorized that when individuals are engaged in right-brain processing of information, it is possible for them to process and store such information passively (that is, without active involvement). Since TV viewing is a right-brain activity (it entails the passive perception of images through the focused eye), TV is a low-involvement medium. Passive learning occurs through repeated exposures to a specific TV commercial, and produces changes in consumer behaviour (such as a product purchase) prior to any change in the consumer's attitude toward the product.

Print advertisements trigger the left side of the brain, which is in charge of reading, speaking, and translating information into mental images; thus newspapers and magazines are high-involvement media.

Passive Learning Results

The right-brain/passive processing of information theory is consistent with the classical conditioning approach. Through repetition, the product is paired with a favourable visual image to produce the desired response: purchase behaviour. According to this theory, in situations of passive learning (generated by low involvement media), repetition is all that is needed to produce the desired response: purchase behaviour. The behaviour itself, in turn, is likely to lead to a favourable attitude change. In marketing terms, the theory suggests that television advertising is likely to be most effective when it is of short duration and frequently repeated. This strategy is consistent with the passive learning generated by TV; it ensures brand familiarity but is not designed to produce detailed evaluation of the message content.

The passive learning model is supported by the growing use of fifteen-second TV commercials. Research has shown that such brief commercial messages are more efficient in terms of cost than longer commercials. A study found that time-compressed commercials are no less effective (in terms of producing intention to buy) than non-time-compressed commercials. (Time compression of commercials can be achieved through the use of an electronic device that compresses audio and visual channels some 20 per cent while retaining normal voice pitch and appropriate balance between pauses and speech.)

The passive learning model also stresses the importance of the visual component of advertising, including the creative use of symbols. Thus highly visual (rather than informational) TV commercials, in-store displays, and packaging have been found to generate familiarity with the brand and induce purchase behavior. One example of this strategy is Procter & Gamble's format for TV advertising of detergents; its commercials have high repetition, are of short duration, and include a number of visual symbols. P&G's large TV advertising budget commands significant shelf space at the retail level. Consumers instantly recognize the product packaging they have passively learned through TV advertising; this familiarity promotes purchase behaviour. Other examples of products that use a similar TV advertising strategy of high-repetition, short-duration commercials that are rich in visual symbolism include Bounty paper towels, Miller Beer, and Kleenex tissues.

Recent evidence confirms the fact that pictorial cues (which activate right brain processing) are more effective for generating recall and familiarity with the product, while verbal cues (which trigger left-brain processing) generate cognitive activity that encourages consumers to evaluate the advantages and disadvantages of the product.

There are limitations to the application of the split-brain theory to marketing strategy. Research suggests that the right and left hemispheres of the brain do not operate independently of each other, but work together to process information. Furthermore, activation research—the methodology for measuring brain activity is highly complex, and the findings are difficult to interpret.

High and Low Consumer Involvement

The preceding section discussed the active processing of information produced by high involvement media (such as magazines) and the passive processing of information produced by low-involvement media (such as TV) and pictorial rather than verbal cues. In this section, we will discuss the degree of information processing produced by high and low consumer involvement with the product or purchase situation.

In this context, involvement is defined as the degree of personal relevance which the product holds for the consumer. High-involvement purchases are those which are very important to the consumer in terms of perceived risk and which prompt the consumer to engage in extensive problem solving. Low-involvement purchases are purchases which are not very important to the consumer, hold little relevance and little perceived risk, and thus lead the consumer to engage in very limited information processing. Two theories that illustrate the concepts of extensive and limited problem-solving for high and low involvement purchase situations are the Central and Peripheral Routes to Persuasion theory and the Social Judgment theory.

CENTRAL AND PERIPHERAL ROUTES TO PERSUASION

The major premise of the Central and Peripheral Routes to Persuasion theory is that individuals are more likely to carefully weigh information concerning a product and to devote considerable cognitive effort to evaluating it when they are highly involved with the product category. The theory suggests that there is a very strong likelihood that consumers will carefully evaluate the merits and/or weaknesses of a product when the purchase is of high relevance to them. Conversely, the likelihood is great that consumers will engage in very limited information search and evaluation when the purchase holds little relevance or importance for them. Thus, for high-involvement purchases, the central route to persuasion—the instigation of considered thought about the product is likely to be a highly effective marketing strategy.. For low-involvement purchases, the peripheral route to persuasion is likely to be more effective. In this instance, because the consumer is less motivated to exert cognitive effort, learning is more likely to occur through repetition and the passive processing of visual cues.

There is a great deal of research support for the high-relevance/high-involvement—low-relevance/low-involvement theory of consumer information processing. For example, a number of studies indicate that high involvement with an issue produces more extensive processing of information about the issue, and that in such situations, the quality of the argument presented in the persuasive message is very influential in the decision outcome. Consumer research supports this evidence. It was demonstrated that highly involved consumers use more ttributes to evaluate brands than less invólved consumers. Consumers tend to apply very simple choice rules (that is, they make a quick and effortless decision) when the purchase is not important and when the product is purchased frequently (and thus presents very little perceived risk.)

The marketing implications of the two-routes-to-persuasion theory is that for high-involvement purchases, marketers should use arguments stressing the strong, solid, high-quality attributes of their products thus utilizing the central (that is, highly cognitive) route. For low-involvement purchases, marketers should use the peripheral route to persuasion, focusing on the method of presentation rather than the content of the message (*e.g.*, through the use of celebrity spokespersons or highly visual and symbolic advertisements).

Social Judgment Theory

The central premise of the Social judgment theory is that an individual's processing of information about an issue is determined by his or her own involvement with the issue. Individuals who are highly involved with an issue and have a strong or definite opinion about it will accept very few alternative opinions (that is, they will have a narrow latitude of acceptance and a wide latitude of rejection). Highly involved individuals will interpret a message which is congruent with their positions as more positive than it actually is (this is known as the assimilation effect), and one that is not congruent as more negative than it actually is (the contrast effect). Persons who are uninvolved with an issue will be more receptive to arguments for and against (they will have a wide latitude of acceptance) or take no position at all (have a wide latitude of non-commitment.)

The marketing implications of the Social judgment theory suggest that highly involved consumers would find fewer brands acceptable (they would be narrow categorizers) and would interpret messages about these brands in a manner congruent with their previous experiences and opinions about the product. The uninvolved consumer will be receptive to a greater number of messages regarding the purchase (will consider more brands and be a wide categorizer). This type of person is less likely to be brand loyal and is a likely target for brand switching.

Evaluation of Involvement Theory for Marketing Applications

While the theories on involvement presented above appear to be straightforward, it has been difficult to operationalize them for marketing strategy applications. This is quite likely due to the fact that they have been developed by information theorists, rather than by marketing theorists, and deal with the processing and learning of information about issues, rather than about products. In accordance with these theories, many consumer researchers now believe that involvement is consumer-related rather than product-related or media-related. That is, it is a function of the consumer's mental state regarding the product, rather than a function of the product itself. Thus, though some consumer researchers have considered high-priced products to be high-involvement products, they are only high involvement in relation to the consumer's state of mind. For example, if the purchase of an automobile presents high perceived financial risk to a consumer, to such a consumer an automobile may be a high-involvement purchase. By the same token, an inexpensive toiletry product like shampoo might be a high-involvement purchase to a consumer with perceived social risk.

A major problem in operationalizing consumer involvement theory is the great variation in the conceptualization and measurement of the consumer's mental state regarding a purchase. For example, a recent review of consumer involvement research revealed more than thirty conceptual and empirical attempts to operationalize involvement. Many psychological and social theories have also been used to explain consumer "involvement." Most consumer researchers agree that there is no single, widely accepted understanding of involvement, because the term has been neither carefully defined nor well conceptualized. One widely quoted study identified familiarity, commitment, and importance of the product as the components of involvement. Another review specified ego involvement, commitment, communication involvement, purchase importance, and extent of information search as the five types of involvement. Some researchers have identified the person, product, and situation as the major components of involvement. Others view low involvement as applicable to purchases where there is little information search and no attitude formation regarding the product prior to the purchase.

In addition to problems of definition, there are also problems of measurement. The measurement of involvement has varied greatly. Researchers who regard involvement as a cognitive state are concerned with the measurement of ego involvement, risk perception, (and importance of the purchase; researchers who focus on the behavioural aspects of involvement measure such factors as the search for and evaluation of product information. Some researchers consider decision time an effective measure of involvement. Others argue that involvement should be measured by the degree of Importance the product has to the buyer. A recent study has concluded that since there really are so many kinds of consumer involvement, efforts should be made to measure an involvement profile rather than a single involvement level. This recommendation is consistent with previous studies which argue that involvement should be measured on a continuum rather than as a dichotomy consisting of two mutually exclusive categories of "high" and "low" involvement.

One study views long-term involvement with a product as leisure behaviour; under this theory, long-term products are considered high-involvement products. Thus durable products which deliver pleasure on a continuing basis (such as cars, stereo equipment, and home computers) are viewed as high-involvement products. However, if high-involvement products are defined as continuous pleasure-giving products, it is just as reasonable to extend the term to non-durables such as cigarettes or chewing gum, since it is obvious that some consumers derive continuous pleasure from these products, as evidenced by their repeat purchases.

At the present time, involvement research is clearly at a crossroads. The thrust of such research thus far seems to have been an attempt to distinguish limited information processing from the classical view of extensive information processing. Indeed, one researcher has concluded that the low-involvement notion is an incomplete learning theory which should be put to rest. However, the view of right-brain/passive information processing does seem to have strong implications for the length, duration, and content of TV advertising.

The issue of personal relevance of the product to the consumer appears to be more complicated. Before the degree of relevance can be measured, the researcher must define exactly what it is that should be measured go, motivation, task involvement, situational variables, or what. It is clear that solid and widely accepted measures of product relevance need to be developed. Of course, too many variables may make it extremely difficult to operationalize the consumer involvement issue in a way that can be realistically integrated into marketing strategy.

Evaluation of Behavioural Theory Vs Cognitive Theory

The new emphasis in marketing circles on the consumer as an information processor revives the long standing dispute among learning theorists about the relative importance of behavioural versus mental processes—the old "nature versus nurture" argument about whether the mind comes equipped with innate ideas or inherited tendencies to think and behave in specific ways, or whether the mind is a blank slate at birth and comes to think only in ways that have been "written" upon it by experience and training. The movie Trading Places, with Eddie Murphy and Dan Ackroyd, depicts this age-old question in an entertaining format, and supports the view suggested by recent research that learning is the product of an interaction between nature and nurture; each is essential, but neither is wholly controlling.

CONSUMER DECISION-MAKING

It is important to remember that not all consumer situations receive (or require) the same degree of information search, If all purchase dccisions required extensive effort, consumer decision making would be an exhausting proccss that left little time for anything else. On the other hand, 'if all purchascs were routine, they would tend to be monotonous and would provide little pleasure or novelty, On a continuum of effort ranging from very high to very low, we can distinguish three specific levels of consumer decision making, *i.e.,* extensive problem solving, limited problem solving, and routinized response behaviour.

Expensive Problem Solving. When consumers have no established critcria for avaluating a product category as specific brands in that category or have not narrowed the number of brands they will consider to a small, manageable subset (the evoked set), then decision-making efforts can be classified as extensive problem solving. At this level the consumer needs a great deal of information to establish a set of criteria on which to judge specific brands and a correspondingly large amount of information concerning each of the brands to be considered.

Limited Problem Solving. At this level of problem solving, consumers already have established the basic criteria for evaluating the product category and the various brands in the category. However, they have not fully established preferences concerning a select group of brands. Their search for additional information is more like "fine-tuning". They must gather additional brand information to discriminate among the various brands.

Routinized Response Behaviour. At this level, consumers have some experience with the product category and a well-established set of criteria with which to evaluate the brands in their evoked sets. In some situations, they may search for a small amount of additional information, in other they simply review what they already know.

Just how extensive a consumer's problem solving task is depends on how well established his or her criteria for selection are, how much information he or she has about each brand being considered, and how narrow the set of brands (the evoked set) if from which the choice will be made. Clearly, extensive problem solving implies that the consumer must seek more information to make choice, while routinized response behaviour implies little need for additional information.

ACT OF MAKING DECISIONS

The act of making a consumer-decision consists of two stages:

1. need recognition.

2: pre-purchase search.

1. Need Recognition. The recognition of need is likely to occur when a consumer is faced with a problem. For example, consider the case of a busy young consulting engineer named David who recently moved from Daytona Beach, Florida, to start with his career in the San Diego, California area. David's new position requires that the travel out-of-state at least three business days a month on engineering consulting assignments. In addition to this new position, David has just enrolled at a local state university as a part time MBA student.

Always on the go, David is open to any product or service that would help him jiggle the 'blur' between his business and private life. For this reason, he has fax machine at home, a notebook computer with a built in modem that alarms him to send and receive documents while travelling, and a small portable cellular telephone. In addition, to his almost constant use, of the telephone, David lived in three different parts of United Kingdom States during the past five years, and now has family and close friends in the more than eight states.

This past weekend, while visiting his sisters, he learned about a new personal telephone service called AT & T Easy Reach, 700 service. His sister had recently started subscribing to it and wanted to show it offer to her "high-tech" brother. As she told him about it, David recalled that he had just received same direct mail from AT & T about the service but had not gotten around to reading it. He also remembered skimming an article in one of the popular business magazines describing personal 800 and 700 numbers for personal or non-business users. He recalled that article mentioned that all three major long-distance telephone companies had some form of personal telephone service. David wondered whether the Easy Reach 700 Service was one of the services described in the article.

His sister was particularly impressed by the pemanent telephone number that a subscriber could continuously us as long as he or she subscribes to the AT&T service. She suggested that David could even request a 'vanity number' for a small one time charge. And the number would be private: AT&T Easy Reach 700 numbers are not listed with directory assistance. She told David that no matter where he lives, he could always have the people he wants reach him by calling his personal Easy Reach 700 number. As she told, him about the service.; David learned that it had many different features in addition to the permanent telephone number. After hearing his sister's almost non-stop description of the new service, David thought that he also might benefit the service because of his frequent travel, and his need to be reached by business associates, personal friends, and relatives. (David has recognized a possible need for a personal telephone service).

Among consumers, there seem to be the different problem recognition Styles. Some consumers are actual state types, who perceive that they have a problem when a product falls to perform satisfactorily. (*e.g.*, a watch no longer keeps accurate time). In contrast, other consumers are desired state types for whom the desire for something new may trigger the decision process. (David in his considerations of a personal telephone service, appears to be desired state consumer).

Need or problem recognition also can be viewed as either simple or complex. Simple problem recognition refers to needs that occur frequently and that can be dealt with almost automatically, such as becoming hungry and purchasing a candy bar from a vending machine. Complex problem recognition, however, is characterized as a state in which problem develops over time, as the actual state and the desired state gradually more apart. For example, after several years of driving a car, the owner may begin to consider trading it in for a new one to avoid growing repair bills.

2. Pre-Purchase Search. Pre-purchase search begins when a consumer perceives a need that might be satisfied by the purchase and consumption of a product. A consumer who senses a need for information on, which to base a choice is in this stage. The recollection of past experiences (drawn from long term memory storage) might provide the consumer with adequate information to make the present choice. On the other hand, if the consumer has had prior experience, he or she may have to engage in extensive search of the outside environment for useful information on which to base a choice.

The consumer usually searches his or her memory (the psychological field) before seeking external sources of information regarding a given consumption related need. Past experience is considered an internal source of information. The greater the relevant past experience the less external information the consumer is likely to need in order to reach a decision. Many consumer decisions are based on a combination of past experience (internal source) and marketing and non-commercial information (external sources). The degree of perceived risk can also influence this stage of the decision process. On high risk situations, consumer is likely to engage in complex information search and evaluation; in low-risk situations, they are likely to use very simple search and evaluation tactics.

An examination of the external search effort associated with the purchase of different product categories (*e.g.* TVS, VCKs personal computers) found that as the amount of total search effort increased, consumer attitudes towards shopping became more positive and more time was made available for shopping. Not, surprisingly, the external search effort was greatest for consumers who had the least amount of product category knowledge. It follows that the less consumers know about a product category and the more important the purchase is to them, the more time they will make available and the more extensive their pre-purchase search activitity is likely to be.

How much information a consumer will gather also depends on various situational factor. Consider the case of David, the consulting engineer who has recognized the need for a personal telephone service. Though he has little exposure to such service (simply hearing about AT&T version from his sister), he believes that such service might make it easier for business associates, friends and family to reach him as he travels around the country on engineering assignments. If he feels that he must make an immediate purchase decision, he might call AT&T's customer service 800 number and order the service. On the other hand, this type of rapid decisions making does not suit everyone. Many consumers prefer to approach a new and somewhat complex'decisions with more deliberation and considerations of the options (*i.e.*, considering competitor's services and/or options that can be added on to the core service). In addition to calling the other two major long-distance companies to find out about their personal telephone service. David might undertake a computer search (remember, he is a "high-tech" person). He might also call his sister and ask her if she still "loves" the service. On the basis of selective perception David might start seeing advertisements for personal telephone services.

As the table given below indicates, a number of factors are likely to increase consumer's prepurchase search. In this specific case of the personal telephone service, a service that is new and evolving, David does not have on going experience on which to draw. Furthermore, a personal telephone service is essentially a discretionary purchase, rather than a necessity, so there is no rush to make a decisions.

Table : Factors that are Likely to Increase Pre-purchase Search

Product Factors

* Long interpurchase time (a long-lasting or frequently used product)
* Frequent changes in product styling.
* Frequent price changes.
* Volume purchasing (large number of units)
* High price.
* Many alternative brands.
* Much variation in features.

Situational Factors

Experience

* First-time purchase
* No past experience because the product is new
* Unsatisfactorily past experience within the product category

Social Acceptability

* The purchase is for a gift
* The product is socially visible

Value-Related Considerations

* Purchase is discretionary rather than necessary
* All alternatives have both desirable and undesirable consequence;
* Family members disagree on product requirements or evaluation of alternatives
* Product usage deviates from important reference group
* The purchase involves ecological considerations
* Many sources of conflicting information.

Product Factors

Demographic Characteristics of Consumer

* Well educated
* High income
* White collar occupation
* Under 35 years of age

Personality

* Low dogmatic (open-minded)
* Low risk perceiver (broad categorizer)
* Other personal factors, such as high product involvement and enjoyment of shopping and search.

Let us consider several of prepurchase search alternatives open to the prospective subscriber to a personal telephone service, such as David. At the most fundamental level, search alternatives can be classified as either personal or impersonal. Personal search alternatives includes more than a consumer's past experience with the product or service. They also include asking for information and advice from friends, relatives, co-workers and sales representatives. For instance, David might speak with Telecommunications manager at his engineering firm and ask her what she knows about personal telephone services. If the services were right not so new, David might investigate whether Consumer Reports might have related different brands of personal telephone services.

The table given below presents some of the sources of information that David might use as part of his prepurchase search. Any of or all of these might be imployed as part of a consumer's search process.

Table: Alternative Prepurchase Information Sources for Personal Telephone Services

Personal	Impersonal
Friends	Newspaper Article
Relatives	Magazine Articles
Coworkers	Consumer Reports
Calling the long distance	Long-distance Telephone companies Information brochures,
Calling the long distance companies customer service 800 numbers,	Information from service ads.

Evaluation of Alternatives. When evaluating potential alternatives, consumers tend to use two types of informations—(1) a ' list" of brands from which they plan to make them (the evoked set) and this criteria they will use to evaluate each brand. The evoked set is generally only a part-a subset of all the brands of which the consumer is aware these brands, in turn, frequently are only a portion of all brands in the market. Making a selection from a sample of all possible brands is a human characteristic that helps simplify the decision-making process.

The criteria consumers to evaluate the brands that constitute their evoked sets usually are expressed in terms of important product attributes. Examples of product attributes that consumers have used as criteria in evaluating nine product categories are listed in the table.

Table: Possible Product Attributes Used as Purchase Criteria for Nine Product Categories

Personal Computers	**35 mm Cameras**	**Air Conditioners**
Processing speed	Autofocusing	BTUs
Price	Built-in-Flash	Efficiency
Type of display	Automatic film loading	Quieteness
Disk size	Lens type	Warranty
Runs on popular software	Size and weight	Price
Laptop or desktop		
Paper Towels	**Colour TVs**	
Strength	Picture quality	
Design	Length of Warranty	
Price	Cable ready	
Colour	Cabinet Style	
Package size	Size of screen	
Absorbancy		
Shaving Cream	**Fountain Pens**	
Fragrance	Balance	
Consistency	Price	

Price	Shape
Size	Smoothness
Smoothness or Shave	Size

Frozen dinners	**Watches**
Taste	Wrist brand
type of main course	Alarms
Type of side dishes	Water resistant
Serving size	Quartz movement
	Size of face

IMPORTANCE OF RELATIONSHIP OF MARKETING

Many firms have established relationship marketing programmes (sometimes called loyal programmes) to foster usage loyalty and a commitment to their company's products and services. Relationship marketing is exceedingly logical when we think that credit card research has shown, that "75 per cent of college students keep their first card for 15 years, and 60 per cent keep that card for life." This kind of loyalty is enhanced by relationship marketing, which at its heart is all about building trust (between the firm and its consumers) and keeping promises ("making promises," enabling promises," and "keeping promises" on the part of the firm and, possibly, on the part of the customer).

Indeed, it is the aim of relationship marketing to create stone lasting relationships with a core group of customers. The emphasis is on developing long-term bonds with customers by making them feel good about how the company interact (*i.e.* does business) with them and by giving them some kind of "personal connection" to the business. A review of the composition of 66 consumer's relationship marketing programmes revealed three elements shared by more than 50 per cent of the programmes, They are: *(1)* Fostering ongoing communication with customers. (73 per cent of the programmes), *(2)* Furnishing loyalty by building extras like upgrades and other peaks (68 per cent of the programmes) and *(3)* stimulating a sense of belonging by providing a "Club membership" format (50 per cent of the programmes).

An analogy can be drawn between two individuals who build an interpersonal relationship and the type of relationship marketeers attempt to build between the company: (or its product) and the consumer. Like personal relationships between individuals who are willing to do favours for each other, "relationship" marketeers offer loyal customers special services, discounts, increased communications and attention beyond the care product or service, without expecting an immediate payback. However, they are hoping that, over time, they will reap the advantages of sustained and increasing transactions with a core group of loyal customers.

Although direct marketing, sales promotion, and general advertising may be used as part of a relationship marketing strategy, relationship marketing stresses long-term. commitment to the individual customer, Advances in technology (*e.g.* VPC scanning equipment, relational database), have provided techniques that make tracking customers' simpler; thus influencing the trend towards relationship marketing.

Many companies call their relationship programmes or "club" and some even charge a fee to join. Membership in a club, may serve as a means to convey to customers the notions of performance and exclusivity inherent in a "committed relationship." Additionally, those firms that charge a fee (*e.g.* the Amcrican Express platinum Card) increase customers investment in the relationship that my, in turn, lead to greater commitment to the relationship and increased usage loyalaty. A remarkable alluring relationship club, are with branches in several continents and with members from all over the world, is the Swatch Collectors Club (*i.e.* "Swatch the Club"). For an $80 annual membership fee, Participants (*i.e.* "Swatchers") receive an exclusive membership Swatch watch; a member's pin and card, journals and newsletter and a variety of other materials all designed to inform and entertain collectors of Swatch Watches.

Airlines and major hotel chains, in particular, use relationship marketing, techniques by awarding points to frequent customers that can be, used to obtain additional goods or services from the company.

This kind of point system may act as an exit barrier, because starting a new relationship would mean giving up the potential future value of the points and starting from ground zero with a new service provider. Moreover, companies have recently been broadening the scope of such relationship programmes.

Ultimately, it is to a firm's advantage to develop long-term relationships with existing customers; because it is easier and less expensive to make an additional sale to an existing customer than to make a new sale to a new consumer. However, the effort involved for the firm in developing and maintaining a customer relationship must be weighed against the expected long-term benefits. Marketeers must determine the "Lifetime value of a customer to ensure that the costs of obtaining servicing and cummunicating with the customer do not exceed the potential profits. The table portrays some of the characteristics of the relationship between the firm and customer, the "Spirit" of relationship marketing.

PURCHASE BEHAVIOUR

Consumers make three types of purchase-trial purchases, repeat purchases, and long-term commitment purchases. When a consumer purchases a product (or brand) for the first time and buys a smaller quantity than usual. This purchase would be considered trial. Thus, a trial is exploratory phase of purchase behaviour in which consumers attempt to evaluate a product through direct use. For instance, when consumers purchase a new brand of mouthwash about which they may be uncertain, they are likely to purchase smaller trial quantities than if it were a familiar brand. Consumers can also be encouraged to try a new product through such promotional Marketing Association of America found that coupons substantially influenced initial trial of products like ready-to-eat cereal, bar soap and salted snacks.

When a new brand is an established product category (toothpaste, chewing gum, or cola) is found by trial to be more satisfactory or better than other brands, consumers are likely to repeat purchase. Repeat purchase behaviour is closely related to the concept of brand loyalty, which most firms try to encourage, because it contributes to greater stability in the marketplace. Unlike trial, in which the consumer uses the product on a small scale and without any commitment, a repeat purchase usually signifies that the product meets with the consumer's approval and that he or she is willing to use it again and in larger quantities.

Trial, of course, is not always feasible. For example, with most durable goods (clothes dryers, freezers, or Microwave ovens), a consumer usually moves directly from evaluation to a long-term commitment (through purchase), without the opportunity for an actual trial.

Consider, Joanne and her decision concerning the selection of an online service. If she wanted to personally try to each of the services in her evoked set—America Online, Prodigy, and Compu serve—she could receive a free trial disk and several free hours of usage from each of these on-line venders. However, she feels that setting up software for each service on her home computer would be just too much of hassle for her. Instead, she asks around her retirement community and finds individual's who subscribe to each. She then visits each of these individuals homes to see, first hand, each on-line service. (Joanne discovers that users of on-line services delight in sharing others their computer systems and what their on-line services delight in sharing others their computer systems and what their on-line services have to offer.) Joanne is especially impressed with how easy it is to "surf the net", using the version of browser software that America On line. Using the disk that she received in the mail that offers her 10 free hairs of trial usage.

Post Purchase Evaluation. As consumers use a product particularly during a trial purchase, they evaluate its performance in light of their own expectations. There are three possible outcomes of these evaluations: *(1)* Actual performance matches expectations, leading to a neutral feeling. *(2)* Performance exceeds expectations, causing what is known as positive disconfirmation of expectation (which leads to satisfaction) and *(3)* Performance is below expectation causing negative disconfirmation of expectations and dissatisfaction.

For each of these three outcomes, consumers expectations and satisfaction are closely linked, that is consumers tend to judge their experience against their expectations when performing a post purchase evaluation. The two go hand in hand.

An important component of post purchase evaluation is the reduction of uncertainty or doubt that the consumer might have had the selection. As part of their postpurchase analyses, consumers try to reassure themselves that their choice was wise one; that is, they attempt to reduce post purchase cognitive dissonance. They do this by adopting one of the following strategies: they may rationalise the decision as being wise, they may seek advertisements that support their choice and avoid those of competitive brands, they may attempt to persuade friends or neighbours to buy the same brand (and thus confirm their own choice); or they may turn to other satisfied owners for reassurance.

The degree of postpurchase analysis that consumers undertake depends on the importance of the product decision and the experience acquired in using the product. When the product lives up to expectations, they probably will buy it again. When the product's performance is disappointing or does not meet expectations, however, they will search for more suitable alternatives. Thus, the consumer's post purchase evaluation "feed backs" as experience to the consumer's psychological field and serves to influence future related decisions.

What was Joanne's post purchase evaluation of America Online? Joanne was pleasantly surprised to how easy it was to install. America Online on her computer. She just followed the directions on the disk and then followed the direction on the screen and within. about 10 minutes she was on-line and had her own e-mall address and password. In no more than about 30 minute from the time she first put the America Online install disk in her disk drive, she had composed e-mail messages to several of her friends and had sent them, in fact, she could not wait to start receiving their replies, not that they would have her e-mail address.

She also had even more fun "surfing the net" then she ever thought she would. Joanne also found the experience of being able to send e-mail to her many friends (and some relatives) anywhere in the world to be great time and cost saver. Additionally, she was very impressed with the amount of investment information she could obtain from America Online-information that would help her both select and keep track of her stocks, bonds, and mutual funds. Although America Online did not offer her specialized, extra cost investment news and services, she found that the investment services it did offer were more than adequate for her needs. For example, she found that she could enter up to 100 investments into her America On line "Portfolio" and each time she opened her portfolio screen she would find updated quotas for each one.

In summary, Joanne is thus far thrilled with her experience as an America Online. user, and she wonders how she ever got along without it!

Lifestyles as a Consumer Decision Strategy

An individual's or family's decisions to be committed to a particular lifestyle (*e.g.* devoted followers of a particular religion) impacts on a wide range of specific everyday consumer behaviour. For instance, The Trends Research Institute has identified "Voluntary simplicity" as one of the top "10 lifestyle trends of the 1990s.

They estimate that by the year 2000,15 per cent of all "boomers" will be seeking a simpler lifestyle with reduced emphasis on ownership and possessions. Voluntary simplifiers are making do with less clothing; fewer credit cards (with no outstanding Balances), and moving to smaller, yet still adequate homes or apartments, in less populated communities. Most importantly, it is not that these consumers can no longer afford their affluence or "lifestyle of abundance", rather, they are seeking new, "reduced", less extravagant lifestyles. A part of this new lifestyle commitment some individuals are seeking less stressful and lower salary careers or jobs. In a recent telephone survey for example, 33 per cent of these contacted claimed that they would be willing to take a 20 per cent pay cut in return for working fewer hours.

Incomplete Information and Non-comparable Alternatives

In many choice situations, consumers face incomplete information on which to base decisions and must use alternatives strategies to cape with the missing elements. Missing information may result from advertisements or packaging that mention only certain attributes the consumer's own imperfect memory of attributes for non-present alternatives, or because some attributes are experimental and can only be evaluated after product use. There are at least four alternatives strategies that consumers can adopt for coping with missing information:

1. Consumers may delay the decision until missing information is obtained. This strategy is likely to be used for high risk decision.

2. Consumers may ignore missing information and decide to continue with current decision rule (*e.g.* compensatory or non-compensatory), using the available attribute information.

3. Consumers may change the customorily used decision strategy to one which better accommodates missing information.

4. Consumers may infer ("construct") the missing information.

In discussing consumers decision rules, we have assumed that a choice is made from among the brands evaluated. Of course, a consumer may also conclude that none of the alternatives offers sufficient benefits to warrant purchase. If this were to occur with a necessity, such as a refrigerator, the consumer would probably either-lower his or her expectations and settle for the best of the available alternatives or seek information about additional brands, hoping to find one that more closely meets predetermined criteria. On the other hand, if the purchase is more discretionary (*e.g.* a second or third pair of jeans), the consumer probably would postpone the purchase. In this case information gained from the search up to that point would be transferred to long-term storage (in this psychological field) and retrived and reintroduced as input if and when the consumer regains interest in making such a purchase:

In applying decision rules, a consumer may at times attempt to compare dissimilar (non comparable) alternatives. For example, a consumer may be undecided about whether to buy a new car or remodel her kitchen, because she can afford either, but not both, expenditures. Another example, a consumer may try to decide between buying a new raincoat or a new pair of shoes. When there is great dissimilarity in the alternative way allocating available funds, consumers abstract the products to a level in which coparison are possible. In the example, cited above, a consumer might weigh the alternatives (new car versus remodelled kitchen or raincoat vs. shoes) in terms of which alternative would offer the most pleasure or which, if either is more of a "necessity".

Decision Rules and Marketing Strategy. An understanding of which decision rules consumers apply in selecting a particular product or service useful to marketeer concerned with formulating a promotional programme. A marketeer familiar with the prevailing decision rule can, prepare a promotional message in format that would facilitate consumer information processing. The promotional message might even suggest how potential consumers should make a decision. For instance, a direct mail piece for a new computer notebook might tell potential consumers "what to look for in a new notebook". This mail piece might specifically ask consumers to consider the attributes to screen size, battery life, price, weight, pointing device, and amount of memory in their purchase decision process.

Consumption Vision. Researchers have recently proposed "consumption vision" as a non-orthodox, but potentially accurate, portray of decision-making for those situations in which the consumer has little experience and problems are not well structured, as well as in which there is a considerable amount of emotions. Under such circumstances, the consumer may turn to a "consumption vision" a mental picture or visual image of specific usage outcomes and/or consumption consequences." Such vision (*e.g.* a prospective bride envisioning a garden wedding versus a wedding taking place on a boat or a consumer visualizing a skiing vacation versus a caribbean vacation) allow consumers to imagine or vicariously participate in die consumption of the product or service prior to making an actual decision. After "trying out" a number of different alternatives in one's mind, so to speak the consumer then makes his or her decision.

CONSUMER DECISION-MAKING

Everyday we make number of decisions concerning different aspects of our daily lives. We generally make these decisions without stopping to think about how we make them and what is involved in the particular decision-making process itself. In the most general terms, a decision is the selection of an option from two or more alternative choices, In other words, a choice of alternatives must be available, for a person to make a decision. When a person has a choice between to make a purchase and not to make a purchase, a choice between brand "M" and brand "N", or a choice of spending time doing, "Y" or "Z", that person is in a position to make a decision. On the other hand, if the consumer has no alternatives from which to choose and is literally forced to make a particular purchase or take a particular action, (then this single "no-choice" does not constitute a decision, such a no "choice decision is commonly referred to as a Hobson's choice".

But in fact, no choice purhcase or consumption situations are fairly rare. For consumers, freedom often is expressed in terms of a wide range of product choices, Thus, if there is almost always a choice, then there is almost always an opportuniry for consumers to make decision. Moreover, experimental consumer research reveals that providing-consumers with a choice when there was originally none can be a very good business strategy, one that can substantially increase sales. For example, when a direct mail electrical applince catalogue displayed two coffee makers instead of just one (*e.g.* the original coffee maker at $149 and a "new" only slightly larger, one at $229), the addition of the second comparison coffee maker seemed to stimulate consumer evaluation that significantly increased the sales of the original coffee maker.

Levels of Consumer Decision-Making

Not all consumer decision-making situtations receive (or require) the same degree of information search. If all purchase decisions required extensive effort, then consumer decision-making would be an exhaustive process that left little time for anything else. On the other hand, if all purchases were routine, then they would tend to be monotonous and would provide little pleasure or novelty. On a continuum of effort ranging from very high to very low, we can distinguish three specific levels of consumers decision-making *(a)* extensive problem solving; *(b)* limited problem solving; *(c)* rouitinized response behaviour.

Extensive Problem Solving. When consumers have no established criteria for evaluating a product category or specific brands in that category or have not narrowed the number of brands they will consider to a small, manageable subset, their decision-making efforts can be classified as extensive problem solving. At this level, the consumer needs a great deal of information to establish a set of criteria on which to judge specific brandsap and correspondingly large amount of information concerning each of the brands to be considered.

Limited Problem Solving. At this level of problem solving, consumers already have established the basic criteria for evaluating the product category and the various brands in the category. However, they have not fully established preferences concerning a select group of brands. Their search for additional information is more like "fine tuning". They must gather additional brand information to discriminate among the various brands.

Routinized Response Behaviour. At this level, consumers have some experience with the product category and a well established set of criteria with which to evaluate the brands they are considering. In some situations, they may search for a small amount of additional information: In others, they simply review what they already know.

Just how extensive a consumer's problem-solving task is depends on how well establihsed his or her criteria for selection are, how much information he or she has about each brand being considered: and how narrow the set of brands is from which the choice will be made. Clearly, extensive problem. solving implies that the consumer must seek more information to make a choice, while routinized response behaviour implies little need for additional information.

Models of Consumers

Four Views of Consumer Decision-Making. We will consider several schools of thought that depict consumer decision-making in distinctly different ways, before presenting an overview model of how consumer makes decisions. The term models of consumers refers to a general "view" or perspective as to how (and why) individuals behave as they do. Specifically, we will examine models of consumers in terms of the foliowing four views:

1. an economic view,
2. a passive view,
3. a cognitive view, and
4. an emotional view.

1. An Economic View. In the field of theoretical economics, which portrays a world. of perfect competition, the consumer has often been characterized as making rational decisions. This model, called the economic man theory, has been criticized by consumer researchers for a number of reasons. To behave rationally in the economic sense, a consumer would have to:

(a) be aware of all available product alternatives,

(b) be capable of correctly ranking each alternative in terms of its benefits and disadvantages, and

(c) be able to identify the one best alternative.

Realistically however, consumers rarely have all of the informaion or sufficiently accurate information or even an adequate degree of involvement or motivation, to make the so-called "perfect" decision.

According to a Leading. social scientist, the economic model of an all rational consuriler is unrealistic for the following reasons:

(a) people are limited by their existing skills, habits, and reflexes,

(b) people are limited by their existing values and goals, and

(c) people are limited by the extent of their knowledge.

Consumers operate in an imperfect world in which 'they do not maximize their decisions in terms of economic considerations, such as price-quantity relationships, marginal utility, or indifference curves. Indeed, the consumer generally is unwilling to engage in extensive decision-making activities and will settle instead for a "satisfactory" deisions, one that is good enough. For this reason, the economic model is oftten rejected as too idealistic and simplistic.

Passive View. Quite opposite to the rational economic view of consumers is the passive view that depicts the consumer as basically submissive to the self-serving interests and promotional efforts of marketeers. In the passive view, consumers are perceived as impulsive and irrational purchasers, ready to yield to the aims and arms of marketeers. At least to some degree, the passive model of the consumer was subscribed to by the hard-driving supersalesman of old, who were trained to regard the consumer as an object to be manipulated. The following excerpt from a 1917 salesmenship text dramatically illustrates the long held belief in the dominance of the salesmen over the unresising, somewhat passive consumer.

In the development of selling process, there are four stages. First, the salesman must secure the prospects undivided attention. Secondly, this attention must be sustained and developed into interest. Thirdly, this interest must be ripened into desire. And Fourthly, all lingering doubts must be removed from the prospects mind and there must be implanted a firm resolution to buy; in other words, the sale must be closed.

The principal limitation of the passive model is that it fails to recognize that the consumer plays an equal, if not dominant, role in many buying situations sometimes by seeking information about product alternatives and selecting the product that appears to offer the greatest satisfaction and at other times impulsively selecting a product that satisfies the mood or emotion of the moment. Motivation, selective perception, learning, attitudes, communication, and opinion leadership serves to support the proposition that consumers are rarely objects of manipulation. Therefore, this simple, and single-minded view should also be rejected as unrealistic.

A Cognitive View. The third portrays the consumer as a thinking problem solves. Within this framework consumers frequently are pictured as either receptive to or actively searching for products and services that fulfil their needs and enrich their lives. The cognitive model focuses on the processes by which consumers seek and evaluate information about selected brands and retail outlets.

Within the context of the cognitive model, consumers are viewed as information processors. Information, processing leads to the formation of preferences and ultimately, to purchase intentions. Consumers also may use a preferences formation strategy that is "other based" in which they allow' another person (*i.e.* trusted friend, an interior decorator, or a expert retail salesperson) to make the selection for them.

In contrast to the economic view, the cognitive view recognizes that the consumer is unlikely to even attempt to obtain all available information about every choice. Instead, consumers are likely to cease their information seeking efforts when they perceive that they have sufficient information about some of the alternatives to make a "satisfactory" decision. As this information-processing viewpoint suggests, consumers often develop short cut decision rules (called heuristics) to facilitate the decision-making process. They also use decision rules to cope with exposure to too much information (*i.e.* information overload).

The cognitive, or problem solving view describes a consumer who falls somewhere between the extremes of the economic and passive views, who does not (or cannot) have total knowledge about available product alternatives and therefore cannot make perfect decisions, but who nonetheless actively seeks information and attempts to make satisfactory decisions.

So cognitive model seems to capture the essence of a well educated and involved consumer who seeks information on which to base consumption decisions.

Importance of Brand Loyalty and Brand Equity in Marketing

A major goal of marketeers interested in how consumers learn is to encourage brand loyalty. Brand loyal customers provide the basis for a stable and growing market share, and can be a major intangible asset, reflected in the purchase price of a company. A study of consumer purchase habits reported that brands with larger market shares have proportionately larger groups of loyal buyers.

As straightforward as it may seem, brand loyalty is not a simple concept. A basic issue among researchers is whether to define the concept in terms of consumer behaviour or consumer attitudes. To cognitive learning theorists behavioural definitions lack precision, since they do not distinguish between the "real" brand-loyal buyer who is intentionally faithful, and the spurious brand-loyal buyer who repeats a brand purchase because it is the only one available at the store. Such theorists say that brand loyalty must be measured by attitudes toward a brand rather than by purchase consistency.

One study measured brand loyalty in three different ways-brand market share, the number of same-brand purchases in a six months period, and the average number of brands bought per buyer. Findings suggest that consumers buy from a mix of brands within their acceptable range. Thus, the greater. the number of acceptable brands in a specific product category, the less likely is the consumer to be brand-loyal to one specific brand. Conversely, products having new competitors, as well as those purchased with great efficiency, are likely to have greater brand loyalty.

Food products found to have over 80 per cent of brand-loyal users include table salt, vinegar, nonstick cooking spray, dry milk, powdered breakfast drinks, and egg substitutes. Non-food grocery products with over 80 per cent brand loyal users include waxed paper, oven cleaners, spot removers, and pet shampoos.

A recent study explored the relationship between perceived differences among brands vis-a-vis brand loyalty for selected products and services and found that brand loyalty is not driven necessarily by perceived differences among brands. Men's cologne, cola drinks, and fast food restaurants (quadrant) have high brand discrimination yet low brand loyalty, whereas headache remedies and shaving cream (quadrantly) have brand discrimination but high brand loyalty. Another study concluded that brand of loyalty is generally time-dependent; that is consumers can be brand-loyal during one period of time and not another.

Some theorists suggest that brand loyalty is correlated with the consumer's degree of involvement. They suggest that high involvement leads to extensive information search and ultimately to brand loyalty, whereas low involvement leads to exposure and brand awareness and then possibility to brand habits, If brand loyalty is defined as commitment clearly the low-involvement consumer could not be considered brand loyal.

Developing Brand Loyalty. Behavioural scientists who favour the theory of instrumental, conditioning believe that brand loyalty results from an initial product trial that is reinforced through satisfaction, leading to repeat purchase, Cognitive researchers, on the other hand, emphasize the role of mental process in building brand loyalty. They belive that consumers engage ill extensive problem-solving behaviour involving brand and attribute comparisons, leading to a strong brand preference and repeat purchase behaviour. Involvement theory suggests that frequent exposure to TV commercials that are rich in visual cues and symbolism and short duration, buttressed by in-store displays, creates a type of brand loyalty for low involvement purchases.

Some studies have indicated there is little defference in demographics among consumers who are brand loyal and those who are not. Others have found that brand-loyal consumers are olders, have higher income, and greater perceived risks. Some ethnic groups appear to be fiercely loyal to certain brands that have traditionally created to their specific market. For example, Hispanics have been loyal to Goya products for generations, making it extremely difficult for other marketeers to gain a freehold in the Hispanic Marketplace.

Marketeers are interested not only in 'how' brand loyalty develops, but in "when" it develops, Research evidence suggests that a great deal of brand loyalty develops quite early in the context of family life. Classic toys, Leo blocks, Barbie dolls, Lionel trains, GI loes were the popular christmas toys in 1988, as baby boomers tried to convey traditional values to their children by buying the toys they best remembered. Indeed, nostalgia has become an important advertisement appeal for this market.

Marketeers must be careful not to impose unilateral changes on product which have a loyal following. The Coca-cola company discovered this in its classic marketing blunder in 1985, when it suffered a furious consumers backlash to its replacement of the original Coca-cola formula with a newly formulated Coke. More recently, Procter & Gamble had to bring back its original green Prell Shampoo after loyal consumers rebelled at a new blue formulation.

Declining Brand Loyalty. Many Marketing Managers are concerned with a growing trend towards brand switching. Among the reasons given for the decline in brand loyalty are consumers boredom or dissatisfaction with a product, the dazzling away of new products that constantly appears in the Marketplace, and an increased concern with price at the expense of brand loyalty. National brand usually command premium prices, a strategy which is at odds with the new focuss on lower prices "value" brands. The market shares of private label brands continues to rise in categories once considered the bastion of brand loyalty. Because of the growing number of private label cigarrete brands, Philip Morris U.S.A. lowered its price for Marlboro cigarettes in an effort to maintain market share. Marketeers also are upgrading their national brands to distinguish them from private labels and promoting them more aggressively.

There also has been tremendous increase in sales promotion "deals". In trying to increase market share many companies have spent a greater proportion of their promotion budget on sales promotion device (*e.g.*. coupons, special price deals, sweepstakes, free samples, point of purchase in display) than on advertising. Yet advertising is an important Medium through which consumers learn product attributes. Although promotional activities may boost sales in the short run, evidence suggests that brand loyal consumers take advantage of such temporary price deals to increase their purchases (thus cannibalizing full-price sales), white deal prone customers who succumbs to the deal inducement are quick to swtich to another brand when the special offer ends or a better deal comes along. Thus, while sales promotion efforts do increase market share in the short run, they are unlikely to hold prone consumers in the long run. Declines in brand loyalty are also attributed to the increase in advertising, increased targeting of specially niches and increased diversity of supermarket shoppers (unmarried men and women husband teenage children).

Many Marketeers believe it is more difficult to establish service brand loyalty than product brand loyalty. Some service organisations have started to promote consistency of operation and convenience in an effort to combat shifting loyalites. Others have adopted such sales promotions devices as frequently-user credits to encourage brand loyalty. For example, the fast food chain Arby's issue club Arby cards which electronically track members' Arby purchases, and awards prizes like food and coupons for either frequently or aggregate sales.

Some Marketeers have given new life to brands suffering declining sales and declining loyalty through product-line and product-form extensions. Tide detergent for example started out as a powdered laundry soap, and was extended to liquid Tide, Tide with Bleach and Ultra Tide, each targeted at a different Market niche. In some cases, brands that have been kept alive through aggressive promotion have been dubbed "dinosaur brands".

Because of the importance of brand imagery to brand loyalty, many Marketeers develop a simple, description promotional line and, through heavy repetition, engrave it consumers memories. By using such everyday advertising tools as mnemonic devices singles, rhymes, and audience participation marketeers increase brand name rehearsal and enhance brand memory even for low-involvement products.

Despite the diversity of viewpoint among leaving theorists, most marketeers are interested in all measures of brand loyalty. They concerned with actual consumer purchasing patterns with consumers belief and opinions concerning their brand and competing brands, and with knowing how important the product is to the consumer. Developing a highly consistent market share of brand-loyal consumers is the ultimate goal of marketing strategy. Discovering how consumers learn about brand and become attached to certain brands assist marketeers in achieving this goal.

Brand Equity. The term brand equity refers to the value inherrent in a well-known brand name. It contributes to acceptance of new product, allocation of preferred shelf space, perceived value, perceived quality, premium pricing options and even to value assets on a company's balance sheet. For all of these reasons, companies have begun to carefully nurture their brand names.

Because a brand that has been promoted heavily in the past remains a cummulative level of native recognition, companies actually buy and sell brand names. Knowing that it is easier to buy than to create a brand name with enduring strength.

Well known brand names are referred to as Mega-brands. Among the best known brands are Campbell's group, Hallmark Cards, United Parcel Service, Her shey's and McDonald's. These names have become "cultural icons", and enjoy powerful advantages over the competitions. Large marketeers have begun to pave down their portfolios of brand name, as Proctor & Gamble did when it folded its $ 66 million white cloud bathroom tissue into its $ 312.5 million Charmin brand, calling it Charmin Ultra. They are also paving down their product categories. For example, RJR Nabisco bought Stella D'oro cookies to complement its Nabisco brand and sold its cold cereal, including shredded wheat, to General Mills, which enhanced General Mills Cereal category.

Because of the proliferation of brands and resulting consumer confusion, major marketeers also are trying to consolidate their brands into global brands product lines, that dominate their categories and marketed in some of the countries. When Gillette acquired Parker Pen Holding Ltd. of Britain, it became the world's largest producer of pens as well as shaving products. The Gillette Company also added a new unifying "Omnimark" Logo to its premium priced brands, "worlds-class vrands, product, people".

Brand equity is important to marketeers because it leads to brands loyalty, to increased market share and ultimately to greater profits. To marketeers, the major function of learning theory is to teach consumers that their product is best, to encourage repeat purchase, and ultimately, loyalty to the brand name.

Importance of Brandin Consumer Decision Making

Evoked Set. Within the context of consumers decision-making, the evokedset refers to the specific brands a consumer considers in making a purchase within a particular product category. (The evoked set is also called the consideration set-up consumer s evoked set is distinguished from his or her inept setup which consists of brand the Consumers excludes from purchase consideration because they are felt to be unacceptable (*e.g.* they are seen as "inferior") and from the inert set, which consists of brands the consumer is indifferent towards because they are perceived as not having any particular advantages. Regardless of the total number of brands in a product category, a consume's evoked set ends to be quite small on average, often consisting of only three to five brands.

The evoked set consists of the small number of brands the consumer is familiar with, and finds acceptable; It is essential that a product be parts of consumer's evoked set if it is to be considered at all. The five terminal positions in the model that do not end in purchase would appear to have perceptual problems. For example, *(1)* Brands may be unknown because of the consumer's selective exposure to advertising media and selective perception of advertising stimuli ; *(2)* Brands may be unacceptable because of poor qualities or attributes or inappropriate positioning in either advertising or product characteristics ; *(3)* Brands may be perceived as not having any special benefits and are regarded indifferently by the consumer; *(4)* Brands, may be overlooked because they have not been clearly positioned or sharply targeted at the consumer market segment under study; and *(5)* Brands may not be selected because they reperceived by consumers as unable to satisfy perceived needs 'as fully' as the brand that is chosen.

In each of these instances, the implications for marketeers is that promotional techniques should be designed to impart a more favourable, perhaps more relevant product image to the target consumer. This may also require a change in product features or attributes (more or better features).

Criteria Used for Evaluating Brands. The criteria consumers use to evaluate the brands that constitute their evoked sets usually are expressed in terms of important product attributes. Examples of product attributes that consumers have used as criteria in evaluating nine product category are listed in the table.

Table: Possible Product Attributes used as Purchase Criteria, for Nine Product categories

Personal Computers	*Sneakers*	*Wristwatch*
Processing speed	Styling	Watch band
Price	Colour	Alarm feature
Type of display	Price	Price
Hard disk size	Air sole	Water-resistant

Amount of memory	High top or low top	Quartz movement
Lap top or desk top	Purpose (*e.g.* basketball)	Size of dial

Telephones	***Colour TVs***	***Frozen Dinners***
Size	Picture Quality	Taste
Warranty	Length of warranty	Type of main course
Memory dialing	Cable ready	Type of side dishes
Hold button	Price	Speaktrphone
Cabiret style	Size of screen	Preparation requirements

35 MM Cameras	***Fountain Pens***	***Men's Dress Shirts***
Auto focus	Balance	Size
Built in flash	Price	Fabric
Automatic filmloading	Gold nib	Colour
Lens type	Smoothness	Collar style
Size and weight	Ink reserve	Cuffstyle

The table given below presents a comparison of consumers by different age groups in terms of ratings of attributes that "Strongly influence" their automobile purchase decisions. Although all consumers, regardless fage, value cars that are reliable and durable,' there are some age differences. For instance, while the youngest car buyers (those from 16 to 29 years of age) are more concerned with owning cars that offer the latest technology, the oldest car buyers (those 50 years of age and older) appear to be the least price conscious to rely more on trusted brand names, and to value "easy to use" factors. Because baby boomers are moving into this older age cohort, automobile makers are increasingly human engineering their cars to make them easier to get into and act of, as well as easier to use.

The Influence of Seleded Automobile Attributes on Purchase Decision (Age)

	Percent Rating as Strongly Influence Age Categories		
	16-29	*30-49*	*50+*
Reliable, works like it should	68	85	73
Long lasting, durable	63	78	72
Easy to fix, maintain	39	49	53
Low Price	40	42	30
Easy to use	38	40	46
Easy to Purchase	33	31	25
Known, trusted, brand name	26	32	43
Latest technology styles	20	13	14
Marty options, features	18	11	13

Source : Laurie Peterson, "The Strategic Shopper" Adweek's Marketing Week (March 30, 1992 18.

When a company knows that consumers will be evaluating alternatives they, sometimes advertisers in away that recommends the criteria that consumers should use in assessing product or service options. For example, an ad for The Bank of New York Challenges the reader to compare the home equity credit lines offered by different banks in terms of a number of specific criteria.

We have probably all gone through the experience of comparing or evaluating different brands or models of a product and findings the one that just feels, 100 ks, and/or performs "right". Interestingly, research shows that when consumers discuss such "right products", there is little or no mention of price, brand names are not often top of mind, items often reflect personality characteristics or child hood experiences, and it is often "love at first sight" In one recent study, the products claimed by research participants to 'just-feel right" included Big Berther golf clubs, old leather briefcase, Post-it notes, and the Honda Accord.

Let's return for a moment to Joanne, the retire who is contemplating subscribing to a computer on-line service. After calling the major on-line service companies for literature on their services, reading the direct mail she received at home and number of magazine articles, and talking to a few knowledgeable friends, Joanne' s evoked set might consists of America On line, Prodigy and Compusive.

On the basis of her recently acquired information, Joanne has tentatively decided that the on-line service she subscribes to should have the following three features; local telephonenumber access, the ability to "Surf the net", and the availability of stock market and mutual find information that she would need to monitor her investments. Evaluating the information supplied by each of the on-line service, Joanne might mentally or on paper construct a table that compares the availability of specific features of the three services in her evoked set. The table shows the data.

Table

Feature	*America Online*	*Compusive*	*Prodigy*
Monthly fee	$9.95/5hr	$9,95/5 hr	$ 9.95/5 hr
Additional hours	$ 2.95	$ 2.95	$ 2.95
Maximum Connect Speed	28,800 bps	28,800 bps	14,400 bps
24-hr, 7 days/week technical support	Yes	No	Yes
On line banking	Yes	No	Yes
Full internet connection	Yes	Yes	Yes
Allows use of good Web browsing software	Yes	No	No

Can check stocks and mutual funds	Yes
Personalized investment news & services	No

As 30 May, 1996

As part of her search process Joanne also has acquired information about other relevant issues (or attributes) that could influence her final choice. For example, she has learned that both America Online and Prodigy Offer 24 hour, 7 days-a week technical support, Compuserve offers more business and reference features and America Online has the most users friendly interface.

Additionally, whereas America online and compuserve will allow to use her modern at its highest speed of 28,000 bps, Prodigy's maximum user speed was at the time of her decision only 14,400 bps.

Consumer Decision Rules. Consumer decision rules often referred to as heuristics, decision strategies brand (or other consumption-related) choices. These rules reduce the burden of making complex decisions by providing guidelines or routines that make the process less taxing.

Consumer decision rules have been broadly classified into two major categories. Compensatory and non-compensatory decision rules. In following a compensatory decision rule, a consumer evaluates brand options in terms of each relevant attribute and computes a weighted or summered score for each brand. The computed score reflects the brand's relative merit as a potential purchase choice. The assumption is that the consumer will select the brand that scores highest among the alternatives evaluated. Table given below clears using a conpensatory decision rule, America On line scrores highest.

A unique feature of a compensatory decision rule is that it allows a positive evaluation of a brand on one attribute to balance out a negative evaluation on some other attribute. For example, a positive assesment of the energy-savings made possible by a particular brand or type of right bulb's may offset an assessment in terms of the bulb's diminished light output.

Feature	America On Line	Compusive	Prodigy
	*Hypothtical Ratings for On-line Servlces**		
* Monthly Fees	6	6	6
* Maximum connect Speed	10	10	5
* 24 hr, 7 day/week technical support	7	5	7
* On line banking	6	4	6
* Full internet connection	9	9	9
* Allows use of good web brousing software	10	5	5
* Can check stocks and mutual funds	10	10	10
* Personalized investment news & services	5	7	7
	63	56	55

*Evaluation are on a ten point scale, a higher number indicates a higher rating.

In contrast, non compensatory decision rules do not allow consumers to balance positive evaluations of brand on one attribute against a negative evaluation on some other attribute. For instance, in the case of energy-saving light bulb, the product's negative (unacceptable) rating on its light output would not be offset by a positive evaluation of its energy savings. Instead, this particular light bulb would be disqualified from further consideration. If Joanne choice of an on-line service was based on maximum connection speed, a non-compensatory decision rule would have eliminated Prodigy.

Three non-compensatory roles are considered briefly here: the conjunctive rule, the disconjunctive rule, and the lexicographic rule.

In the following a conjunctive decision rule the consumer establishes a separate, minimally acceptable level as a cut of point for each attribute. If any particular brand falls below the cut off point on anyone attribute, the brand is eliminated from further consideration. Because the conjunctive rule can result in several acceptable alternatives, it becomes necessary in such cases for the consumer to apply an additional decision rule to arrive, at a final selection, for example, to accept the first satisfactory brand. The conjunctive rule is particularly useful in quickly reducing the number of alternatives to be considered. The consumer can then apply another, more refined decision rule to arrive at a final choice.

The disconjunctive rule is the "mirror image" of the conjunctive rule. In applying this decision role, the consumer also establishes, a separate, minimally acceptable level as the cut of point for each attribute (which may be higher than one normally established for a conjunctive rule), In this case, if a brand alternative meets or exceeds the cut off established for anyone attribute, it is accepted. Here again a number of brands might exceed the cut off point, producing a situation in which another decision rule is required. When this occurs, the consumer may accept the first satisfactory brand as the final choice or apply some other (perhaps more suitable, decision, role,

In following a lexicographic decision rule, the consumer first ranks the attributes in terms of perceived relevance or importance. The consumer then compares the various brand alternatives in terms of the single attribute that is considered most important. If one brand scores sufficiently high on this top-ranked attribute (regardless of the score on any of the other attributes), it is selected and the process ends. When, there are two or more brand alternatives, the proccss is repeated with the second highest ranked attribute (and so on), until reaching the point that one of the brands is selected because it exceeds the others on a particular attribute.

With the lexicographic role, the highest ranked attribute (the one applied first) may reveal something about the individual's basic consumer (or shopping) orientation, For instance, "buy the best" rule might indicate that the consumer is quality oriented; a "buy the most prestigious brand" rule might indicate that the consumer is status oriented a "buy the least expensive" rule might reveal that the consumer is economy minded.

A variety of decision roles appear quite commonplace. Accord to a consumer survey, pine act of ten shoppers who go to store for frequently purchased items possess a specific shopping strategy, for saving money. The consumer, segment and the specific shopping rules that these segments employ are:

1. **Practical Loyalists.** Those who look to for ways to sare on the brands and products they would buy anyway.

2. **Bottom line Price Shoppers.** These who buy the lowest-priced item with the little or no regard for brand.

3. **Opportunistic Switchers.** Those who' use coupons or sales to decide among brands and products that within their evoked set.

4. **Deal Hunters.** Those who look for the best "bargain" and are not brand loyal.

We have considered only the most basic of an almost infinite number of consumer decision rules. Most of the decision rules described here can be combined to form new variations. It is likely that for many purchase decisions; consumers maintain in long-term memory overall evaluations of the brands in their evoked sets. This would make assessment by individual attributes unnecessary. Instead, the consumer would simply select the brand with the highest perceived overall rating. This type of synthesized decision rules is known as the affect referral decision rule and may represent tbe simplest of all rules.

The table given summurizes the essence of many of the decision rules, in terms of the kind of mental statements that Joanne, our retired school teacher might make in selecting an on-line information service.

Hypothetical Use of Popular Decision Rules in Making an On-Line Service Decision

Decision Rule	*Mental Statement*
Compensatory rule	"I selected the on-line service that came out best when I balanced the good ratings against the bad ratings."
Conjunctive rule	"I picked the on-line service that had no bad features."
Disjunctive rule	"I selected the on-line service that excelled in at least one attribute." "I looked at the feature that was the most important to me and chose the on-line service that ranked highest on that attribute."
Affect referral rule	"Everything they do is outstanding, so I decided to buy their-on-line services".

MODEL OF CONSUMER DECISION-MAKING

This section presents an overview model of consumer decision making that reflects the cognitive (*i.e.* problem-solving) consumer and, to some degree the emotional consumer. The model is designed to tie together many of the ideas on consumer decision making and consumption behavior. It does not presume to provide an exhaustive picture of the complexities of consumer decision making. Rather it is designed to synthesize and coordinate relevant concepts into significant whole.

Input. The input component of our consumer decision-making model draws on external influences that serve as sources of information about a purticular product and influence a consumer's product-related values attitudes and behaviour. Chief among these input factors are the marketing mix activities of organizations that attempt to communicate the benefits of their products and services to potential consumers, and the non marketing socio cultural influences, which, when internalized, affect the consumer's purchase decisions.

Marketing Inputs. The firm's marketing activities are a direct attempt to reach inform and persuade consumers to buy and use its products. These inputs to the consumer's decision-making process take the form of specific marketing mix strategies that consists of the product itself (including its package, size and guarantees), mass-media advertising, direct marketing, personal selling and other promotional efforts, pricing policy; and the selection of distribution channels to move the product from the manufacturer to the consumer.

Ultimately, the impact of a firm's marketing efforts in large measure is governed by the consumer's perception of these efforts. Thus, marketeers do well to remain diligently alert to consumer perceptions by sponsoring consumer research, rather than to rely on the intended impact of their marketing messages.

Sociocultural Inputs. The second type of input, the sociocultural environment, also exerts a major influence on the consumer. Sociocultural inputs consists of a wide range of non-commercial influences. For example, the comments of a friend, an editorial in the newspaper, usage by a family member, or an article in Consumer Reports are all specific and direct no commercial sources of information. The influences of Social Class, culture, and sub-culture, although less tangible, are important input factors that are internalized and affect how consumers evaluate and ultimately adopt (or reject) products.

The unwritten codes of conduct communicated by culture subtly indicate which consumption behaviour should be considered "right" or, "wrong" at a particular point of time. For example, until the 1970, most men would not have considered using hair colouring or hairspray. Now use of these products is fairly commonplace among men.

A Simple Model of Consumer Decision-Making

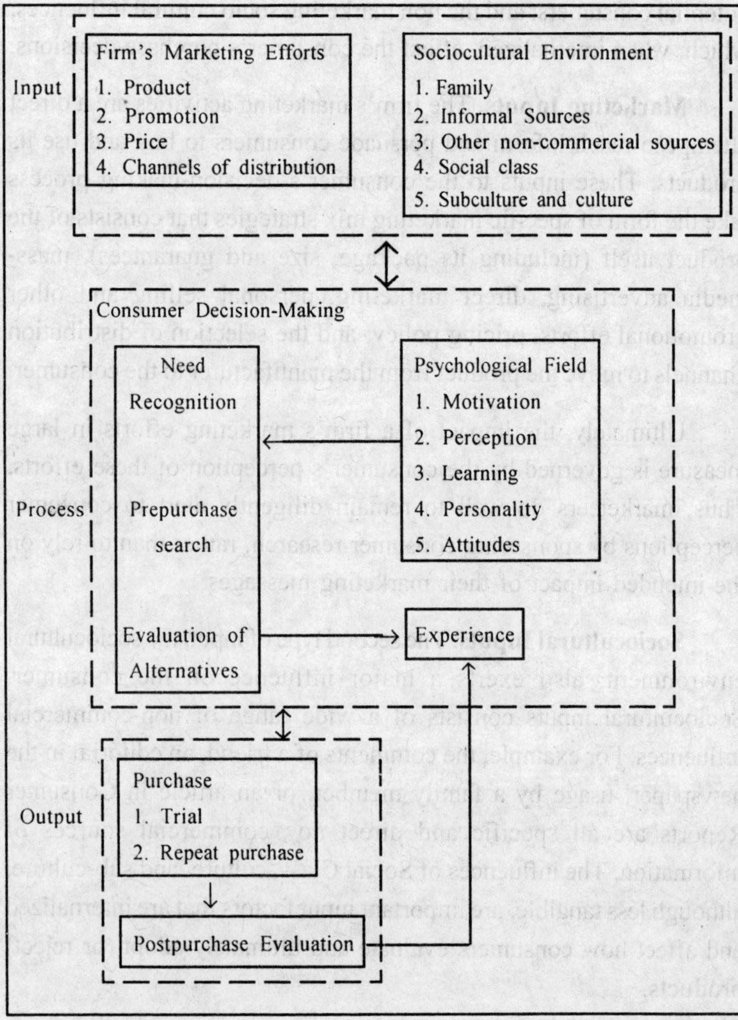

Unlike the firm's marketing efforts, socio-cultural inputs do not necessarily support the purchase or consumption of a specific product but may influence consumers to avoid a product. For example, in some areas of the country and in some articles, circles, animals rights, activists have discouraged women from buying and wearing furs.

The cumulative impact of each firm's marketing efforts, the influence of family, friends, and neighbours; and society's existing code of behavior are all inputs that are likely to affect what consumers purchase and how they use what they buy. Because these influenes may be directed to the individual or actively sought by the individual, a two headed arrow is used to link the input and process segments of the model.

Process. The process component of the model is concerned with how consumers make decision. To understand this process, we must consider the influence of the psychological concepts. Psychological field represents the internal influences (motivation, perception, learning, personality, and attitudes) that affect consumers decision-making process (what they need or want, their awareness of various product choices, their information-gathering activities and their evaluation of alternatives). The act of making a consumer decision consists of three stages: *(1)* need recognition *(2)* Prepurchase search, and *(3)* evaluation of alternatives.

Need Recognition. The recognition of a need is likely to occur when a consumer is faced with a "problem". For example, consider the case of newly retired couple, Arthur and Joanne, who have recently sold their home in a suburb of Boston and relocated to Tampa, Florida. Although Arthur is looking forward to spending time on the golf course, Joanne (a former kindergarten teacher) has been promising herself for the past 2 years that she was going to learn how to send and receive-e-mail and access to internet, using their home computer (which has formally used only for letter writing and for making birthday cards to send to the couple's grandchildren). Some of her friends who are already retired have told her how convenient and inexpensive it is to keep in touch via-e-mail, and they have also spoken to her about the wealth of free information available on the internet-everything from apple pie recipes to zoo visiting hours. One friend in particular, Robert (who is also a retired teacher) a "technology lover" (a person heavily interested in technology, including computers and internet), has been encouraging Joanne "to take the plunge and subscribe to an on-line service". Recent research exploring older consumers on line computer behaviour has revealed two different types of "cyberseniors" technology lovers versus technology users.

Now, let us return to Joanne she is also interested in being to check on the performance of the couple's current investments in several stocks and mutual funds. Moreover, her friends have told her that the easiest way to' gain access to e-mail and the Internet is by subscribing to an on-line service. (Joanne has recognized a possible 'need for an on line service).

Because Joanne had been talking about subscribing to an on line service for a while, for Mother's Day her children and grandchildren presented her with a new, external 28,800 bps model, and they even attached it to her computer and telephone line for her.

Among consumers, there seem to be two different needs or problem recognition styles. Some consumers are actual state types, who perceive that they have a problem when a product fails to perform satisfactorily (*e.g.* a wrist watch no longer keep accurate time). In contrast, other consumers are desired slate types, for whom the desire for something new may trigger, the decision process. (Joanne in her consideration of an on-line service, appears to be a desired state consumer).

Prepurchase Search. Prepurchase search begins when a consumer perives a need that might be satisfied by the purchase and consumption of a product. The recollection of past experiences (drawn from long term, memory storage) might provide the consumer with adequate information to make the present choice. On the other hand, when the consuiner has had no prior experience, he or she may have to engage in extensive search of the outside environment for useful information on which to base a choice.

The consumer usually searches his or her memory (the psychological field depicted in the model) before seeking external sources of information regarding a given consumption-related need. Past experience is considered an internal source of information. The greater the relevant past experience, the less external information the consumer is likely to need to reach a decision. Many consumer decisions are based on a combination of past experience (internal sources) and marketing and non-commercial information (external sources). The degree of perceived risk can also influence this stage of the decision process. In high-risk situation; consumers are likely to engage in complex information search and evaluation, in low-risk situations, they are likely to use very simple search and evaluation tactics.

An examination of external search effort associated with the purchase of different product categories (*e.g.* TVs, VCRs, or personal computers) found that, as the amount of total search effort increased, consumer attitudes, towards shopping became more positive, and more time was made available for shopping. Not surprisingly the external search effort was greatest for consumers who had the least amount of product category knowledge. It follows that the less consumers know about a product category and the more important the purchase is to them, the more they will make available and the more extensive their prepurchase search activity is likely to be. Additionally, by conducting focus groups and other consumer research on how expectations of a product influence consumers subsequent interpretation and evaluation of product information, firms are assisted in their efforts to devise better products and to promote their products strongest points.

How much information a consumer will gather also depends on various situational factors. Consider the case of Joanne, the retired kindergarten teacher who has recognized a need for an on-line computer service. Although she has little exposure to such services (simply hearing about these services from friends neighbours), she believes that such a service would provide her with the link she needs to the. Internet and make it easy for her to send and receive e-mail and to keep track of her family's investments. If she feels that she must make an immediate purchase decision, then she might call each on-line venders 800 number, speak to a consumer service representative, and select one on that basis alone. On the other hand, this type of rapid decision-making does not suit everyone. Many consumers prefer to approach a new and somewhat complex decision with more deliberation and consideration of the options (*i.e.* considering competitors service andlor options that can be added into the core service). In addition to calling the on-line services to find out about the features and services offered by each, Joanne might go to the local library and try to find a number of magazines articles that have reviewed these services. She might also talk to some friends, neighbours (former and present), and/or relatives who she thinks subscribe to one or more on line services. On the basis of selective perception, Joanne might start seeing ads and direct mail for computer on-line services.

Evaluation of Alternatives. When evaluating potential alternatives, consumers tend to use two types of informations: *(1)* a "list" of brands from which they plan to make their selection (the evoked set) and *(2)* the criteria they will use to evaluate each brand. Making a selection from a sample of all possible brands is a human characteristic that helps simplify the decision-making process.

Table: Comparison Cybersenior Technology Lovers Versus Technology Users

	Technology Users	**Technology Lovers**
Computer Behaviour		
Time spent on line	Less Hours	More Hours
On-line purchase behaviour	Little	More
Other on-line activities	Less	More
Resource Availability		
Time available	No difference	No difference
Money available	No difference	No difference
Space available	No difference	No difference
Others (health, Caregiver)	No difference	No difference

Personal Characterstics		
Attitudes	Less positive	More positive
Involvement	Less Involvement	More Involvement
Impact of computers	Less Impact	More Impact
Innovator	Less	More
Travel more than others	No difference	No difference
Happier than others	Less	More
Collector	No difference	No difference
Computer are magical	No difference	No difference
Financially better off	No	Yes
Healthier than others	No	Yes
Cognitive age Vs Chronological age	The same	Younger
Computer experience	Less	More
Locus of Control	Generally in Control	Very much in Control
Need for cognition	Less	More
Need for novelty	Less	More
Need to communicate	Perhaps (not computers)	Yes
Education	College	College
Life Satisfaction	Less satisfied	Moe satisfied
Life styles	No difference	No difference

Source: Charles McMellon, Leon Schiffman, and Elaine Sherman, "Consuming Cybersenior: Some Personal and Situational Characteristics that influence their on-line behaviour.

NICOSIA MODEL OF CONSUMER DECISION-MAKING

The Nicosia model focuses on the relationship between the firm and its potential consumers. In the broadest terms, the firm communicates with consumers through its marketing, messages (advertising), and consumers communicate with the firm by their purchase response. Thus the Nicosia Model is interactive in design. The firm tries to influence consumers and the consumers-by their actions or (inactions) influence the firm.

Figure

Field 1. From the source of a message to the consumer's attitude.

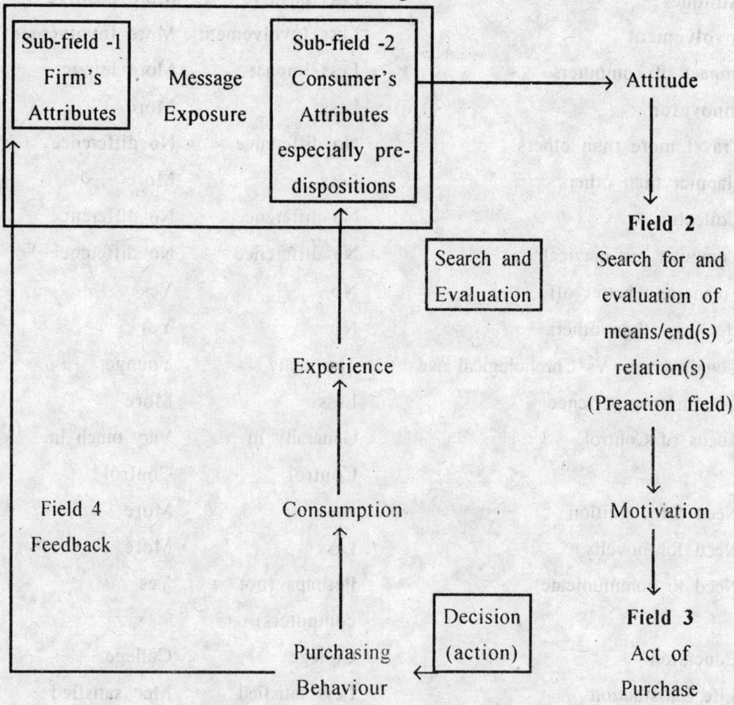

In its original form, the Nicosia Model is an elaborate computer flowchart of the consumer decision-making process. In the above figure a summary flowchart that highlights the full model. The Nicosia model is divided into four major fields: *(l)* the consumer's attitude based on message exposure, *(2)* the consumer's product search and evaluation, *(3)* the act of purchase, and *(4)* feedback in the form of consumer experience to both the firm and consumer.

Field 1: The Consumer's Attitude: Based on the Firm's Message. The first field of the Nicosia model is divided into two sub-fields. Subfield 2 includes aspects of the firm's marketing environment and communications effort that affect consumer's attitudes, such as product attributes, the competitive environment, characteristics of relevant mass media, the choice of copy appeal, and characteristics of the target market. Subfield 2 specifies various consumer characteristics (*e.g.* personality, experience) that mediate reception of the firm's promotional messages.

The output offield is an attitude towards the product based on the consumer's interpretation of the message.

Field 2: Search and Evaluations. The second field of the Nicosia's model deals with the search for relevant information and evaluation of the firm's brand in comparison with alternative brands. The output of this stage is motivation to purchase the firm's brand. (Of course, evaluation could also lead to rejection of the firms brand, however, the model illustrates, a positive response).

Field 3: The Act of Purchase. In the third field, the consumer's motivation towards the firm's brand results in purchase of the brand from a specific retailer.

Field 4: Feedback. The final field consists of two important types of feedback from the purchase experience-one to the firm in form of sales data, and the other to the consumer in the form of experience (satisfaction or dissatisfaction). The consumers experience with the product affects the individual's attitude and predisposition concerning future message from the firm.

Howard-Sheth Model. The Howard-Sheth model is a major revision of an earlier systematic effort to dewelop a comprehensive theory of consumer decision-making. This model distinguishes among three levels of learning (*i.e.*, stages of decision-making).

1. Extensive problem solving takes place when the consumer's knowledge and beliefs about bra,nds are very limited or non-existent, and he or she does not have specific brand preference. Here the consumer actively seeks information concerning a number of alternative brands.

2. Limited problem solving takes place when the consumer's knowledge and beliefs about the brands are only partially established, and he or she is not fully able to assess brand differences in order.

to arrive at a preference. Some comparative brand information is sought, although the decisions criteria are likely to be fairly well defined.

3. Routinized response behaviour occurs when the consumer's knowledge and beliefs about the brand and its alternating are well established, and the consumer is predisposed to the purchase of one particular brand.

Table 1 summarizes the main characteristics of each of these three stages of decision-making.

A simplified version of the basic Howard-Sheth model is shown in Figure A-2. The model consists of four major sets of variables *(1)* inputs, *(2)* perceptual and learning constructs, *(3)* Outputs, and *(4)* exogenous (external) variables.

Inputs. The input variables consists of three distinct types of stimuli (information sources) in the consumer's environment. Physical brand characteristics (significative stimuli) and verbal or visual product characteristics (symbolic stimuli) are furnished by the marketeer in the form of product or brand information. The third type of stimulus is provided by the consumer's social environment (family, reference graph, social class). All three types of stimuli. provide inputs concerning the product class or specific brands to the prospective consumer.

Table 1 Characteristics of the Three Stages of Decision-Making

Stage	*Amount of Information Needed Prior to Purchase*	*Speed of Decision*
Extensive Problem Saving	Great	Slow
Limited Problem Saving	Moderate	Moderate
Routinized Response Behaviour	Little	Fast

Perceptual and Learning Constructs. The central component of the Howard Sheth model consists of psychological variables that are assumed to operate when the consumer is contemplating, a decision. These constructs are treated as abstractions and are not operationally defined or directly measured. Some of the variables are perceptual in nature and are concerned with how the consumer receives and processes information acquired from the input stimuli and other parts of the model. For example, stimulus ambiguity occurs if a consumer is unclear about the meaning of information received from the environment; perceptual bias occurs if the consumer distorts the infomation received so that it fits his or her established needs or experiences.

Learning constructs serve the function of concept formation. Included in this category are the consumer's goals, information about brands in the evoked set, criteria for evaluation alternatives, preferences, and buying intentions. The proposed interaction (linkages) between the various perceptual and learning variable and the variables in other segments of the Howard-Sheth model has its distinctive character.

Outputs. The model indicates a series of output that correspond in name to some of the perceptual and learning construct variables (attention, brand comprehension, attitudes intention), in addition to the actual purchase.

Exogenous Variables. Exogenous variables are not directly part of the decision-making process and are not shown in model presented here. Relevant exogenous variables include the importance of the purchase, consumer personality traits, time pressure and financial status.

❐

4

Information Search Strategy and Market Segmentation

The field of consumer research is developed as extension of the field of marketing research focusing almost exclusively on consumer behaviour rather than on other aspects of the marketing process. Just as the findings of marketing research there used to improve managerial decision-making, so too were the findings of consumer research. The initial reason for studying consumer behaviour was to enable marketeers to predict how consumers would react to promotional messages, and to understand why they made the purchase decision they did.

The Modernist Era. The era in which the field of consumer research developed is known as the modernist era. Researchers who endorse the assumptions upon which modernism is based are called positivists. The data collected are quantitative in nature and lend themselves to sophisticated statistical analysis.

The Development of Motivational Research. Despite their assumptions that consumers were logical problem solvers who engaged in careful thought processe to arrive at their consumption decisions, researchers soon realized that consumers were not always consciously aware of why they made the decisions they did. Even though they were aware of their basic motivations, consumers were not always willing to reveal these reasons.

As early as 1939, a Viennese psychoanalyst named Earnst Dicttar began to use Freudian psychoanalytic techniques to uncover the hidden motivation of consumers. Till the late 1950s, his research methodology, which has come to be known as motivational research was widely adopted by marketcers advertising agencies. Motivational research requires highly trained intervocal analyst to collect data and to analyse research findings. Because sample sizes are necessarily small, findings cannot be generalized to larger populations. Motivational research findings are highly subjective, because they are based on analyst interpretation. Used primarily to obtain new ideas for promotional campaigns, motivational research is considered to be qualitative research findings to predict consumer actions based on variolls promotional inputs.

Postmodernism. A number of academicians from the field of consumer behaviour, as well as from other social science disciplines from which the consumer behaviour field developed, have become more interested in the act of consumptions than in the act of buying. They view consumer behaviour as a subset of human behaviour, and increased understanding as a key to reducing some of the ills associated with consumer behaviour (the so-called "dark side" of consumer behaviour) such as addiction, shoplifting, alcoholism, and compulsive buying behaviour. Interest in consumer experiences has led to the term experimentalism, and the researchers who adopt this paradigm are known as experimentalists, postmodernists, or interpretivists.

Interpretivists Rescarch. Interpretivists engage in qualitative research. Among the research methodologies they use are ethnography, semiotics, and depth interviews. Ethnography is a tcchnique borrowcd from cultural anthropology in which thc researchers place themselves in the society under study in an effort to absorb the meaning of various cultural practices. Ethnography lends itself easily to the study of all kinds of consumer behaviour, including how individuals buy product and services. Ethnology has been used in interpertivist studies to discover the meanings of objects accumulated by the homeless. Interpretivists are also very interested in semiotics the study of symbols and the meanings they convey. Consumer researchers use semiotics to discover the meanings of various consumption behaviours and rituals. It is important to understand the meanings that non-verbal symbols may hold for the target audience to be certain that symbols enchance, rather than inhabitat, the persuasiveness of the message. Depth interviews are an important part of the interpretivist's research process. However, interpretive research findings are often unique to the specific researchers/ consumer interaction.

MAJOR STEPS IN CONSUMER RESEARCH

The major steps in the consumer research include *1.* defining the objectives of the research, *2.* collecting and evaluating secondary data, *3.* designing a primary research study, *4.* collecting primary data, *5.* analysing the data, and 6. preparing a report on the findings.

Dcveloping Rescarch Objectives. The first stop in the consumer research prosess is to define carefully the objectives of the study to segment the market for wide-screen television? To find out consumer attitudes about cellularphones? To determine what percentage of men use cologne? It is important for the marketing manager and the researcher to agree at the outset on the purposes and objectives of the study to ensure the research design is appropriate. A careful thought out statement of objectives helps to define the type and level of information needed.

For example, if the purpose of the study is to come up with new ideas for products or promotional campaigns, then a qualitative study is usually undertaken, in which respondents spend a significant amount of time face to face with highly trained professionals moderator who also does the analysis. Because of the high costs of each interview, a fairly small sample of respondents is studied thus, the findings are not projectable to the market place. If the purpose of the study is to find out how many people in the population use certain products and how frequently they use them, then a quantitative study that can be computer analyzed is undertaken.

Collecting Secondary Data. A search for secondary information generally follows the statement of objectives in any data originally generated for some purpose other than the present research objectives. It includes findings based on research done by outside organisation as well as data generated in house for earlier studies or even customer information collected by the firm's sales or credit departments. Locating secondary data is called secondary research

Sccondary research sometimes provides sufficient insight into the problem as hand to eliminate the need for primary research. Most often, it piovides clues and direction for the design of primary research. Govt. agencies, private population data firms, marketing research companies and advertising agencies are important sources of secondary market data.

Designing Primary Rescarch. The design of a research study is based on the purposes of the study if descriptive information is needed, then quantitative study is likely to be undertaken if the purpose is to get new ideas, then a qualitative study may be in order. Because the approach for that type of research differs in terms of method of data collection, sample design, and type of data collection instrument used, each research approach is discussed separately before.

Data Collection. Qualitative studies usually require highly trained social scientists to collect data. A quantitative study generally uses a field staff that is either recruited and trained directly by the researcher or contracted from a company that specialises in conducting field interviews. In either case, it is aften necessary to verify whether the interviews have, in fact, taken place. This is sometimes done by a postcard mailing to respondents asking them to verify. They participated in an interview on the data recorded on the questionnaire form. Completed questionnaires are reviewed on a regular basis as the research study progresses to ensure that the recorded responses are clear, complete and legible.

Analysis. In qualitative research, the modertor or test administrator usually analysis the responses received. In quantitative research, the researcher supervises the analysis. Open-ended responses are first coded and quantified, then all of the responses are tabulated and analyzed. Although it is possible to tabulate and analyze up to 200 responses without the use of a computer most surveys are computer analyzed using sophisticated analytical techniques, the computer can process multiple correlation and cluster the data by released demographic charactertistics.

Report Preparation. In both qualitative and quantitative research, the research report includes a brief executive summary of the findings. Depending on the assignments from marketing management the research report may not include recommendations for marketing action. The body of the report includes a full description of the methodology used and for quantitative research, also includes tables and graphics to support the findings. A sample of the questionnaire is usually included in the appendix to enable management to evaluate the objectivity of the findings.

DATA COLLECTION METHODS

There are three basic ways to collect primary data in quantitative research:

1. Observation Rescarch. Observational research is an important method of consumer research, because marketeers recognize that the best way to gain an in-depth understanding of the relationship between people and products is by watching them in the process of buying and using products. Many large corporations and advertising agencies use cultural anthropologist to observe and often video-tape consumers in stores, nails and their own homes (*i.e.*, to engage in anthrographic research). By watching people, observational researchers gain in a better understanding of what a product symbolize to a consumer, and greater insight into the bond between people and products that is the essence of brand loyalty. Observational research also provides valuable inputs into product advertising. For example, when observational research showed that most people greet their mail carriers as first name friends, the United States Postal Service began prominently featuring mail carriers in its advertisements. Toyota found that many customers saw cars as art objects, so it worked that theme into early advertisements for its Lexus automobile. Observational research is widely used by interpretivist research to understand the buying and consumption process.

2. Experimentation. It is possible to test the relative sales appeal of many types of variables such as package designs, prices, promotional offers or copy themes through experiments designed to identify cause and effect. In such experiments (called casual research), only one variable is manipulated at a time (the independent variable), while all other elements are kept constant. A controlled experiment of this type ensures that any difference in results (the dependent variable) is due to different treatments of the variable under study and not to extraneous factors. For example, if a marketeer wanted to test the sales appeal of three different colour packages, he or she might select three supermarkets (or group of supermarkets) matched in terms of size, appearance, and type of neighbourhood and place a display of green packages in one, blue packages in the second, and red in the third. In each instance the design of the packages is held constant. If one store sells significantly more units of the product than the others during a specific time frame, the researcher could conclude that the difference in sales was due solely to the specific colour of package, since all other factors (such as price, type of consumer, type of promotional appeal) were kept constant, experiments could also be conducted in a laboratory with the use of special instrumentation, such as eye cameras that study the eye movement of subjects as they view competitive advertisements.

3. Surveys. If researchers wish to ask consumers about their purchase preferences, they can do so in person, by mail, or by telephone. Each ofthese survey methods has certain advantages and certain disadvantages that the researcher must weigh in selecting the method of contact. Personal Interview surveys most often take place in the home or in retail shopping areas. The latter, referred to as mail intercepts, have become much more frequent of late because of the high incidence of not-at-home working women and among those who do not work, fears of allowing a stranger into their homes.

Telephone surveys are often used to collect consumer data, though the high incidence of working woman has limited their use. Evenings and weekends are often the only times to reach the working homemaker, who tends to be less responsive to calls that interrupt dinner, television viewing, or general relaxation. The difficulties of reaching people who have unlisted telephone numbers has been solved through random digit dialling and the costs of a widespread telephone survey are often used by using toll free WATS lines. Other problems arise, however, from the increased use of answering machines to screen calls especially among the young affluent market segment.

Mail surveys are conducted by sending questionnaires directly to individuals at their homes. A number of commercial research firing that specialize in consumer surveys have set up 'panels' of consumer who, for a token fee agree to complete the research company's mail questionnaires on a regular basis. Sometimes panel members are also asked to keep diaries of their purchase.

Data Collection Instruments. For quantitative research, the primary data collection instrument is the questionnaire, which can be sent through the mails to selected respondents for self administration or administered by a trained interviewer in person or by telephone.

Consumers are often reluctant to take the time to respond to surveys. For this reason, researchers have found that questionnaires must be interesting, objective, unambiguous, easy to complete and generally non-burdensome in order to motivate respondents to answer truthfully and completely. To enhance the analysis and facilitate the classification of response in to meaningful categories, questionnaires include both questions that are relevant to the purpose of the study as well as pertinent demographic questions. To assure validity, questionnaires are presented and 'debugged' before widespread distribution. The format of the questionnaire, and the wording and sequence of the questions, affect the validity of the responses and in the case of mail questionnaires, the number of response received.

Comparative Advantages of Mail, Telephone and Personal Interview Surveys

	Mail	*Telephone*	*Personal Interview*
Cost	Low	Moderate	High
Speed	Slow	Immediate	Slow
Response rate	Low	moderate	High
Geographic Flexibility	Excellent	Good	Difficult
Interview bias	N/A	Moderate	Problematic
Interview Supervision	N/A	Easy	Difficult
Quality response	Limited	Limited	Excellent

The questionnaire itself can be disguised or undisguised as to its true purpose; a disguised questionnaire sometirnes yields more truthful answers and avoid responses that respondents may think are expected or sought. Questions can be open-ended (requiring answers in the respondent's own words) or closed ended questions yield more insightful information but are more difficult to code and analyse closed ended questions are relatively simple to tabulate and analyze but the answers are limited to the alternative response provided (*i.e.* to the existing insights of the questionnaire designer). Great care must be taken in working each question to avoid biasing the responses. The sequence of questions also important the opening questions must be interesting enough to 'draw' the respondent into participating they must proceed in it logical order and classification questibns should be placed at the end, where they are more likely to be answered. Questionnaires usually offer respondents confidently or anonymity in order to dispel any reluctance about self disclosure.

Sometimes, instead of a list of question, the data collection instrument presents a series of statements to which respondents are asked to indicate their degree of agreement or disagreement, these are often called inventories. Researchers sometimes present respondents with a list of products or product attributes to which they are asked to indicate their relative feelings or evaluation. The instruments most frequently employed to capture this evaluative data are called attitude scales and include Likert scales semantic differential scales and rank order scales.

The Likert Scale is by far the most popular form of attitude scale because it is easy for researchers to prepare and to interpret and simple for consumers to answer. They check or write the number corresponding to their level of 'agreement' or 'disagreement' to each of a series of statement that describes the attitude object under investigation. The figure given below presents an example of five, point Likert scale. Note that the scale consists, of an equal number of agreement/disagreement choices on either side of a neutral choice. A principal benefit of the Likert scale is that it gives the researcher the option of considering the responses to each statement separately, or of combining the responses to produce an overall, summitted score, Because of this property the Likert scale is often called a summated scale.

Instructions:

Please place the number which best indicates how strongly you, agree or disagree with each of the following statemems about shopping at flea markets in the space to the left of the statement.

1. Agree strongly
2. Agree
3. Neither Agree nor Disagree
4. Disagree
5. Disagree strongly.

............a It is fun to shop at a flea market.

............b. Products often cost more than they are worth.

............c. It is a good place to meet friends and neighbours.

............d. Many of the sellers are rude and aggressive.

............e. There is no waiting for delivery.

............f. Most flea markets are difficult to reach.

............g. There are no taxes to be paid.

Like the Likert scale the semantic differential scale is relatively easy to construct and administer. The scale typically consists of a series of bipolar adjectives (such as good/bad, hot/dislike, expensive/inexpensive) that are anchored at the ends of an odd numbered *e.g.* 5 or 7 point) continuum. Respondents are asked to evaluate a concept (*e.g.*, a product or company) on the basis of each attribute by checking the point on the continuum that best reflects their feelings or beliefs. Sometimes an even numbered scale is used in order to eliminate the option of a neutral answer Semantic differential profits are also used to compare consumer perceptions of competitive products and to indicate areas for product improvement when perceptions of the existing products are measured against perceptions of the "ideal" product.

With rank-order scales, subjects are asked to rank items such as products (or retail stores or companies) in order of preference in terms of some criterion such as overall quality or value for the money. Rank, order scaling procedures provide important competitive information and enable marketeers to identify needed areas of improvement in product design or product positioning.

Sampling. An integral component of a research design is the sampling plant. Specifically, it addresses the three questions—When to survey (the sampling unit), how many to survey (the sampie size), and how to select them (the sampling procedure).

Deciding whom to survey requires that the universe or boundaries of the market which data is sought be defined so that an appropriate sample can be selected (*e.g.* working mothers). Interviewing the correct target or potential target market is basic to the validity of the study.

The size of the sample is dependent both on the size of the budget and the degree of confidence that the marketeer wants to place in the findings.

The larger the sample, the more likely the responses will reflect the total universe under the study, It is interesting to note, however, that a small sample can often provide highly reliable findings, depending on the sampling procedure adopted.

If the researcher wants the findings to be projectable to the total population, then a probability sample should be chosen, if it is sufficient to have the findings "representative" of the population, then a non-probability sample can be selected.

A. The following are six brands of candy bars. We are interested in learning your preference for each of these brands. Place A1 alongside the brand you would be most likely to buy, A2 alongside the brand you would next be most likely to buy Continue doing this until you have remked all six brands.

............Hershey Chocolate Bar

............Snickers

............Three Musketeers

............M & Ms

............Mounds

............Twix

B. Hank the following electric razors from 1 to 6 in terms of closeness of shave.

............Remington

............Norelco

............Shick

............Braun

............Panasonic

............Ranson

C. We are interested in knowing how much you enjoy each of the following four types of TV. professional sports programmes. Please rank them from 1-4, where 1 means that you enjoy more and means that you enjoy it least.

............Baseball

............Football

............Basketball

............Hockey

DATA COLLECTION

Qualitative studies usually require highly trained social scientists to collect data. A quantitative study generally uses a field staff that is either recruited and trained directly by the researcher or contracted from a company that specializes in conducting field interviews. In either case, it is often necessary to verify whether the interviews have in fact taken place. This is sometimes done by a postcard mailing to respondents asking to verify that they participated in an interview on the date recorded on the questionnaire form. Completed questionnaires are reviewed on a regular basis as the research study progresses to ensure that the recorded responses are clear, complete and legible.

Table: Probability and Non-probability Sampling Designs

Probability Sample	
Simple random sample	Every member of the population has a known and equal chance of being selected.
Stratified random sample	The population is, divided into mutually exclusive groups (such as age group) and random, samples are drawn from each group.
Cluster (area) sample	The population is divided into mutually exclusive groups (such as blocks), and the researcher draws a sample of the groups to interview.
Non Probability Sample	
Convenience Sample	The researcher selects the most accessible population members from whom to obtain information (*e.g.* students in classroom)
Judgement Sample	The researcher uses his or her judgement to select population members who are good sources for accurate information (*e.g.* experts in the relevant field of study).
Quota Sample	The researcher interviews a prescribed number of people in each of several categories (*e.g.* 50 men and 50 women).

ANALYSIS

In qualitative research, the moderator or test administrator usually analyzes the responses received. In quantitative research, this 'researcher supervises the analysis, open-ended responses are first coded and quantified (*i.e.*, converted into numerical scores); then all of the responses are tabulated and analyzed. Though it is possible to tabulate and analyze up to 200 responses without the use of a computer, most surveys are computers analyzed using sophisticated analytical techniques. The computer can process , multiple correlations and cluster the data by selected demographic characteristics.

Report Preparation. In both qualitative and quantatitive research report includes a brief executive summary of the findings. Depending on the assignment from marketing management, the research report may or may not include recommendations for marketing action. The body of the report includes a full description of the methodology used and for quantitative research, also includes tables and graphics to support the findings. A sample of the questionnaire is usually included in the appendix to enable management to evaluate them objectivity of the findings.

MARKET SEGMENTATION

Market segmentation can be defined as the the process of dividing a potential market into distinct subsets of consumers with common needs or characteristics and selecting one or more segments to target with a distinct marketing mix.

Before the widespread adoption of marketing concept, the prevailing way of doing business with consumers was through mass marketing.

BASES FOR SEGMENTATION

The first step in developing a segmentation strategy is to select the most appropriate base(s) on which to segment the market. Following are the bases of market segmentation—*(i)* Geographic segmentation, *(ii)* Demographic Segmentation, *(iii)* Psychological

Segmentation, *(iv)* Socio-cultural Segmentation, *(v)* Benefit Segmentation.

Geographic Segmentation

Region	North, South, East, West.
City size	Major metropolitan areas, small cities, towns.
Density of Area	Urban, rural.
Climate	Temperate, hot, humid.

Demographic Segmentation

Age	Under 11, 12, 17, 18-34,35-49, 50-64, 65-74
Sex	Male, Female
Marital Status	Married, single, divorced, living together, widowed
Income	Under \$15,000, \$15,000-\$24,999, \$25,000-\$39,999, \$40,000-\$64,999 and over.
Education	Some High school, some college, P.G.
Occupation	Professional, blue-collar, white-collar agricultural.

Psychological Segmentation

Needs-Motivation	Shelter, safety, affection, sense of selfworth
Personality	Extroverts, Introverts, aggressive.
Perception	Low risk, moderate risk, high risk.
Attitudes	Positive attitude, Negative attitude.

Socio-Cultural Segentation

Culture	Indian, American, Bangladesh, Pakistan.
Sub-Culture Religion	Hindu, Sikh, Muslim, Christian
Social Class	Lower, middle, upper.
Benefit Segment	Convenience, prestige, economy, value for the money.

Geographic Segmentation. It calls for dividing the market into different geographical units as nations, states, regions, cities or neighbourhoods. The company can decide to operate in one or a few geographic areas or operate in all but pay attention to local variations in geographic needs and preferences.

In short, geographic segmentation is useful for many marketeers. It is relatively easy to find geographically-based differences for many products. Geographic segments can be easily reached through local media.

Demographic Segmentation. It consists of dividing the market into groups on the basis of demographic variables such as age, gender, family size, family life cycle, income, occupation, education, religion, race and nationality.

Age and Life Cycle Stage. Consumers wants and capacities change with age. For example-Alabe Products, a toy manufacturer realised this and designed different toys for babies as they move through various stages from three months to one year.

General foods applied age segmentation strategy to dog food. General foods formulated four types of canned dog-food: *(1)* cycle, for puppies, *(2)* cycle 2, for adult, *(3)* cycle 3, for overweight dogs and *(4)* cycle 4, for older dogs.

Gender. This segmentation has long been applied in clothing, hair dressing, cosmetics and magazines.

Income segmentation is an another long standing practice in such, product and service categories as automobiles, boats, clothing, cosmetics and travel.

However, income does not always predict the best customers for given product. Blue-collar workers were among the first purchaser of colour T. V. sets, it was cheaper for them to buy these sets than to go to movies and restaurants.

Psychographic Segmentation. In this segmentation buyers are divided into different groups on the basis of social class, life style and/or personality.

Social Class. The social class has a strong influence on the person's preference in cars, clothing, home furnishing, leisure activities, reading habits, and so on. Many companies design products and/or services for specific social classes.

Life Style. The goods that consumers consume express their life styles. Companies making cosmetics, alcoholic beverages and furniture are seeking opportunities in life-style segmentation. Marketeers are increasingly segmenting their .markets by consumer life-styles. For example:

* Volkswagen has designed lifestyle automobiles a car for "the good citizen" emphasizing economy, safety and ecology; and car for the "car freak" emphasizing handling and variability.
* Manufacturers of women's apparel are following Du Points advice and designing different clothes for the "plain women" and "fashionable women" and the "manly women".
* Cigarette companies have developed brands for "defiiant smoker", the "casual smoker" and the "careful smoker".

Personality. Marketeers have used personality variables to segment markets. They endow their products with brand personalities that correspond to consumer personalities. For example in the late fifties, Fords and Chevrolets were promoted as having different personalities. Ford buyers were identified as "independent, impulsive, masculine, alert to change and self confident, while Chevrolet owners were conservative, thrifty, prestige conscious, less masculine and seeking to avoid extremes" currently. Nike is using the personality of certain athletes, such as basketball star Michael Jordan as a brand identifier to attract his fans.

Socio-Cultural Segmentation. Socio-cultural variables provide further bases for market segmentation. For example, consumer markets have been sub-divided into segments on the basis of family life-cycle, social class, culture, sub-culture and cross culture.

Family Life-cycle. Segmentation is based on the assumptions that many families pass through similar phases in their formation, growth and final dissolution. At each phase, the family unit needs different products. Family life-cycle includes relative age, income and employment status. It also includes marital and family status.

Social Class. The concept of social class implies a hierarchy in which individuals in the same class generally have the same degree of status while members of other classes have either higher or lower status.

Culture, Sub-culture and Cross Culture. Some marketeers have found it useful to segment their domestic and international markets on the basis of cultural heritage.

Marketeers who use cultural segmentation stress specific, widely hold cultural values with which they hope consumers will identify *e.g.* for Americans freedom of choice and individuality. Cultural segmentation is particularly successful in international marketing, but in such instances, it is important for the marketeer to understand fully the beliefs, values and customs of the countries in which the product is marketed (*i.e.*, the cross cultural context).

Often, a product is altered or reformulated for different cultural markets. For example, Nestle, a Swiss company that sells coffee worldwide, makes a strong brew for the Italian market and a weaker coffee for the United States market. Sometimes it is merely custom that divides cultural segments. Greeting cards, sold without verses in Europe, usually are sold with verses in the United States.

Benefit Segmentation. Examples of benefits that are commonly used includes, belonging, healthy aerobic workout, a sense of "doing good" (care) financial security, relief of dryskin.

Changing life-styles play a major role in determining the product benefits that are important to consumers. For example, Micro-wave oven was the perfect solution to the needs of dual income household.

Benefit segmentation can be used to position various brands within the same product category. For example, close-up with a social appeal that stresses bright teeth is targeted to young people. Aim is targeted to parents as a good targeting toothpaste that will encourage children to brush longer.

Behavioural Segmentation. Under this segmentation buyers are divided into groups on the basis of their knowledge, attitude, use or response to a product.

Occasions. Buyers can be distinguished according to occasions when they develop a need, purchase a product, or use a product. For example, air travel is triggered by occasions related to business, vacation, or family. An airline can specialise in serving people for whom one of these occasions dominates. Thus charter airlines serve people who fly for group vacation.

This segmentation also helps firms expand product usage. For example, orange juice is most usually consumed at breakfast. An orange juice company can try to pomote drinking orange juice on other occasions-lunch, dinner, midday.

Loyalty Status. A market can be segmented by consumer-loyalty patterns. Consumers can be loyal to brands (Coca-Cola) and other entities. Buyers can be divided into four groups according to their brand loyalty status. *(1)* Hard-core loyals, *(2)* Split loyals, *(3)* Shifting loyals, *(4)* Switchers.

A brand loyal market is one with a high percentage of hard-core brand loyal buyers. Thus the tooth-paste market and the beer market are fairly high brand loyal market.

It is difficult to gain more market share and hard to get in.

A company should study the characteristics of its own hard-core loyals. Colgate finds that its hard-core loyals are more middle class, have larger families and are more health conscious. This pinpoints the target market for Colgate.

By studying its split loyals, the company can pinpoint which brands are most competitive with its own. If many Colgate buyers also buy Crest, Colgate can attempt to improve its positioning against Crest by using direct comparison advertising.

In shifting loyals market a company can learn about its marketing weaknesses and hope to correct them.

Attitude. Five attitude groups can be found in a market: enthusiastic, positive, indifferent, negative and hostile.

This determines that how much time a company should spend with these groups.

Companies thank enthusiastic buyers and remined them to buy. They reinforce those who are positively disposed. They try to win the attending indifferent buyers.

They spend no time to change the attitudes of negative and hostile buyers.

Use-Related Segmentation. An extremely popular and effective form of segmentation categorizes consumers in terms of product, service, Or brand usage characteristics, such as wage rate, awareness status and degree of brand loyalty.

Rate of usage segmentation differentiates among-heavy users, medium users, light users and non-users of specific product, service or brand.

Marketeers also consider the current versus the future potential of consumer segments when setting marketing strategy.

Non-users represent a special challenge. Marketeers have to decide:

1. Whether non-users are a potentiality worth-while segment, or
2. whether the resources needed to convert them into users can be better spent in trying to lure present users away from competitive products.

Awareness status encompasses the notion of consumer awareness, interest level or buyer readiness. Marketeers have to determine whether potential consumers are aware of the product, interested in the product, or need to be informed about the product.

Criteria for Effective Targeting of Market Segments

Idtentification. To divide the market into seperate segments on the basis of common needs or characteristics that is relevant to the product or service, the marketeers must be able to identify the relevant characteristics.

Some segment variables such as geography (location) or demographies (age, gender, occupation, race) are relatively easy to identify.

Others, such as education, income or marital status, can be determined through questionnaires.

Still other characteristics, such as benefits sought or life-style, are more difficult to identify.

Sufficiency. It must have a sufficient number of people for promotional campaign to specific needs or interst or a market segment.

Stability in terms of demographic and psychological factors and needs.

Type of Psychographic Variables. Psychographics are often referred to as AIOs.

A : Activities (*i.e.*, how the consumer or family spends time)

I : Interests (the consumer's or family's preferences and priorities *e.g.*, home, fashion, food),

O : Opinions (how a consumer feels about a wide variety of events and issues-politics, social issues, the state of education, the future).

In a psychographic research study, consumers usually are asked to reveal their personal or their family's reaction to a variety of statements. For example if Gillette decided to evaluate the target market for its successful Sensor razor in terms of psychographic characteristics, it might be using the following statements to capture individual and family predispositions (inclinations) toward the Sensor razor system.

Personal Statements

— I'm a demanding person.

— For me seeking perfection in what I do is really not important.

— When I wake up in the morning, my appearance is uppermost on my mind.

— When it comes to the way I dress, I am not particularly fashion conscious.

Family Statements

— "Good" grooming is important to all members of my family.

— Members of my family frequently comment about how good I look after I shave.

— We are a particularly good-looking family.

— We are more likely to try new products than most of our friends and neighbours.

— I imagine that we buy and use more grooming products than other people we know.

Respondents are asked to evaluate such statements in terms of their degree of agreement (*e.g.* strongly agree, agree, disagree-strongly disagree).

They may be asked to indicate the degree of importance (*e.g.*. very important, slightly important, unimportant).

In addition to reflecting either personal or family activities, interests, and opinions, psychographic statements can be designed to be either general or product-specific.

For example, a study aimed at examining the practice of including snacks in children's lunch boxes might include such general statements as these:

— "My children could eat the same thing for luch everyday."

— "My children are always telling me what their friend's mother make them for lunch."

— "My children prepare their own school lunches most of time."

Product Specific Statements

"When I was child, my mother regularly gave me a snack as part of my school lunch."

"When choosing lunchtime snack for my children, I select it as if I am selecting food."

Both types of statements suply valuable insights regarding consumer's attitude. However, while the general statements focus on broader perceptions preferences and attitudes.

The product-specific statements pertain directly to the product and its use.

Classification of Different types of psychographic statements for a T.V. viewership study

	Individual/personal	Family/Household
General	"I am the kind of person who hangs out at home a 'lot."	"We really must be couch potatoes, we are always staying home."
	"Give me, a good reason and I will have a party:"	"We will buy anything that will bring the family together."
Product Specific	"My idea of a good evening is to stay home and relax in front of the T.V."	"We have real limits 'as to how much T.V. we allow ourselves to watch."
	"I can watch 10 hrs, of T.V. and not know it."	"We eat our meals as a family while watching T.V."

SEGMENT STRUCTURAL ATTRACTIVENESS

A segment might have desirable size and growth but lack profit potential. Porter has identified five forces that determine the intrinsic long-run profit attractiveness of a market or segment. The company has to appraise this impact on long-run profitability of five groups: industry competitors, potential entrants, substitutes, buyers and suppliers. The five threats they pose are as follows:

1. Threat of Intense Segment Rivalry. A segment is unattractive if it already contains immerous, strong, or aggressive competitors. The picture is even worse if the segment is stable or declining, if capacity additions are done in large/increments, if fixed costs are high, if exit barriers are high or if competitors have high stakes in staying in the segment. These conditions will lead to frequent price-war, advertising battles and new-product introductions and will make it expensive for companies to compete.

2. Threat of New Entrants. A segment is unattractive if it is likely to attract new competitors who will bring in new capacity, substantial resources and a drive for market-share growth. The question boils down to whether new entrants can easily get in. They will cumbent firms. The lower the barriers to entry and incumbent willingness to retaliate, the less attractive the segment. A segment's attractiveness varies with the height of the entry and exit barriers. The most attractive segment to be one in which entry barriers are high and exit barriers are low. Few new firms can enter the industry, and poor-performing firms can easily exit. When both entry and exit barriers are high profit potential is high but is usually accompanied by more risk because poorer-performing, firms stay in and fight it out. When entry and exit barriers are both low then firms easily enter and leave the industry and the returns are stable and low. The worst case is when entry barriers are low and exit barriers are high: here firms enter during good times but find it hard to leave during bad times. The result is chronic overcapacity and depressed earnings, for all.

Figure. Five Forces Determining Segment Structural Attrativeness

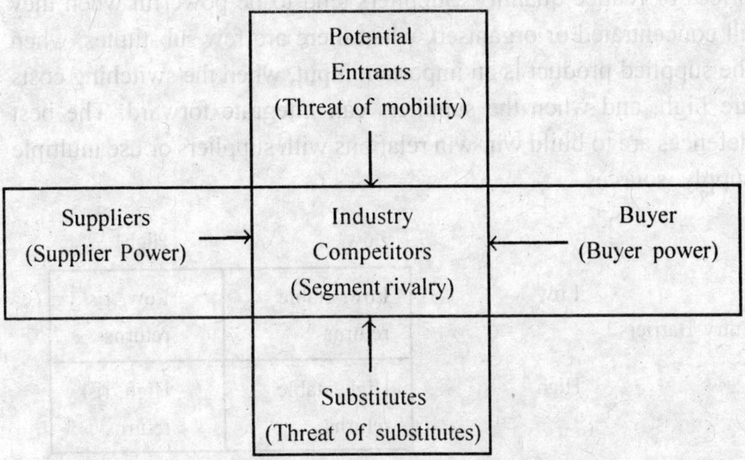

3. Threat of Substitute Products. A segment is unattractive when there are actual or potential substitutes for the product. Substitutes place a limit on the potential prices and profits that a segment can earn. The company has to watch closely the price trends in the substitutes. If technology advances or competition increases in these substitute industries, prices and profits in the segment are likely to fall.

4. Threat of Growing Bargaining Power of Buyers. A segment is unattractive if the buyer possess strong or growing bargaining power. Buyers will try to force prices down, demand more quality or services and set competitors against each other, all at the expense of seller profitability. Buyers bargaining power grows when they become more concentrated or organised, when the product represents a significant fraction of the buyers, costs, when. the product is undifferentiated when the buyers swiching coste are low, when the buyers are price sensitive because of lowprofits or when the buyers can integrate backward. In defence, sellers might select buyers who possess the least power to negotiate or switch suppliers. A better defense consists of developing superior offers that strong buyers cannot refuse.

5. Threat of Growing Bargaining Power of Suppliers. A segment is unattracting if the company suppliers are able to raise prices or reduce quantity. Suppliers tend to be powerful when they all concentrated or organised, when there are few substitutes, when the supplied product is an important input, when the switching costs are high, and when the suppliers can integrate forward. The best defences are to build win-win relations with suppliers or use multiple supply sources.

		Low	High
Entry Barriers	Low	Low, stable returns	Low, risky returns
	High	High, stable returns	High, risky returns

Company Objectives and Resources. Even if a segment is large, growing, and structurally attractive; the company needs to consider its own objectives and resources in relation to that segment. Some attractive segnents could be dismissed because they do not mesh with the company long-run objectives. Even if the segment fits the company's objectives, the company must consider whether it possess the requistie skills and resources to succeed in that segment.

Each segment has certain success requirements. The segment should be dismissed if the company lacks one or more necessary competences and is no position to acquire the necessary competences. But even if the company possesses the requisite competence, it needs to develop some superior advantages. It should enter only market segments where it can offer superior value.

Selecting the Market Segment. Having evaluated different segments the company must now decide which and how many segments to serve. That is the problem of target market selection. The company can consider five patterns of target market selections.

Single Segment Concentration. In the simplest case, the company selects a single segment. Volkswagen concentrates on the small car market and Richard D. Irwin on the economics and business texts market. Through concentrated marketing the firm achieves a strong market position in the segment owing to its greater knowledge of the segment's needs and the special reputation it gains. Furthermore, the firm enjoys operating economies through speciallizing its production, distribution and promotion. If it captures leadership in the segment, the firm can earn a high return on its investment.

At the same time, concentrated marketing involves higher than norm all risks. The particular market segment can turn sour. For example, when young women suddenly stopped buying sportswear it caused Bobbie Brook's earnings to fall sharply. Or a competitor may invade the segment for these reasons, many companies prefer to operate in more than one segment.

Selective Specialization. Here the firm selects a number of segments, each objectively attractive and appropriate, given the firm's objectives and resources. There may be little or no synergy between the segments, but each segment promises to be a money maker. This strategy of multisegment coverage has the advantage of diversifying the firm's risk. Even if one segment becomes unattractive, the firms can continue to earn money in other segments.

Product Specialization. Here the firm concentrates on making a certain product that sells to several segment. An example would be a microscope manufacturer that sells microscopes to universily laboratories, government laboratories and commercial laboratories, The firm makes different microscopes for these different customer groups out avoids manufacturing other instruments that laboratories might use. Through this strategy, the firm builds up a strong reputation in the specific product area. The downside rise would occure if microscopes were supplemented by an entirely new technology.

Market Specialization. Here the firm concentrates on serving many needs of a particular customer group. An example would be a firm that sells an assortment of products for university laboratories; including microscopes, oscilloscopes, Bunsen burners and chemical flasks. Th firm gains a strong reputation for specializing in serving this customer groups and becomes a channel for all new products that this, customer group could feasibly use. The downside risk would occur if university laboratories suddenly had their budgets £ut and reduced their purchases.

Full Market Coverage. Here a firm attempts to serve all customer groups with all the products that they might need. Only large firms can undertake a full market coverage strategy. Examples would include IBM (computer market), General Motors (vehicle market) and Coca-Cola (drink market).

Large firms can cover a whole market in two broad ways, namely, through undifferentiated marketing or differentiated marketing.

Undifferentiated Marketing. The firm might ignore market segment differences and go after the whole market with one market offer. It focuses on what is common in the needs of buyers rather than on what is differentiated. It designs a product and a marketing programme that will appeal to the broadest number of buyers. It relies on mass distribution and mass advertising. It aims to endow the product with a superior image in people's minds. An example, of undifferentiated marketing is the Coca-Cole Company's early marketing of only drink in one bottle size in one taste to suit everyone.

Undifferentiated marketing is defended on the grounds of costs economies. It is seen as the marketing counterpart to standardization and mass production in manufacturing transportation costs. The undifferentiated advertising programme keeps down advertising costs. The absense of segment research and planning lowers the costs of marketing research and product management. Presumably, the company can turn its lower costs into lower prices to win the price-sensitive segment of the market.

Nevertheless, a growing number of marketeers have expressed strong doubts about his strategy. Gardner and Levy, while acknowledging that "some brands have very skillfully built up reputations of being suitable for a wide variety of people'" noted that "it is not easy for a brand to appeal to stable, lower-middle-class people and at the same time to be interesting to sophisticated, intellectual upper-middle class buyers it is rarely possible for a product or brand to be all things to all people.

When several competitors practice undifferentiated marketing, the result is intense competition in the largest market segments and undersatisfaction of the smaller ones. Kuehn and Day have called this tendency to go after the largest market segment the "majority fallacy". The recognition of this fallacy has led firms to increase their interest in entering smaller neglected market segments.

Differentiated Marketing. Here the firm operates in several market segments and design different programmes for each segment. General Motors claims to do this when it says that it produces a car for every purse, purpose, and personality. And IBM offers many hardware and software packages for different segments in the computer market. Consider the case of Edison Brothers.

Edison Brothers operates nine hundred shoe stores that fall into four different chain categories, each appealing to a different market segment. Chandler's sells higher-priced shoes. Baker's sells moderate-priced shoes. Burt's sells shoes for budget shoppers, and Wild pair is oriented to the shopper who wants very stylished shoes. Within three blocks on State Street in Chicago are found Burt's, Chandler's and Baker's. Putting the stores near each other does not hurt them because they are aimed at different segments of the women's shoe market. This strategy has made Edison Brothers the country's largest retailer of women's shoes.

Differentiated marketing typically creates more total sales than undifferentiated marketing. "It is ordinarily demonstrable that sales may be increased with a more diversified product line sold through more diversified channels". However, it also increases the costs of doing business. The following costs are likely to be higher.

Product Modification Costs. Modifying a product to meet different market segment requirements usually involves some R & D engineering, and/or special tooling costs.

Manufacturing Costs. It is usually more expensive to produce, say, ten units of ten different products than 100 units of one product. The longer the production set up time for each product and the smaller the sales volume of each product, the more expensive it becomes. On the other hand, if each model is sold in sufficiently large volume, the higher costs of setup time may be quite small per unit.

Administrative Costs. The company has to develop separate marketing plans for the separate segments of the market. This requires extra marketing research, forecasting, sales analysis, promotion, planning and channel management.

Inventories Costs. It is more costly to manage inventories containing mans products than few products.

Promotion Costs. The company has to reach different market segments with different prrmotion programme. This increases promotion-planning costs and media costs.

Since differentiated marketing leads to both higher sales and higher costs, nothing can be said in general regarding the profitability of this strategy. Companies should be cautious about oversegmenting their market. If this happens, they may want to turn to counter segmentation or broadening the customer base. Johnson & Johnson, for example, broadened its target market for its baby shampoo to include adults. And Beecham launched its Aquafresh toothpaste to attract simultaneously three benefit segments those seeking fresh breath, whiter teeth, and cavity protection.

Figure. Three Alternative Market Selection Strategies

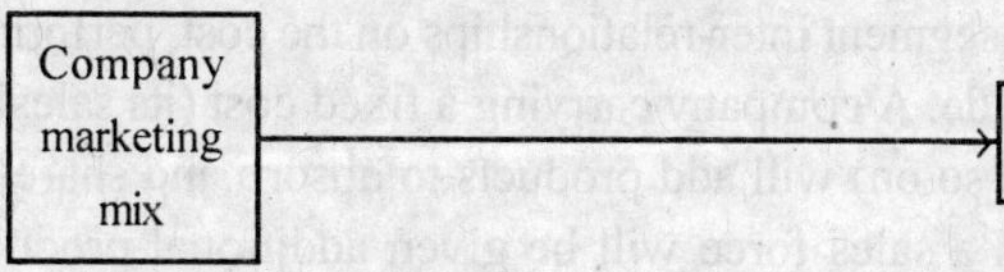

(a) Undifferentiated Marketing.

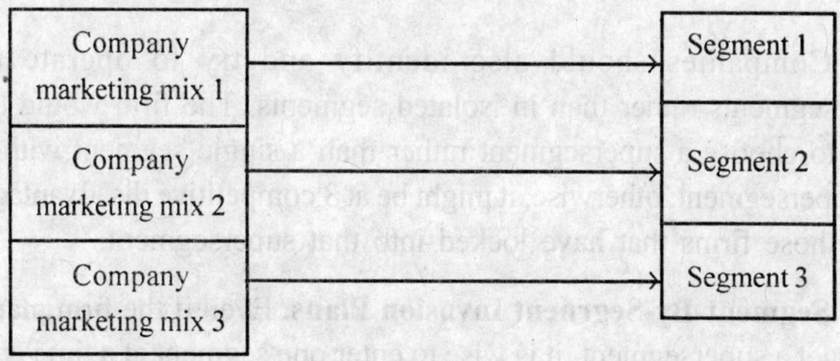

(b) Differentiated Marketing.

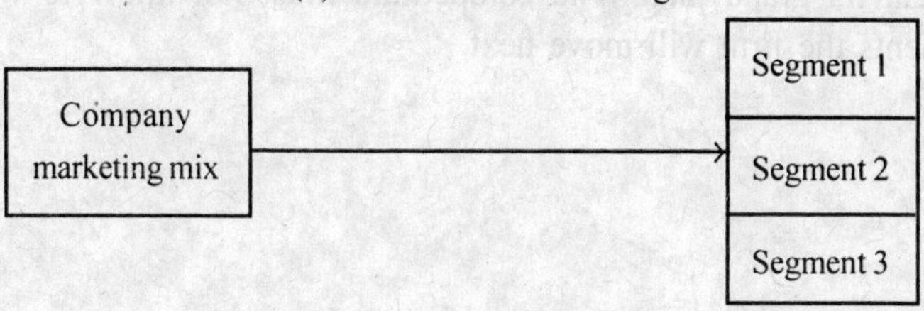

(c) Concentrated Marketing

Additional Consideration in Evaluating and Selecting Segments. Three other considerations must be taken into account in evaluating and selecting segments.

Ethical Choice of Market Targets. Market targeting sometimes generates controversy. The public is concerned when marketeers take unfair advantage of vulnerable groups (such as children) or disadvantaged groups (such as inner-city poor people), or promote potentially harmful products. Marketeers need to proceed in a socially responsible way when these issues may arise.

Segment Inter-relationships and Super-segments. In selecting more than one' segment to serve, the company should pay close attention to segment inter-relationships on the cost, performance and technology side. A company carrying a fixed cost (its salesforce, store outlets, and so on) will add products to absorb and share some of the cost. Thus a sales force will be given addjtional products to sell, and a fast food outlet will offer additional dishes. This is a search for economies of scope, which can be just is important as economies to scale.

Companies should also identify and try to operate in supersegments rather than in isolated segments. The firm would be wise to choose a supersegment rather than a single segment within the supersegment; otherwise, it might be at 3 competitive disadvantage with those firms that have locked into that supersegment.

Segment-By-Segrnent Invasion Plans. Even if the firm plans to target a supersegment, it is wise to enter one segment at a time and conceal its grand plan. The competitors must not know to what segments the firm will move next.

❒

5

Consumer Behaviour and Advertising

Customer or consumer is the central theme of our marketing system. For a product to sell at all, with or without advertising, it must appeal to and satisfy, some needs for some consumers at léast as well as competing items. These need dominate the behaviour of the consumers. The producer or manufacturer should identify these motives, which prompt them to purchase the product offered or he can offer the product wanted by them *i.e.*, a complete product satisfying their needs. Thus, it is a buying motive that prompts the buyer to buy the article. Such motives may be fear, desire for money, vanity, pride, fashion, possession, sex or romance, affection or comfort.

Behaviour of each individual differs. Each individual behaves in a particular manner as directed by his inner motive. The marketer or advertiser must identify the motives which govern the behaviour of the consuming public before going for the advertising for his product. It helps the designing of an advertising programme. By studying the consumer behaviour, the advertiser or the advertising agency can take a decision about the media of advertisement apppeal to be made, market segment where to advertise and the type of advertisement.

Advertising is not a magic capable of causing people to things which they do not need or want. It simply helps people to retionalise purchases of products they want, but do not need in the strcit economic sense. Thus, advertising simply transforms the want into the motive that motivates the buyer to purchase the product the company offered if the product or the brand satisfies the need of the buyer. If wants or needs ar stronger, the chancel for its sale exists. If the product is capable of satisfying only the comparatively weak and less basic needs or wants, there is not so much advertising opportunity. The extent of advertising opportunity thus, varies with the strength of the basic underlying needs or wants that are satisfied by the product or brand.

The consumer behaviour is subject to change overtime due to social and cultural influences. It makes an attitude in the long run.

CONSUMER BEHAVIOUR — DETERMINANTS

What is Consumer Behaviour?

Consumer behaviour may be defined as the acts of individuals in obtaining and using goods and services, including the decision processes that precede and determine these act. This definition includes both the ultimate consumers and the industrial users. The behaviour of these two consumers differ a lot. A major difference in the purchasing behaviour of industrial consumer is that additional influences can be exerted on the industrial purchasing agent from within the organisation. Our approach of consumer behaviour is to view it as a decision process, and the act of purchasing is one of the acts in the process. In order to understand consumer behaviour clearly, we must understand the events that precede and follow from purchase act. Consumer behaviour results from individual and environmental influences. Consumers often purchase the goods and services which they want others to accept. Behaviour is therefore determined by the individual's psychological make up and the influence of others. Thus, behaviour is the result of the interaction of the consumer's personal influences and the pressures exterted upon them by outside forces in the environment.

Determinants of Consumer Behaviour

There are four basic determinants of consumer behaviour:

1. Individual Needs. The starting point in the purchase decision process is the recognition of a felt need. A need may be defined as the lacking of something useful. An individual always has innumerable unsatisfied needs. These needs become motives later on because everybody is motivated by needs or wants. Psychological studies indicate that all human activities including buying behaviour are directed towards satisfying certain basic needs. All individuals do not act exactly in the same war in their efforts to fulfil their needs. These actions not only depend upon the nature of the basic needs but they are modified by the individual's particular environmental and social backgrounds.

All Needs are Basic. There is no unanimity upon the list of basic needs among the psychologists. The need classification of Maslow is the most popular and is known as 'Maslow's Hierarchy of Needs'. Maslow has classified basic needs in the hierarchical order as follows:

(1) Physiological needs, *(2)* Safety needs, *(3)* Belongingness and love needs, *(4)* Esteem needs, *(5)* Self actualisation needs, *(6)* Desire to know and understand, and *(7)* Aesthetic needs. According to Maslow,' an individual normally tries to satisfy his needs strictly in the order given in the list. Thus bying behaviour of a person may be determined on the basis of the stage of his needs. Some of the needs are natural and some others are acquired during the life time.

2. Drive or Motive. When a need or want is not satisfied it leads to a drive. The food need for instance, lead to hunger drive Drive is a state of tension where individual tries to find the ways to satisfy the drive. Drives are, in effect the reasons underlying certain behaviour patterns. Drive tension leads to behaviour that will satisfy the need or want and thereby reduce the drive tension.

A drive is a strong stimulus that motivates the individual. Depending on the cues—products, signs, advertisements, and other stimuli relevant to the situation-existing in the environment, the individual chooses some specific response in an effort to satisfy the drive. The specific response to be chosen depends upon the cues and the previous experience. Reinforcement in the learning process occurs when the response is followed by satisfaction, *i.e.*, a reduction in the derive tension. Reinforcement strengthens the relationship between the environmental cue and the response. Similar response may be repeated next time when the drive occurs and such repeated reinforcemement leads to the development of a habit, thereby making a decision process a routine for the individual.

Thus a motive can be defined as an urgent for which an individual seeks satisfaction. It becomes a buying motive when the individual seeks satisfaction through the purchase of something. It is, thus, an inner urge that moves or prompts a person to some action.

3. Perception. Perception is the image or the formalised impressions residing in the minds of the individuals about different products, brands, producers, retailers and of themselves. Patterns of buying behaviour are greatly influenced by these perceptions. As perception affects the buying behaviour, marketers take them into account in drafting promotional plans and programmes. There are two types of image in the minds of consumers *(i)* self image, and *(ii)* brand image.

Self image is a picture of himself in the mind of individual *i.e.*, the kind of person he considers himself to be or the kind of person he imagines that others consider him to be. Different people have different kinds of self image that gives rise to market segmentation along psychlogical lines. A basic level of motivation research is that in many buying situations, an individual prefers to buy those products or brands whose images appear consistent with his or her self image.

Brand image is the impression of a particular brand in the minds of the consumers. Through long continued use of particular advert sing and selling appeals many brands have accuired definite image in the minds of the public such as Dalda for the vanaspati ghee or surf for the detergents. The management should also take advantage of the brand image.

The perception of incoming stimuli is greatly affected by the attitudes to these stimuli.

4. Attitudes. Attitude governs the response to a stimulus and leads to behaviour, usually to action. An attitude cannot be neutral.

To have attitude means some involvement in being ready for action. Attitude immediately defines the position of a person for or against a thing.

Importance of Consumer Behaviour in Advertising

Consumer behaviour plays a very crucial role in advertising. Before preparing an advertising plan, an advertiser or the advertising agency must be aware of the behavioural pattern of the consumers. The success of the programme depends greatly on the behaviour study of the consumers. The study of consumer behaviour determines the media of advertising or media mix to cover the market segments where it can influence the consumer behaviour and induce the consumers to take a decision to purchase the product.

The Consumer Behaviour Study also Recogoises the Drives that should be Satisfied. The advertiser may improve his product so as to satisfy the particular drive. For example, during disturbances on local or regional levels, a safety drive emerges in the minds of the people having some previous belongings. The insurer may introduce new policies in order to provide safety against disturbances taking the drive as the main stimuli for the action. Thus consumer behaviour helps advertiser improve the products or services or introduce new products or services in order to satisfy the needs.

The Idea of Scientific Advertising has been Developed by the Study of Consumer Behaviour. Scientific advertising means properly planned advertising based on serious deliberations or overall factors that have a bearing upon its success. It implies the development and use of a fact finding approach to the formation and execution of an advertising programme. It avoids pure emotional methods' that predominated the earlier advertisements. Consumer behaviour study has shaped the advertisements in a scientific manner. The message or the appeal, contained in a scientific copy of advertisement can only be made influential if it touches the inner soul of the consumer or if it is timely responding to what the consumer wants to purchase or desires to purchase at a particular juncture. The appeals may be changed with the changing behaviour of the people. So, change in the attitude due to change in habits or fashion may lead to a change in advertising appeal.

Consumer Behavioural Science Deals with Characteristics of Human Behaviour. Marketing belongs to human behaviour as it deals with buying decisions. Advertising is socio-psychological art. The advertisement writer like a teacher has to study psychology behind human behaviour in respect of satisfaction of wants. Harlow Gate thought advertising a new field for psychological work and one of the great and increasing importance. Consumer psychologists are interested in the behaviour of group consumers rather than the behavioural patterns of single individuals. There are four principal areas of interes:

(i) Decision making in the market place.

(ii) Change in attitudes and behaviour of consumers.

(iii) Influence of time and uncertainty, and

(iv) Studies of group belongings.

The consumer is believed to be sovereign. The advertiser must adopt to the basic disposition of the consumer and behaviour changes results when the basic dispositions are either favourable or at least neutral with respect to the suggested 'Change.' Hence consumer reacts to the offerings of the market in the ways he believes to be in his best interest.

One school of thought holds that consumers behave in a manner, consistent with their self concepts, that is:

(a) The kind of person that one believes he or she is; and

(b) The kind of person that one believes that others think he or she is.

According to this self concept theory consumers develop life styles (behaviour patterns) that are in accordance with their self concepts. They purchase and use goods and services most congruent with their self concepts. The objective of marketer tends to follow this theory is to ear mark the self concepts embraced by target consumers and provide a marketing mix which are compatible with their self concepts. An individual's self image is a good motivating force. People buy certain product only to express how they feel about themselves.

Some marketers believe the insights into the personalities of target consumers are useful in understanding and predicting consumer behaviours. The term personality refers to that combination of enduring Psychological traits that characterise the individual and distinguish him from others in the way he perceives, acts upon and interacts with the environment. Personality traits include degree of aggresivenes, dominance, adventuresomeness, hostility flexibility, responsibility, sociability, obstinacy and patience etc. Each individual has different combination of traits which make his personality different from others. Further these traits are consistent or enduring rather than continually changing and permanent. Our concern is more with the essence of personality and with the reasonable assumption that an individual's personality makes him respond consistently to similar stimuli. Logic suggests that personality should be closely associated with consumer behaviour. It would see, for instance, that persons having similar personalities would tend to purchase and consume similar products and services. Research to date has not substantiated this view.

COGNITIVE PSYCHOLOGY

Cognition Means Knowledge of Something. Cognitive psychology, thus, focuses on the human's desire to know. The underlying notion in this theory is that behaviour is a function of cognition (knowings), which are nothing other than ideas, bits of knowledge, values and beliefs held by the individual. One authority describes cognition as "those processes by which any sensory input is transformed, reduced, elaborated, stored, recovered or used".

The cognitive psychology has been very nicely summed up by Mr. Markin as—"The human organism, and especially the focus of our inquiry the consumer, is a sensory processing and data gathering organism. His behaviour stems from his goal striving and his aspirations. He is not so much driven to acts of choice by his goals and aspiration. Consumers learn they modify their behaviour overtime. What was sufficient cause or motivation in one situation, may for numerous reasons no longer be interpreted or perceived as sufficient justification for action or similar action in a subsequent situation. Thus, it can be seen that motivation, learning and perception lie at the core of the consumer cognitive process."

Cognitive structures and processes provide two functions:

(i) They are purposive in that they serve the individual in his attempt to achieve satisfaction of needs.

(ii) They are regulatory in that they determine in large meassure the direction taken in the consumer's steps towards his attempt to attain the satisfaction of his initiating needs.

Cognitive Dissonance

An individual always uses his cognitive psychology but in certain circumstances, it is not so. According to Leon Festinger, the human beings, at times, act in such a way which is against their wishes or knowledge. They know that their actions have certain advantages and disadvantages even though they keep the balance between knowledge and action, which are quite against each other. In doing so they are not bothered about others opinions or beliefs Such actions take them to behave with consonance. In other words, dissonance exists, and an individual will try to have a balance by changing behaviour or if behaviour cannot be changed, opinions ,will be changed. After making the decision, persons tend to expose themselves to information that they perceive as likely to support the choice and to avoid information that may favour the rejected alternatives.

The process of dissonance reduction explains why few justify the actions of others. It implies that people are quite receptive to message that help reduce dissonance and resistent to one that might, increase it.

Congnitive dissonance causes frustration and anxiety. There are certain devices, called 'Defence Mechanism' which are generally used to protect the person concerned from frustration and anxiety. These are of four kinds—*(a)* Repression, *(b)* Sublimation, *(c)* Compensation, *(d)* Rationalisation.

(a) **Repression.** Repression means denial of a motive or goal anything involved in any anxiety situation-by exerting control over the motive. It.is a method of dealing with motivational conflicts by excluding from conscious awereness, thoughts or feelings that cause pain or shame. The person concerned avoids the action by forgetting the motive or it may be self deceptive for the existence of a motive. Conflict still remains but anxiety is relieved. The best example of repression is that of sex which is repressed motive.

(b) **Sublimation.** It means substitution of an activity to satisfy a motive. As for sex urge which is not fulfilled due to any reasoninternal disturbance or external obstacles may be sublimated by substitution of music, religion or other social activities, acceptable to him. It will help relieving tension by substituting one type of response for another.

(c) **Compensation.** It makes up a loss or privation. This mechanism enables us to overcome or make up a feeling of inadequacy or inferiority. It has a substitute activity for a frustrated motive. Compensation means offsetting the failure or loss of selfesteem in one activity by fruitful efforts in another area of endeavour.

(d) **Rationalisation.** In this mechanism, when a person is not successful in fulfilling his motive, he accepts a less acceptable real motive and thus he rationalises his motive.

Cognitive Psychology and Advertising

Cognitive psychology and advertising are closely related. Consumer is said to be a thirster of knowledge. Producers try to find out more about people and about the product they use in their daily lives.

The consumer solves the problem. Advertising is one source of such information and to be effective, it must be in proper psychological terms. In this way both consumers and producers get knowledge about each other and the products through advertising.

The cognitive dissonance theory is also useful in the planning and designing of different advertising programmes. It is the advertiser who must know the behaviour of consumer if be is frustrated and is not able to satisfy his needs through the existing goods and services. The advertiser should develop his product or introduce a new product, may be a substitute which can be able to meet the demands of those poor people. Such introduction is made to the public through advertising. Messages should take into account the idea of dissonance, advertisement copy designed skillfully may be an effective appeal to such consumers.

In this way cognitive psychology and cognitive dissonance theories may be applied to advertising field also to get the best of the money.

SOCIAL AND CULTURAL INFLUENCES ON CONSUMER BEHAVIOUR

Man is a social animal. His needs and motives are greatly influenced by the croups in the society. As one experiences needs, he seeks to satisfy them. The pattern of interelated motives and attitudes that determine his response is acquired largely from groups. Groups may be formal and informal. Beginning with our early learning family may be taken as the primary group. Other groups are formed later in the society. Consumer behaviour is largely influenced by these social groups.

An advertise must study the group behaviour before reinforcing or changing the consumers' attitude. The action or response desired must conform to the standards of the group to which the target consumer belongs. The desired action or attitude must have the approval of that group. If group approval is not there, the desired action is not likelly to take place. On the other hand, if the strong group approval is present, for a particular action, this will be the most inclined action to choose. There may other equally desirable actions, but they cannot be taken up in absence of group approval. We shall study in the following lines various social groups and the culture that influence the consumer's behaviour:

1. Family. Most of our attitudes are developed in the family. It represents one of the strongest sources of group influence for the individual consumer. Attitudes of individuals are formed by parents and other members of family towards the products, brands and retail outlets certainly influence of each family member is important when products for family use are purchased. The relative importance of each spouse in the purchase of various housebold durables, such as homes and automobiles, has received much attention.

Almost every person in the society is a member of two families during his life time: One into which he is born and the other, he eventually forms after marriage. The establishment of new household upon marriage results in new marketing opportunities due to new demands of furniture, cots, utensils etc.

A second market is established for the parents who are left alone when childern move away from home. They need pleasure in leisure. Such equipment may be developed to help such parents *e.g.*, gardening equipment, ridio, tape-recorder, etc.

Traditionally, the wife goes for the majority of the family purchases of household items such as food, clothing etc., since the husband works during most of the day. Even though, the preferences of childern and husband may have influenced her decisions, she usually continues to be responsible for the purchases. The husband traditionally has had the final authority in purchasing durables. Even where the decisions are shared by both, mostly the husband is concerned with the functional characteristics of the item while the wife evaluates its style and appearance.

The role of childern is also important in influencing the decisions as they grew older. Their early influence is centred around toy purchases. Younger ones prefer to so for kulfi or ice-cream or other eatables of their choice. They also influence the decisions of their parents as regards their clothing, tailoring as they grew younger. The childem's relative influence on major family purchases also increases with age. A teenager may influence the decision while purchasing a household durable like T.V., car, etc. This influnce very much depends upon his knowledge about the product and its use.

2. Reference Groups. It is but natural for individuals to act in a manner associated with their status in life or with a status to which they aspire. This selfawareness leads us to identify ourselves with certain reference groups. A reference group is a group of people with which an individual identitries himself to the point whrere the group becomes a norm, a standard, or a point of reference. These groups are referred to as a standard of behaviour for their attitudes.

Reference groups may be formal in nature as found in church or in social organisations or informal such as friendship. Reference groups generally adopt certain objects as symbols and these objects are desired by group members.

Group membership is no pre-requisite for group influence in directs their purchase behaviour. Individuals after refer these groups for their purchase decisions even though they are not members. of the group. This partially explains the use of athletes in advertisements even though few have necessary skills.

Reference groups are such groups to which individual looks for guidance for proper behaviour. Such reference group exerts some degree of control over his individual mental and physical conduct. Such groups are the family, service groups (Rotary organisations) social groups (clubs), work groups etc. Small groups that involve freqcent face to face interaction (family and work groups) influence the behaviour of their members.

Aspiration groups are also of interest. The individual does not belong to these groups but aspires to become a member. In some cases, a reference group is only one individual where the standards of such reference individual influence the behaviour of the consumer.

Thus some consumers wear clothings tailored by University Tailors, others like Dilip Kumar's hair style, yet otbers walk like Raj Kapoor or Dev Anand or commit actionless murder like Phoolan Devi.

Reference groups may be social, economic or professional groups. Such groups may vary in size also from one person to an entire profession or political party. The individual may be a member of that group in whole or in part for confirmation; or in some cases for the self assurance that he is acting in opposition to their views.

Reference groups may be classified in the following three categories:

(a) **Standard Groups.** Such groups serve as a standard with which we compare ourselves. We may feel poor compared to those who are richer or rich when compared to poorer.

(b) **Aspiration Groups.** The individual does not belong to this group but be wants to get in and imitates that status symbols and buying behaviour of the group to which he aspires to belong. This may be higher social groups such as of revolutionaries.

(c) **Groups whose Prospectives are Assumed.** An individual may adapt The views are standards or norms of the group without intending to belong to it. For example, we may adapt the opinion of a congress leader without dreaming of achieving his popularity or talent. Conversely, a member of minority group may adopt the values of majority group to which he dislikes most.

The advertiser must identify these reference groups and their forms and standard which are expected to be adopted by their members or aspirants.

3. Role of Opinion Leader. Katz and Lazarsfeld developed the concept of opinion leaders. They believe that opinion leaders exist at all levels in the society who are trend setters. These leaders are first to purchase The product newly introduced in the market and others follow the suit. They become the first hand source of information in the group. They are leaders because their opinions are respected within the group and often sought after for advice.

The diffusion of information by opinion leaders is a two step flow of communication. They get the ideas and information from the mass media including radio and television and then pass it on to opinion followers in the leaders sphere of influence.

In this way the place of opinion leaders is very important for the advertiser because they disseminate information and advice. The adverther must identify the opinion leaders or likely opinion leaders as information outlets for the introduction of new products. Some marketer aim promotion efforts at opinion leaders because their opinions are respected and followed by other members of the reference group. So, a marketer while designing marketing mix, must keep in mind the interest and patronage of the opinion leaders so that they may persue the other members of the group.

At this juncture, there is one practical problem that it is very difficult to locate opinion leaders in the group. Moreover, it is also not easy to identify one opinion leader for all products. If one leader is influential for one product, be may not be so influential for another product.

4. Culture. Culture may be defined as "concept that includes a set of learned beliefs, values, attitudes, habits and forms of behaviour that are shared by a society and are transmitted from generation within that society," Culture represents the ideas values, attitudes, artifacts, and symbols governing the behaviour of a member of the group. It determines many of the responses that individuals make in given situations. It is a completely learned and handed down way of life that gives each society its own peculiar flavour. Thus each culture has its own peculiar characteristics which separate one culture from the other. Culture may be identified as:

(a) Continental culture such as Asian culture or European culture.

(b) National culture as Indian culture or Russian culture.

(c) Regional culture as East and west cultures.

Further we may identify sub cultures based on race (Aryan or vor Dravid culture) on religion (Hindu, Jain, Sikh, Christian, Jews, Parsi cultures), on state of origin (U.P. culture or Punjab culture), 'or on place of origin (Lucknow culture, Delhi culture).

Culture does not have a static list of characteristics, beliefs or traditions. It is alive, moving or changing. It reats to pressure from within or from outside. Resistance to these pressures cause conflicts between members of different culture. Cultural changes may result from technological advancements. Introduction of LPG (Liquified Petroleum Gas) has changed the old methods of cooking thus shifting to a new culture. Education and travel substantially influence the culture, Education attaches value to the new ideas and theories that are quite unknown earlier. Travel also influence the culture. As more and more young people experience life in other countries, they adopt new values.

The core values of Indian culture include Government reliance, easy life, religious convictions, husband dominated families, parent-centered household, respect for elders, savings for the future, sexual chastety, security, contentment and non-violence etc. We should not stereotype all citizen by using our own cultural background and relating them to the men belonging to different states alike. Cultural differences in different attitudes and mores.

Our advertising is very much influenced by different cultures and sub-cultures. The alert advertising manager should recognise these sub-cultures that may form different market segments. He should seek of increase an understanding of their motivations, needs. and attitudes. Much of the fashionable popularity of products or ideas reflects, not a cultural change but a temporary fascination. The trick is to spot long term trend behind the fad. Tight jeans or bell-bottom may come and go but the trend towards masculinity may continue with a significant cultural meaning. The women's liberation may die down, but the long term trend towards equality and male female relationship on new terms will continue. Thus the advertiser should try to set the long term trend that may represent a cultural change or he should be cautious enough to introduce his products in the light of these short term and long term cultural changes.

5. Social Classes. The population of a country can be logically divided into manageable groups on some basic similarities of age, occupations, income, sources of income, types of homes and location of homes. These groups may be called 'social classes', The members of a given social class hold comparable positions in the socio-economic system who hold generally similer attitudes, beliefs and value and patterns of behaviour. We can group the population of India into upper, middle and lower social classes containing persons with particular demographic and life style characteristics.

Occupation is the most important determinant of the social class Doctors, Engineers, I.A.S. officers have been granted greater prestige than clerks, drivers etc. in the society. In addition, members of the particular occupational group have similarities in values, beliefs and opinions, tastes and behaviour within a particular group, the success of individual determines his status in the society. A highly successful engineer may be put in a high social class than an unsuccessful one or one who is not so successful. The members of a given social class share many fundamental values. The means that segmentation by social class is a distinct possibility.

Interpersonal relationships too, are important determinants of the social class of an individual. It is a day to day experience that the members of the same class tend to become friends to entertain one another socially, and to maintain close day to day relationship and personal contacts.

Differences among social classes exist in attitudes, goals. prohibited behaviour, perception means of gaining information, the role of family members in decision making and in numerous other areas of behaviour. Thus each social class is diffrrent in behaviour values and beliefs.

Since social classes encompasses groups of people who share similar life style, market segmentation is highly useful in advertising planning. This is not to suggest that every marketers should use social classes for this purpose but they should gather information about social classes to see whether social classes fòrm the basis of market segmentation.

Social classes may be used as a determined of media to be used. Different journals or newspapers are used by different social classes, the advertiser can choose the media most suitable for the product. The drug advertiser will prefer to advertise in a journal meant for medical practitioners or medical representatives.

6. Life Style. Anotber important influence on consumer behaviour is lifestyle that is largely derived from the influence of the family. In many ways, the term is closely akin to individual differences. The term describes a distinctive mode of living. The concept goes far beyond the characterisations that result from a person's social class. This describes how go about their daily routine. It is a problem how people allocate their time on different activitive of daily life, rather than how they spent their money, although the two problems are interelated in many instances. What is important to individuals may be reflected by their actions. We may see that two persons belonging to the same social class and possessing the same demographic characteristics are very much different in their life style.

The life style research can be highly useful in designing and development of advertising strategy and copy. It provides data dealing with such demographic variables as sex, age, and income or studies of consumer attitutes about the product and its use.

Thus, the advertising strategist attempts to learn as much as possible about the social and cultural influences on target consumers' behaviour. It will help much in designing and preparing the advertisement copy and the appeal in the rigbt perspective effectively. By studying social and cultural influences, on the behaviour of the people The advertiser can take a decision about the media to be used. These insights combine to permit better communications.

ATTITUDE

Attitude is the most important variable in social Psychology. Attitudes govern the response to a stimulus and lead to behaviour, usually to action. G. Allport has defined the attitude as "as neutral mental state of rediness to respond, which is organised through experience and exerts a directive or dynamic influence on behaviour." Thus attitude means involvement readiness to action. Attitude indicates The likings and dislikings of the people about a particular product. It states the person's position for or against a product or whether it is friendly or hostile. Belief is a must in attitude. An attitude cannot be said to exist without a belief.

Components of Attitudes

There are three main components of attitude. These are cognitive (awareness, comprehension and knowledge), affective evaluation, liking), and conative (action tendency).

(1) Cognitive Component. The cognitive component is what the individual knows or believes about the product. We are not only concerned with the beliefs about the characteristics of the object. but more of less, about its evaluations also. It is important to evaluate the object in terms of its qualities *i.e.,* whether the object is good or bad, moral or immoral or neccessary or unnecessary. Without belief (knowing the object and framing an opinion about it) attitude cannot take shape.

(2) Affective Component. The affective component is the individual's emotional reaction to the object *i.e.* whether individuals like the object or not or to know whether they have favourable or unfavourable attitude towards the object. This component states why the objects carry a positive view.

(3) Gonative Component. This component is the behavioural part of the attitude, the readiness to respond with action. If the attitude is negative, it will adversely affect the behaviour of the person. The response may range from ignoring the object stimulus to aggresively attacking it conversely, a positive attitude towards the object is a good omen. It may result in praise, and, hopefully for the marketer in the purchase of the product.

Each of these three components of attitude varies according to the situation and the person. Every-one in effect, does not have a good or bad attitude or love or hate attitude towards every product in the market. Attitude may range from indifferences to passion with many complexities along the way. Attitudes, good or bad, are learned and do not spring up all of a sudden. Experience teaches us what is good or what is bad. We learn this in our family or family plays a very important role in forming an attitude in the begining and later on peer group influences or forms our attitude.

Attitudes do not function in isolation. They interact with perception, thinking, feeling, and reasoning. By selecting from the constant bombardment of stimuli, we organise our world in an attempt to maintain our sanity and search for meaning in our environment.

Attitude Formation and Change through Mass Communication

As we have explained above that an advertiser has three alternatives towards the consumer attitude depending upon how the product doing *i.e. (i)* confirm the existing positive attitude *(ii)* change the existing negative attitude, and *(iii)* creating new and positive attitude for the new product. How can an advertiser be successful in dirccting the consumer attitude, depends upon various factors to be takcn into account in preparing and designing the advertising programme. The factors in each of the above situations are:

(1) Creating Positive Attitude

The objective of creating positive attitudes motivates much advertising development in situations involving an entry of new product or brand. Creating positive attitude can also be a worth while objection in case of established product. The following creative styles and approaches can be used for this purpose.

(a) Message Focus. A message can be designed to focus a receiver's attention. The focus may be on the source *i e.,* who is explaining the message. But care should be taken that the source and what he or she is communicating by actions, voice, and role position should be in agreement and is able to attract the receiver's attention. An alternative may be to concentrate on generating emotional reactions in a receiver by putting him or her in a pleasant mood, enhancing and bolstering his or her ego, or using some type of emotional appeal. There is one more alternative. A receiver's attention can be directed mainly to the claim being made which are based on widely accepted principles and logic. Thus, the main objective of this style is to focus the attention of the receiver to the message.

(b) Conclusion Drawing. The messages are designed in such a way as to leave something out of a message. It will arouse the curiosity among the prospective and motivation to inquire further about the brand, thus, advertistd. The messages for this, purpose may be 'cool' when they are unstructured such as viewers are told a fragment of the story so that each person must fill in from imagination or 'hot' when they are structured, logical and sequential. This style is more appropriate to build a long range image, when the basic product is emotional (perfumes, make-up) or when a product has no apparent differential advantage over the competionrs' brands.

(c) One sided Versus Two sided Messages. Should an advertiser present only one side (favourable) or both sides (favourable and unfavourable information on the issue) of an argument? The decision depends upon many factors concerning the nature of the overall message and the audience to which it is addressed. It is, however, considered that two sided message is more effective in attitude change than one-sided message. The laboratory studies suggest that one-sided messages are generally more effective among lower educated group and among those having favourable disposition toward a product. Two sided messages often tend to be more effective with a higher educated group and among those having no positive predisposition.

(d) Comparative Advertising. Comparative advertising is a form of advertising that incorporates two sided approach. It compares two or more specifically named or recognisable brands of the same generic product class and makes the comparisons in terms of one or more specific product attributes. It is a recently developed style. This type of advertising provides the consumer with more information and thus improves consumer decision-making. From advertiser's point of view comparative advertising is not favoured by the manufacturers of leading brand. A brand in second and third place, might, on the other hand use this technique to try to convince people of its superiority over the leader. But the attributes chosen as the basis for comparison must be carefully research, and the claims made must be capable of substantiation.

(e) Emotional Appeals. The persuasiveness of advertising can often be enhanced by stimulating various kinds of emotions such as fear, love, hate, humour, sexual desire etc. Fear and humour appeals are most common in developing a particular mood for message delivery.

(i) Fear Appeals. A message stressing the unfavourable Physical consequences of not taking a suggested course of action can have an adverse effect on attitude if this fear appear is too intense. An advertiser can try to induce behavioural change by emphasising either positive or negative appeals or by a combination of both. For example, in a campaign designed by a fire insurance company it may emphasise its positive aspects its low cost, services offered by the company friendliness and so on-or stress the negative aspects of not getting insurance. The danger of losing one's belongings due to fire. Negative appeals are fear appeal and use the strategy of increasing a person's anxiety about not using a product or service. Even though a fear appeal of some kind is used in wide variety of product categories. The most obvious cases are those involving a product designed to protect an individual from loss of property or loss of health, friends, states, job, position and so forth. In this category are personal-care-products (soaps, cosmetics, toothpaste. deodorants etc.) or home making products (food and appliances). Failure to use them poses the threat of health and of not being a good homemaker. The fear appeals can be particularly effective if individuals have been previously exposed to positive arguments or for those whose arousal or anxiety about the product is low and for those who would not normally search for information about the product.

(ii) Humour Appeals. Many advertisements use some form of humour and there is a great deal of opinion expressed concerning the desirability or lack thereof of using humour. A study by Lynch and Hartman suggests eight kinds of humour in advertising relating to general knowledge, sophistication, sensitivity, simplicity, visualisa. tion, cuteness, staging and abstra:tion. Following general views can be expressed about advertising humour—*(i)* humorous messages attract attention; *(ii)* humorous messages may detrimentally affect. comprehension; (iii) humour may distract the audience yielding an increase in persuasion; *(iv)* humorous appeals appear to be persuasive, but the persuasive effect is, at best no greater than that of serious appeals; *(v)* humour tends to enhance source credibility; *(v)* audience characteristics may confound the effects of humour; *(vi)* a humorous context may increase the persuasive effect of a message; and *(viii)* to the extent that a humorous context functions as a positive reinforcer. a persuasive communication placed in such a context may be more effective.

(f) Source Creadibility. Typically, there is a positive relationship between source credibility and the confirmation of attitude, consumers seem to place greater confidence in a trust worthy source and hence are more receptive to what is said. The message should be form a person who is known for an expert and un biassed views.

A doctor could be an expert in recommending a drug product, for example, but the influence would be less if listeners or viewers considered his recommendations to be biassed by the monetary rewards involved. Similarly, there is a substantially reduced tene dency to accep a discrepant message when the source is of moderate or low credibility. It is also obviously possible that one source is credible for some audiences (for example teenngers) may be less credible for others (for example adults or old). A credible source has the potential to register a strong and lasting belief and be a very significant part of an advertising message.

(g) Source Attractiveness. Source attractiveness is also significant in attitude change. Attractiveness concerns the receiver's preceptions of the prestige of the source, the degree to which the source is similar to the receiver, and the physical attractiveness of the source. Prestige, derive from past achivements, reputation. wealth, political power etc. in the society Kapil Dev, for example is very prestigious for advertisements of sports materials. This aspects perates because of the human tendency to be attracted to and influenced by prestigeous person. Physical attractiveness also help in changing the attitude. All other things being equal, the stronger the physical attractive all raction of the source, the greater the liking will be the persuasive impact. The similarity and physical attractiveness both are affected by the relevance of the source to the product or object advertising situation. Thus, for example attractive female models may result in greater intention to buy perfume among males.

(2) Building Resistant Attitudes

We now turn the next notion concerning attitude change. In this notion attempts are made to resist individuals to switch on to the competitors' brand. This problem is more acute when The advertiser has developed favourable patronage and shared the market. He therefore, should sustain the present position. In attitude cheory, terms, how can we induce those who are currently loyal to our brand to remain loyal? This may be called sustaining function of advertising.

A consumer can be made more resistant to competitive appeals either by attempting to make a brand offering more attractive or by attempting to train the consumer to withstand the persuasive efforts of competitors. From the first viewpoint, for example, one strategy would be to anchor beliefs about the brand to other beliefs that the consumer values highly *i.e.*, mantaining self esteem or ego or second. alternative may be to emphasise the risks involved in not using the brand or the brand may be otherwise positioned as a means of defence. The goal of such approaches would be to try to increase the degree to which the consumer made a private commitment to continue using the brand.

The second alternative of attempting to train a consumer to withstand competitive appeals has been the subject of some empirical work in marketing in order to make an attempt to diffuse the advertising messages of competitors. The diffusion of adverting messages should be thought similar to the diffusion of germs in the spread of the disease through a population. It requires a complete check up of the body (market) and then to suggest an effective dose (arguments in message) of medicine. It has been demonstrated that pre-exposure to weakened forms of counter argument is more effective in building up resistance to strong subsequent attacks than is prior presentation of supportive arguments.

Refutational Approach. This is another approach in building resistant attitudes. It refers to the process of explicitly or implicitly stating competitive appeals and then refuting them. The usual advertisements deal exclusively with brand benefits, not making any reference to the competitive brands but the refutational advertisements first deal with competitors claims and then refute them. In nolmal situations the advertisements simply stating the qualities of the product without refering to the competitors products are more effective but refutational advertisements are superior in situations where we take into account the longer run impact of advertising and the competitive environment in which most advertisements are read or viewed. There may be three reasons why refutational messages appear to work

(i) They are more stimulating than supportive messages.

(ii) They refute counter claims and thus make the competitive attacks appear less credible when they appear. Statements of counter claims can arouse dissonance or imbalance. The refutation can restore balance.

(iii) Refutational messages do contain some supportive information.

(3) Changing Negative Attitude

The goal of changing existing negative attitude towards a brand is too difficult to achieve. In some very special circumstances, an advertiser may want to consider changing negative attitudes towards a brand. Changing negative attitude is a very difficult and costly tasle. In such situations, there is one approach in psychology that is likely to be effective. When a person is very much involved in an issue and when he sees or hears an argument that runs counter to his own position on it, that person will tend to resist the argument by constructing a set of reasons for supporting the original position. In effect, the individual argues to himself against the persuasive intent of the conflicting message. In advertising, this position can be seen when consumer is committed to the arguments of competitive advertiser. The refutational approach discussed above is one means of withstanding counter arguments by immunising the committed consumers againts competitive attacks. This may help in changing the negative attitude of consumers into positive attitude.

Any how, this is quite difficult to change the negative attitude of consumers towards a brand. It generally occurs in the decline stage of the product life cycle. In such circumstances it is better to allow the product die down and think of introducing a new brand or product in place of the original one. It will prove economical. The advertiser should try to develop the positive attitude towards new product tbrough extensive adverting programmes rather to spend much money in changing the negative attitude.

Thus attitude is a very typical phenomenon in advertising. The whole art and science of adverting revolves round the attitude. The advertisers always try to develop a positive attitude towards their products or brands and want to change the negative attitude.

HIERARCHY OF EFFECTS MODEL

The advertising is a mass communication and that communication is only a part of total marketing effort. The consumer behaviour can be developed or changed through an effective communication process. There are various steps each one is the effect of previous step, through which a consumer may be persued to purchase the goods and services offered. Many models have been developed to clarify the communication process. The best known and the most frequently used model is 'Hierarchy of Effects Models.' This model has been developed by Lavidge and Steiner.

In this model, they have described advertising as a force that must more people up a series of steps. There, are six stages in the adoption process-Awareness, knowledge, liking, preference conviction and final decision *i.e.,* purchase, thus, starting from their being unaware of the products existence, on to their actual purchase of it.

The first step is awareness. An individual starts at some point by being unaware of the brand's presence in the market. The initial task is get awareness of the product. There are several ways to measure awareness. If an individual say that he has heard of the brand, it means, he is aware of the presence of the brand in the market.

The Second Step is Knowledge. It implies that the purchaser must know about the specific characteristics and appeals of the brand. How does it differ from the competitors brands? Whom is it supposed to benefit? Thus, the buyer must gather a neutral knowledge or cognitive bits of the product.

Next step comes liking when a person stores some knowledge about the various brands of the product available in the product, only then, he can make his liking. This step helps in creating brand image. This step, however, is multi-dimensional. Rarely is there a single dimension that will measure a brand image adequately, for a person will usually have some knowledge or impression of more than one aspects of it.

The fourth step is preference. The buyer will decide the preferences or rank the brands before making an attitude to purchase.

The next step is attitude or conviction step and invenes between image or preference step and final action. The development of attitude is both rich and useful. There are several ways to measure attitude one is action orieted and might involve intensions to buy or rank order preference. Another may be like-dislike feeling. A third approach would take into consideration the fact that an object consists of several attributes. A customer may like some of them and not other.

The last step is action phase *i.e.,* an overt move by the customer. He makes a final decision to purchase the article. It may be possible at this stage that customer may try a brand for the first time and ask for the literature.

These are six steps in the Hierarchy of Effects model. The first two steps 'awareness' and 'knowledge' are positive and relate to information of ideas. The next two steps 'taking' and 'preference' have to do with favourable attitude or feelings towards the product. The final two steps 'conviction or attitude' and 'purchase' are action oriental. That is decision to purchase the product finally.

These three advertising functions divide the behaviour into three dimensions—*(i)* coguitive—intellectual, mental or rational state, *(ii)* affective-emotional or feeling state, *(iii)* conative or motivational-striving state treating objects as positive or negative.

Change in Sequence

The hierarchy of effect model assumes that there is a logical progression from stimulus to response. In most of the case. The logic seems true. But, it appears that some consumers in certain circumstances skip some steps or move in a different sequence. If research in a particular market indicates that the buyer behaves like this natural the promotion plans of the marketer should be adopted to suit the target customers' buying behaviour. But this not an easy task.

There may be two models where a buyer deviates from the basic steps of hierarchy of effects models such models are—*(1)* Action First Medel, and *(2)* Quick Decision Model.

1. Action First Model. This model shows that some consumers buy first as soon as they gain awareness of the brand or the product and then they come to know the basic characteristics of the brand. If they are satisfied with the use of the product, they perhaps like and prefer the product. If their attitude and brand image are favourable only then confirmation takes place. The buyers behave in this way perhaps because the decision is overwhelming to them. After the purchase they read the advertisements and brochures relating to the brand purchased and of the competitors brands to learn that is so good or not good about the brand they have purchased. If they are satisfied with the use of the brand their attitude becomes positive, confirming their decision and they may create a positive attitude about the producer and the product by words of mouth.

2. Quick-Decision Model. There is another model in the series that escapes the steps in Hierarchy of Effects model. This model is named 'Quick Decision Model. This model is relevant if consumers are regularly bombarded with stimuli about products which are seen not very important or very, different from its competitors. Many convenience goods where consumers feel that a serious evaluation of the product is not necessary, are purchased in this way. As soon as consumers come to know about the product, they get the knowledge about the physical characteristics of the product and decide to purchase it. Here, after the purchase, they feel if it meets their needs or they should purchase it again. During the consumption process attitude changes may move the consumers towards liking or even prefering. the product. Here promotion efforts are necessary or useful in promoting brand recognition and creating brand image so that the brand may be selected in the first place in future. At this stage, consumers may understand the advantage and subtle differences of the product. Eventually, they may be convinced and their decision is confirmed. They then may carry their positiveattitudes by word of mouth.

The Effects of Involvement

Several studies have suggested that the use of 'Hierarchy of Effects model is limited to conditions of high involvement un the part of consumers. It was recognised that, the high involvement of consumer with he product or the message acts as a moderator variable in the communication process. According to this theory an individual processes the advertising in one of the two ways one process called 'High-Involvement Hierarchy' and the other Low

Involvement Hierarchy' High Involvement Theory corresponds to Hierachy of Effects model as discussed above. It exposes first some cognitive change which gives rise to a change in effects and finally a change in behaviour. On the contary 'Low-Involvement Hierarchy begins with a cognitive change, followed by a change in behaviour, then a change in effect. The two involvement hierarchy models may be diagrammed thus:

High Involvement	**Low-Involvement**
Exposure	Exposure
|	|
Cognition	Cognition
|	|
Affect	Behaviour
|	|
Behaviour	Affects

The high involvement model sometimes assume, that people have some prior attitude towards the brand or the product and they act according to their belief. They sometime act to rationalise their attitude. The low-involvement model on the other hand assumes that people are passive learners and their behaviour is not preceded by strong beliefs about the product. It is claimed that the product involvement is affected by the degree of consumer commitment the importance of and familiarity with a product on the consumer's part, and the degree of differentiation in the product.

The advertising themes are different in both types of involvements. In high involvement, the role of advertising is to create favourable attitude towards the product or brand. Print media can be used extensively repetition of messages and appeals is not required and clear-cut advertising themes can be developed. On the contrary, in low involvement case, the main aim of advertising is to create awareness. The use of short messages and frequent repetition strategy in broadcast media are recommended.

❐

6
Consumer Motivation

Motivation can be defined as the driving force within individuals that imples them to action. This driving force is produced by a state of tension, which exists as the reslt of an unfulfilled need. Individuals strive both consciously and sub-consciously to reduce this tension through behaviour that they anticpate will fulfil their needs and thus relieve them of the stress they feel. The specific goals they select and the patterns of action they undertake to achieve their goals are the results of individual thinking and learning.

The specific course of action that consumers pursue and their special goals are seiected on the basis of their thinking processes and previous learning. For that reason, marketeers who understand motivational theory attempt to influence the consumer's cognitive processes.

Needs. Every individual has needs. Some are innate, others are acquired. Innate needs are physiological; they include the needs for food, for water, for air, for clothing, for shelter and for sex. Because they are needed to sustain biological life, the biogenic needs are considered primary needs or motives.

Acquired needs are needs that we learn in response to our culture or environment. These may include needs for self-esteem, for prestige, for affection, for power and for learning. Because acquired needs are generally psychological, they are considered secondary needs or motives. They result from the individual's subjective psychological state and from relationships with others. For example, all individuals need shelter from the elements; thus finding a place to live fulfills an important primary need for a newly transferred executive.

However, the kind of residence she rents or buys may be the result of secondary needs. She may seek a place in which she and her husband can entertain Huge groups of people; she may want to live in an exclusive community to impress her friends and family. The house an individual ultimately purchases thus may serve to fulfil both primary and secondary needs.

Goals. Goals are the sought after results of motivated behaviour. Our discussion of motivation is in part concerned with generie goals, that is, the general classes or categories of goals that consumers select to fulfil their needs. Marketeers are even more concerned with consumer's product specific goals, that is, the specifically branded or labelled products they select to fulfil their needs.

The Selection of Goals. For any given need; there are many differnt and appropriate goals. The goals selected by individuals depend on their personal experiences, physical capacity, prevailing cultural norms and values, and other goal's accessibility in the physical and social environment.

For example, an individual may have a strong hunger need. If he is a young college athlete, he may envision a thick sirlm steak as his goal object; if his doctor has advised him to avoid red meat, he may settle for a thick Tuna Steak instead. If he has a toothache, he may not be able to chew a teak he may have to select hamburger. If he has never tasted steak, if it is outside his realm of personal experience, he probably would not even think to steak but instead would select a food that has previously satisfied his hunger.

Finally, the goal object has to be both socially acceptable and physically accessible. If our college athlete was having dinner with his mother, she might frown on his eating red meat and insist to eat fish or chicken instead. If he were shipwrecked on an island with no food provisions or living animals, he could not realistically select steak as his goal object, although he might fantasize about it. If he were in India, were cows are considered sacred, he would not be able to eat steak, because to do so would be considered a sacrilege. He would have to select a substitute goal more appropriate to the social environment.

An individual's own perception of himself or herself also serves to influence the specific goals selected. The products a person owns, would like to own, or would not like to own are often perceived in terms of how closely they reflect (are congruent with) the person's self image A product that is perceived as matching a consumer's self image has a greater probability of being selected than one that is not. Thus, a man who perceives himself as young and "with it" may drive a Porsche; a woman who perceives herself as rich and conservative may drive a Mercedes. The types of houses people live in the cars they drive, the clothes they wear, the very food they eat these specific goal objects are often chosen because they, symbolically reflect the individual's self-image while they satisfy specific needs.

Interdependence of Needs and Goals. Needs and goals are interdependent neither exists without the other. However, peope are often not as aware of their needs as they are of their goals. For example a teenager may not consciously be aware of his spcial needs but may join a photography club to meet new friends. A local politician may not consciously be aware of a power need but may regularly run for public office. A woman may not recognize her achievement needs but may strive to have the most successful real estate office in town.

Individual's are usually somewhat more aware of their psychological needs. Most people know they are hungry or thirsty or cold and they take appropriate steps to satisfy these needs. The same pople may not consciously be aware of their needs for acceptance, for self-esteem, for status. They may, however, sub-consciously engage in behaviour that satisfy these psychological (acquired) needs.

Positive and Negative Motivation

Motivation can be positive or negative in direction. We may feel a driving force oward some objector condition, or a driving force away from some object or condition. For example, a person may be impelled towards a restaurant to fulfil a hunger need and away from motorcycle transportation to fulfil a safety need.

Some psychologists refer to positive drives as needs, wants, or desires and to negative drives as fears or avessions. However, although positive and negative motivational forces seem to differ dramatically in terms of physical (and sometimes emotional activity, they are basically similar in that both serve to initiate and sustain human behaviour. For this reason, researchers often refer to both kinds of drives or motives as needs, wants, and desires. Some theorists distinguish wants from needs by defining wants as product pecific needs. Thus, to use an earlier example, a person may experience thirst (a need); she may want Lipton's Iced Tea as a means of alleviating her thirst.

Goals, too, can be positive or negative goal positive goal is one toward which behaviour is directed and thus is often referred to as an approach object. A negative goal is one from which behaviour is directed away and this is sometimes referred to as an avoidance object. Since both approach and avoidance goals can be considered objects to motivated behaviour, most researchers refer to both simply as goals. Consider this example, A middle age a woman may have a positive goal of fitness and so she joins a health club to work out reguarly, her husband may view getting fat as a negative goal and so he joins a road runners club. In the former case, the wife's actions are designed to achieve a positive goal health and fitness, in the latter case, her husband's action is designed to avoid a negative goal a flabby physique.

Sometimes people become motivationally aroused by a threat to or elimination of a behavioural freedom (*e.g.* the freedom to make a product chice without undue influence from a retailer). This motivational state is called psychological reactance and is usually manifested by a negative consumer response. For example, in 1985 when the Coca-Cola company changed its traditional formula and introduced 'New Coke", many people reacted negatively to the fact that their "freedom to choose" had been taken away, and refused to buy the New Coke. Coca-Cola management responded to this unexpected psychological reaction by reintroducing the original formula as "Classic' Coke".

Rational Versus Emotional Motives. Some consumer behaviourists distinguish between socalled rational motives and emotional (or nor rational) motives. They are the term rationality in the tradional economic sense, which assumes that consumers behave rationally when they carefully.consider all alternatives and choose those that given them the greatest utility. In a marketing context, the term rationality implies that consumers elect goals based on totally objective criteria, such as size, weight, price or miles per gallon. Emotional motives implies the selection of goals according to personal or subjective criteria (*e.g.* the desire for individuality, pride, fear, affection, status).

The assumption underlying this distinction is that subjective or emotional criteria do not maximize utility or satisfaction. However, it is reasonable to assume that consumers always attempt to select alternatives that, in their view, serve to maximize satisfaction. Obviously, the assessment of satisfaction is a very personal process, based on the individual's own need structure, as well as on past behavioural and social experiences. What may apper irrational to an outside observer may be perfectly rational in the context of the comsumer's own psychological field. For example, a product purchased to enhance self image (such as fragrance) is a perfectly rational form of consumer behaviour. If behaviour does not appear rational to the person at the time it is undertaken, obviously he or she would not do it. Therefore, the distinction between rational and emotional consumption motives is not always warranted.

Consumer researcher who subscribe to the positivist perspective tend to view all consumer behaviour as rationally motivated and they try to isolate the causes of such behaviour so that they can predict, and thus influence, future behaviour. Experimentalists are interested in studying the hedonistic pleasures that consumption behaviour provides, such as fun, or fantasy, or sensuality. The study helps consumer to gain insights and understanding of the consumer in his or her own unique circumstances.

DYNAMIC NATURE OF MOTIVATION

Motivation is a highly dynamic construct that is constantly changing in reaction to life experiences.

Needs and Goals are Constantly Changing. Needs and goals are constantly growing and changing in response to an individual's physical condition, environment, interactions with others and experiences. As individuals attain their goals, they develop new ones. If they do not attain their goals, they continue to strive for old goals or they develop substitute goals. Some of the reasons why need driven human activity never ceases include the following : *1.* Existing needs are never completely satisfied; they continually impel activity designed to attain or maintain satisfaction *2.* As needs become satisfied, new and higher-order needs emerge that cause tension *3.* People who achieve their goals set new and higher goals for themselves.

Needs are Never Fully Satisfied. Most human needs are never fully satisfied. For example, at fairly regular intervals people experience hunger needs that must be satisfied. Most people regularly seek companionship and approval from others to satisfy their social needs. Even more comple psychological needs are rarely satisfied. For example a person may partially or temporarily satisfy a power need by working as assistant to the CEO of a fortune 500 company; but this small taste of power may not sufficiently satisfy her need, and so she maystrive for her own decision-making position in the company. In this instance, temporary goal achievement does not adequately satisfy the need for power, and the individual strives harden in an effort to satisfy the need more fully.

New Need Emerge as Old Needs are Satisfied. Some motivational theorists believe that a hierarchy of needs exists and that new, higher-order needs emerge as lower-order needs are fulfilled. For example, a man who has largely satisfied his basic psychological needs may turn his efforts to achieving acceptance among his new nighbours by joining their political clubs and supporting their candidates.

Having achieved acceptance, he then mey seek recognition by giving lavish parties or making large charitable contrbutions.

Marketeers must be attuned to changing needs. Car manufacturers who stress the prestige value of their automobiles may fail to recognize that many consumers now look elsewher to satisfy need for prestige, for example through charitable gift giving or public service. For this reason, manufacturers of prestige cars might do better if they stressed other need satisfactions as real sons for buying a new model.

Success and Failure Influence Goals. A number of researchers have explored the nature of the goals that individuals set for themselves. In general, they have concluded that individuals who sucessfully achieve their goals usually get new and higher goals for themselves; that is, they raise their levels of aspiration. This is probably due to the fact that success makes them more confident of their ability to reach higher goals. Conversely, those who do not reach their goals sometimes lower their level of aspiration. Thus, goal selection is often a function of success and failure.

Substitute Goals. When an individual cannot attain a specific goal or type of goal that he or she anticipates will satisfy certain needs, behaviour may be directed to a substitute goal. Although the substitute goal may not be as satisfactory as the primary goal, it may be sufficient to dispel uncomfortable tension. Continued deprivation of a primary goal may result in the substitute goal assuming primary goal status. A man who has stopped drinking whole milk because he is dieting may actually begin to prefer skim milk.

Defense Mechanism. People who cannot cope with frustration often mentally redefine the frustrating in order to protect their self-image and defend their selfesteem. For example, a young woman may yearn for a milk coat she cannot afford. The coping individual may select a less expensive fur such as muskrat, or a cloth coat with a fur collar. The person who cannot cope may react with anger towards her boss for not paying her enough money to buy a fur, or she may decide that wearing the fur of animals is a barbaric custom in which she will not participate. These last two possibilities are examples, respectively, of aggression and rationalization, defence mechanisms people sometimes adopt to protect their egos from feelings of failure when they do not attain their goals. Other defence mechanism include regression, withdrawal, projection, autism, identification and repression.

Frustration. Failure to achieve a goal offer results in feelings of frustration. At one time or another everyone has experienced the frustration that comes from the inability to attain a goal. The barrier that prevents attainment of a goal may be personal to the individual or it can be an obstacle in the physical or social enviornment. Regardless of the causes, individuals react differently to frustrating situations. Some people are adaptive and manage to cope by findings their way around the obstacle or, if that fails, by selecting a substitute goal. Others are less adaptive and may regard their inability to achieve a goal as a personal failure and experience feelings of anxiety. An example of adoptive behaviour would be the college student who would prefer to own a sports car but settles for second hand Sedan.

Rationalization. Sometimes individual redefines a frustration situation by inventing plausible reasons for being unable to attain their goals. Or they may decide that the goal really isn't worth pursuing. Rationalizations are not deliberate lies since the individual is not fully aware of the cognitive distortion that occurs as a result of the frustrating situation. For example, consumers who cannot quit smoking may convince themselves that they are smoking less if they switch of low-tar cigarettes.

Aggression. Individuals who experience frustration may resort to aggressive behaviour in attempting to protect their self-esteem: This was aptly illustrated by two British Yachtsmen who, disappointed at their poor showing in a sailing competition, burned their boat and swan ashore. Frustrated consumers have boycotted manufacturers in efforts to improve product quality and boycotted retailers in efforts to have prices lowered.

Regression. Sometimes people react to frustrating situations with childish or immature behaviour. A shopper attending a bargain sale, for example, may fight over merchandise and resort to tearing a garment that another shopper will not relinquish, rather than allow the other person to have it.

Withdrawal. Frustration is often resolved by simply withdrawing from the situation. A person who has differently achieving officer status in an organisation may simply guilt that organisation. Furthermore, he may rationalize his resignation by deciding the organisation is not true to its stated ideals and the other members are somewhat shallow. In addition, he may decide he can use time more constructively in other activities.

Autism. Autism or autistic thinking, refers to thinking that is almost completely dominated by needs and emotions, with little effort made to relate to reality. Such day dreaming, or fantasizing, enables the individual to attain imaginary gratification of unfulfilled needs. A person who is who shy and lonely, for example, may daydream about a romantic love affair.

Projection. An individual may redefine a frustrating situation by projection blame for his or her own failures and inabilities on other objects or persons. Thus, the golfer who misses a stroke may blame the caddie or her golf clubs; the driver who has an automobile accident may blame the other driver or the condition of the road.

Identification. Sometime's people resolve their feelings of frustration by sub-consciously identifying with other persons or situations they consider relevant Marketeers have long recognized the importance of this defence machanism an often use it as the basis for advertising appeals. That is why slice-of-life commercials and advertisements are so popular. Such advertisements usually portray a stereotical situation in which an individual experiences a frustration and then overcomes the problem that has caused and frustration by using the advertized product. If the viewer can identify with the frustrating situation, he or she may very likely adopt the proposed solution and by the product advertised. For example, a fellow who has difficulty in attracting dates may decide to use the same mouthwash, shampoo or clothing that "worked" far the man in the commercial interest. Interestingly enough, use of the product may increased his self-confidence sufficiently to enable him to achieve his goal.

Multiplicity of Needs. A consumer's behaviour offen fulfils 'more than one need. In fact, it is more likely that specific goals are selected because they fulfil several needs. We buy clothing for protection and for modesty; in addition our clothing fulfils an enormous range of personal and social needs. Usually, however, there is one overriding need that,initiates behaviour. For example, a man maystop smoking because he wants to rid himself of a chronic cough; he also may be concerned about cancer. In addition, his girlfriend may be "turned off" by the smell of cigarette smoke. If the cumulative amount of tension produced by each of these three reasons is sufficiently strong, he will stop smoking. However, just one of the reasons may serve as the triggering mechanism; that would be the prepotent need.

Repression. Another way that individuals avoid the tension arising from frustration is by repressing the unsatisfied need. Thus, individuals may "forget" a need; that is they force the need out of their conscious awareness. Sometimes represented needs manifest themselves indirectly. A couple who cannot have children may surround themselves with plants or pets.

Need and Goals Vary among Individuals. One cannot accurately infer motives from behaviour. People with different needs may seek fulfilment through selection of the same goals, while people with the same needs may seek fulfilment through different goals. Similarly, five people may be driven by the same need to seck fulfilment in different ways. The first may seek advancement and recognition through a professional career, the second may become active in the league of women voters, the third may join a health club, the fourth may take professional dane lession and the fifth may seek attention by monopolizing classroom discussion.

IMPORTANCE OF NEEDS AND MOTIVATION IN CONSUMER' BEHAVIOUR

Marketeers do not create needs though in some instances they may make consumers more keenly aware of unfelt needs. Successful marketeers define their markets in terms of the needs they presume to satisfy, rather than in terms or the product they sell. This is a market oriented rather than a production oriented, approach to marketing.

A marketing orientation focuse on the needs of the buyer; a production orientation focuses on the needs of the seller. The marketing concept implies that the manufacturer will make only what it knows people will buy, a production orientation implies that the manufacturer will try to sell what it decides to make.

Human needs. Consumer needs are the basis of all modern marketing. Needs are the essence of the marketing concept. The key to a company's survival, profitability and growth in a highly competitive marketing environment is its ability to identify and, satisfy unfulfilled consumer needs better and sooner than the competitor.

Motivation. Motivation can be described as the driving force within individuals which impels them to action.

Model or Motivational Process

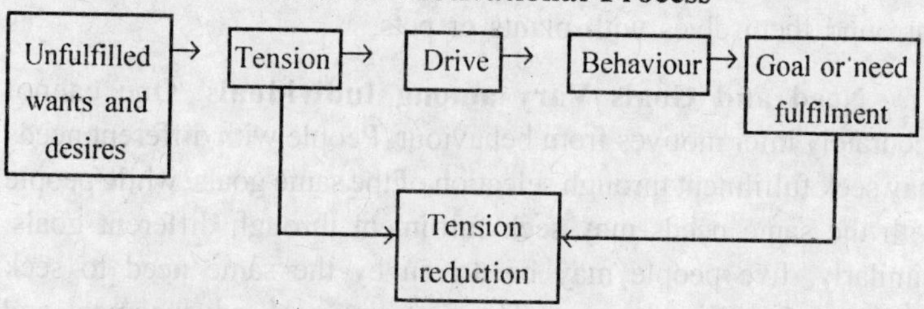

The specific course of action that consumers pursue and their specific goals are selected on the basis of their thinking process (*i.e.*, congnition) and previous learning. For that reason, marketeers who understand motivational theory attempt to influence the consumer's cognitive processes.

Needs—

—Some needs are innate, others are acquired.

—Biogenic needs are considered as, primary needs or motives.

—Acquired needs are needs that we learn in response to our culture or environment. These may include need for self-esteem for prestige, for affection, for power and for learning.

Since these needs are generally psychological/psychogenic, they are considered secondary needs or motives.

Goals—

Goals are sought after results of motivated behaviour.

—Generic goals-that is, the general classes or categories of goals that consumers select to fulfil their needs.

—Product specific goals that is, the specifically branded or labelled products they select to fulfil their needs.

Selection of Goals. depends upon individual's personal experiences, physical capacity, prevailing cultural, norms and values and goal's accessibility in the physical and social environment.

Individual's self image also influences the goal's selection.

Positive and Negative Motivation. Motivation can be positive or negative in direction.

A positive goal is one towards which behaviour is directed often referred to as an approach object.

A negative goal is one from which behaviour is directed away, and thus is sometimes referred to as an avoidance object.

Sometimes people become motivationally aroused by a threat to or elimination of a behavioural freedom (*e.g.* the freedom to make a product choice without undue influence from a retailer). This motivational state is called psychological reactance and is usually manifested' by a negative consumer response. When the Coca-Cola company changed its traditional, formula and introduced "New Coke", many people reacted negatively to the fact that their "freedom to choose" had been taken away and refused to buy the New Coke: Coca-Cola management responded to this unexpected psychological reaction by reiptroducing as "Classic Coke".

Rational *Vs.* Emotional Motives. The term rationality is used in the traditional economic sense which assumes that consumers behave rationally when they carefully consider all alternatives and choose those that give them the greatest utility.

Emotional motives imply the selection of goals according to personal or subjective criteria *e.g.* the desire for individuality, pride, lear, affection, status.

MASLOW'S THEORY OF MOTIVATION

Abraham Maslow has explained that why people are driven by particular needs at particular times? Why does one person spend considerable time and energy on personal safety and another on pursuing the esteem of others?

His answer is that human needs are arranged in a hierarchy, from the most pressing to the least pressing.

In their order of importance, there are physiological needs, society needs, social needs, esteem needs and self-actualization needs.

A person will try to satisfy the most important needs first. When a person succeeds in satisfying an important need, it will cease being a current motivator, and the person will try to satisfy the next-most important need.

Maslow's theory helps the, marketeers to understand how various products fit into the plans, goals, and lives of potential consumers.

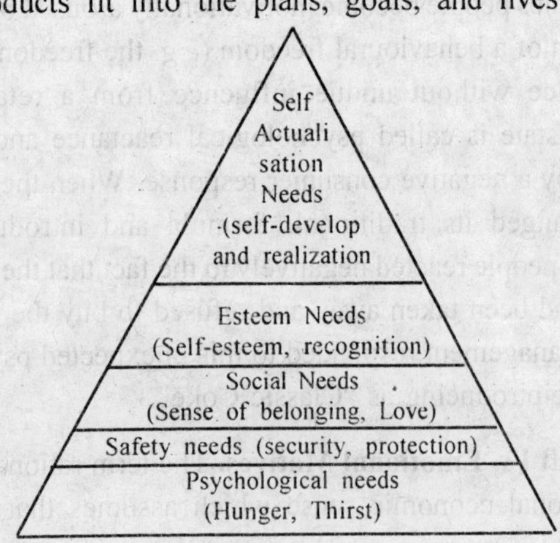

Physiological Needs. In the hierarchy-of-needs theory the first and most basic level of needs is physiological.

According to Maslow, physiological needs are dominant when they are chronically unsatisfied. "For the man who is extremely and dangerously hungry, no other interest exists but food. He dreams food, he remembers food; he thinks about food, he emotes only about food, he perceives only food and he wants only food."

Safety Needs. These needs are concerned with much more than physical safety. The include order, stability, familiarity, control over one's life and environment and certainty. Health is also a safety concern.

Social Needs includes such needs as love, affection, belonging and acceptance. Advertisers of personal care products often emphasize this appeal in their advertisements.

Egiostic Needs. These needs can take either inward or an outward orientation or both. Inwardly-directed ego needs reflect an individual's need for self acceptance, for self esteem, for success, for independence, for personal satisfaction with a job well done.

Outwardly-directed ego needs include the needs for prestige, for reputation, for status, for recognition from others.

Need for Self-Actualization. According to Maslow most people do not statisfy their ego needs sufficiently to ever move to fifth level the need for self-actualisation. In Maslow's words "what a man can be, he must be."

Evaluation of the Need Hierarchy. This is a useful tool for understanding consumer motivations and is readily adaptable to marketing strategy.

— Physiological needs—house, food, clothing.

— Safety and security needs—Insurance.

— Social needs—personal cafe products (cosmetics, mouthwash, shaving cream.)

— Ego needs—Luxury products, furs or jewels or big cars.

— Self—actualisation training:

Application of this Thory. Segmentation Application.

Positioning Application. That is deciding how the product should be perceived by prospective consumers. This application of the heed hierarchy relies on the that no need is ever fully satisfied, that it always continues to be somewhat motivating. Safety, for example, is a continuing need.

Most manufacturers of luxury cars use Status appeals (Impress your friend), companies self-actualizing appeals ("you deserve the very best") or even social appeals (the whole family can ride in luxurious comfort). To find a unique position among its luxury competitors, some automobile comfort have used safety appeal in advertisements directed to well-to-do executives ("when your wife is driving the two children home on a dark and stormy night, you can relax if she is driving the mercedes.")

Conclusion. The hieraruchy offers useful, comprehensive framework for marketeers trying to develop appropriate advertising appeals for their products. It can be adopted in two ways:

(a) it enables marketeers to foctus their advertising appeals on a need level that is likely to be shared by a large segment of the prospective audience.

(b) it facilitates product positioning or repositioning interest in buying a computer? We can guess that Ram has satisfied his physiological, safety and social needs. His computer interest might come from a strong need for more esteem from others or from a higher need for self-actualization.

HERZBERG'S THEORY OF MOTIVATION

Herzberg developed a "two factor theory" of motivation, which distinguishes dissatisfiers (factors that cause dissatisfaction) and satisfiers (factors that cause satisfaction).

This theory of motivation has two implications. First, sellers should do their best to avoid dissatisfaction such as a poor training manual or a poor service policy.

Secondly, the manufacturer should identify the major satisfiers or motivators of purchase in the computer market and supply them. These satisfiers will make the major differences as to which computer brand the customer buys.

Perception. How the motivated person actually acts is influenced by his or her perception of the situation. One might see a fast talking computer sales-person as aggressive and insincere. Another shopper might see the same as intelligent and helpful.

Why do people perceive the same situation differently? The fact is that we apprehend a stimulus object through sensations.

Motivational Research

The term motivational research, which, should logically include all types of research into human motives, has becomes a "'item of art" used to refer to qualitative research designed to uncover the consumer's sub-conscious or hinden motivations. Based on the promise that consumer are not always aware of the reasons for their actions; motivational research attempts to discover underlying feelings; attitudes and emotions concerning product, service or brand use. The table given below represents the "personalities" consumers have attributed to selected products uncovered through motivational research studies.

Table: Selected Product Prcrsonality Profiles Uncovered by Motivational Research

Banking.	An expression of feminity and motherhood; banking evokes pleasant/nostalgic memories of the oders pervading the house when one's mother was banking. To many, a woman is sub-consciously and symbolically going through the act of giving birth when banking a cake, and the

	most fertile moment occurs when the baked product is pulled out of the oven.
Ice-Cream.	Ice-Cream is associated with love and affection. It desires particular potency from childhood memories, when it was given to a child for being "good" and withheld as an instrument of punishment People refer to ite-cream as something they "love" to eat, ice-cream is a symbol of abundance; people prefer round packaging with an illustration that runs around the box panel because it suggests unlimited quantity.
Power Tools.	Power Tools are a symbol of manliness. They represent masculine skill and competence and are often bought more for their symbolic value than for active do it, yourself applications. Ownership of a good power tool or circular same provides a man with feelings of omnipotence.

Source. Adapted from\Handbook of Consumer Motivations by Ernest Dichter

Development of Motivational Research. Sigmand Freuds psychoanalytic theory of personality provided this basis for the development of motivational research. This theory was built on the premise that unconscious needs or drives-especially biological and sexual drives are at the heart of human motivation and personality. Freud constructed his theory from patients' recollections of early childhood expariences, analysis of their dreams and the specific nature of their mental and physical adjustments problems.

Early Motivational Research. Dr. Ernest Dichter, formerly a psychoanalyst in Vienna, adapted Freud's psychoanalytical techniques to the study of consumer buying habits, Up to this time, marketing research had focused on what consumer did (*i.e.* quantitative, descriptive studies) rather than on why did it. Marketeers vere quickly fascinated by the glib, entertaining and usually surprising explanations offered for consumer behaviour, especially since many of these explanations were rooted in sex. For example, marketeers were told that cigarettes and life saver commodities were bought because of their sexual symbolism, that men regarded covertible cars as surrogate mistress, that women baked cakes to fulfil their reproductive yearnings. Before long, almost every advertising agency on Madison Avenue had a psychologist on staff to conduct motivational research studies.

Limitations of Motivational Research

By the early 1960s, marketeers realised that motivational research had some drawbacks. Because of the intensive, nature of qualitative research, samples necessarily were small; thus there was concern about generalising findings to the total market. Also, marketers soon realized that analysis of projective tests and depth interviews was highly subjective. The same data given to three different analysts could produce three different reports, each offering its own explanation of the consumer behaviour examined. Critics noted that many of the projective tests that were used had originally been developed for clinical purposes, rather than for studies of marketing or consumer behaviour. Other consumer theorists had noted additional inconsistencies in applying Freudian theory of the study of marketing consumer behaviour. First, psychoanalytic theory was structured specifically for use with disturbed people, while consumer behaviourists were interested in explaining in the behaviour or "typical" consumers. Second, Freudian theory was developed in an entirely different social,context while motivational research was introduced in 1950s post war America.

Fimally, too many motivational researchers imputed exotic reasons to rather, prosaic consumer purchases. Marketeers began to question their recommendations (*e.g.* is it better to sell a man a pair of suspenders as a means of holding up his pants oras a "reaction to castration anxiety" ? Is it easier to persuade a woman to buy a garden hose to water her lawn or as a symbol of "genital competition for the female ?"). Motivational researchers often came up with sexual explanations for the most mundane activities. For example, an ad showing a hostess behind a beverage taste filled with large bottles of soft drinks was commended by a leading motivational researcher for its "clever' use of phallic symbolism."

Motivational Research Today. Despite these criticisms; motivational research is still regarded as an important tool by marketeers who want to gain deeper insights into the whys consumer behaviour than conventional marketing research techniques can yield. There is new and compelling evidence that the unconscious is the site of a far larger portion of mental life than even Freud envisioned. Research studies show that the unconscious mind many understand and respond to non-verbal symbols, form emotional responses and guide actions largely independent of conscious awareness. The new science of semiotics is concerned upto the conscious and sub-conscious meaning of non.verbal symbols to consumers. These insights are usually obtained through motivational research.

❐

7

Problems of Advertising and Consumer Choice

When bishops are asked for their views on sin they apparently reply that they are against it. Many economists would give the same reply if asked about advertising. In the field of macro-economics, the monetarists do battle with the Keynesians over the main causes and mechanisms of inflation. But in an adjoining field a no less intense conflict continues between those who see advertising as one component of the basic right of free speech and information, a means of undermining existing monopolies, and those who believe that it destroys consumer sovereignty, buttresses market power and wastes resources.

By coincidence advertising in an economy like the UK amounts to roughly 2 per cent of GNP very similar to estimates of the direct welfare losses from monopoly. An initial reaction might be, therefore, why such a great fuss over a comparatively small amount? There are two answers to this query. First, as Johnson (1970) firmly points out, any micro-economic magnitude will almost by definition, be only a small fragment of a macro-economic quantity like GNP. The second and related point is that the direct costs of a particular activity may bear very little relation to its importance and influence. The costs of maintaining and running the Houses of Parliament are a much smaller fraction of GNP but few would doubt their power to affect profoundly the lives of all citizens.

In this area, where aesthetics may get the better of the economics, giant companies have not surprisingly taken the full force of the opponents' attack. For although heavy advertising (for a variety of well known reasons) is confined to a narrow range of industries producing consumer goods, these are usually the industries where the largest companies dominate or have rapidly come to dominate. For example, the greater part of the outputs of manufactured foods, drink, tobacco, household detergents, cars and petrol is produced by members of the hundred largest companies and is also heavily advertised.

Within the framework of orthodox economics there is the defence that by advertising, the largest companies are providing information to consumers about existing and new products and this assists in the process of innovation and change. If the world is viewed as basically one of short-run monopolies, then advertising may be an important lever, making existing demand curves more elastic, as discerning consumers are tempted by rival products. On the other hand at least since Chamberline (1962) wrote in the 1930s the more widely held orthodoxy has been that advertising differentiates one firm's products from those of close rivals and therefore has both the purpose and effect of making individual demand curves less elastic. In addition, in oligopolistic industries with differentiated products, advertising while making for intense rivalry amongst existing firms, actually hinders the entry of new competitors, deterred by the formidable costs of establishing a viable market share.

There is a much more heretical view which gives advertising a more dramatic role in modern society. This view, recently associated with the name of Professor Galbraith, sees advertising as the main device by which the large companies control consumer demand so that it meshes in completely with their own production plans. The controllers of the companies can thus achieve their over-riding objective of stable growth. Underlying this vision of modern industry is the notion that the demands themselves are created by the combined efforts of the manufacturer and his advertising agent. Since most consumers expenditure in wealthy economies does not go to meet some primal need such as for food and shelter then, it is argued, the vast majority is spent on fulfilling artificial, frivolous and unnecessary wants. The implications of this view are far reaching and needless to say have not gone unchallenged. We examine the claims and counter claims in section three.

Advertising and Competition

We can consider two main issues in the controversy over advertising and competition. First does advertising in oligopoly generate barriers to new entry sufficient to allow a joint monopoly return to existing firms applying a minimum of respect for their mutual interests? Secondly, does competition through advertising lead in oligopoly to a wasteful use of resources? We examine these issues in turn looking first at the a priori arguments and then the empirical evidence.

Some of the main conclusions of Chamberlin's Theory of Monopolistic Competition (1962) have not retained that position of central importance with which they were initially greeted. The famous 'excess capacity' theorem is now treated either as a rather special (and not particularly important) case or shown merely as an intermediate stage on the road to a more stable equilibrium (see for example Dewey, 1969). But an important effect of the book has been to focus attention on selling costs in general and advertising in particular as a crucial aspect of competition and one which may have important implications for public policy. Perhaps ironically, in view of the interest originally provoked by Chamberlin's 'large group' case (where a large number of producers selling differentiated but close substitute products were in competition) the main controversy today essentially concerns the 'small group' case of a few large firms competing mainly through advertising. A landmark in this phase of the discussion was the publication in 1956 of Bain's work on barriers to new competition. His empirical findings still form the basis for one side of the conventional wisdom on advertising and competition, and both in the US and UK have been quoted at one time or another by official agencies to back up their reports on individual industries.

Bain defined the condition of entry as the advantages of established sellers in an industry over potential entrant sellers, these advantages being reflected in the extent to which established sellers can persistently raise their prices above a competitive level without attracting new firms to enter the industry (Bain, 1956). He thus viewed entry conditions as a structural characteristic and in theory they could vary over a whole range of values. At one extreme entry conditions may be so easy that existing firms would have no scope. for maintaining prices above competitive levels. At the other extreme their advantages may be so great that, so long as they can (tacitly) agree on a joint profit-maximising strategy, then prices can be maintained at the equivalent of the monopoly level. The entry barriers would effectively prevent the emergence of new competition. Between these two extremes there might be a great number of different levels of impediment to potential entrants. Bain identified product differentiation advantages that existing firms might have, as one of the main factors governing the condition of entry. In his initial conception these were viewed quite widely and included superior product designs protected by patents, favourable distributive outlets as well as accumulative preferences of buyers for established brand names and company reputations (Bain, 1956). Although he concludes from his empirical work that in consumer-goods industries advertising was the most important source of product differentiation advantages, he was careful to maintain in his final assessment that 'product differentiation' was a complex concept and indeed that it may be that:

> Advertising per se is not necessarily the main or most important key to the product differentiation problem as it affects intra-industry competition and the condition of entry. Although instances are found in which it is, we many need in general to look past advertising. to other things to get to the heart of the problem. (Bain, 1956)

Later writers have been much less cautious in their approach and in their anxiety to pin down the effect of advertising have allowed these other characteristics of product differentiation to be elided altogether from their analysis. In this way Bain's finding (1956) that product differentiation is the most important barrier to entry, has almost casually been converted into the much narrower view that advertising may be the most important barrier. This view has recently been justified by Mann (1974) on grounds of manageability and econometric convenience. A sceptical bystander may feel that the last reason is rather similar to that given by the drunken man searching for his door key under a street lamp. He explains with the impeccable logic of the intoxicated that he dropped the key over the other side of the road in the dark but was looking over this side where there was more light.

Since Bain wrote, suggesting rather tentatively that there may be a direct correlation between entry conditions, other structural characteristics (such as the level of concentration) and the performance of industry as reflected in the persistent mark-up of price over long-run average costs (measured by the rate of return on capital or sales) a fairly continuous stream of articles have filled the academic journals attempting to measure the relationship. It would be satisfying to record at this point that empirical studies have reached a number of reasonably firm conclusions that command general support. Unfortunately on this subject perhaps more than others, the positive methodology so enthusiastically embraced by many applied economists since the mid 1950s has served merely to accentuate differences. rather than settle them, as we shall see below.

Part of the explanation for differing hypotheses and empirical results may be a certain lack of clarity over what constitutes a barrier to entry, especially in the case of advertising. In an important monograph on advertising and competition Comanor and Wilson (1974) quote the Bain definition which we have already given above and then add that this is consistent with a rather different definition given by Stigler:..a barrier to entry may be defined as a cost of producing ... which must be borne by a firm which seeks to enter an industry but is not borne by firms already in the industry (Stigler, 1968). This emphasis on the differential advantages of existing firms over new entrants and not merely on the costs of entry which may have been required of established firms in the part, is emphasised by Comanor and Wilson. They argue, for example, that as existing firms were 'first in the field' they have advantages that cannot be neutralised by entrants investing an amount comparable to the present value of existing firms' past advertising outlays. Entran s will have to spend more. When existing firms were creating the market for their product they will have met little resistance and may have been able to proceed at a more lei surely pace than new entrants can now allow themselves for the latter are confronted by the established brand preferences of consumers. To capture a viable market share the entrant has, on this view, to spend proportionately more than existing firms to win customers away from established brands. By coming late to the field the entrant must 'shout louder' to make his voice heard above the insistent clamour of the existing brands. But the Comanor and Wilson view probably overstates the case of advertising and entry barriers. They allow existing firms a comparatively easy passage into their position of dominance on the ground that they were 'creating the market' and were the first in the field, while entrant firms run into the opposition of existing brands. This complete antithesis between existing firms and entrants is underlined: 'When existing firms entered the market, their entry was probably associated with an innovation of some sort or with a period of rapid growth of demand... Prospective entrants in the present, unaccompanied by innovation, faced different contingencies' (Comanor and Wilson, 1974). This seems to be a much too simplified view of the competitive process especially in that comparatively narrow range of consumer goods industries on which Comanor and Wilson concentrate. In these industries product innovation (supported by heavy promotional outlays), although not of the world-shaking kind, is the very essence of competition and is a frequent occurrence. New products are just as likely to run into consumer resistance whether they come from an entrant or not. The cycle of new products partially superceding existing products and so on is a more or less continuous process and not one which has been laid down for all time a decade or so beforehand.

The Comanor and Wilson suggestion that existing firms also tend to have an advantage since they were the first to make a new product acceptable to consumers can also be stood on its head. Once a certain type of new product, say soapless detergent or wrapped bread is accepted it seems just as convincing to argue that entrants would have less difficulty overcoming consumer scepticism and ignorance that greeted the initial promotional efforts of the innovators. Once the produce is familiar, therefore, entrant firms may actually reap part of the benefit that, 'by rights', belong to the innovator. A priori, therefore, there seems little ground for the view that advertising creates a differential advantage for existing firms.

Comanor and Wilson (as well, incidentally, as most other researchers outside of Chicago) add a further strand to their argument. Economies of scale in advertising, in the form of both reduced prices charged by the media for larger volumes of repeat messages and also of the greater effectiveness of messages beyond a certain volume per unit of time, may further increase entry barriers. But this extension of the idea beyond that of differentially higher costs of new firms clearly does not square with Stigler's definition. In fact he explicity rules out scale economies as forming a useful part of the definition of entry barriers. Certainly the substantive issues raised by them, especially policy issues, seem more clearly defined if scale economies are treated simply as a possible determinant of firm size rather than an impediment to new competition. Indeed this argument has often been used to support the view that advertising and concentration will be positively correlated. If economies of scale in advertising (and related selling costs) are substantial then this would lead, over time, to the survival of only a few giants. Without denying, therefore, that the past advertising expenditures of existing firms may continue to have an important effect after they were incurred and that there may be important economies of scale in advertising we can remain sceptical of the hypothesis that treats advertising per se as an important barrier to the entry of new competition. Our scepticism is based on two points, *(a)* advertising is only one part (and possibly an insignificant part) of the much wider concept of product differentiation, as discussed by Bain, and *(b)* there is little ground for believing that advertising by a firm 'first in the field' with a particular product gains a differential cost advantage over potential rivals (see also Schemalensee, 1974).

Unfortunately for many of those researchers who have worked with great diligence and ingenuity to test the relationship between advertising and concentration the results have so far been singularly anaemic. At best, the observed relationship has been weak and at worst non-existent, with the issue clouded inevitably by the interaction of many other factors. Telser's scepticism of the validity of the hypothesis was apparently matched by his results (Telser, 1964). But others have complained that his measurement of the variables may have been too gross (industries too widely defined, for example) and caused the negative results. Their own more refined measurement, they claimed, produced a definite and positive relationship (Mann et al., 1967). Subsequent empirical work (surveyed by Comanor and Wilson, 1979) has unfortunately done little to settle the controvers'y.

Instead the emphasis has tended to shift back to the more fundamental problem first tackled by Bain: the relationship between profitability and advertising. If intensive advertising makes an important contribution to high entry barriers then this will be reflected in persistently high profits with possibly important implications for resource allocation. As we have raised doubts about the likelihood of advertising giving existing firms a differential cost advantage we are sceptical about this interpretation of any links between advertising intensity and profits. Comanor and Wilson, amongst others, argue extensively of a positive relationship and their empirical analysis supports this view. They summarise their main finding as follows: Industries characterised by heavy advertising earn profit rates that are typically between 3 and 4 percentage points higher than those in other industries. This differential represents up to a 50 per cent increase in rates of return. They argue further that as long-run average costs in the manufacturing sector are probably constant over the relevant range of output for the market leaders, then their results imply that prices in industries selling heavily advertised products, exceed marginal costs. Furthermore their later results were robust enough to stand up to an energetic critique mounted by Brozen that in their original article profit rates were overestimated since no account was taken of the capital value of past advertising outlays. Most students of advertising are agreed that it has similar characteristics to capital investment. In effect it earns a return for a number of years after the expense is incurred. Hence it should be treated like any other capital asset and depreciated over a number of years not simply treated as a current expense as it is for accounting purposes. Rates of return on capital, therefore, that do not include the capital value of advertising assets in the denominator will, on this argument, be biased upwards. Profitability comparisons between industries where advertising is heavy and those where it is not, will favour the former. But this is simply a result of the bias and not of barriers to entry.

In the event, when Comanor and Wilson adjusted the measurement of profits to take account of this point their results were little changed: profitability was positively related to advertising intensity. Similar results were obtained by Weiss, although he was somewhat more circumspect in his interpretation: 'It is possible that the net relationship between advertising and profit rates would fall to non-significance if ads could be depreciated over more reliable lives' (Weiss, 1969). The issue is therefore left unsettled because if there are grounds for disagreement about how fixed assets should be depreciated, a fortiori there will be disagreement about the true rate of decay of advertising assets.

Recently a more subtle point on the interpretation of any positive relationship between advertising and profitability has been made. One response to the result that profits are correlated with heavy advertising might be to ask whether the firms concerned could increase their profits simply by increasing their advertising? If that were true we may wonder why advertising formed such a small part of GNP. Comanor and Wilson attempt to dispel any such idea with the following explanation:

> Advertising in this analysis acts as a proxy for product differentiation, or, more specifically, for the product and market characteristics that permit heavy advertising expenditures to differentiate effectively the products of a firm from those of its rivals. Although these product and market characteristics are not easily measured, they are typically characterised by heavy advertising expenditures. (Comanor and Wilson, 1974).

Those who feel that this comes uncomfortably close to circular reasoning\are in good company: Comanor and Wilson (1979) have themselves conceded the point. All that we really know, therefore, from such research is that certain product and market characteristics determine both advertising and profitability but we do not know what they are.

The alternative hypothesis on the basic issue is that advertising is a means of entry into imperfect markets for new competitors and that in its absence prices would be even higher. Far from being a barrier to entry, therefore, advertising is seen as a key to entry. An interesting study which supports this view is one by Benham (1972). He compared the price of spectacles in states in America that allowed advertising of the product with those that had banned it. He found that prices in the states without advertising were about twice as high as in the others, where advertising was permitted. The wider market developed by advertising allowed larger sales volumes, smaller margins, and lower prices. Compared with the cross section analysis of forty-one industries by Comanor and Wilson this study refers to only one industry and perhaps for that reason may be considered of rather limited applicability. More studies of this kind would clearly be highly desirable, but there must be very few products which allow such clear-cut (almost laboratory-like) divisions between advertised and non-advertised regions.

Some writers have suggested that there may be significant differences between manufacturer and retailer advertising. The information content in the latter (as in the case study of spectacles) may be much higher than in the former (the Comanor and Wilson sample) and, therefore, genuinely reflect pro-competitive forces. Others have suggested that within consumer goods there may be different categories which are affected in distinct ways by advertising. The demand for 'convenience' goods of low unit price and purchased at the most accessible outlets without much thought for price and quality comparisons may be much more amenable to advertising than 'shopping' goods which are highly priced and where the gains from price and quality comparisons easily outweigh the costs of searching.

In view of these complexities a certain degree of agnosticism is indicated. As a recent reviewer of the literature put it:

> The differences between the two schools of thought are not as irreconcilable as they might at first appear. There is no contradiction in believing both that advertising is crucial in facilitating firms' entry into new markets and that these entry costs might be steep enough to discourage entry. It is not inconsistent to hold that indivisibilities associated with advertising on nation-wide television create market power in certain industries, but that a government policy to severely curtail advertising in these industries would cause prices to become even higher. (Butters, 1976)

Agnosticism, however, has not found favour amongst most observers of this emotive subject. Advertising is heaviest in oligopolistic, consumer goods industries because it can be used as a major competitive instrument in place of price changes. As is well known from the theory of oligopoly, overt price competition can be extremely damaging for the firms concerned and therefore may only be used in exceptional circumstances. It is therefore argued that advertising, with its less clear-cut and predictable result can be used extensively by rival firms in their struggle for an increased market share without undermining the price structure. In these industries indirect methods. of price co-ordination may be relatively easy to maintain because firms know the dangers if they are upset. It may be much more difficult to reach agreement on limiting and restraining advertising expenditures, for the same kind of reason that makes it almost impossible for the super powers to agree on nuclear-arms control. A price cut can be matched quickly, precisely and with certainty. An increase in advertising may have a much less determinate outcome. Some campaigns, for no apparent reason capture much more public attention than others, equally expensive. Monitoring the outcome of a particular advertising campaign is also much less precise than that of an (unmatched) price change. On this view there is an ever present temptation, therefore, to spend just that much more to ensure a major rival does not gain an advantage.

For these reasons it is often claimed that advertising in consumer goods industries is 'excessive' and leads to waste. Thus Scherer is led from the hypothesis that the competing advertising claims by firms in oligopoly may cancel each other out and lead to a waste of resources to the unwarranted conclusion that the prime offenders include 'soap, proprietary drug, cosmetic and toilet goods, cigarette, cereal, beverage and automobile industries', (Scherer, 1980). The clear inference that we are invited to make is that most of the reasources used in these industries' advertising campaigns are wasted. Presumably the reason for listing these industries is that their advertising sales ratios are high. The list would be similar for the UK or any other 'advanced' economy. There is still a good deal of controversy over whether, even in principle, the volume of advertising may be excessive (see, for example the exchanges provoked by Dixit and Norman (1978). It is extremely hazardous, therefore, to attempt to measure the extent to which reasources devoted to advertising lead to a social loss.

Nevertheless, Comanor and Wilson carry the Scherer view several stages further by estimating the social costs (welfare loss) of 'excessive' advertising. They suggest that advertising is excessive in some industries first because of the extreme skewness of its inter-industries incidence and secondly because of the correlation between profit rates and advertising-sales ratios. As we have already observed, all that these points suggest is that there are some product and market characteristics, as yet not fully understood, that determine both advertising and profits., It is not a justification for concluding that advertising leads to social waste. Comanor and Wilson's estimates of the social costs of 'excess' advertising amounted to about 1.5 per cent of the value added in consumer-goods manufacturing which puts them roughly at 0.6 per cent of GNP. To this they add an estimate of a similar size attributable to the maintenance of sub-optimal capacity that advertising allows. They conclude that advertising accounts directly and indirectly fora large proportion of the total costs of market power in consumer goods industries and that these costs are especially concentrated in a small group of industries.

We have indicated above that we are less than happy with the logical foundations on which these conclusions rest. That unease is compounded when we read in a more recent study which attempts to measure the social costs of monopoly power that all of advertising is added to the welfare loss. This takes the extreme view of advertising as merely an instrument for security market power (Cowling and Mueller, 1978). Comanor and Wilson at least restricted their estimates to those industries which had, in their judgment, high advertising-sales ratios. Not surprisingly the estimates of the social costs ot monopoly in this later study are much larger than in most previous efforts.

Before turning to the subject of advertising and consumer choice it is perhaps appropriate to mention briefly policy towards advertising, although policy matters are dealt with more fully in part three of the book. Recent experience in the UK of restrictions on the use of cigarette advertising illustrates the general point that unless policies are well thought out they may have the opposite effect from that intended. The decision to end cigarette advertising on the commercial television channel was made on health grounds. But the restriction was the signal for the tobacco companies to redouble their efforts elsewhere. Resources formerly used in television advertisements were channelled into sponsorship of a wide range of regular sporting events. The first irony was, therefore, the unholy alliance of an apparently lethal product with activities designed to promote bodily health. The sècond irony had a special British flavour. The BBC which of course carries no direct advertisements prides itself on the breadth and excellence of its sports coverage. No sooner, therefore, do tobacco companies sponsor a new event, in show-jumping, snooker, cricket, tennis or rugby league (with the accompanying brand name, image, rand advertising hoarding in the arena itself) than the BBC arrives to give it comprehensive coverage. Not only is the association between sport and smoking maintained but it is promulgated on a television channel which has to deny, because of its Charter, direct access to other advertisers. Truly a masterstroke for the advertising agent and a perfect example of a policy misfiring.

It might be argued that in a private enterprise economy if there is widespread dissatisfaction with the information provided by advertisements and frequent complaints that consumers are led into purchases that they subsequently regret, an industry would spring up providing, for. a fee, unprejudiced information based on scientific tests of advertised products. If the extent of the dissatisfaction was genuinely great then, on this argument, firms in this 'information' industry would make handsome returns, producers of inferior brands would have to mend their ways or see their market share dwindle and consumers would no longer be deceived. It is true that organisations of this kind do exist both in the UK and the USA but they are usually non-profit-making bodies and hitherto have had rather limited appeal. Certainly subscribers to Which? the magazine of the Consumers Association in the UK are miniscule compared with the number of regular customers for advertised products.

Unfortunately we cannot conclude from this that the lack of response on the part of information-providing firms or information-seeking consumers necessarily signifies general satisfaction with the current state of advertising. The reason lies in the 'public good' attributes of the kind of information that such agencies or firms can provide. If the Consumers Association offers the results of its tests to one subscriber that, for example, on a number of relevant criteria Brand X is the 'best buy' then the use of this information by the subscriber in no way diminishes its value to the subscriber's friends, neighbours, casual acquaintances and so on. Indeed if the subscriber regards himself as in the vanguard of protecting consumers interests, he may well feel it is his duty to give the information to as many people as possible. In contrast there is a flourishing trade in market research carried out by specialist agencies and commissioned by producers. To know what consumers expect from a breakfast cereal, deodorant, or toilet soap will be useful to the manufacturer when planning his packaging and marketing strategy. Clearly he has a strong incentive to keep this information to himself otherwise any competitive advantage may be lost.

Thus the non-exclusive nature of unbiased information on consumer products means that there will be too little investment in its provision. For this reason policy discussions of advertising usually include proposals for government funded agencies to undertake the necessary testing and publicity to make up for the shortfall in private investment (*e.g.*, Mann et al., 1967; Scherer, 1980). They are often accompanied by other suggestions for direct or indirect measures that will curb the volume of advertising.

Advertising and Consumer Choice

The disagreements that we have so far reviewed in this chapter have, by and large, been within the mainstream of neoclassical theory. Central to the dispute has been the role of product differentiation and especially advertising in the competitive process. The power that advertising may confer was seen either as a means of barring the entry of new competition or alternatively as a key to effective entry. We have so far heard little about the consumers themselves, except that they may desire access to more unbiased information.

The consumer plays a much more important role in what is claimed to be a more profound attack on advertising mounted over a number of years and through successive volumes by Galbraith. The main thrust of his attack is on the notion of consumer sovereignty in modern, wealthy societies. According to the conventional view, in market economies resources are allocated to their most important uses in order to meet the most urgent needs in response to consumer demand. Changes in testes will be reflected in upward pressure on prices, lower stocks and lengthening waiting lists for those products favoured by an increase in demand while the reverse will occur for those products now relatively unpopular. As a result more resources will be devoted to the production of the first group of goods and less to the second group. As the whole of economic activity is devoted to the satisfaction of consumers' wants, the greater the bundle of goods and services consumers can buy the higher will be their utility or welfare, ceteris paribus.

According to Galbraith the logic of this argument fails once it is recognised that the wants themselves are being created by the same process by which they are satisfied. For many products in wealthy economies demand no longer arises spontaneously in the breast of the consumer but is implanted there by the wiles of the advertising industry. Like Iago sowing the seeds of discord in the noble soul of Othello, so the road-side hoarding; the television commercial and the full-colour newspaper spread creates dissatisfaction with his current possessions in the pliable mind of the consumer. In this way he becomes the servant of the producer instead of the other way round, as the conventional wisdom has it. Now, argues Galbraith, if consumer demand is really the creation of the producer in order that his production, growth and profit plans may be fulfilled, it is a short step to recognise that we can no longer assume that the more of these kinds of goods the consumer has, the higher his level of satisfaction. The goods in question are those heavily advertised which we have discussed above.

This apparent reversal of the roles of production and consumption by which 'wants depend on the process by which they are satisfied' Galbraith called, in his early work, the 'Dependence Effect'. It is integrated into the main argument in his last book in this area which contains the important statement:

> Production is great not necessarily where there is great need; it may be where there is great capacity for managing the behaviour of the individual consumer or for sharing symbiotically in the control of the procurement of public goods and services, all in the interest of bureaucratic growth. This is in sharp contrast with the neo-classical view of power which holds that power restricts output in the manner of the classical monopoly. But a moment's thought directed to the areas of abundance in the economy-automobiles, weapons, soaps, deodorants and detergents will suggest that the present analysis is not in conflict with common observation and common sense. (Galbraith, 1975)

This passage has been quoted because it helps us to see the implications of Galbraith's argument. Prices are no longer any guide to what needs to be produced and hence in the allocation of resources.

As prices can no longer be relied upon even as rough benchmarks against which 'needs' are to be gauged some other mechanism will have to be substituted. Since we cannot rely on benign providence we shall, presumably, have to depend on committees of wise men who will be able to decide for everyone what 'need' in an 'exclusive or dominant sense' is. What a heavy responsibility for the wise men but what a comfort for the consumer to be relieved of the onerous task of choosing between different brands in their multi-coloured packets. For the wise men will surely eliminate much waste and make certain that everyone has access to the uniform and standard products.

If Galbraith's view is taken seriously the logical outcome would seem very close to this caricature. But very few producers would recognise themselves amongst those supermen portrayed by Galbraith. Similarly very few consumers whether they frequent senior common rooms or the local discotheque (or perhaps both) would recognize the demeaning portrait painted of them. Although many producers may at times wish they had such powers to control demand for their products, few if any come within hailing distance of such mastery. To take one of the very few industries that Galbraith mentions to illustrate his argument, motor cars, both in the United States and Europe (and particularly Britain) the well-established and firmly entrenched enterprises which over the years have spent millions of pounds advertising their brand names and made them household words have recently been groaning under the burden of intense competition from Japanese models. In the space of very few years names which were formerly unknown have captured more, than a tenth of the British market. To argue that this merely demonstrates the powers of advertising, since the Japanese campaign was launched with heavy promotional expenditures, misses the point at issue. It is not logical to argue simultaneously that firms are in control of the demand for their products which they themselves have created yet at the same time to hold that they are at the mercy of any determined competitor using methods similar to their own. Nor is it sufficient to suggest that it is not the position of the individual firms which is in question but that of all firms in the industry for in many cases what constitutes an 'industry' is very difficult to define. Over time changes in demand, technology, or income levels decimates the size of some industries and multiplies that of others. At one period products that are regarded as close substitutes and hence (conceptually) belonging to the same industry may at a later period be regarded as more distant substitutes.

> The joint but unco-ordinated efforts of the producers merely creates one element of the environment by which wants of the consumer are shaped. It is because each individual producer thinks that the consumers can be persuaded to like his products that he endeavours to influence them. But though this effort is part of the influence which shapes consumers' tastes, no producer can in any real sense 'determine' them. (Hayek, 1979)

There is, however, a much more fundamental criticism of the Galbraith position. The essence of the argument, after all, rested on the notion that most consumers' expenditures in wealthy economies are spent on satisfying wants that are far from 'basic'. Soapless detergent, perfume, electric toothbrushes and so on would do little to help Robinson Crusoe keep body and soul together. Since most expenditures are on products that do not have this life and death urgency then psychologically grounded desires take over. Hence, says Galbraith, the vulnerability of the consumer to the allurements of the advertising man.

If psychologically grounded desires take over as soon as basic needs for food and shelter are met the scope for the advertising industry is great indeed. If further, the goods and services that go to meet these 'desires' may all be regarded as illegitimate or at least as not improving man's utility, then the greater proportion of GNP of many societies for many decades if not for several centuries must fall into this category. A moment's reflection, however, suggests that the Dependence Effect rests on a very shaky foundation.

> The innate wants are probably confined to food, shelter and sex. All the rest we learn to desire because we see

> others enjoying various things. To say a desire is not important because it is not innate is to say that the whole cultural achievement of man is not important. (Hayek, 1979).

All of the great works of art in architecture, literature, music and painting fail the Galbraithian test of meeting a real or genuine 'need' and therefore man is no better off with them than without them. His welfare would be improved if the reasources devoted to the creation of works of art were made to serve some more 'useful' purpose.

The argument has only to be stated to demonstrate its absurdity and yet it is logically the same as that which Galbraith invites us to accept in the case of other, humbler artefacts. In most societies most of the time the demand for the great majority of products is culturally determined rather than derived from an innate need. We leave the last word to Hayek:

> Professor Galbraith's attempt to give an apparent scientific proof for the contention that the need for the production of more commodities has greatly decreased seems to me to have broken down completely. With it goes the claim to have produced a valid argument which justifies the use of coercion to make people employ their income for those purposes of which he approves. (Hayek, 1977)

We ended the previous section by noting that there may be a case for non-profit making agencies to increase the supply of unbiased information because of its 'public good' characteristics. Similarly we conclude this section with a brief comment on the view that some forms of private consumption should be encouraged by public subsidy. In view of the general tenor of the last few pages which has favoured the notion that the consumer still knows his own mind best despite the efforts of advertisers it may come as a surprise to read general support for public expenditure of this kind.

Perhaps the most eloquent advocate has been Tibor Scitovsky who has for some time warned of the dangers of taking a too uncritical view of the sanctity of consumers choice as expressed in the market. He recognises the enormous benefits that have been brought by economies of scale but he also points to an important drawback. The widespread application of mass production techniques while lowering unit costs also raise wages and this makes it costly and possibly uneconomic to produce on a small scale and cater for specialised, minority tastes. As a consequence, they may have become comparatively neglected and unless given special treatment may die out altogether. Scitovsky argues that this may have undesirable consequences for the development of the preferences of the majority. As we have already said most tastes in advanced economies are learnt rather than innate. If the market economy is catering to a wide variety of tastes, consumers have the opportunity of learning from those with highly developed or informed tastes. Consumers who now have such tastes were once not in that happy position and thus have the considerable advantage of experiencing both states:

> I cannot claim that an informed person's tastes are better by any test, than an uninformed person's, or that they are more conducive to happiness or more appropriate to the atomic age; but I can claim that they are based on knowledge of a wider range of alternatives, which includes the alternatives, available to the uninformed person. (Scitovsky, 1964)

But in the wake of important economies of scale in mass production, the market alone may fail to cater for specialist, minority tastes with the eventual consequence that majority tastes may be based on a progressively narrower range of alternatives simply because the example and knowledge of other preferences-poetry over pushpin, mountaineering over sunbathing, baroque over rock music, or whatever are almost totally lacking. In order, therefore, that 'specialist' tastes may compete on an almost equal footing with 'general' tastes and perform this important educational function some public support for these artistic and sporting activities can be justified. Scitovsky underlines this point by observing that such activities only yield up their full 'pleasures' after perhaps a long period of relative 'pain'. Most artistic and sporting pursuits involve this reversal of the usual sensations in consumption (immediate pleasure or satisfaction) and therefore many potential consumers for the lack of information, practice, or expert example, may 'under-consume' on a whole range of activities. The case for subsidy may thus be further strengthened. Other commentators who have ventured to write on 'Economics and the Arts' have frankly admitted that the question of subsidy is not one which can be answered by reference to scientific economics, but is one of basic political philosophy. Peacock tries to fit the arguments in favour of subsidy into a 'public goods' or 'externalities' framework but is not very happy with the results (Peacock, 1976). The case for subsidy is recognised in varying degrees by the governments of most wealthy economies (although as Scitovsky points out there is little correlation between wealth and public expenditure on the arts) and ironically by many of the largest companies who are increasingly using their shareholders money to underwrite Shakespeare, art exhibitions, and concerts. To some extent, therefore, they are helping to offset the adverse effects that scale economies in mass production may have on the formation of public taste.

Conclusion

Advertising has always had an uneasy place in neo-classical economics which much of the time assumes perfect knowledge of the opportunities available to consumers. On the other hand, the main rationale of advertising is usually claimed to be precisely to fill gaps in consumer knowledge by bringing to their attention the goods and services on offer. As a result there is bound to be some ambiguity and conflict about the proper role of advertising, especially if it is conceded that consumers may derive genuine utility from product variety which will entail branding and other product differentiation activities.

In recent years the older controversies about the possibility of separating the persuasive from the informative content of advertising and precisely where production costs cease and selling costs begin, have largely given way to a discussion of the nature and importance of product differentiation (particularly by advertising) in creating barriers to the entry of new competition. Given that effective entry barriers allow existing firms to maintain prices in excess of long-run average costs, then to the extent that product differentiation contributes to such barriers, it impairs the competitive process and requires some policy response. In this chapter we noted that for this argument to hold, advertising and related activities had to give some differential advantage to the established firms over potential entrants, otherwise the latter could simply match the (past and present) expenditures of the former and win a viable market share. On a priori grounds a differential advantage from advertising seems difficult to sustain and the empirical evidence is mixed. If we unravel the statistical problems that have frequently led to claims and counter-claims about the efficiency or iniquity of advertising, there is some evidence that certain product and market characteristics lead to both high advertising and high profits but as yet we do not really know what they are or in what direction the causation flows. On the other side there is some case-study material that suggests that advertising may tend to keep prices lower than they might otherwise be. More investigations of this kind are really needed before we can be confident about their general applicability.

We are inclined to reject entirely the Galbraithian thesis that in affluent societies wants are created by the process by which they are satisfied and that therefore 'it can no longer be assumed that welfare is greater at an all round higher level of production than at a lower one'. Most wants in all societies except those in the most piteous poverty are learned rather than innate but this makes them no less urgent or desirable. On the contrary, some of those acts of consumption which by common consent involve participation in the greatest achievements of man-the arts-depend so much on learning, practice, and example that they require direct intervention in the market with subsidies.

❐

8

Consumer Perception and Information Processing

Whatever message we communicate through advertisement, the first thing is that it must enter the mind of the receiver so that he may be persued to buy the product. Until and unless the message is entered in the mind of the receiver, he cannot be in a position to gain the knowledge about product or create or change an attitude or image about product or producer. This part of communication process is referred to as perception. There are two prerequisites for a successful advertising message first, an individual must be exposed to it and pay some attention to it. Second he must interpret it in the way in which advertiser intends it to be interpreted. Perception, therefore is the process by which an individual maintains contact with his environment. An individual receives stimuli through various senses and interprets them, is known as pereption. Thus, it has two stage attention and interpretation. There are two important factors that influence the perception stimulus and individual factors. Perception is always referred to selectiveness. Only selective stimuli are perceived.

Perceptual skills are learned through experience and therefore, advertiser must pay some attention to learning process. As soon as is percieved the perceiver wants to learn about the product characteristics. If he is satisfied, and gains some advantages of using the product over the competitors product which he was using earlier, he may purchase the product. Thus a relationship between stimulus and response is learning. The success of learning process may be imagined from *(i)* receptivity of learner's mind and *(ii)* the environment of learning. As learning is quite slow in the beginning, repetition of pessage is necessary. It helps in changing attitude in favour of the product.

If, after learning, the attitude of the public is changed, it is good for the profitability and stability of company. The acceptance or rejection of a new product as in other words, the image of the product further diffuse the information about the characteristics a among other people. This is called diffuion of information. There are too many theories of diffusion.

This chapter dealer with this three aspects of communication-Perception learning and diffusion.

Perception Process

A perception starts as soon as the message is released for on ward transmission to the destination. Before a message can transfer knowledge, create or change an image. create or change an attitude or precipitate behaviour, it must enter the mind of the receiver. This part of communication process is referred to as perception and is itself a process made up of elements, flows and forces that enhance or inhibit messages to which an individual is exposed.

Perception has been defined as "the process by which an individual maintains contact with his environment." In other words it is "the process whreby an individual receives stimuli through the various senses and interprets them," Stimuli here can refer to sets of advertisements to a single advertisement or to a portion of an advertisement.

There are two important prerequisites for a successful advertising message. First ao individual must be exposed to it and pay some attention to it. Second, he or she must interpret it in the way, the advertiser intended it to be interpreted. Each represents, in some sense a perceptual barrier through which many advertisewents fail to pass. Some advertisements fail to stimulate sense organs in the recipient to a minimum threshold level of interest and awareness. There are some other advertisements the meaning of which are distorted by the recipient in such a way that the effect of the advertisement is quite different what the advertiser intended. Both these elements-attention by the receivers and the desired effect are necessary to make the message or advertisement successful. Thus the perception process as conceptualised in figure 1 includes two stages attention and interpretation. The perception process is influenced by such stimulus characteristics as its size intensity message, etc. and by the variables reflecting the differences accross people, such as their needs, attitudes values and interests.

The Perception Process

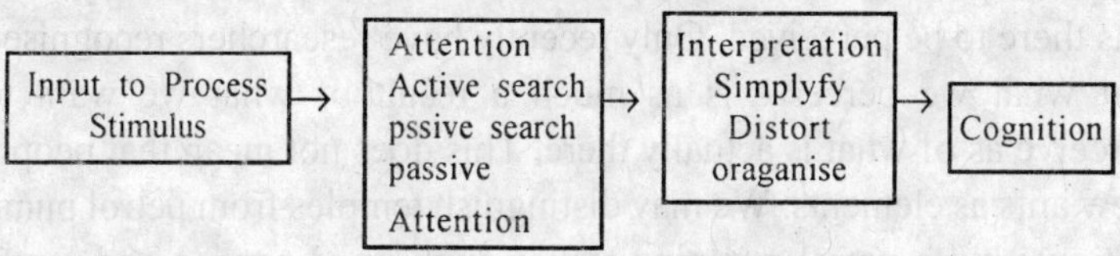

Fig. 1

The first stage in the perception process is the attention filter. An individual overtly or accidentally avoids exposure to stimuli. The receiver reads only certain publications, see only selected television programmes and listens to radio programmes which he or she thinks to be interesting or which affect his or her needs, attitudes, values and interests. Furthermore, most stimuli (advertisements) to which a person is exposed, are screened out or remain unseen, un listened or unread because he or she considers them uninteresting and irrelevant. Thus only a small fraction of all advertisements are exposed to a given person. Also only a portion of those advertisements to which an individual is exposed will get through the attention filter.

The second stage in the perception process is the interpretation process. An individual organised the stimulus contents into his or her own models of reality, models that may be very different from those of other individuals or of the sender. In doing so, the person often simplifies, distorts, organises and even creates stimuli. The output of this process is a cognitive awareness and interpretation of the stimulus a cognition.

Individual beaviour resulting from motivation is affected by how we perceive the stimuli. Perception has the meaning that each person attributes in incoming stimuli received through the five senses.

To Perceive is	To see To hear To touch To taste To smell	Some	Thing Event Idea

Psychologists previously assumed that perception was an objective phenomenon, that is, an individual can perceive only what was there to be perceived. Only recently have researchers recognised that what we perceive is as much a result of what we want to perceive as of what is actually there. This does not mean that people view ants as elements. We may distinguish temples from petrol pump stations; but a petrol pumping station with good service and repair facilities, is perceived quite differently from an ordinary petrol pumping station having no such facilities. Thus, the perception is not what the advertiser intends to be perceived but the receiver perceives what they want to perceive out of what is actually there and thus their self concept, group pressures, role, and reference groups influence the perception to a great extent.

Factors that Influence the Perception Process

There are two types of factors that influence our perception process.

(1) Stimulus Factors. These are inputs to the process. Stimulus factors are characteristics of the physical object that affect both stages attention and interpretation of the process. Such factors are size intensity, colour, shape, message, novelty, position and context; and

(2) Audience or Individual Factors. These factors reflect individual characteristics or differences. These factors include not only sensory processes but also past experiences with similar items, and basic motivations and expectations. Factors to be considered are informations needs attitudes, values, interests, confidence, social context and cognitive style.

These factors can be depicted in the following way:

Stimulus Conditions	***Audience Conditions***
—Intensity	—Attitudes
—Size	—Values
—Message	—Interests
—Position	—Confidence
—Context	—Social Context
	—Cognitive Style.

The process of perception is not identical across people, even, for the same stimalus. On the contrary, there are extreme differences among people in terms of their exposure to what they are attracted and how they interpret information. A most important aspect of the study of the perceptual process is to determine what variables explain these differences. Thus different people will perceive differently the same stimulus at different times according to their needs, interests, values, attitudes and confidence.

Principles or Perception

Perception is the process by which an individual receives, interprets and responds to stimuli in his environment. From the advertising point of view, it is the process by which a mental impression is formed from the stimuli within the consumers field of awareness. The comumer attaches significant meaning to what is observed because this meaning depends upon personal experience, memories, beliefs, fantasies and so on. No two people have the same meaning of any given observation. Let us approach the problem of understanding perception by four principles.

(1) Perception is Selective. An individual will perceive selectively. In other words, he will not perceive all the stimuli. He will perceive only those stimuli which concern him.

(2) Perception is Organised. Perception is well organised in the indivisual because it has meaning for the indvidual. Perceptions do not represent confusion.

(3) Perception Depends upon Stimulus Factors. The nature of the physical slimulus itself helps determine perception. Various stumulus factor's such as size, colour, intensity, position and context affect the perception of the message. It is, therefore relevant whether an advertisement in a magazine is in colour or black and while a full page or a half from the perception point of view.

(4) Perception Depends Upon Personal Factors. Personal factors such as needs, moods memory experiences and values, affect the message reception. What the individual brings to the situation governs perception the ability to see or hear the message. A person who is interested in cricket is more likely to perceive an advertisement for stereo equipment than one for power back saw. A person's need at the moment will also determine perceptual selectivity. The thirsty man is more likely to perceive an advertisement for cold drink during a match. Past experience also shows that people have developed a taste for product preferences and therefore, like to see some ads than others.

Perhaps, the most significant aspect of perception from marketer's point of view is its selectivity. The individual consumer perceives a product in terms of its brand image resulting from .experience with the product and any promotion or advertising. The product name, package, design, and consumer's behaviour all contribute to the consumer's perceptual performance.

Product price also has special significance. Every customer has two price limits in his mind a lower limit and an upper limit. Any thing above the upper limit is expensive and will fainh perceiving the customers. Any price below lower limit will create doubt about quality of the product. The price perception is only part of the total brand image to be maintained.

SELECTIVE PERCEPTION

The manufacturer most of ten bombard the target consumers with commercials on T.V. and advertisements through difference media but all are not perceived by them. Most of them are ignored, many are seen or viewed uninterestingly and probably a few are retained in the mind. The main problem of every marketer is how to stimulate the target consumers or in other words, what are those stimuli which consumers may respond to. How can they gain the attention of the individual so that he may read and perceive the message in the advertisement? There are two basic factors (stimulus and individual) that affect the selectivity of the message (which we have discussed in the previous questions) *i e.*, size, colour, intensity, position and the needs, motives, attitudes etc. decide the perception process. As every individual is different in motives, interest attitudes etc., so he selects only those ads that meet his requirements. Thus, there is a great deal of selectivity going on, in the process of perception. A popular word in the lexicon of the consumer behaviourist is 'Selective Perception'. Three kinds of selectively occur:

(i) Selective Exposore. The customer attempts to encounter only those media and messages that interests him and are important to him and consistent with his deeply held values and beliefs. He will not attend to the exposures which are not in agreement with his beliefs and values.

(ii) Selective Perception. The customer will 'see' or 'hear' ideas, messages and appeals which, are relevant to him and can sereen out others. It generally happens that persons do not see or view the advertisements that do not interest him or concern him at the time. Either they take them lightly or read hurriedly or do not see them at all. It means they have not perceived the message or appeal.

(iii) Selective Retention. The people will remember what they like to remember and the rest they forget. It is neither desirable nor feasible to remember what is irrelevant for them.

These selective processes (as explained above) help to explain why some people are not all affected by advertising even by offensive advertising because they do not care to see and remember the advertisement messages.

A person's attitudes and pre-disposition to wards the market in question affect these selective processes. Furthermore, decisions that the consumer in currently making and typically concerned about will affect the pre-dispositions which are relevant. For example, if a consumer is thinking about buying a scooter, he will perceive the message in advertisements relating to scooters and the people attitude towards the extisting brands of scooters available in the market. He will not even see advertisements concerning land dealings.

In case of introduction of new product in the market, the manufarcturer will bombard. the target consumers with commercials or advertisements on T.V. and in magazines with a view to inform and perceive the target consumers. In the beginning, it brings a little change in sales because for a quite some time, the most of the consumers would have no knowledge of the new product, though heavily advertised Why? Because this information simply never penetrated their perceptual filters. Consumers perceive incoming stimuli on a selective basis. They perceive only those incoming stimuli which they wish to perceive of in other words which serve their interests with such selectivity at work, it is easy to see the importance of the marketer's efforts to obtain a consumer franchise, for his product in the form of brand loyalty. Satisfied customers will lot like to seek much information about competing products. If this information is forced upon them, they will not pass it to others through their perceptual filters. They will tune out such information which is not in accord with their beliefs and expectation.

SUBLIMINAL PERCEPTION

Subliminal perception is a stage of sub-conscious level of awareness. It is possible to communicate with persons without their being aware of the communication. The words Drink Campa Cola flashed at the cinema screen frequently during the interval only for one second the message may be too short to be recognised at the conscious level. Still it may increase the sale of Campa Cola. This is why, the advertising agencies become intensely interested in subliminal perception. It avoid perceptual screens of viewers the goal of original research in this area was to induce the buyers of consumers goods without their awareness of the source of motivation. But later findings have not been successful. The subliminal advertising has been widely condemned throughout the world over. It is unlikely to conclude that such advertising will induce the buyers and will increase sales except in such cases where buyer himself is interested in purchasing the item. There are several reasons for this:

(a) Stimulus factors are absent in such type of advertising which are very necessary to gain attendance.

(b) Only a very short message can be transmitted.

(c) Individuals vary greatly in their thresholds of awareness. Message transmitted in such cases for one person may not be perceived at all by other people who have not seen it on the screen. Moreover, when exposed subliminally, the message may carry a confused version. For example, the message 'Drink Campa Cola, may go unseen by some viewers. Some others may take it as 'Drink Coca Cola' or Drink Cocoa etc., and in this way competitors may gain. Contrary to earlier research, it has been established that consumers cannot be forced to purchase what they do not want to purchase.

Thus, subliminal advertising is not used in the present day advertising world.

Attention in Perception Process

The term attention can be viewed as the state of focussing one's mind upon something. When consumers attend to advertising, they focus their perception upon it. They distinguish advertising from other elements of environments. Attention can also refer to as an information filter a screening mechanism that controls the quantity, and nature of information. Often advertivers experience difficulty in gaining attention of target consumers who are encircled with an infinite number of stimuli to which an individual could be exposed and an infinite variety of parts or components of a stimulus to which he or she might attend. Clearly, it is possible for an individual to absorb only a small fraction of the available stimuli. The advertiser, generally, are faced with the need for taking steps to make their' advertisements stand out and say or do something to attract consumer's attention in the midst of all this clutter of competing stimuli.

One or the ways of gaining attention is to design the advertisement copy in such a way that consumers may take it different from other elements in the environment. The marketers will try to induce consumers to attend to the advertisement by designing the message and utilising the media that is quite different from others. Usually, target consumers are likely to attend to those ads which are in colour', that feature a well known personality, that are larger than others (in print media), or louder than others (in broadcast media). If the target consumers perceives a particular type of advertisement in preference to others, it means, it is effective in capturing the attention of consumers and they themselves differentiate it from the others to which they are exposed. Exposure is a must without exposure, there can be no communication.

Only a small percentage of the exposed advertisements get through the attention filter *i.e.*, are actually 'seen' or 'attended to'. The attention filter operates at three levels of effort and consciousness:

(a) Active Search. At one extreme level is the process of active search where in the receiver actually seeks information. He or she might collect information through opinions of friends and relactives or search through old newspapers and magazine, not generally read.

(b) Passive Search. This is another extreme where the receiver seeks for information only from sources to which he or she is exposed during the normal course of events.

(c) Passive Attention. The final level might be called passive attention. In such cases, the receiver does not make any serious attempt to obtain the information because he or she does not need it. But some information may nevertheless enter the system.

Motives which Stimulate Consumer to Obtain Information

At all the three levels, it would be appropriate to search why a person obtains information. There may be as many reasons as there are situ,ations and individuals. However, it is instructive to examine four general motives for attending to informative stimuli.

In a sense, these are audience conditions influencing attention. Four motives are:

(1) Information that has Practical Value

Advertising, undoubtedly, is a source of information. Psychologists are of the view that people do expose themselves to information that has practical value of them. The information seeker" or target audience are in a practical need for product information and effective advertisements tend to fulfill this need. Such information is used in making decisions. If an advertisement contains certain information of practical value, people will actually search it out in certain circumstances and will be willing to read the copy to others.

Advertisements that provide useful information, enhance the company image. For examaple, Indian Oil, Corporation disseminates information to its customers that may help the consumers against any risk from the gas leakage. Burnkrant applies a general theory of motivation that the behavioural tendency to process information is based upon three factors:

(i) Information need for some product which are costly, complex or some what unknown because they are new or for some other reason.

(ii) The second factor is expectancy hat processing a particular stimulus will lead to relevant information exposure.

(iii) The third would It measure of the value of the message as a source of relevant information. It is measured in terms of goodness or badness of the message as an information source.

(2) Information that Supports : The Consistency Theories

It is a psychological truth that people have a preference for supportive information and avoid non-supportive or discrepant information. For example, here is a statement of a comedian Dick Gregory "I have been reading so much about cigarettes and cancer that I quite reading." It means drives or motives that do not support the customer's view, he disregard them. We can term this type of derive as 'selective exposure'.

Selective exposure can be explain here by the consistency theories such as dissonance theory, which suggest that people have a cognitive drive to develop consistent cognitions and behaviours about the existence of conflicting cognitive elements is discomforting and that people will try to reduce it. One mechanism to reduce dissonsnce is selective exposure that is perceive such exposures which are supportive to their views and avoid which are not.

Sometimes, involuntary exposures threaten the selective exposure that tend to increase due to non-supportive information. If a person receives any negative information about the brand or product he is loyal to he will become sensitive to information that supports his view that the brand is quite reliable. In such cases, the advertiser might therefore stand ready to respond immediately to any negative information, his customers are likely to receive or received. Such a campaign would capitalise on selectivity and could be very ffective.

In combating such selective exposure, the advertiser can offer rewards, contests or premium to get people to read the message. An alternative is to approach a certain segments of markets indirectly through opinion leaders and rely on words of month to reach others. Another approach may be to broaden the media used *i.e.* to use certain non-conventional media inspite of high cost of advertisement per thousand.

(3) Information that Stimulates—The Complexity Theories

A third motivation is to obtain variety to combat boredom. The argument is that when an individual's stimulation level in sufficiently low, he will cease screening out discripant information, and actually seek out information that is complex, novel, and even inconsistent with his existing attitudesh Theories supporting this view are termed 'complexity theories' Mr. Maddi, who holds prime position a complexity theorist, has put forth the theory as follows:

> "Its essence is that novelty, unexpectedness, change and complexity are pursued because they are inherently satisfying. The definition of novelty and unexpectedness must stress the difference between existing cognitive content and current or future perceptions and hence, the experience of variety is very likely to also be the experience of inconsistc:ncy".

This theory is based on the very reasonable assumption that people get bored and are motivated to reduce that boredom by seeking stimuli that are novel, unusual, and different. People are always curious what is around them and this curosity will influence exposure patterns. In other words, they may be motivated to seek out information that does not support their positions.

The complexity theories have empirical support of their own. Studies have revealed that when a new element is introduced in the environment. People are very much anxious to know about it. Studies have also indicated that variety, in the form of novelty and unexpectedness is pleasurable whereas completely predictable events become boring. It is thus obvious that advertising should avoid being predictable, esspecially in situations wherein selectivity can easily operate to screen out advertisements. Another empirical conclusion is that variety is not only pursued and enjoyed, but is actually necessary to normal living.

(4) Information that Interests

People are attracted to the information that interests them or in turn, they are interested in subjects with which they are involved or people or situations with which they are identified. In an attempt to attract attention, an advertiser can adjust the stimulus the advertisement and its environment. Studies show that people are more apt to look and remember things in which they are interested than things in which they are not. Normally people are interested in information concerning benefits that they feel are important in a product. He, thus, applies benefit segmentation to the task of penetrating the attention barrier.

A most effective approach for gaining interest is to run an advertisement about the person or persons to whom it is directed, mentioning the name and discussing his activities. Advertisements can be developed with which people can readily identify. For example, an insurance company runs a series of advertisements in which agents may be presented in a most personal way. Their hobbies and life styles may be discussed in a manner that made it easy for readers to identify with them. Such advertisements of course, are sure to have an enormous impact on the company's agents.

Another approach is to present a communication involving topical issues those in which the audience is likely to be heavily involved.

An advertiser should not forget that to attract attention is no his only concern. It will be worthless if attention diverts interest from the important aspect of the message. In particular, it is not useful to attract an individual with a highly interesting subject if the brand and its message get lost in the process.

The adoption level theory suggests that it is not to focal stimuli that determine perception, but also the contextual stimuli (background) and residual stimuli (Past experiench). Attention is enhanced when the stimulus deviates markedly from that level. Thus, a colour advertisement will attract more attention than it is seen in black and white environment. In an advertising context, a humourous advertisement may attract attention. if it is surrounded by more conventional copy approaches. However, if many humorous advertisements are involved, the attraction will be less.

Thus, there are four motives that stimulate the audience to read the advertisements or that attract the attention of the people. These motives are—*(i)* information of practical value, *(ii)* information that supports the audience view, *(iii)* information that stimulates or *(iv)* information that gain interest.

INTERPRETATION PROCESS

Interpretation is the second prerequisite of the perception process. By interpretation, we mean that the target audience must carry the same meaning of the message that the advertiser wants to communicate. In other words the audience must interpret the message in the way the advertiser wants it to be interpreted. If it is not interpreted in that way, the whole efforts and cost go waste.

Two concepts from the Gestalt psycholology help up to understand the interpretation process. The first is that stimuli are perceived as a whole. What is important in an advertisement interpretation is the total impression that it leaves on the minds of the audience. The second is that an individual has a cognitive drive towards an orderly cognitive configuration. We shall now discuss these two concepts *(i)* organised whole and *(ii)* cognitive drive in detail.

(1) The Organised Whole

The stimuli should be viewed as a whole and not in parts. Various experiments draw conclusions that even when the stimuli are incomplete, people seem to strive to form a complete impression of a person or object. Advertising copy does not necessarily have to tell the whole story, an individual will naturally fill in the gap to form an impression. The studies indicated that stimuli are seen in interaction. The intelligence of different persons will differ. Because of such interaction effects, the total impact of an advertising campaign needs to be considered. An appeal or an advertisement may prove effective by itself, but it may not be effective in terms of the whole campaign. Studies show that there are some attributes that are more central to the conceptual process than others. Experiments also indicated that first few traits formed a context within which others are interpreted: Thus, an advertiser should be concerned with the first impression that advertisement generates.

The stimuli are viewed as a total configuration suggests that brand must be considered as an organised whole. Thus alteration or addition of a single component may indeed a fact the total configuration. We might see that there are interactions among various dimensions. If one dimension is changed or a new dimension added, the perception of the brand along the others may change radically to consumers. If perception is indeed an organised whole, then the system of interrelationship among components stimuli has meaning of its own. All the stimuli could change, but if the relationship among entities remain, the perception may not be affected.

The concept of orgnised whole also dictates that perception of a stimulus cannot be considered in isolation from its context. The selling of the stimulus is part of the total field and will influence the perception. A salty expression would be perceived quite differently at a football game that it would be in the middle of wedding ceremony.

The context of an advertisement will effect how it is perceived. Advertisement appeared on advertising vehicles will have different perception. The feature material in a specific edition may create a mood that will effect interpretation. Furthermore, the company involved and all its interactions with an audience member will also affect interpretation.

(2) The Cognitive Drive

The next important tenet of the Gestalt Psychology is that there is a cognitive drive to obtain a good configuration one that is simple, familier regular meaningful, consistent and complete. The following principles are related to the cognitive drive:

(a) Closure. If a subject realises that something is missing from a picture or from a copy the audience will fill in the gap. This process is called 'closure.' Strong perception may be seen in closure copy. An advertiser can use the closure process to make a campaign more effective. A 60 second commercial may be run several times on T.V. To combat forgetting, a shorter spot of 5 or 10 seconds long may be spotted. A viewer may visualise the omitted materials. Thus, the material contained in the 60 second commercial will have been transmitted in a much shorter time, reducing the risk of boring the viewer.

Another use of closure concept is leaving a well known jungle uncompleted. Those exposed will have a strong cognitive drive to effect closure by mentally completing the jungle.

Closely Related to closure is the process of interpreting an ambiguous stimuli. The interesting part of the process is the involvement of participants. The advertiser will leave the advertisement ambiguous in any of ways. An advertisement has three main components a picture, a written message and the brand name. The ambiguity can be introduced into any of these elements. This ambiguity with stimulate sufficient interest to sustain cognitive activity necessary to figure it out. But achivertisement should not be too ambiguous.

(b) Assimilation Contrast. Another principle of perceptual psychology is called assimilation contrast. Thus principle is used by the audience member to remove ambiguity from a stimulus. A host of audience conditions may influence interpretation among themselves. Here values, brand preference, social situations cognitive styles and cognitive needs are of importance. For example, some people have a need for cognitive clarity, a need to impose meaning and organisation on their experiences with the world. Such people tend to exert a greater effort to understand an ambiguous communication than those with low need for cognitive clarity. It is useful to attempt to measure advertising, specially while it is being developed to determine its impact on the attention and interpretation stage of the perception filter. Among the approaches to the measursement of interpretation in a pre-test is the direct questioning of those exposed in a laboratory setting, for example projective techniques such as word association and instructured interviews.

LAERNING PROCESS

Psychologists believe that learning is possible in all human behaviour. Gary Stener defines learning as "all those changes in behaviour that results from previous behaviour in similar situations". There is a confusion in its meaning when we try to discover how learning works. The most importants theory from advertising point of view is the 'stimulus response approach'. According to this approach 'learning is what takes place when a link is established between a particular stimulus and a particular response'. Drivers stopping their vehicles at red light, and audiences applauding a performance are examples of stimulus-response learning.

Learning Process and its Important Variables

Perceptual skills are learnt and this fact has led some advertisers to pay special attention to learning process. Learning theorists have isolated a number of steps in the learning process. Learning process begins with a drive a strong stimulus that motivates the individuals to learn. Depending on the cues ads, signs and other stimuli relevant to the situation existing in the environment the individual chooses certain specific response in an effort to satisfy the drive. The specific response thus chosen depends very much on the cues and previous experience. Man behaves in the way in which hé satisfied the drive earlier.

The reinforcement of the learning process occurs when the response is followed satisfaction *i.e.*, a reduction in drive tension. Reinforcement strengthens the relationship between the environmen-!al cue and the response, and may lead to similar response next time the drive occurs. Repeated reinforcement leads to the development of a habit. It becomes a routine for the satisfaction of the drive.

John Dollard and Neal Miller have formulated the stimulus-response relationship in more sophisticated term by breaking it down into four important variables of learning process. They are drive, cue, response and reinforcement. The term drive refers to inner need of an individual that invites action. For example, hunger, fatique, fear, insecurity and so on. These inner drives call for action. A cue is a stimulus in the environment that stimulates an individual to work. A commercial on T.V. providing a solution to the inner drive may be the cue. If hunger is a drive, a commercial for pulao or biscuits may be a cue. Cue links the drive and the response. The response is the action of an individual what he does in response to the cue. For a hungry man, getting something to eat as suggested in the cue is a response.

Reinforcement is the strengthening of the cue-response relationship and is directly related to the degree of satisfaction the response beings to the original drive. The individual reinforces the response, if degree of satisfaction is high otherwise he seeks alternatives. If a response is reinforced regularly, the result is habit formation. We can depict these four vatiables as follows.

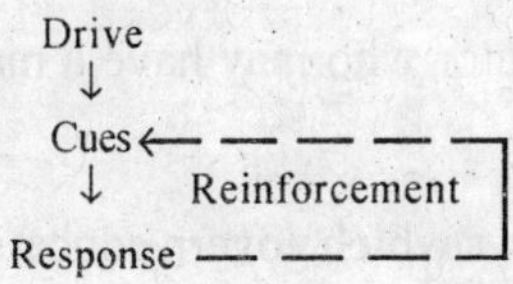

Fig. 2 Important ariables in learning Process

The above description seems to be very simple and straight forward. But, it is not so, if we consider the possible alternative response. The response may be immediately or deferred. If cur response is immediate, our hungry consumer, watching a pulao commercial may immediately go to the kitchen or out to some restaurant and may have some pulao to satisfy his hunger. Or, if the commercial simply focusses attention on hunger drive it may lead the consumer to any response necessary to satisfy the need *i.e.*, he may go to chicken or nons or any other ordinary food. On the other hand, if our hungry consumer is observing fast on that day, he may negate the need for food.

Regardless of the immediate response, the consumer may respond several days later when he goes for shopping. Remembering how appealing it was in the commercial he may look for it in a restaurant. At this, point another intriguing element intervenes, if the consumer notices that the ordinary cooked rice is cheaper than the advertised pulao. This may act as a cue to his drive of economy. The response would be to buy ordinary cooked rice unless the advertisement convinced him that his need would be better satisfied by paying extra for pulao. Anticipating and dealing with such chains of stimuli-response relationship is one of the most absorbing elements of the advertising.

The learning theory is that body of interrelated principles which deals with human money. The notion that the learning theory may be relevant to and helpful in in advertising, suggests, the role of the advertiser as:

(a) disseminator of information;

(b) an audience;

(c) a disseminator who may have a measurable impact on the audience.

The learning laws which govern education may be conveniently applied to advertising.

Every advertiser is interested in knowing that his advertising messages are doing well. If he fails in his mission to get the audience learned, from his budget allocation, it means, the advertiser is guilty of misappropriating the budget.

How to know whether Learning is Efficient or Ineffective

How an advertiser comes to know whether or not learning is efficient or totally ineffective depends upon two factors:

(a) The 'receptivity' of the learner's mind; and

(b) The environment of learnings.

(a) The Receptivity of Learner's Mind. The receptivity means grasping power of the learner's mind and that depends upon two important elements—*(i)* interest level and *(ii)* the intellectual capacity to grasp things. The disseminator has no control or little control over the receptivity of the learner's mind. There are no doubt, certain techniques to develop interest and draw attention of the learner, but these techniques will not be of much help unless the learner has some prime interest in the first place.

(b) The Environment of Learning. The second element for the effectiveness of learning is the environment of learning the conditions under which the exposure is made, can, to a large extent, be controlled by the disseminator. The body .of laws or principles that we call the learning often specifies the best environment for effective learning.

The average person is exposed to several messages each day. Indeed such messages are so obiquitous that we may seem to have come a long way towards developing a filter within ourselves that reduces our annoyance to tolerable levels. Thus, there are certain advertiserments that attract our attention most while there are others that draw our attention not to that degree. The most memorable commercial exposure, the commercial message that produces the most lasting learning experience, is in some way differentiated from the run of the mill commercials. The laws of the learning theory suggest the manner in which differentiation may be developed and exposed. Instead of tall claims of quality, the learning theory suggests that we can associate the product with some other product which is well established in the minds of people. For an advertisement of cadbury chocolate; we may advertise like. Rolls Royce is a car-Cadbury is a chocolate. This manner of conveying the notion of quality utilises the psychological law of belonging. The learning percept that specifies that ideas or objects that are naturally related and organised into meaningful relationship can be remembered better than those that have no logical connection.

❐

9

Communication Strategy

To develop its communications strategy, the sponsor must establish the primary communications objectives. These might consist of creating awareness of a source, promoting sales of a product, encouraging (or discouraging) certain, practices attracting retail patronage, reducing post-purchase dissonance creating good will, a favourable image, or any combination of these and other communications objectives.

Selecting the appropriate audience is an essential component of a communications strategy. Since individual has his own traits, characteristics, interests, needs, experience and knowledge, it is essential, that the sponsor segment the audience into groups that are homogeneous in terms of some relevant characteristics. This enables the marketeer to create specific messages for each target group, and run them in specific media that are seen (or heard) by each target group. It is unlikely that a marketeer could develop a single message that would apeal simultaneously to total audience. Efforts to use "universal" appeals phrased in simple language that all can understand invariably in unsuccessful advertisements to which few people: Since it enables the marketeers to sailor marketing communications to the specific needs of groups of people, market segmentation overcomes some of the problems inherent in trying to communicate with mass audiences. Let us take the example of the problem of hostile audience. Even though people tend to avoid viewpoints opposite to their own, there are times when it makes sense to advertise to hostile audiences. Though it may not change the beliefs of those fully persuaded, an advertisement can prevent others from being infected with some degree of hostility. A study of a 1986 Chenon campaign directed at hostile audiences indicated that the company's promotional efforts resulted in more positive attitudes a well as increased sales of the firm's gasoline. The campaign's greater impact in terms of attitude change and increased purchase behaviour was observed among a market segment described as inner directed those consumers who think for them selves.

Companies that have many adverse audiences sometimes find it useful to develop a communication. Strategy that consists of an overall communicatioris message to all their audiences, from which they spin off a series of related messages targeted directly at the specific interests of each individual segment.

To main in private communications with all their publics, most large organizations employ public relations counsellors, or establish heir own public relations departments, to provide favourable information about the company and to suppress unfavourable information of good public relations person will develop a close working relationship with editors and programme directors of all the relevant media in order to facilitate editorial placement of desired messages. Publicity campaign design to promote the image of the company are becoming increasingly popular and marketeers have developed methods to monitor and increase their effectiveness.

MEDIA STRATEGY

Media strategy is an essential component of a communication plan. It calls for the placement of advertisements in the specific media read, viewed or heard by selected target markets. To accomplish this, advertisers develop through research, a consumer profile.

Further, before selecting specific media vehicles, advertisers must select a general media category that will enhance the message they wish to convey, which category the marketeers selects depends on the product or service to be advertised, the market segments to be reached, and the advertising objectives, rather than select one media category to the exclusion of others many advertisers use a multi-media campaign strategy, with one primary category carrying the major burden of the campaign and other categories providing supplemental support.

Many research studies have pointed out the comparative effectiveness of one medium over others for variousproducts, audiences, and advertising objectives. In general, the findings have been inconclusive. Each media category has certain advantages and disadvantages that the marketeer must consider it developing a media strategy for a specific campaign. Some media categories are more appropriate vehicles for certain products or messages than others. For example, a retailer who wants to advertise a clearance sale should advertise in local newspapers, since that is where consumers are accustomed to looking for sales announcements.

Once marketeers have identified the appropriate media category, they can then choose the specific medium in that category that reaches their intended audiences. The major issue marketeers must consumer when selecting specific media are overlapping audiences, the characteristics of the audiences and the effectiveness of their advertisements.

Since many media, specially those with similar editiorial features and formats have overlapping audiences the characteristics of the audiences and the effectiveness of their advertisements.

Since many media have identified those with similar editorial features and formats have overlapping audiences, advertisers usually place their advertising messages simultaneously or sequentially in a number of media with similar audience profils. This enables them to achieve both react and frequency. The term react refers to the number of different people or households that are exposed to the advertisement, frequency refers to how often they are exposed to an individual number of a target group over an agreed upon time period. The effective react thresholds suggests that 45% of the target group should be reacted over the agreed upon time period. Figure given below illustrates how an advertisement in two similar media vehicles is likely to reach a unique audiences in each medium, as well as an overlapping segment which reads both magazines and thus receives two exposures.

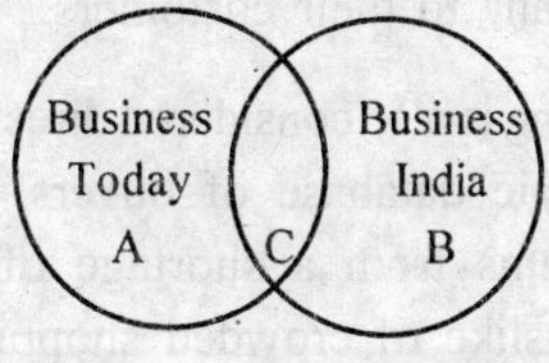

Overlapping Readership of Magazines with Similar Audience Profiles

Marketeers use various syndicated marketing research services to obtain data on media audiences their demographies, product purchses, brand preferences. Many marketeers have adopted a media strategy called precision targeting. This strategy has been facilitated by media that seek a specific niche for themselves in the market place by catering to the needs and interests of a highly specific target segment.

Direct mail and direct marketing are excellent example of precision targeting. Direct mail is advertising that is sent directly to the mailing address of a target customer. Direct marketing is not a mediam but marketing technique that uses various media for the purpose or soliciting a direct response from a consumer. A major advantage of direct marketing is its ability to generate measurable responses. This capacity enables direct marketeers to measure the profitability of their efforts directly through such variables as cost per enquiry, cost-per-sale, and income per advertisement, and to evaluate the timing and frequency of companies.

A prime objective in direct marketing is to build and constantly refine as electronic database of qualified buyers. This is done by soliciting both enquiries and direct others.

Many people are concerned that the direct marketing practice of preserving and building the shopping histories of customers in their database is an invasion of privacy. Mail order catalogues are a prime example of direct marketing sent through the mails to carefully homed databases. Given the huge amount of competition in the field, some category retailers are trying to engage in relationship marketing by including in their catalogue editorial content that they think will make them more "human" to their customers.

Electronics shopping is also considered direct marketing because it generates an electronic database of buyers. The popularity of electronic shopping stems from a shortage of free tittle among working women and dislike of crowded shopping mails. In some cases, consumers simply find lone home shopping all entertaining every to relax in the comform of their homes. Some advertisers using fax machines to reach an upscale educated market through numbers listed in fax phone books.

Clearly marketeers must be familiar with the characteristics of their audiences, the characteristics of their products and the characteristics of media in order to make wise media choices.

COMPONENTS OF COMMUNICATION

The sender who is the initiator of the communication, can be a formal or an informal source. A formal source is likely to represent either a for profit or a not-for-profit organisation, an informal source can be a parent or a friend who gives a product information or advice. As we know that consumers often rely on informal communication sources in making purchase decision because, unlike formal sources, the sender apparently has nothing to gain from the receiver's subsequent actions. For that reason, informal word-of-mouth communication tends to be highly persuasive. Research shows that consumers prefer personal information sources when they buy services, because they have greater confidence in such sources. (Source—Keath B. Murrey, "A Test of Services Marketing Theory: Consumer Information Acquisition Activities").

The receiver of formal communications is likely to be a targeted prospect or a customer. There are also many intermediary and even uninterested audiences for marketing communications. Examples of intermediary are wholesalers, distributors and references, who have sent trade advertising designed to persuade them to order and stock merchandise and relevant professionals who have sent professional advertising in the hopes that they will specify or prescribe the marketeers' products. Unintended audiences include everyone who is exposed to the message, whether or not they are specifically targeted by the source. These unintended audiences often include publics that are important to the marketeer, such as shareholders, creditors, suppliers, employees, bankers and the local community in addition to the general public. It is important to remember that no matter hpwlarge the audience, it is composed of individual receivers, each of whom interprets the message in his or her own special way.

The media or communications channel can be interpersonal an informal conversation between two friends, or a formal conversation between a salesperson and a customer. The media can be impersonal—a mass media such as a newspaper or television programme. Mass media are generally classified as print though electronic media are becoming more important daily. News modes of interactive communication that permit the audiences of mass media to provide direct feedback are beginning to blur the distinction between interpersonal and impersonal communication. For example, in some communities consumers can do their grocery shopping electronically as the TV camera scans the grocery shelve. Home shopping networks are expanding. Dramatically, as consumers demonstrate their enthusiasm for TV shopping. Direct marketeers-also called database marketeers seek individual responses from advertisements place in all the mass media: broadcast, print, electro as well as from direct mail.

Despite the general use of the term "mass media" to describe impersonal media there is, a growing trend towards demassification as publishers shift their focuses from large, general interest audiences to smaller more specialized audiences. Some media try to create "captive' audiences. For example one communications company is providing free television equipment and programming to school districts that agree to run their special "School" channel, which includes two minutes of paid commercials, during class time.

The message can be verbal or non verbal, or a combination of two. A verbal message, whether it is spoken or written, can usually contain more specific product (or service) information than a non-verbal message. Sometimes a verbal message is combined with an illustration or a demonstration and together they may provide more information to the receiver than either would alone.

Sometimes, non-verbal information takes the form of symbolic communication. The study of semiotics is the study of the meanings implied by signs and symbols. Marketeers often try to develop logos or symbols that are associated exclusively with their products. The Coca-Cola company, for example, had trade marked both the word "Coke'; in a specific typographic style and the shape of the traditional Coke bottle-and both are instantly recognizable to consumers as symbols of the company's best-selling soft drink.

Non-Verbal communications take place in interpersonal channels as well as in impersonal channels. For example, a good salesperson usually is alert to non-verbal feedback provided by consumer prospecs. These may take the form of facial expressions or bodily movements. Because senders often can "read" meaning into such bodily reactions, these non-verbal actions sometimes are referred to as "body language".

Feedback is an essential component of both interpersonal and impersonal communications. Prompt feedback permits the sender to reinforce, to change or to modify the message to ensure that it is understood in the intended way.

Feedback from Interpersonal Communications and Feedback from Impersonal Communicatons

Marketing communications are usually designed to persuade a target audience to act in a desired way (to purchase a product to vote for a spceific candidate, to pay income tax early), the ultimate test of marketing communications is the receiver's response. For this reason, it is essential for the sender to obtain feedback as promptly and as accurately as possible. Only through feedback can the scholar determine if and how well the message has been received.

An important advantage of interpersonal communication is the ability to obtain immediate feedback through verbal as well as non-verbal cues. Experienced communicators are very attentive to feedback and constantly modify their message based on what they see or hear from the audience. Immediate feedback is the factor that makes personal selling to effective. It enables the salesperson to factor the sales pitch to the expressed needs and observed reactions of cach prospect. Similarly, it enables a political candidate to selectively stress specific aspects of his or her platform in response to questions posed by prospective voters in face-to-face meetings. Immediate feedback in the form of inattention serves to alert the college professor to the need to awaken the interest of a dozing class, thus, the professor may make a deliberately provocative statement such as "This material will probably appear on your final exam."

Feedback is just as important a concept in interpersonal (mass) communications as it is in interpersonal communications. Indeed, because of the large sums of money expended on mass media, may people consider such feedback even more essential than interpersonal feedback. The organisation that initiates the communication must develop some method for determining whether its mass communications are, infact, received by the intended audience. Understood in the intended way, and successful in achieving the intended objectives.

Unlike interpersonal communication mass communications feedback is rarely direct, instead, it is usually inferred. Receivers buy (or do not buy), The advertised product they renew (or do not renew) their magazine subscriptions, they vote (or do not vote) for the political candidate. Senders infer how persuasive their messages are from the resulting action (or in action) of the targeted audience.

Advertisers often try to gauge the effectiveness of their messages by conducting audience research to find out which media are read, which television programmes are viewed and which arvertisements are remembered by their target audience. If feedback mindcates that the audience does not note or miscomprehends the advertisement, the sponsor has the opportunity to modify or revise the message so that the intended communication does in fact take place.

Mass communications feedback does not have the timeliness of interpersonal feedback. Other commercial sources are constantly seeking innovative methods to find out quickly how effective their consumer advertising is. For example, an important feedback mechanism for food and other packaged goods is based on the Universal Product Code (UPC) and tied to computerized each registers. Super market Scanner data can be combined with data from other sources to measure the correlation between advertisements, special promotions and sales.

The Niclsen SCANTRACK household panel service is an integrated tracking system that pulls together, all the casual factors of consumer purchasing—advertising, promotion and retailer activity in an effort to track the specific cues that induce people to buy certain products. Niclsen has provided household panel members with hand-held scanners that they use to scan the UPC Code of each item they buy and the coupons they redeem. By equipping the households with TV meters as well, Niclsen can report to subscriber how often each family views its commercials and which newspapers, magazines and coupon mailings they receive. The data input records price increases and in-store specials and provides information as to brand switching, the 'level of product usage, and repeat purchases. Most importantly, it provides the feedback necessary to evaluate the effectiveness of a marketing communications strategy and indicates precisely which part of the marketing communications strategy, and indicates precisely which part of the marketing campaign, if any needs revision.

Another type of feedback that companies seek from mass audiences is the degree of customer satisfaction or dissatisfaction with a product purchase. They try to discover and, correct any problems that occur as swiftly as possible in order to retain the brands image of reliability. Many companies have established 24 hour hot lines to encourage comments and questions from their consumers.

Advertising effectiveness research called copy testing can be done before the advertising is actually run in media or after it appears. Pretests are used to determine which, if any, elements, of an advertising message should be revised before major media expenses are incurred. Post-tests are used to evaluate the effectiveness of an advertisement that has already run and to see which elements, if any, should be changed to improve the impact of future advertisements.

One popular method for evaluating the effectiveness of magazine advertisements is through syndicated service called the Starch Readership Service. Readers of a given issue, of a magazine are asked to point out which advertisements they noted, which they associated with the sponsor and which they 'read most. The resulting readership score is meaningful when compared too semilar-sized advertisements to competitive advertisements and to the marketeer's own prior advertisements. There is evidence, that high noted starch scores are correlatad with a favourable attitude toward the advertised brand and a positive brand purchase intention. Thus, starch scores may have solidity beyond immediate processing of the advertisements and may indicate more lasting communication effects for the brand.

IMPORTANCE OF FEAR APPEAL IN ADVERTISING

Fear is an effective advertising appeal often used in marketing communications. Some researchers have found a negative relationship between the, intensity of fear appeals and their ability to per:.uade, so that strong fear appeals tend to be less effective than mild fear appeals. A number of explanations have been offered for this phenomenon. Strong fear appeals concerning a highly relevant topic (*e.g.* cigarette smoking) cause the individual to experience cognitive dissonance practice or by rejecting the unwelcome information. Since giving up a comfortable habit is difficult, consumers more readily reject the threat. Thus they do by a variety of techniques, including denial of its validity, the belief that they are immune to personal disaster.

According to another research there is a positive relationship between fear and persuasiveness. They believe that what individuals focus on controlling the danger nither than controlling fear there is greater probability of accepting the messages recomendation. In some cases, marketeers found that advertisements for condoms that stressed protection against AIDS were not as effective as condom advertisements that did not mention the dreaded disease. For that reason, some condom-marketeers changed their advertising approach from fear appeals to humour, discount promotions and appeals directed at particular ethnic and life style segments.

One study showed that moviegoers who were given prior knowledge of the upcoming frightening events in a movie were more intensely frightened and, upset by the movie than people who were not forewarned. This demonstrates the role of expectations or mind-set on consumer perceptions and should be factored into the creation of effective advertising message.

HUMOUR IN ADVERTISING

Many marketeers use humours appeals in the belief that humour will increase the acceptance and persuasiveness of their advertising communications. Other marketeers avoid the use of humour because they fear their product will become an object of ridicule the consumers will laugh at them rather than with them. A number of studies have outlined the advantages and limitations of advertising messages. A recent review of the impact of humour on advertising has concluded that:

- — Humour attracts attention
- — Humour does not harm comprehension
- — Humour is not more effective at increasing persuasion
- — Humour does not enhance source credibility
- — Humour enhances "liking"
- — Humour that is relevant to the product is superior to humour unrelated to the product.
- — Audience factors (*e.g.* gender, ethnicity, age) affect the responses to humours advertising appeals.

— The nature of the product affects the appropriateness of a humorous treatment.

— Humour is more effective with existing products than with new products.

— Humour is more approprivate for low-involvement products and "feeling oriented" products than for high-involvement products.

There is evidence that audience characteristics may confound the effects of humour, perhaps the wisest policy for marketeers humorous advertising treatments to be certain of their appropriateness for the audiences and the product.

The effect of humour may be confounded on the characteristics of the audience. For example, younger, better educated and professional people are receptive audience for humorous messages. Humorous commercials seem to work best when presented in an action adventure environment, rather than in a situation comedy environment.

The wiser policy for marketeers to follow is to use humour selectively for products and audiences that seem to lend themselves strongly to this approach.

A study that examined the behavioural impact of humours promotions within a field setting found that relevant humour patronage are a negative impact.

SEX IN ADVERTISING

In highly permissive society, sex in advertising seems to promote the print media and the air waves. Sex in advertising ranges from the blatancy of nudes and obvious double entendre to devices so subtle it takes a trained observer to recognize them.

A study that compared sexual portrayal in magazines in 1964 versus 1984 found that the percentage of advertisements with sexual content did not change over the 20 year period, although the type of portrayal did. By 1988 however sex had become less explicit in advertising, as the public's fear of AIDS caused advertisers to turn to more romantic and less overfly sexual-themes. Sexual imagery is not likely to disappear from television commercial and print advertisements during the late 1990s, but it is likely to be handled more subtly than in the previous decade. There are many instances in which advertisers who have used sex as a thematic appeal have been very successful. Another instances, such as advertising has proved either damaging or simply ineffective. Consumer reaction to advertisements with sexual appeals is difficult to predict. Many psychologists believe that the skilful manupulation of sexual appeals in visual images in copy or in both may arouse subconscious desires that manifest themselves in the purchase of goods or services. Although sexual themes may attract a reader's attention, they rarely encourage curiosity about the product. A study found that mere product related thinking occurred in response to non-sexual appeals and that visual sexual elements in the advertisement more likely to be processed than the verbal content, drawing cognitive processing away from product or message evaluation. Those findings support the notion that sexual advertising appeals detract from the processing of message content.

Further, one study of sexually oriented advertisements compared the recall scores of advertisements that used sexual elements *(1)* as an attention getting device, *(2)* to display the product funetiga, *(3)* as fantasy images and *(4)* symbolically. It found that advertisements that used sexual themes and sexual elements solely as attention getting devices proved to have the lowest brand-recall scores. Advertisements in which sexual themes were presented as post of a fantasy fulfilment enjoyed good recall scores. Still better recall sources were obtained by advertisements that used sexual elements to demonstrate product function such as ads for bras or lingerie. The advertisements that received the highest recall scroes were those that used sexual elements symbolically, such as an advertisement for Eve cigarettes that featured the picture of a lighted cigarette lying horizontally across the top of an apple.

Further, men and women respond differently to sex in advertising. For example, perceptions among men of an ad's sexiness depend on the extent of nudity portrayed. For women, romantic content is the primary determinent an advertisement is "sexy". Even more interesting are gender differences regarding brand recall. Though extremely sexy advertisements negatively impact brand recall for women as well as men. Researchers have found that women can view advertisements that produce a high level of sexual arousal cannot remember anything about the product.

One thread seems to run through all the research findings regarding sex in advertisement, the advertiser must be sure that the product, the advertisement the target audience and the use of sexual themes and elements all work together. When sex is relevant to the product, it can be an extremely patent copy theme.

Betiman's Information Processing Model of Consumer Choice

Bettman's model of consumer choice portrays the consumer as possessing a limited capacity for processing information. When faced with a choice, the consumer rarely undertakes very complex analysis of available alternatives. Instead, the consumer typically employs simple decision strategies. These simplifying decision rules enable the consumer to arrive at a choice by sidestepping the overly burden some task of assessing all the information available about all the alternatives.

The Bettman model consists of a number of interrelated now charts that depict the various dimensions of the consumer choice process. The overview of the Bettman model in figure illustrates its seven basic components, *(1)* processing capacity, *(2)* motivation, *(3)* attention and perceptual encoding, *(4)* information acquisition and evaluation, *(5)* memory, *(6)* decision processes, *(7)* consumption and learning process. In addition the model includes mechanisms that continually scan the environment and receive and respond to interruptions.

Processing Capacity. The processing capacity component of the Bettman model presumes that individuals have only a limited capacity for processing information. Thus in making choices, consumers are likely to find complex computations and extensive information processing particularly difficult or burdensome. To deal with these demands, consumers are likely to select choice strategies or rules of thumb that make product selection an easier and less taxing process.

The processing capacity component influences the other major components of the model. This has important implications for the kinds and scope of choice strategies consumers are likely to employ.

Motivation. Since consumer choice is conceived as being purposeful, motivation is a central component of the Bettman model. It influences both the direction and the intensity of consumer choice and stimulus the consumer to seek the information required to evaluate and make a choice (*e.g.* a purchase).

Motivation provides momentum by means of a hierarchy-of-goals mechanism and scanner-and-interrupt mechanism. The hierarchy-of-goals mechanism is a dynamic force that takes the form of a series of intermediate subgoals that lead to a desired end state a choice. This mechanism is consistent with the notion of limited capacity; it suggests that a consumer gains experience in a particular choice area, he or she will no longer have to employ an elaborate hierarchy of goals to arrive at a decision. Instead, acquired experiences eventually provide the consumer with the basis for employing less demanding decision rules. Thus the goal-hierarchy mechanism channels the consumer's efforts in making a choice. Because companion scanner-and-interrupt mechanisms are linked to all the components of the Bettman. model, they will be discussed after we have considered the other components.

Attention and Perceptual Encoding. The attention and perceptual encoding components are closely tied to and heavily influenced by the consumer's goal hierarchy. There are two types of attention-voluntary attention, which is a conscious allocation of processing capacity to current goals, and involuntary attention, which is more of an automatic response to disruptive events. Each of these different types of attention influences how individuals progress in reaching goals and making choices.

The perceptual encoding clement is an extension of the attention component. It accounts for the process by which the consumer organizes and interprets perceived stimuli and provides insights into the need for additional information.

Memory. Memory is the component through which all information flows; it is where a consumer first begins the search for information on which to base a choice. If the internal information is insufficient, then the consum undertakes external search. Acquired information is stored either in short-term storage or in long term storage.

Decision Process. The Bettman model stresses that different types of choices are normally made in conjunction with the fulfilment of specific components of the model. Thus the choices made during the decision processes component are a particular form of choice rather than the choice. Specifically, this component deals with the application of heuristics or rules of thumb in the evaluation and selection of a specific brand.

The portion of the model emphasizes that the specific heuristics a consumer employs are influenced by both individual factors (*e.g.*, personality differences) and situational factors, thus, it is unlikely that a particular decision rule will be consistently employed by the same consumer in different situations, or by different consumers in the same situation.

Consumption and Learning Processes. The consumption and learning component of the Bettman model is concerned with the future utilization acquired after the purchase choice has been made and the selected alternative consumed. Such consumption experiences not only provide the consumer with information to be applied to future choice situations, but also provide the basis for developing or refining heuristics.

Scanner-and-Interrupt Mechanisms. Throughout the Bettman model are Scanner-and-interrupt mechanism that receive all tkms of messages from the environment. The scanner is continuously open to relevant information from the environment, the interrupt mechanism deals with messages that interfere with the process of making a choice.

SHETH-NEWMAN-GROSS MODEL OF CONSUMPTION VALUES

The Sheth-Newman Gross model of consumption values was recently developed to explain "why" consumers make the choices they do. Compared with the other comprehensive models explored in this appendix, if has fewer component parts and stresses a series of specific measurement approaches to secure the necessary consumer input required to test and apply the model. For this reason the Sheth-Newmen-Gross model is particularly relevant to the understanding and segmentation of markets. The model concentrates on assessing consumption relevant values that explain why consumers choose to buy or not to buy a specific product, why consumers choose one product type of over another, and why consumers choose one brand over another. The model can be applied to consumer choices involving a full range of product types.

The Sheth-Newman-Gross model is rooted in three central propositions: *(1)* consumer choice is a function of a small number of consumption values, *(2)* specific consumption values make differential contributions in any given choice situation; and *(3)* different consumption values are independent. Figure given below identifies the five consumption values that are the core of the model; namely, functional value, social value, emotional value, epistemic value and conditional value.

The Five Values Influencing Consumer Choice Behaviour.

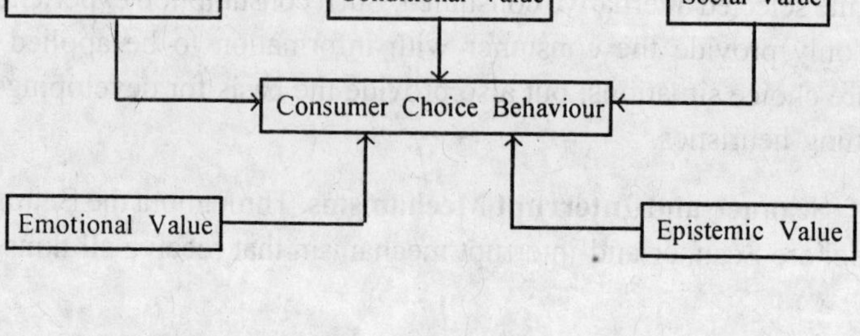

Functional Value. The functional value of a consumer choice is the perceived functional, utilitarian, or physical performance utility received from the choice's attributes. Functional value is particularly associated with economic utility theory, popularly expressed in terms of "rational economic man". At the heart of the functional value are such consumer-relevant atttitubes as reliability, durability, and price. For exmaple, the decision to purchase a particular automobile might be based on purchase price and promised fuel economy.

Social Value. The social value of a choice is the perceived utility acquired because of the association between one or more specific social groups and a consumer's choice. A consumers schoice gains social value by being linked with positively or negatively stereotyped demographic, socio-economic, and cultural ethnic groups. Choices involving highly visible products and goods or services to be "social shared" are often driven by social value.

Epistemic Value. The epistemic value of a choice is the perceived utility that comes from the choice's ability to foster curiosity, provide novelty and/or satisfy a desire for knowledge. New purchase and consumption experiences, especially, offer epistemic value, however, even a simple "change of pace" also provides the consumer with epistemic value.

Emotional Value. The emotional value of a choice is the perceived utility acquired from its capacity to stimulate the consumer's emotions or feelings. A choice acquires emotional value when associated with specific feelings or when it triggers or sustains those feelings. Products and services are frequently associated with emotional responses.

Conditional Value. Finally, the conditional value of a choice is the perceived utility acquired by a choice as an outcome of some particular situation or circumstances facing the consumer. For instance, some products are associated with a particular time or event (*e.g.* coffee at breakfast). Some products have specific climatic or location benefits. Some are associated with "once in lifetime" events and some are used only in emergency "situations (*e.g.*, a dentist on a Sunday afternoon).

The model proposed that consumer choice behaviour may be influenced by any of all of these five consumption values. As already noted, the attractiveness of the Sheth-Newman Gross model lies in the fact that the developers have not only considered the conceptual consumption of the model, but have also given considerable attention to how the five components values should be measured in the case of different consumer-choice situations. This makes the model of significant value to both consumer researchers and marketing practitioners.

❑

10

Consumer Attitudes and Attitude Change

Every time consumers are asked whether they like or dislike a product (*e.g.*, Classic Coke), a service (*e.g.*, Lawn King), an advertising theme (*e.g.*, AT&T's "Reach Out and Touch Someone"), or a particular retailer (*e.g.*, Banana Republic), they are being asked to express their attitudes. Within the realm of consumer behaviour, attitude research has been employed to study a wide range of critical marketing strategy questions. For example, attitude research is commonly undertaken to ascertain the likelihood that consumers will accept a proposed new-product idea, to gauge why a firm's target audience has not reacted more favourably to its revised promotional theme, or to learn how target customers are likely to react to a proposed change in the firm's packaging and label.

In fact, it is difficult to imagine any consumer research project that does not measure some aspect of consumer attitudes. As an outgrowth of this pervasive interest in consumer attitudes, it is not surprising that attitudes have received so much attention in the consumer behaviour literature.

In this chapter we will discuss the reasons' why attitude research has had such a pervasive impact on consumer behaviour. We will also discuss the properties that have made attitudes so attractive to consumer researchers, as well as some of the common frustrations encountered in conducting attitude research. Particular attention will be given to a number of important models relating to the structure and composition of attitudes. Finally, we will review the approaches frequently employed to measure consumer attitudes. We will continue our discussion of attitudes by focusing on the central topics of attitude formation and attitude change, and on a number of related issues.

What are Attitudes?

As the opening sentence of this chapter implies, attitudes are an expression of inner feelings that reflect whether a person is favourably or unfavourably predisposed to some "object" (*e.g.*, a brand, a service, a retail establishment). As an outcome of some psychological processes, attitudes are not directly observable, but must be inferred from what people say or from their behaviour. Consumer researchers therefore tend to assess attitudes by asking questions or making inferences from behaviour. For example, if a, researcher determined from questioning a consumer that the individual has consistently bought Panasonic products and recommends them to friends, the researcher would be likely to infer a positive attitude toward Panasonic products.

This illustration suggests that a whole universe of consumer behaviour sconsistent purchase, recommendations to others, top rankings, beliefs, evaluations, and intentions are related to attitudes. What, then, are attitudes? According to one popular definition, an attitude is a learned predisposition to respond in a consistently favourable or unfavourable manner with respect to a given object. Each part of this definition is an important property of an attitude and is critical to understanding the role that attitudes play in the examination of consumer behaviour.

The Attitude "Object"

The word object in our adopted definition of attitude is designed to be interpreted broadly. Anyone of many more specific concepts might be substituted in its place-issues, actions, behaviour, practices, persons, or events. In examining consumer behaviour, we would be inclined to substitute 'consumer' or marketing-related concepts, such as product category, brand, service, advertisement, price, or retailer.

In conducting attitude research, we might even be more specific. For example, if we were interested in ascertaining shoppers' attitudes toward a number of major mass merchandisers, our "object" might include Sears, J.C. Penney, and K mart; if we were examining consumer attitudes toward a number of major brands of soap, our "object" might include Dial, Ivory, Irish Spring, and Palmolive.

Attitudes Have Consistency

Another characteristic of an attitude is that it is relatively consistent with the behaviour that it reflects. However, we should avoid confusing consistency with permanence. Attitudes are not necessarily permanent; they do change. We will explore attitude change in the next chapter.

It is important to illustrate what we mean by consistency. Normally we expect consumer attitudes to correspond with behaviour; that is, if a segment of consumers report that they especially like Kodak film, we expect that they will buy Kodak film. Similarly, if these consumers are not particularly fond of Fuji film, we do not expect them to buy this brand of film. Thus, when consumers are free to act as they wish, we anticipate that their actions will be consistent with their attitudes. However, circumstances are not always uniform. Therefore we must consider the influence of the situation on consumer attitudes and behaviour.

Attitudes Are a Learned Predisposition

There is general agreement that attitudes are learned. This means that attitudes relevant to purchase behaviour are formed as an outgrowth of direct experience with the product, information acquired from others, and exposure to mass media (*e.g.*, advertising). Closely related to the idea that attitudes are learned is the realization that attitudes are not synonymous with behaviour, but reflect either a favourable or an unfavourable evaluation of the attitude object. As a pre. disposition, attitudes might have a motivational quality; that is, they might propel the consumer toward a particular behaviour.

Attitudes Occur Within a Situation

It is not immediately evident from our definition that attitudes occur within and are affected by the situation. Situations are events or circumstances that, at a point in time, influence the relationship between attitudes and behaviour. A situation can cause consumers to behave in a manner seemingly inconsistent with their attitudes. For instance, let us assume that a consumer purchases a different brand of coffee each time his inventory runs low. Although his brand switching may seem to reflect a negative attitude or dissatisfaction, it actually may have been influenced by a specific situation—the need to economize. Although the consumer may have a strong preference for Maxwell House coffee, a tight budget may influence him to purchase whatever brand is on "special" at the supermarket.

The opposite is also true. If a consumer purchases a can of Brim each time her supply runs low, we may erroneously infer that she has a favourable attitude toward Brim. On the contrary, the consumer may dislike the taste of Brim but may be following doctor's orders to reduce the amount of caffeine in her diet. She therefore regards Brim favourably as a means of accomplishing this goal.

In a similar vein, individuals can have different attitudes toward a particular behaviour, each corresponding to a particular situation. A man may feel it is suitable to eat lunch at McDonald's but may not consider it appropriate for dinner. In this case, McDonald's has its "time and place," which functions as a boundary indicating those situations when McDonald's is acceptable. However, if the individual is coming home late one night, feels exhausted and hungry, and spots a McDonald's, he may just decide to have "dinner" there. Why? Be cause it is late, he is tired and hungry, and McDonould's is convenient. Has he changed his attitude? Probably not.

In recent years, attention has been given to how consumer attitudes vary from situation to situation. For instance, one study examined whether consumer preferences for different fast-food chains operating in a midwestern city (*e.g.*, Arby's, Burger King,

McDonald's, and Wendy's) varied in terms of four eating situations (*i.e.*, lunch on a weekday, snack during a shopping trip, evening meal when rushed for time, and evening meal with family when not rushed for time). The results revealed some distinct differences in consumer preferences for the various fast-food restaurants, depending upon the anticipated eating situation. McDonald's, for example, was the frontrunner across all four eating situations, whereas Wendy's was found to be strongest with consumers who were seeking a place to have evening dinner with the family when not in a rush. The findings suggest that Wendy's might emphasize increasing consumer acceptance as a nice place to take the family for a leisurely (and inexpensive) dinner.

Tricomponent Attitude Model

Motivated by a desire to understand the attitude-behaviour relationship, behavioural scientists, especially social psychologists, have endeavoured to construct models that capture the underlying dimensions of an attitudes To this end, the focus has been on specifying more precisely the composition of an attitude in order to better explain or predict behaviour.

Attitudes are frequently portrayed as consisting of three major components: a cognitive component, an affective component, and a conative component (see Figure 1).

Structural Models of Attitudes

Now that we have defined what attitudes are and elaborated on their basic properties, it is appropriate that we examine several important attitude models: the tricomponent attitude model, single-component attitude models, and multi-attribute attitude models. Each of the models provides a somewhat different perspective as to the number of component parts of an attitude, and how those parts are arranged or interrelated.

The Cognitive Component

The first component of the tricomponent attitude model consists of a person's knowledge (cognitions) and perceptions that are acquired by a combination of direct experience with the attitude-object, and related information secured from various sources. This knowledge and resulting perceptions frequently take the form of beliefs; that is, the consumer believes that the attitude-object possesses various attributes and that specific behaviour will lead to specific outcomes.

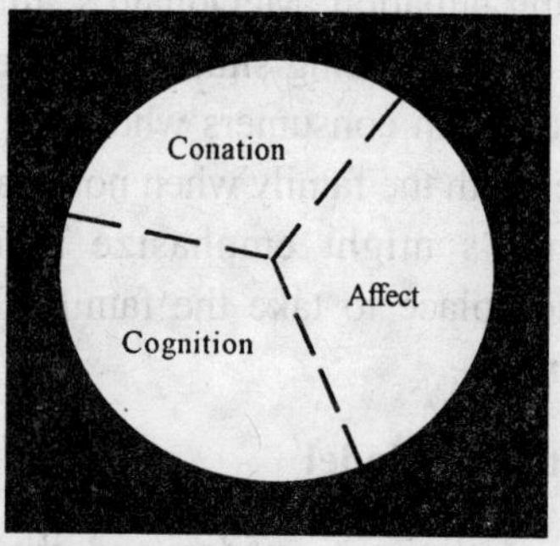

Figure 4. A Simple Representation of the Tricomponent Attitude Model

While capturing only a portion of a consumer's belief system toward two brands of mouthwash, Figure 2 illustrates just how complex a consumer's belief system can be. It is interesting that, with the exception of the attribut6 "dentist," the same basic attributes for both brands are included in the consumer's belief system. However, the beliefs about several of the attributes are different. For instance, the consumer sees Scope as tasting "sweet like a soft drink," whereas Listerine is perceived as tasting "like medicine." Also, the consumer does not. necessarily evaluate the same basic belief similarly for each brand. For example, with regard to long-lasting quality, Scope is evaluated positively, while Listerine is evaluated negatively.

The Conative Component

Conation, the final component of the tri-component attitude model, is concerned with the likelihood or tendency that an individual will undertake a specific action or behave in a particular way with regard to the attitude-object. According to some interpretations, the conative component may include the actual behaviour itself.

In marketing and consumer research, the conative component is frequently treated as an expression of the consumer's intention to buy. Buyer intention scales are employed to assess the likelihood of purchasing a product or behaving in a certain way.

Single-Component Attitude Models

In contrast to the tri-component perspective, researchers subscribing to a single-component attitude model treat the affective, or feeling, component as the attitude itself.

Following this viewpoint, a consumer's attitude toward various brands of 35mm cameras would be equal to the individual's overall evaluation of the comparative merit (*e.g.*, good versus bad, positive versus negative, favourable versus unfavourable) of the brands being considered (*i.e.*, the consumer's evoked set).

The single-component attitude model is especially popular with marketing researchers who want to save time and space by including a single evaluative scale on a questionnaire. However, although it is uncomplicated, the single-component model fails to provide useful insights as to what influences or explains a consumer's evaluative rating. To illustrate, two consumers may possess the same positive attitude (*i.e.*, the same level of affect) toward Dial soap, with quite different salient beliefs. One may like it because of its deodorant protection, while the other may like it because of its pleasant fragrance. Unless the researcher measured each consumer's beliefs and evaluations about each attribute of Dial, all that would be known is that both possess the same basic attitude or level of affect toward Dial soap. Thus we would be left in the dark as to the underlying knowledge and beliefs the consumers bring to bear in arriving at their overall assessment. Moreover, we would not be provided with any relevant insights about the relationship between their evaluations and the consumers' intention to buy.

To overcome the shortcomings of the single-component attitude model, attitude researchers have suggested a compromise between the broadly conceived tri-component attitude model and the narrowly focused single-component model. The resulting modified single-component attitude model still considers affect to be the attitude, but includes cognition and conation as interrelated and important factors that influence the affective component (see Figure 2). In a sense, the modified model is a rearrangement of the tri-component model with the affect component treated as the attitude, and the two other components downgraded to supporting roles.

Modified single-component attitude models are also called multi-attribute attitude models.

Multi-Attribute Attitude Models

Multi-attribute attitude models are particularly appealing to both consumer researchers and marketing practitioners because they examine attitudes in terms of selected product attributes or beliefs. While there are many variations of this type of attitude model, those proposed by Fishbein and his associates have stimulated the greatest amount of research interest. We have selected three Fishbein models to consider here because of their potential merit in applied consumer behaviour research: the attitude-toward-object model, the attitude-toward-behaviour model, and the theory of reasoned action model.

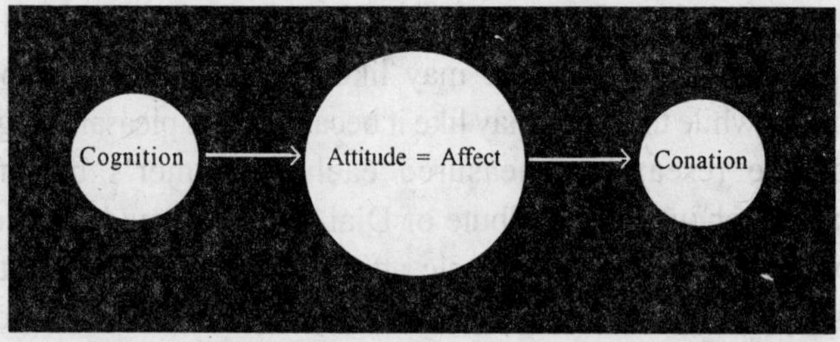

Figure 2

The Attitude-Toward-Object Model

The attitude-toward-object model is especially suitable for measuring attitudes toward a product or specific brands (*i.e.*, the object). In accordance with this model, a consumer's attitude is defined as a function of the presence (or absence) and evaluation of a number of product-specific beliefs or product attributes possibly possessed by a product or specific brands of a product. Following from this, consumers will generally have favourable attitudes toward those brands they assess as having an adequate level of positive attributes, and unfavourable attitudes toward those brands they feel have an inadequate level of desired attributes or too many negative attributes. Table 1 lists two different belief systems (one favourable and the other unfavourable) for two different consumers.

The Fishbein attitude-toward-object model is usually depicted in the form of the following equation:

$$\text{Attitude}_0 = \sum_{i=1}^{n} b_i e_i$$

where Attitude_0 is a separately assessed overall measure of affect for or against the attitude-object (*e.g.*, a product, brand, service, retail establishment); b_i is the strength of the belief that the attitude-object contains the *i*th attribute (*e.g.*, the likelihood that Duncan Hines cake mix tastes "homemade"); e_i is the evaluative dimension associated with the *i*th attribute (*e.g.*, how good or bad is the quality of being "homemade"); and Σ indicates that there are n salient attributes over which the bi and e_i combinations are summated.

Tabel 1. Two Hypothetical Bellief Systems Concerning IBM Personal Computers

Consumer 1 (mainly negative)
IBM PCs are expensive.
IBM PCs are too complex.
IBM PCs are used by businesses.
IBM PCs are high quality.

Consumer 3 (mainly positive)

IBM PCs are high quality.
IBM PCs are dependable.
IBM PCs are used by businesses.
IBM PCs are worth the investment.

Source: Inspired by Icek Ajzen and Martin Fishbein, understanding Attitudes and Predicting Social Behaviour (Englewood Cliffs, N.J. Prentice Hall, 1980).

Before moving on to the next model proposed by Fishbein and his colleagues, it should be pointed out that numerous modified versions of the Fishbein attitude-toward-object model have been suggested in the consumer behaviour and marketing literature. These models, which have been referred to as "ad hoc" or "intuitive," frequently examine the relationship between some overall evaluation of a brand (*e.g.*, preference, affect, intention, or brand choice) and a combination of consumer beliefs as to the brand's possession of specific product attributes and the importance attached to these attributes. As a group, these intuitive models can be criticized for not faithfully testing the attitude models that were borrowed from social psychology.

The Attitude-Toward-Behaviour Model

The focus of Fishbein's attitude-toward-behaviour model is the individual's attitude toward behaving or acting with respect to an object, rather than the attitude toward the object itself.

The appeal of the attitude-toward-behaviour model is that it seems to correspond more closely with actual behaviour than does the attitude-toward-object model. For instance, knowing a consumer's attitude about the act of purchasing a $40,000 BMW car (*i.e.*, attitude toward the behaviour) is more revealing about the potential act of purchasing than simply knowing the consumer's attitude toward the car (*i.e.*, attitude toward the object). This seems logical, for a consumer might have a positive attitude toward the $40,000 car, but a negative attitude as to the prospects of purchasing such an expensive automobile.

The attitude-toward-behaviour model is depicted by the following equation:

$$\text{Attitude}_{(beh)} = \sum_{i=1}^{n} b_i e_i$$

where $\text{Attitude}_{(beh)}$ is a separately assessed overall measure of affect for or against carrying out a specific action or behaviour (*e.g.*, buying, preparing, or serving a Duncan Hines cake); b_i is the strength of the belief that an ith specific action will lead to a specific outcome (*e.g.*, that the preparation of a Duncan Hines cake will indeed taste "homemade"); e_i is an evaluation of the ith outcome (*e.g.*, the "favourableness of a cake tasting homemadc); and Σ indicates that there are n salient outcomes over which the bj and e_i combinations are summated.

Theory of Reasoned Action Model

The theory of reasoned action builds on the earlier research conducted by Fishbein and his associates. It represents a comprehensive arrangement of attitude components integrated into a structure that is designed to lead to both better prediction and better explanations of behaviour. Like the basic tri-component attitude model, the theory of reasoned action incorporates a cognitive component, an affective component, and a conative component; however, these are arranged in a pattern different from that of the tri-component model.

Figure 4 is a model of the theory of reasoned action. Examine it carefully. Working backward from behaviour (*e.g.*, the act of purchasing a particular product or brand), the model suggests that the best predictor of behaviour is intention to act. Thus if consumer researchers were solely interested in predicting behaviour, they would directly measure intention (*i.e.*, use an intention-to act scale). However, if they were also interested in understanding the underlying factors that contribute to intention to act in a particular consumer situation, they would look behind intention and consider the factors that lead to intention; that is, the consumer's attitude-toward-behaviour and the subjective norm.

Continuing with the same basic logic, attitude-toward-behaviour can be directly measured as affect (*i.e.*, a measure of overall favourability toward the act of purchasing a product or brand). Further, as with intention, we can get behind the attitude to its underlying dimensions (see the discussion of the attitude-toward-behaviour model).

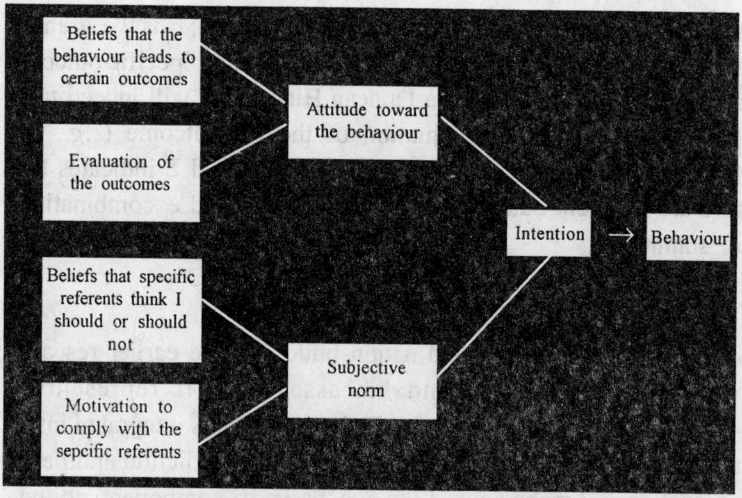

A Simplified Version of the Theory of Reasoned Action

Figure 3

In accordance with this expanded model, to understand intention we must also measure the subjective norm that influences an individual's intention to act. A subjective norm can be measured directly by assessing a consumer's feelings as to what relevant others (family, friends, roommates, co-workers) would think of the action being contemplated; that is, would they look favourably or unfavourably on the anticipated action? Within a consumer behavior context, if a college student were considering purchasing micro-stereo equipment for his dormitory room and stopped to ask himself what his parents or roommate would think of such behaviour (*i.e.*, approve or disapprove), such a reflection would constitute his subjective norm.

As with an attitude, consumer ressarchers can get behind the subjective norm to the underlying factors that are likely to produce it. They accomplish this by assessing the normative beliefs that the individual attributes to relevant others, as well as the individual's motivation to comply with each of the relevant others. For instance, consider the student who is contemplating the purchase of micro-stereo equipment. To understand his subjective norm about the anticipated purchase, we would have to identify his relevant others (parents and roommate); his beliefs as to how each would respond to his purchase of the equipment (*e.g.*, "Mom and Dad would consider the purchase extravagant, but my roommate would love it"); and finally, his motivation to comply with his parents and/or roommate.

The above discussion and examples suggest that the theory of reasoned action is a series of interrelated attitude components (*i.e.*, beliefs precede attitude and normative beliefs precede subjective norms; attitudes and subjective norms precede intention; and intention precedes actual behaviour).

Consistent with the theory of reasoned action, an attitude is not as strongly or as directly linked to behaviour as intention is linked to behaviour. In part, this flows from the observation that intention is usually more highly associated with behaviour than is attitude.

Why study attitudes at all, if intention is ultimately a better predictor of behaviour? The answer is simple: Intention may be a better predictor, but it does not provide an adequate explanation of behaviour. If marketers want to understand why consumers act as they do, they require something more than a basically mechanical measure of what consumers expect to do (*e.g.*, their buying intentions). Similarly, a measure of affect may predict an attitude; however, marketers usually want to know the underlying or salient attributes or beliefs that produce the specific attitude.

THE MEASUREMENT OF ATTITUDES

Observation of Behaviour

Since we cannot get inside consumers' heads to observe their attitudes directly, we must rely on indirect measures of attitudes. One such measurement approach is to observe consumers' behaviour and to infer their attitudes from their behaviour.

The practice of inferring attitudes from behaviour is done constantly, not only by professional researchers, but by each of us in the course of our daily lives. For instance, if you were to observe that the person ahead of you on the supermarket checkout line was buying five cans of Bumble Bee tuna, you might conclude that several members of the shopper's family liked the brand.

In much the same way as you might informally observe and draw conclusions from another's behaviour, so do professional researchers observe behaviour. The difference is that they are trained observers and they scrutinize consumer behaviour in order to draw conclusions that will become part of a research report.

Although observational research is quite useful, drawing conclusions about consumers' attitudes from their behaviour is often quite difficult and very likely to be subjective. For instance, the shopper who was observed purchasing five cans of tuna fish might have done so to take advantage of the store's special low price, rather than because family members particularly liked the brand.

It is difficult for an observer, even a highly trained one, to be confident about inferring attitudes from a single action, in a single situation. However, if the researcher were to observe the same behaviour at different points in time (*e.g.*, see the same shopper purchase the same brand of tuna fish on subsequent trips to the supermarket), or see the shopper purchase the tuna fish under different circumstances (*e.g.*, when the brand was not on store special), then the researcher might be more confident that the behavior reflected a positive attitude. Since researchers seldom have the opportunity to observe the same consumers repeatedly, it is common practice to employ observations as a supplement to other research approaches, rather than as the primary research method.

Qualitative Research Methods

Attitude researchers have found qualitative research methods, especially depth interviews and focus group sessions, to be very useful in understanding the nature of consumers' attitudes.

While these two research methods differ in composition both are closely associated with motivational research and have their roots in the psychoanalytic and clinical aspects of psychology. In particular, both stress open-ended and free-response types of questioning that stimulate respondents to reveal their inner thoughts and beliefs.

These two popular qualitative research methods are regularly employed in the early stages of attitude research to pinpoint relevant product-related beliefs or attributes. To illustrate, let us assume that as a result of several focus group sessions, a leading marketer of erasable ballpoint pens notices that users are more interested in the ease of erasing errors than in the longevity of the pen. This finding suggests that the pen company, in advertising its pen, should stress the ease of erasing errors, rather than the long life of the pen.

As the illustration implies, depth interviews and focus groups are frequently conducted to determine which product or brand attributes potential product users are likely to use in judging alternative brands. A sample of product attributes associated with four different product categories. Such lists of attributes are often developed from depth interviews, focus group sessions, and related forms of qualitative research.

Self-Report Attitude Scales

The most common way of assessing consumer attitudes is through the administration of a questionnaire containing attitude scales. While a great many attitude-scaling procedures have been proposed, the three most popular are Likert scales, semantic differential scales, and rank-order scales.

Likert Scales

The Likert scale is by far the most popular form of attitude scaling because it is easy for researchers to prepare and uncomplicated for consumers to respond. Likert scales can be recognized by their characteristic "agreement" scale, which provides respondents with tbe opportunity to indicate their degree of agreement or disagreement with a series of statements that fully describe the attitude-object under investigation. A sample of Likert scales as they were employed in a consumer attitude survey of flea market shopping experiences.

A principal attraction of Likert scales is that they give researchers the option of treating the response to each attitude statement as a separate scale, or combining the responses of items that pertain to the same basic attitude dimension into a composite or weighted attitude score. It is because of this feature that Likert scales are frequently referred to as summated scales.

Semantic Differential Scales

Similar to the Likert scale, the semantic differential scale is relatively easy to construct and administer. The scale typically consists of a series of bipolar an tonyms (adjectives or phrases, such as good-bad, liberal-conservative, like-dislike, sweet-sour, high priced-low priced) which, when anchored at the ends of a 5-point or 7-point scale, provide respondents with an opportunity to evaluate a concept (*e.g.*, United Airlines, 7-Eleven stores, All-Temperaturė Cheer). The major feature of the semantic differential is that it lends itself to the creation of profiles of consumer attitudes that can be depicted in graphic form.

A popular application of the semantic differential scaling procedure is in the examination of shoppers' attitudes toward competitive retail establishments. Such studies are frequently referred to as store image studies.

Rank-Order Scales

As its name implies, a rank-order scale has subjects rank a set of attitude-objects (*e.g.*, brands of peanut butter) in terms of some criterion (*e.g.*, fresh taste). Rank-order scaling procedures are especially suitable in attitude measurement because they allow consumers to evaluate alternative brands, and thus they are an important way of assessing brand preference or brand choice.

ATTITUDE FORMATION

How do young people form their initial attitudes toward using computers in general, an Apple, AT&T, or IBM computers in particular? How do family members and friends, admired celebrities, and mass media advertising influence the establishment of attitudes about owning and using personal computers? Why do some attitudes seem to be maintained indefinitely (*e.g.*, a positive attitude toward a particular political party)? The answers to such questions are important to marketers, for unless they have some idea of how attitudes are formed, they are unlikely to be able to understand or affect consumer attitudes or behaviour.

Our examination of attitude formation is divided into three areas: the learning of attitudes, the sources of influence on attitude formation, and the impact of personality on attitude formation.

Learning of Attitudes

When we speak of the formation of an attitude, we are referring to the shift from no attitude toward a given object (*e.g.*, a banana) to some attitude toward it (*e.g.*, a banana is a fruit to put in breakfast cereal). To understand this shift (attitude formation) requires an appreciation of the basic learning processes involved. We will briefly focus on how attitudes are learned by considering how the learning theories discussed in relate to attitude formation.

Classical Conditioning

An originally neutral stimulus, such as the brand name for a new product, can produce a favourable or unfavourable attitude if it is repeatedly followed by or associated with a reward or punishment. The idea of family branding is based on this form of attitude learning; by giving a new brand of perfume, Coco, the benefit of a well-known and respected family name—Chanel perfume—the marketers are counting on an extension of the favourable attitude already associated with the Chanel brand name to the new product.

Similarly, marketers who associate their new products with well-known and respected celebrities are trying to create a positive bond between the celebrity who already enjoys a positive attitude and the "neutral" new product. They hope to transfer recognition and goodwill from the celebrity to their product so that potential consumers will more quickly acquire a positive attitude toward the new product. This is the theory on which licensing is based.

Instrumental Conditioning

Consumers can purchase a brand without having an attitude toward it. They may buy a brand,. for instance, because it is the only product of its kind left on a store shelf; or they may make a trial purchase of a new brand from a product category they feel does not warrant more information than an awareness of its existence. If they find the brand satisfactory, they may eventually develop a favourable attitude toward the brand.

Cognitive Learing Theory

In situations where consumers are quite involved in a purchase decision, cognitions (knowledge and beliefs) are likely to be a major input in the formation of attitudes. If a shopper who is interested in a new video camera learns that automatic focusing and low light level capability are two essential attributes of a fine-quality video camera, and that certain of Panasonic's video cameras possess these two features, then the shopper could be expected to form a positive attitude toward Panasonic video cameras. Generally speaking, the more information (up to a point) an individual has about a product or service, the more likely he or she is to have an attitude toward it—either positive or negative.

Information Processing

As an outgrowth of cognitive learning theory, the focus of the information processing framework centers on the limits of consumers' abilities or interests to process purchase-related information. Consumers often use only a relatively small amount of the information available to them. Experimental research suggests that the summation of the three most important beliefs about a product dominates when it comes to the formation of attitudes, and that less important beliefs provide little additional input.)

Sources of Influence in Attitude Formation

Although learning theories tell us how attitudes may be established, identification of the sources from which consumers obtain information, advice, and influence is also important. The principal sources that affect the formation of consumer attitudes include experience, personal influence, and mass media.

Direct and Past Experience

The primary means by which attitudes are formed toward goods and services are through the direct experience of trying and evaluating them. Recognizing the importance of direct experience, marketers frequently attempt to stimulate trial of new products by offering cents-off coupons or even free-trial samples. Their objective is to get consumers to experience the new product and then to evaluate it. If a product proves satisfactory, it is likely that consumers will form positive attitudes and possibly purchase the product when they again have need of it.

Personal Influence

As we come in contact with others, especially family, close friends, and admired individuals (*e.g.*, a respected teacher), we acquire attitudes that influence our lives. The family is an extremely important source of influence when it comes to the establishment of attitudes, for it is the family that provides us with many of our basic values and a wide range of less central beliefs. For instance, children growing up in France might initially dislike wine as a beverage; but by observing other family members, they generally learn to enjoy it with most of their meals. In a similar manner, young American children who are exposed to sweet foods and candy as part of their daily diet often retain a taste for (and positive attitude toward) sweets as adults.

Exposure to Mass Media

It seems inevitable that in a country where people have easy access to newspapers and an almost infinite variety of general and special-interest magazines and television and cable channels, mass media advertising would be an important source of information to influence our attitudes.

Personality Factors

In addition to recognizing the critical role that learning theory plays in the understanding of attitude formation and the contribution that various sources of information make in influencing consumer attitudes, it is also important to realize that personality plays an important role in attitude formation. Introverted individuals, for instance, are likely to express their introversion in negative attitudes toward flashy cars, dancing classes, group tours, and public activities. Similarly, consumer attitudes toward new products and new consumption situations are strongly influenced by their own personality characteristics.

ATTITUDE CHANGE

As we begin our discussion of attitude change, it is important to recognize that what we have said about attitude formation is also basically true of attitude change. That is, attitude changes are learned, they are influenced by personal experience and other sources of information, and personality affects both the receptivity and the speed with which attitudes are likely to be altered.

Strategies of Attitude Change

Altering consumer attitude is a key strategy consideration for most marketers. If a marketer is in the fortunate position of having its brand possess the lion's share of the market, the overriding goal is likely to be to fortify the existing positive attitudes of its customers so that they will not succumb to the blandishments of competitors and defect. For instance, in product categories like yogurt, where the Dannon brand has dominated for years, or mustard, where Gulden's has dominated, most competitors take aim at the market leaders when developing their own marketing strategies.

To understand the dynamics of attitude change, we will examine a number of attitude change strategies that can be classified under the following categories: *(1)* changing the basic motivational function, *(2)* associating the product with a specific group or event, *(3)* relating to conflicting attitudes, *(4)* altering components of the multi-attribute model, and *(5)* changing beliefs about competitors' brands.

Changing the Basic Motivational Function

One way of changing attitudes toward a product or brand is to make new needs prominent. One attitude change theory that demonstrates how changing basic motivations can change attitudes is known as the functional approach. With this approach, we classify attitudes in terms of four functions: the utilitarian function, the ego-defensive function, the value-expressive function, and the knowledge function.

The Utilitarian Function. We hold certain brand attitudes partly because of the brand's utility. If a product has helped us in the past, even in a small way, our attitude toward it tends to be favourable. One way of changing attitudes in favour of a product is by showing people that it can solve a utilitarian goal they may not have considered. To illustrate, while clothing ads normally stress fashion, the advertisement for Bion II fabric coating stresses its utilitarian benefits (*i.e.*, it allows body heat and vapor to escape).

The Ego-Defensive Function. We want to protect our self-concept from inner feelings of doubt. Cosmetics and personal hygiene products, by acknowledging this need, increase their relevancy to the consumer and heighten the possibility of a favourable attitude by offering reassurance to the consumer's self-concept. Dry Idea, an aerosol anti-perspirant and deodorant, applies the ego-defensive function in a magazine ad that states: "Gain Control: Never Let Them See You Sweat".

The Value-Expressive Function. Attitudes are one expression of general values, lifestyle, and outlook. If a consumer segment generally holds a high evaluation (*i.e.*, a positive attitude) towards being "in fashion," and high-fashion clothing and accessories are treated as symbols of that lifestyle, then attitudes toward fashion and fashionable clothing will reflect these positive attitudes. If a consumer segment holds a low evaluation of the "fashionable life," however, this segment will have negative attitudes toward the lifestyle that faddish fashion symbolizes.

The Knowledge Function. Individuals have a strong need to know and understand the people and things with whom they come in: contact, especially if they think they might influence behaviour. The "need to know," a cognitive need, is important to marketers concerned with product positioning. Indeed, most product and brand positionings are attempts to satisfy consumers' needs to know and increase their positive attitudes toward the brand by clarifying its advantages over competitive brands. For instance, ads for secret, a deodorant targeted to women, point out that a woman's pH level can be higher than a man's. The inclusion of color photographs showing differences in male and female pH levels appeals to the knowledge function and is designed to positively influence female attitudes toward secret deodorant. One consumer-oriented study that applied the four-function framework to an examination of attitudes toward playing tennis found it to be useful, and susgests that different consumers may like or dislike the same product or service for different reasons. For instance, although two consumers might both have very positive attitudes toward a head tennis racquet, one may be responding to the fact that the racquet provides greater control (a utilitarian function), while the other may be reacting to the masculine image of the sports celebrities used in head's advertising (an ego-defensive function).

Relating to Conflicting Attitudes

Attitude change strategies can also be designed to take advantage of actual or potential conflict between attitudes. Specifically, if consumers can be made to see that their brand attitude is in conflict with another more basic attitude, they may be "forced" to change their evaluation of the brand.

A simple theoretical notion-balance theory shows how this attitude change mechanism works. It assumes that individuals attempt to avoid inconsistency and instead seek consistency, balance, or harmony. Specifically, balance theory proposes that consumers sub-consciously alter their attitudes in such a way as to place their attitudes in balance. In general terms, the theory can be thought of as a triangular relationship between an individual and two attitudes that are initially in conflict. To illustrate how balance theory works, let us consider two friends, Peter and John, their attitudes toward a brand of toothpaste, and one friend's attitude toward the other. The key attitudinal relationships are: *(1)* Peter's attitude toward Colgate toothpaste, *(2)* Peter's attitude toward his friend John, and *(3)* John's attitude toward Colgate toothpaste.

There are several instances where Peter's attitude might change in direction:

1. Peter initially has a negative attitude toward Colgate, and John, an admired dentist friend, recommends Colgate. This personal/professional endorsement is likely to represent a strong case for Peter to change his preliminary negative attitude to a positive attitude toward Colgate.
2. Peter initially has a positive attitude toward Colgate, and his friend John, who happens to be a dentist, recommends Crest. This situation also represents a strong, case for attitude change. Here Peter's initially positive attitude toward Colgate may be replaced by a favourable attitude toward Crest.

The key to changing attitudes by relating them to other attitudes is to choose object-attitudes that are very strong and clearly conflicting with the one the marketer wishes to change. For instance, if consumers really respect a particular medium (*e.g.*, The Wall Street journal), they may re-evaluate their negative attitude toward a particular product that advertises in the medium. Similarly, if a product endorsement by an admired person is both strong and in conflict with a consumer's preexisting views, it may effect an attitude change.

BEHAVIOUR PRECEDING ATTITUDES

Our discussion of attitude formation and attitude change has stressed the traditional "rational" view that consumers develop their attitudes prior to actions (*e.g.*, "know what you are doing before you do it"). There. are alternatives to this attitude-precedes-behaviour perspective, which upon careful analysis are likely to be just as logical and rational. We will consider two alternatives, cognitive dissonance theory and attribution theory, each of which provides a different explanation as to why behaviour might be expected to precede attitudes.

Cognitive Dissonance Theory

According to cognitive dissonance theory, discomfort or dissonance occurs when a consumer receives new information concerning a belief or an attitude that is in conflict with the original belief or attitude. For instance, when consumers have made a commitment to buy a product, particularly an expensive one such as an automobile, the unique positive qualities of the brands not selected remind the consumers that they may not have made the wisest choice. Because purchase decisions often require some amount of compromise, such feelings of cognitive dissonance especially when occurring after a purchase (*i.e.*, postpurchase dissonance) are quite normal; nevertheless, they are likely to leave consumers with an uneasy feeling about their prior beliefs or actions.

Post-purchase dissonance is discussed here within the context of changes in behaviour leading to changes in attitudes because the conflicting thoughts or dissonant information that follow a purchase are seen as prime factors that induce consumers to change attitudes so that they will be consonant with the actual purchase behaviour. Thus attitude change is seen as an outcome of behaviour.

To illustrate how attitude change occurs within the context of post-purchase dissonance, let us return to the toothpaste example II The thought (*i.e.*, the belief) that "All fluoride toothpastes taste bad" is dissonant with the behaviour of using Colgate Toothpaste daily. To reduce the dissonance arising out of this conflict, the consumer can elect one or both of the following basic strategies: *(1)* introduce new cognitive beliefs supporting the original attitude or behavior, or *(2)* reevaluate the conflicting beliefs to create consonance. To make the daily use of Colgate consonant with the negative belief of unpleasant taste, the consumer, can introduce a new supportive belief—*e.g.*, "The reason why I had no cavities on my last visit to the dentist was because I have been using a toothpaste with fluoride." Alternatively, the consumer may reevaluate the dissonant belief and reject it—*e.g.*, "I don't mind the taste of fluoride toothpaste." .

What makes post-purchase dissonance relevant to marketing strategists is the premise that dissonance propels consumers to take steps to reduce the unpleasant feelings created by the rival thoughts.

A variety of tactics are open to consumers to reduce post-purchase dissonance. The consumer could rationalize the decision as being wise, seek out advertisements that support the choice (while avoiding those of dissonance-creating competitive brands), try "selling" friends on the positive features of the brand, or look to satisfied owners for their reassurance.

In addition to such consumer-initiated tactics to reduce post-purchase uncertainty, a marketer can relieve consumer dissonance by including messages in its advertising specifically aimed at reinforcing consumer decisions, offering a stronger guarantee or warranty, increasing the number and effectiveness of its services, or providing detailed brochures on how to use its products correctly.

Attribution Theory

As a group of loosely interrelated social psychological principles, attribution theory attempts to explain how people assign causality to events in terms of either their own behaviour or the behaviour of others. In other words, a person might say "I contributed to Cancer Care, because it really helps people in need," or "He tried to persuade me to buy that unknown washing machine because he makes a bigger commission." In attribution theory, the underlying question is why: "Why did I do this?" "Why did he try to get me to switch brands?" This process of making inferences about one's own or another's behaviour is a major component of attitude formation and change.

Attribution theory portrays attitude formation and change as an outgrowth of people's interpretations of their own behaviour and experiences.

Self-Perception Theory

Of the various perspectives on attribution theory that have been proposed, individuals' inferences or judgments as to the causes of their own behaviour, kdown as self-perception theory, are a good beginning point for a discussion of attribution.

In terms of consumer behaviour, self-perception theory suggests that attitudes develop as consumers look at and make judgments about their oum behaviour. Simply stated, if a woman observes that she routinely purchases The Wall Street journal on her way to work, she is apt to conclude from such behavior that she likes The Wall Street journal (*i.e.*, she has a positive attitude toward this newspaper).

Internal and External Attributions. Drawing inferences from one's own behaviour is not always as simple or clear-cut as the newspaper example might suggest. To appreciate the complexity of self-perception theory, it is useful to distinguish between internal and external attributions. Let us assume that you have just finished baking your first apple pie and that it is delicious. If upon tasting this "masterpiece" you think to yourself, "I'm really a naturally good baker," this statement would be an example of an internal attribution. It is an internal attribution because you are giving yourself credit for the outcome (*e.g.*, your ability, your skill, or your effort). That is, you are saying, "This pie is good because of me." On the other hand, if you were to conclude that the successful apple pie was due to factors beyond your control (*e.g.*, ingredients, the assistance of a friend, or just "luck"), this would be an example of an external attribution. Here you might be saying, "This pie is good because of b ginner's luck."

This distinction between internal and external attributions may be of strategic marketing importance. For instance, it would generally be in the best interests of a firm such as Pillsbury if bakers, especially in-experienced ones, internalized their successful baking experiences. If they internalize such positive experiences, it seems more likely they will repeat the behaviour and perhaps start baking on a regular basis. Alternatively, however, if they were to externalize their success, it would be preferable that they attribute it to Pillsbury ingredients, rather than to an incidental environmental factor such as "beginner's luck," or a friend's "foolproof" recipe.

According to the principle of defensive attribution, consumers are likely to accept credit personally for success (internal attribution), and to credit failure to others or to outside events (external attribution). For this reason, it is crucial that marketers offer uniformly high-quality products that allow consumers to perceive themselves as the reason for the success-*i.e.*, "I'm competent." Moreover, a company's advertising should serve to reassure consumers, particularly in-experienced ones, that its products will not let them down but will make them "heroes" instead.

Foot-in-the-door Technique. Self-perception theorists have explored situations where consumer compliance with a small or simple request affects subsequent attempts to gain compliance with a more substantial request. This strategy, which is commonly referred to as the foot-in-the-door technique, is based on the premise that individuals look at their prior behaviour (compliance with the minor request) and come to the conclusion that they are the kind of person who says yes to such requests (*i.e.*, an internal attribution). If effective, such self-attribution serves to increase the likelihood that they will say yes to the more substantial request. Someone who donates $5 to Cancer Research may be persuaded to donate a much larger amount if properly approached. The initial donation is, in effect, the foot-in-the-door.

Applications of the foot-in-the-door technique have concentrated on how specific incentives (*e.g.*, cents-off coupons of varying amounts) ultimately influence consumer attitudes and subsequent purchase behaviour. The research has generally found that different-size incentives tend to create different degrees of internal attribution, which in turn lead to different amounts of attitude change. For instance, individuals who try a brand without any inducements, or individuals who repeatedly buy the brand, are progressively more likely to infer increasingly positive attitudes toward the brand from their respective behaviors (*e.g.*, "I buy this brand because I like it"). In contrast, individuals who try a free sample are least committed to changing their attitudes toward the brand ("I tried this brand because it was free").

Attributions Towards Others

Although consumer researchers usually focus most of their attention on self-perception theory, they are also interested in understanding attributions toward others. Attributions toward others would seem to have a wide variety of potential applications within the realm of consumer behaviour and marketing. As suggested earlier in this section, every time a person asks "Why?" about a statement or action of another person—a family member, a friend, a salesperson-attribution theory is relevant. For example, if a husband and wife were in an audio store contemplating the purchase of a new compact stereo system, the salesperson's recommendation that they purchase a Pioneer system. which cost $300 more than the one they were initially considering would logically lead to the question "Why?" If the couple conclude that the salesperson has suggested it because of its superior features, then they are likely to judge the salesperson's motives as "sincere" and will possibly purchase the more expensive model. However, if they conclude that the salesperson is interested only in the greater commission from selling th more expensive model, then they might judge the salesperson as "insincere" and be unlikely to buy the more expensive model. Indeed, they might leave and go elsewhere because they no longer trust the salesperson or the store. The consumer is really asking, "Is the salesperson trying to sell me the more expensive model because of the superiority of the model or because of the increased commission?"

Attributions Towards Things

Attributions toward things also have considerable appeal for consumer researchers, especially since a product or service can be thought of as a "thing."1? It is in the area of judging product performance that consumers are most likely to form product attributions. Specifically, they want to find out why a product meets or does not meet their expectations. In this regard, they could attribute the product's success (or failure) to themselves, to the product itself, to other people or situations, or to some combination of these factors.

How We Test our Attributions

After making initial attributions of a product's performance or a person's words or actions, we often attempt to determine if the inference we made is correct. According to a leading attribution theorist, individuals acquire conviction about particular observations by acting like "naive scientists"; that is, by collecting additional information in an attempt to confirm (or disconfirm) prior inferences. In collecting such information, they often employ the following criteria:

1. **Distinctiveness.** The consumer attributes an action to a particular person or product if the action occurs when the person or product is present, and does not occur in its absence.

2. **Consistency over time.** Each time the person or product is present, the consumer's reaction must be the same, or nearly so.

3. **Consistency over Modality.** The reaction must be the same even though the situation in which it occurs varies.

4. **Consensus.** The action is perceived the same way by other consumers.

A consumer behaviour example illustrates how each of these criteria are used to assess inferences about product performance and people's actions. If a homeowner (let us call him Jim) who prides himself on his lawn observes that his grass seems to be more evenly cut with his new Lawn-Boy mower than with his former lawnmower, he is likely to credit the new Lawn-Boy for the improved appearance of his lawn (*i.e.*, distinctiveness). Furthermore, if Jim finds that his new Lawn-Boy produces the same high-quality results each time he uses it, he tends to be more confident about his initial observation (*i.e.*, the inference has consistency over time). Similarly, he will also be more confident if he finds that his satisfaction with the Lawn-Boy extends across a wide range of other related tasks, such as mulching grass and picking up leaves (*i.e.*, consistency over modality). Finally, Jim will have still more confidence in his inferences to the extent that his friends who own Lawn-Boys have also had similar experiences (*i.e.*, consensus).

Much like Jim, we go about gathering additional information from our experiences with people and things, which we use to test our initial inferences.

Clearly, attributions are quite relevant to consumers' satisfaction with a product, a salesperson, or even a retail establishment. Moreover, since attributions are closely associated with consumer satisfaction, we can expect that an attribution perspective is likely to become more popular as we increasingly look at the public policy effects of advertising substantiation, packaging legislation, sales cooling-off laws, and product liability practices.

❐

11

Personality and Buying Behaviour

Marketeers have long been intrigued by the possibili!y of appealing to consumers in terms of personality traits. They have felt that what consumers purchase and when and how they consume, are likely to be influenced by personality factors. For this reason, advertising and marketing people have frequently depicted specific personality traits or characteristics in their advertising messages.

Carl Gustav jung defines personality as "Personality is the supreme realization of innate individuality of a particular living being".

Some have emphasized the, dual influence of heredity and early childhood experience on personality development others have stressed broader social and environmental influences and the fact that personalities develop continuously over time. Some theorists prefer to view personality as a unified whole others focus on specific traits. The wide variation in view points makes it difficult to arrive at a single definition. However, we propose that personality be defined as those inner psychological characteristics that both determine and reflect how a person responds to his or her environment.

The emphasis in this definition is on inner characteristics those specific qualities; attributes, traits, factors and mannerisms that distinguish an individual from oher individual. Therefore, the identification of specific personality characteristics associated with consumer behaviour may be highly useful in the development of a firm's market segmentation strategies.

The Nature of Personality

Personality Reflects Individual Dfferences. Because the inner characteristics that constitute an individual' s prsonality are unique combination of factors, no two individuals are exactly alike. Nevertheless, many individuals tend to be similar in terms of a single personality characteristics. For instance many people can be described as "high" in sociability, while others can be described as "low" sociability. Personality is in useful concept because it enables us to categorize consumer into different groups on the basis of single trait or a few traits. If each person were different in all respects, it would be impossible to group consumers into segments and there would be little reason to develop standardized products and promotional campaigns.

Personality is Consistent and Enduring. An individual's personality is commonly thought to be both consistent and enduring. Indeed, the mother who comments that "her child has been stubborn from the day he was born" is supporting the connection that personality has both consistency and endurance. Both qualities are essential for marketeers to explain or preduct consumer behaviour in terms of personality.

The stable nature of personality suggests that it is unreasonable for marketeers to attempt to change consumers personalities to confirm to certain products. At best, they may learn which personality characteristics influence specific consumer responses and attempt to appeal to relevant traits inherent in their target group of consumers.

Even though an individual's personality may be consistent, consumption behaviour often varies considerably because of psychological, socio-cultural and environmental factors that affect behaviour. For instance, while an individual's personality may be largely stable, specific needs of motives, attitudes, reactions to group pressures and every responses to newly available brands may cause a change in the person's behaviour.

Personality is only one of a combination of factors that influence how a consumer behaves.

Personality Can Change. Although personality tends to be consistent and enduring, 'it may still change under certain circumstances. For instance an individual's personality may be altered by major life events, such as the birth of a child, the death of a loved one, a divorce, or a major career promotion. An individual's personality changes not only in response to abrupt events, but also as a part of a gradual maturing process.

Freudian Theory of Personality. Sigmund Freud's psychoanalytic theory of personality is the cornerstone of modern psychology. This theory was built on the premise that unconscious needs or drives, especially sexual and other biological drives, are at the heart of human motivation and personality. Freud constructed his theory on the basis of patient' s recollections of early childhood experience, analysis of their dreams and the specific nature of their mental and physical adjusment problems.

Id, Superego and Ego. Based on his analyses, Freud proposed that the human personality consists of three interacting systems the id the superego and the ego: The id was conceptualized as" a "warehouse" of primitive and impulsive drives—basic physological needs such as thirst, hunger and sex for which the individual seeks immediately satisfaction without concern for the specific means of satisfaction. In contrast to the id, the superego is conceptualized as the individual's internal expression of society's moral and ethical codes of conduct. The superego's role is to see that the individual satisfies needs in a socially acceptable fashion. Thus, the superego is a kind of "brake" that restrains or inhibits the impulsive forces of the id.

Stages of Personality Development. In addition to specifying astructure for personality, Freud emphasised that an individual's personality is formed as he or she passes through a number of instinct stages of infant and childhood development. These are the oral, and phallic, latent and genital stages. Freud lebelled four of these stages of development to conform to the area of the body on which he believed the child's sexual instincts are focused, at the time.

Oral State. The infant first experiences social contact with the outside world through the mouth (*e.g.* eating, drinking, sucking). A crisis develops at the end of this stage when the child is weaned from the mother's breast or from the bottle.

Anal Stage. During this stage, the child's primary source of pleasure is the process of elimination. A second crisis develops at the end of this stage when parents try to toilet train the child.

Phallic Stage. The child experiences self oriented sexual pleasure during this phase with the discovery of the sex organs. A third crisis occurs when the child experie ces sexual desire for the parent of the opposite sex. How the child resolves this crisis affects later relationships with the persons of the opposite sex and with authority figures.

Latency Stage. Freud believed that the sexual instincts of the child *i.e.,* dormant from about age 5 until the beginning of adolescence and that no important personality changes occur during this time.

Genital Stage. At adolescence, the individual develops a sexual interest in persons of the opposite sex, beyond self-oriented love and love for parents.

According to Freud, an adult's personality is determined by how well, he or she deals with the crisis that are experienced while passing through each of these stages. For instance, If a child's oral needs are not adequately satisfied at the first stage of development, the person may become fixated at this stage and as an adult display a personality that includes such traits as dependence and excessive oral-activity (*e.g.*,gum chewing and smoking). When an individual is fixated at the oral stage, the adult personality may display other traits, such as an excessive need for neatness.

Freudian Theory and "Product Personality". Researchers who apply Freud's psychoanalytic theory to study consumer personality and to stress the idea that human drives are largely unconscious and that consumers are primary unaware of their true reasons for buying what they buy. These researchers tend to focus on consumer purchases and/or consumption 'situations, treating then as a reflection and an extension of the consumer's own personality.

Brand Personality. Consumers tend to ascribe various descriptive "personality like" traits or characteristics the ingredients of brand personalities to different brands in a wide variety of product categories.

Consumers not only ascribe personality traits to products and services, but also they tend to associate personality factors with specific colours. In some cases, various products, even brands, associate a specific colour with personahty like connotations. For example, Coca-Cola is associated with red, which connotes excitement. Mans fast food restaurants use combinations of bright colours, like red, yellow and blue, for their roadside signs and interior designs. In contrast, fine dining restaurants tend to use sophisticated colours like grey, white, shades of tane, or other soft, pale, or muted colours to reflect fine leisurely service.

Table: The Personality like Associates of Selected Colours

Colour	Personality Link	Marketing Insights
Blue	Commands respect, athority	America's favoured colour IBM holds the title to blue Associated with club soda Men seek products packaged in blue Houses painted blue, are avoided Low-calorie, skim milk Coffee in blue can perceived as 'mild'
Yellow	Caution, novelty, temporary warmth	Eyes register it fastest Coffee in yellow can tasted "weak" Stops traffic Sells a house
Green	Secure, natural, relaxed or easy going, living things	Good work environment Associated with vegtables and chewing gum

		Canda dry ginger ate sales increased when it changed sugar-free package from red to green and white.
Red	Human, exciting, hot passionate strong	Makes food "smell" better Coffee in a red can perceived as "rich" Women have preferred bluish red Men have a preference for yellowish red Coca-cola "owns" red
Orange	Powerful, affordable, informal	Draws attention quickly
Brown	Informal and relaxed masuline, nature	Coffce in a dark-brown can was "too strong". Men seek products packaged in brown
White	Goodness, purity, chastity, cleanliness, delicacy refinement, formality	Suggests reduced calories Pure and wholesome food Clean, bath products, feminine
Black	Sophisticated, power authority, mystery	Powerful clothing High tech electronics
Silver, Gold Platinum	Regal, wealthy, stately	Suggests premium price.

JUNGIAN PERSONALITY TYPES

Carl Jung was a contemporary and colleague of Freud. His contribution to modern psychology is extensive and his theories and insights pertaining to personality types are especially relevant to consumer behaviour. Jung's personality types have been made particularly useful for marketeers by the Myers Briggs Type Indicator (a personality inventory) that measures the following pairs of Jungian inspired psychological dimension : 1. sensing-intuiting, 2. thinking-feeling 3. extroversion-introversion and 4. judging perceiving. Each of these four, pairs of dimension reflect too distinctly different personality characteristics that offer a picture as to how consumer respond to the world around them.

The attempt to match each psychological dimension from all pairs with each psychological dimension in all other pairs would result in too many different combinations of personality types for productive study. To avoid the extreme complexity, a consumer researcher recently investigated the consumption relevance of just two pairs of dimensions (*i.e.,* sensing intuiting and thinking-feeling). The sensing (S) and intuiting (N) dimensions capture new consumers, find about "things" (obtaining and processing information) and the thinking (T) and feeling (F) dimensions are opposite ways of making decisions (decision styles). By cross tabulating the specific characteristics of the two pairs of psychological dimensions, four possible personality types are derived.

Table: Selected Jungian Personality Types

	Thinking (T)	Feeling (F)
Sensing	Sensing-thinking (ST)	Sensing-feeling (SF)
Intuiting	Intuiting-thinking (NT)	Intuiting-feeling (NF)

By creating a consumer-specific personality inventory, it would be possible to learn how these four personality types impact on consumer information processing, consumer decision-making and other consumption related issues-personality-related insights that would enable marketeers to better satisfy consumer needs.

For instance, imagine four individuals (corresponding to the four Jungian personality types) facing the investment decision to purchase some stocks. The ST and SF types would tend to conscience study balance sheets and financial performance to secure their facts. However, the ST (sensing thinking). Consumer would arrive at his or her own decision and might eventually use a discount broker. In contrast, the SF consumer would want to include the recommendations of others as part of the decision and would be more likely to use a full-service brokerage house. The NT and NF consumers would be more likely to make their stock selections intuitively or in terms of a "hunch". NT consumers would rely heavily on their imaginations, yet would carefully think out all of the options. Although NF consumers would rely on their imaginations while considering options, the ultimate decision might be expected to reflect inputs from others (*e.g.* comments overheard in some social setting, such as a cocktail party).

NEO-FREUDIAN THEORY

Several of Freud's colleagues disagreed with his contention that personality is primarily instinctual and sexual in nature. Instead, these neo-Freudians believed that social relationships are fundamental to the formation and development of personality. For instance, Alfred Adler viewed human beings as seeking to attain various rational goods, which he called styles of life. He also placed much emphasis on the individual's efforts to overcome feelings of inferiority (*i.e.* to strive for superiority).

Harry Stack Sullivan, another neo-Freudian stressed that people continuously attempt to establish significant and rewarding relationships with others. He was particularly concerned with the individual's efforts to reduce tension, such as anxiety.

Like Sullivan, Karen Horney was also interested in anxiety. She focused on the impact of child parent relationships, especially the individual's desire to conquer feelings of anxiety. Horney proposed that individual's be classified into three personality groups; Complaint, Aggressive and Detached.

1. Complaint Individuals are there who move towards others (they desire to be loved, wanted and appreciated).

2. Aggressive individual are those who move against others (they desire to excel and win admiration).

3. Detached individuals are those who move away from others (they desire independence, self-reliance, self sufficiency and freedom from obligations).

A personality test based on Horney's theory (*i.e.* the CAD) has been developed and tested within the context of consume behaviour. The initial can research uncovered a number of tentative relationships between college student's scares and their product and brand usage patterns. For instance, highly complaint students were bound to prefer name brand products, such as Bayer aspirin, students classified aggressive shared a preference for Old Spice deodorent over the brands (seemingly because of its masculine appeal); and highly detached students or ved to be heavy tea drinkers (possibly reflecting their desire not to conform). More recent research reveals that children who scored high in self-reliance—who preformed to do the things independently of others (which is similar to being detached persons)—were less likely to be very brand loyal and up to a point, were more likely to try different brands.

It is likely that many marketeers have used some of these neo-Freudian theories intuitively. For example, marketeers who position their products'or services as providing an opportunity to belong or be appreciated by others in a group or social selling would seem to be guided by Horney's characterization of a complaint individual.

JUNGIAN THEORY

Cast Jung was a contemporary and colleague of Freud. His contribution to modern psychology is extensive and his theories and insights pertaining to personality types are relevant to consumer behaviour Jung's personality types have been made particularly useful for marketeers by the Myers Briggs Type Indicators that measures the following pairs of Jungian inspired psychological dimensions: *(1)* Sensing intuiting, *(2)* thinking-feeling, *(3)* extroversion-introversion, and *(4)* Judging-perceiving. Each of these four pairs of dimensions reflects two distinctly different personality characteristics that offer a picture as to how consumers respond to the world arround, them. The attempt to match each psychological dimension from all pairs with each psychological dimension in all pairs would result in too many different combinations of personality types for productive study. So avoid this extreme complexity, a consumer researcher recently investigated the consumption relevance of two pairs of dimensions (*i.e.* sensing-in tuiting and thinking-feeling). The Sensing (S) and Intuiting (N) dimensions capture how consumers find out about things, and the thinking (T) and feeling (F) dimensions are opposite crays of making decisions. By cross tabulating the specific characteristics of the two pairs of psychological dimensions, four possible personality types are derived. Table given below summarizes the main characteristics of each of these four Jungian personality types.

SUMMARY CHARACTERISTICS OF SELECTED JUNGIAN PERSONALITY TYPES

Sensing-Thinking (ST)

— Rational in decision-making

— Logical and empirical in viewpoint

— Makes decision following an "objective" orientation

— Heavily weighs economic considerations—most price sensitive

— Will extend considerable effort to search for decision-making information

— Risk avoider

— Materialism reflects personal or private motives

— Short-time horizon in making decisions

Sensing-Feeling (SF)

— Empirical viewpoint

— Propelled by personal value raller than logic

— Makes decisions following a "subjective" orientation

— Likely to consider others when making a decision

— Shares risk with others

— Materialism reflects how objects will impact on others.

— Short-time horizon in making decisions

Intuiting-Thinking (NT)

— Takes a broad view of personal situation or world

— Relies heavily on imagination, yet uses logic in approaching decisions

— Imagines a wider range of options in making a decision

— Weighs options mentally

— Willing to take risk or be speculative in decisions

— Long-time horizon in making decisions.

Intuiting-Feeling (NF)

— Takes a broad view of personal situation or world

— Imagine a wide range of options in making a decision

— Highly "people oriented"—likely consider other's views

— Makes decisions following a subjective orientation

— Least price sensitive

— Risk seeking

— Indefinite time horizon in making decisions.

Using a psychological inventory, such as the Myres-Briggs Type Indicators, or by creating a consumer specific personality inventory it would be possible to learn how these four personality type impact on consumer information processing, consumer decision making, and other competition related issues-personality related insights that would make able marketeers to better satisfy consumer needs.

FREUDIAN THEORY

Sigmund Freud's theory was built on the premise that unconsciousness needs to drive; especially sexual and other biological drives, are at the heart of human motivation and personality. Freud constructed his theory on the basis of patient's recollections of early childhood experiences, analysis of their dreams, and the specific nature of their mental and physical adjustment problems.

Id, Superego, and Ego. Based on his analysis, Freud proposed that the human personality consists of three interacting systems the id, the superego, and the ego. The id, was conceptualized as a "wordonse" of primitive and impulsive drives basic physiological needs lack as thirst, hunger and sex-for which the individual seeks immediate satisfaction without concern for the specific means of satisfaction.

In contrast to the id, the superego is conceptualised as the individual's internal expression of society's moral and ethical codes of conduct. The superego's role is to see that the individual satisfies needs in a socially acceptable fashion. Thus, the superego is a kind of "brake" that restraints or inhibits the impulsive forces of the id.

Finally, the ego is the individual's conscious control. It functions as an internal monitor that attempts to balance the impulsive demands of the id and the socio-cultural constraints of the superego.

Stubborn from the day he was born, is supporting the contention that personality has both consistency and endurance. Both qualities are essential for marketeers to explain or predict consumer behaviour in terms of personality.

The stable nature of personality suggests that it is unreasonable for marketecrs to attempt to change consumer's personalities to conform to certain products. At best, they may learn which personality characteristics influence specific consumer responses and attempt to appeal to relevant traits inherent in their target group of consumers.

Even though an individual,'s personality may be consistent, consumption behaviour often varies considerably because of psychological, sociocultural, and environmental factors that affect behaviour, for instance, while an individual's personality may be largely stable, specific needs or motives, attitudes, reactions to group pressures, and even responses to newly available brands may cause a change in the person's behaviour. Personality is only one of a combination of factors that influence how a consumer behaves.

Personality Can Change. Although personality tends to be consistent and enduring, it may still change under certain circumstances. For instance, an individual's personality may be altered by major life events, such as birth of a child; the death of a loved one, a divorce, or a major career promotion. An individual's personality changes not only in response to abrupt, events, but also in others too.

Representation the Inter-relationships Among The ID, EGO and Superego

Stages of Personality Development. In addition to specifying a structure for personality, Fraud empnasized that an individual's personality is formed as he or she passes through a number of distinct stages of infant and childhood development. These are the oral, anal, phallic, and genital stages. Freud labelled four of these stages of development to conform to the area of the body on which he believed the child's sexual instincts are focused at the time.

Oral Stage. The infant first experiences social contact with the outside world through the mouth. A crisis develops at the end of this stage when the child is weaned from the mother's breast or from the bottle, there are other stages also such as oral stage,phallie stage, latency stage and genital stage.

Freudian Theory and 'Product Personality'

Researchers who apply Freud's Psychoandlytic theory to the study of consumer personality tend to stress the idea that human drives are largely unconscious and that consumers are primarily unaware of their true reasons for buying what they buy.

These researchers tend to focus on consumer purchases and for consumption situations treating tnem as a reflection and an extension of the consumer's own personality. In other words, one's appearance and possessions how well groomed one is, what one wears, carries, and displays are taken to reflect the individual's personality.

Brand Personality. Consumers tend to ascribe various descriptive "personality like" traits or characteristics the ingiedients of brand personalities to different brands in a wide variety of product categories. A brief case.

Consumers not only ascribe personality traits to products and services, but also they tend to associate personality factors with specific colours. In some cases, various products, even brands, associate a specific colour with personality like connotations. For instance, Coca-Cola is associated with red, which connotes excitement. Yellow is associated with "novelty", and black frequently connotes "Sophistcation". For this, brands wishing to create a sophisticated person or an upscale or premium image use labelling or packaging that is primarily black, still further, a combination of black and white has the power of communicating that a product is carefully engineered, high technology, and sophistcated in design.

TRAIT THEORY

Trait theory constitutes a major departure from the basically qualitative measures that typify the Freudian and neo-Freudian movements (*e.g.* personal observation, self-reported experience, dream analysis, projective techniques).

The orientation of trait theory is primarily :quantitative or empirical it focuses on the measurement of personality in terms of specific psychological characteristics called traits. A trait is defined as "any distinguishing relative enduring way in which one individual differs from another."

Accordingly, trait theorists are concerned with the construction of personality tests (or inventories) that pinpoint individual differences in terms of specific traits.

Selected single trait personality tests (which measure just one trait, such as self confidence) are increasingly being developed specifically for use in consumer behaviour studies. These tailor-made personality tests measure such traits as consumer innovativeness (how receptive a person is to new experiences), consumer susceptability or interpersonal influence (SVSCEP) gauges how consumers respond to social influence), consumer materialism (assess the degree of consumer's attachment to "world" possessions) and consumer ethnocentrism (CETSCALE identifies consumer's likelihood to accept or reject foreign-made products).

Based on experience using personality inventories to understand consumption-related behaviour, researchers have learned that it is generally more realistic to expect personality to be linked to how consumers make their choices and to the purchase or consumption of a broad product category, rather than a specific brand. For example, there is more "likely to be a relationship between personality and whether or not an individual owns a convertible sports car, than between personality and the brand of convertible sports car purchased.

SELF IMAGE

Consumers have a number of enduring images of themselves. These self-images, or "perceptions of self" ar very closely associated with personality in that individuals tend to by products and services and patronize retailers, with images or "personality" that closely correspond to their own self-images.

One or Multiple Selves. Individual consumers have been thought to have "a single self and to be interested in products and services that satisfy that single self. However, research indicates that it is more accurate to think of the consumer in terms of multiple self or multiple selves. The change of thinking reflects the understanding that a single consumer is actually quite likely to act quite differently with different people and in different situations. For instance, a person is likely to behave differently at a museum opening at school, at work, with parents, or with friends at a night club. The healthy or normal person is likely to be a somewhat different person in each of these different situations or social roles. In fact, acting exactly the same in all situations or roles is likely to be a sign of an abnormal or unhealthy person.

In terms of consumer behaviour, the idea that an indiviual embodies a number of different "selves" (*i.e.*, has multiple self-images) suggests that marketeers should target their products and services to consumers within the context of a particular itself".

The Make up of the Self Image. Consistent with the idea of multiple self-images each individual has an image of himself or herself as a certain kind of person with certain traits, habits, possessions, relationships and ways of behaving. As with other types of images and personality, the individual's self-image is unique, the outgrowth of that person's background and experience. Individuals develop their self-images through interactions with other people initially their parents and then other individuals or groups with whom, they relate over the years.

Products and brands have symbolic value for individuals, who evaluate them on the basis of their consistency (*i.e.*, congruence) with their personal pictures or images of themselves. Some products seem to match one or more of an individual's self-images others seem totally alien. It is generally held that consumers attempt to preserve or enhance their self-images by selecting products with "images" or "personalities" they believe are cogment with their own self-images and avoiding products that are not.

A variety of different self-images have been identified in the consumer behaviour literature. One popular model depicts four specific inds of self-images: *1.* actual self-image (*i.e.* how consumers in fact see themselves), *2.* ideal self-image (*i.e.* how consumers would like to see themselves), *3.* social self-image (*i.e.* how consumers feels others to see them) and *4.* ideal social self-image (*i.e.* how consumers would like to others to see them). Other research had identified a fifth type of self-image, expected self-image (it how consumers expect to see themselves at some specified future time). The expected self-image is somewhere between the actual and ideal self-images. It is somewhat like a future-oriented combinations of "what is" (the actual self-image) and what consumers would like "to be" (the ideal self-image). Moreover, because expected self-image provides consumers with a realistic "opportunity" to change the "self", it is likely to be more valuable to marketeers than the actual or ideal self-image as a guide for designing and promoting products.

In different contexts (*i.e.* in different situations and/or with respect to different products), consumers might select a different self-image to guide their attitudes or behaviour. For instance, with some everyday household products, consumers might be guided by their actual self-images, whereas, for some socially enhancing or socially conspicuous products, they might be guided by their self-image. When it comes to a so-called fantasy product, they might be guided by either their ideal self-images or ideal social self-images.

The concept of self-image has strategic implications for marketeers. For example, marketeers can segment their markets on the basis of relevant, consumer self-images and then position their products or services as symbols of such self-images. Such a strategy is fully consistent with the marketing concept. In that marketeer first assess the needs of a consumer segment (with respect to both the product category and to an appropriate symbol of self-image), and then proceeds to develop and market a product or service that meets criteria.

The Extended Self. The inter-relationship between consumer's self-images and their possessions (*i.e.* objects they call their "own") is an exciting topic for consumer research. Spcifically, consumers' possessions can be seen to "confirm" or "extend" their self-images. For instance, acquiring a desired or sought after tennis raquet serve to expand or enrich Mary's Image of "self". Mary might now see herself as being more competitive, more fit, and more successful, "because she added the tennis raquet to her "inventory" of self-enhancing, possessions. In a similar way, if the fountain pen that Steve received as a gift from his grandfather were stolen, Steve is likely to feel diminished in same way. Indeed the loss of a prized possession may lead Steve to "grieve" and to experience a variety of emotions such a frustration, loss of control, the feeling of being "violated", even the loss of magical protection.

The above examples, suggest that much human emotions can be connected to valued possessions. In such cases, possessions can be considered extensions of the self. It has been proposed that possessions can extend the self in a number of ways:

1. actually, by allowing the person to do things that otherwise would be very difficult or impossible to accomplish (*e.g.* problem-solving using a computer),
2. Symbolically, by making the person feel better or "bigger" (*e.g.* receiving an employee award for excellence),
3. by conferring status or rank (*e.g.* status among collectors of rare work or art because of the ownership of a particular masterpiece),
4. by bestowing feelings of immorality by leaving valued possessions to young family members (this also has the potential of extending the recipients "selves"), and
5. by endowing with magical powers (*e.g.*, a came pin inherited from one's aunt might be perceived as a magic amulet bestowing good luck when it is worn).

Altering the Self. Sometimes consumers wish to change themselves to become a different or "improved" self clothing, grooming aids and all kinds of accessories (*e.g.* cosmetics, jewellery) offer consumers the opportunity to modify appearancess and thereby to alter their "selves". In using "self-altering products"; consumers are frequently attemptining to express their individualism or uniqueness by creating a new self, maintaing the existing self (or preventing the loss of self) and extending the self (modifying or changing the self). Sometimes consumers use self altering products or services to conform to or take on the appearance of a particular type of person (*e.g.* amilitary person, a physician, a business executive, or a college professor).

Altering one's self, particularly one's appearance or body parts, can be accomplished by cosmetics hair restlying or colouring, switching from eye glasses to contact lenses (or the reverse), or undergoing cosmetic surgery.

When it comes to, altering one's self, both male and female consumers are open to the idea. According to a study, 45 per-cent of women and 33 per-cent of men would consider cosmetic surgery. By using these options, it is possible to create a "new" or "improved" person. Some people also call upon image consultants to achieve an appropriate and mutually agreed-upon self-image. Image consultants provide clients with advice on such personal attributes as clothing, colour, presentation, appearance, posture, speaking skills.

Vanity and Consumer Behaviour. Closely related to self-image is the idea of personal vanity. Using a recently developed vanity scale, researchers have investigated both physical vanity (an excessive concern for and/or a positive or even inflated view of one's personal achievements). Thus, for they have found these two ideas related to materialism, use of cosmetics, concern and country club membership.

Table: Sample Items from a Variety Scale

Physical-Concern Items
1. The way I look is extremely important to me.
2. I am very concerned with my appearance.
3. It is important that I always look good.
Physical-View Items
1. People notice how attractive I am.
2. People are envious of my good looks.
3. My body is sexually appealing.
Achievement-Concern Items
1. Professional achievements are an absession with me.
2. Achieving greater success than my pears is important to me.
3. I want my achievements to be recognized by others.

Achievement-View Items

1. My achievements are highly regarded by others.
2. I am a good example of professional success.
3. Others wish they were as successful as me.

Personality Influences the Consumption Behaviour of the Consumer

Personality traits proved useful in differentiating between consumer innovators and non-innovators include consumer innovativeness, dogmatism, social character, optimum stimulation level and variety novelty seeking.

Consumer Innovativeness. However, receptive consumers are to new products, new services of new practices is quite important to both consumers and marketeers for both can benefit from the right instruments to gauge the lavel of consumer innovativeness because

Table: A Consumer Innovativeness Scale

In general, I am among the last in my circle of friends to buy a new (rock albums #) when it appears**

If I heard that a (new rock album) was available in the store, I would be interested enough to buy it.

Compared to my mends, I own few (rock albums).

In general, I am the last in my circle of friends to know the (titles of the .latest rock albums).**

I will buy a new (rock album), even of I haven't heard it yet.

I known the names of (new rock acts) before other people do.

The product category and related wording is altered to fit the purpose of the researcher.

** Items with an (**) are negatively worded and secored inversely.

Source: Ronald E. Goldsmith and Charles. F. Hofacker. "Measuring Consumer Innovativeness."

such personality trait measures provide sights into the nature and boundaries of a consumer's willingness to innovate. The table given below presents a six-item measure of consumer innovativeness that is specially designed to be flexible in terms of the boundaries or domain being studied (*e.g.,* broad product, category, personal computers, sub product category, portable computers;—type, notebook computers).

Dogmatism. Dogmatism is a personality trait that measures the degree of rigidity individuals display towards the unfamiliar and towards information that is contrary to their own established belifs. A person who is highly dogmatic approaches the unfamiliar defensively and with considerable discomfort and uncertainty. At the other end of the spectrum, a person who is low in dogmatism will readily consider unfamiliar or opposing beliefs.

Consumers who are low in dogmatism (open minded) are more likely to pefer innovative product to established or traditional alternatives. In contrast highly dogmatic (closed minded) consumers are more likely to choose established, rather than innovative product alternatives.

It is likely that highly dogmatic consumers will be more accepting of ads for new products or services that contain an authoritative appeal. To this end, marketeers have used celebrities and experts in their new-product advertising to make it easier for potentially reluctant consumers (non innovators) to accept the innovation. In contrast, low dogmatic consumers (who are frequently high in innovativeness) seem to be more receptive to messages that stress factual differences and product benefits.

Social Character. The personality trait known as social chracter has its origin in sociological research, which focuses on the identification and classification of individuals into distinct socio-cultural types. As used in consumer psychology, social character is a personality trait that ranges on a continuum from inner-directness to other directness. Available evidence indicates that inner-directed consumers tend to rely on their own "inner" values or standards in evaluating new products and are likely to be consumer innovators. Conversely, other directed consumer tend to look to others for direction on what is "right" or "wrong"; thus, they are less likely to be consumer innovators.

Inner and other directed consumers also may be attracted to different types of promotional messages. Inner directed people seem to prefer ads that stress product features and personal benefits (enabling them to use their own values and standards in evaluating products) while other directed people seem to prefer ads that feature a social environment or social acceptance (in keeping with their tendency to look to others for direction). Thus, other directed individuals may be more easily influenced of their natural inclination to go beyond the cotent of an ad and think in terms of likely social approval of a potential purchase.

Optimum Stimulation Level. Some people seem to prefer a simple, uncultured, and calm existence, while others seem to prefer an environment crammed with novel, complex and unusual experiences. Consumer research has examined how such variations in need for stimulation may be influenced by selected personality traits and how, in turm, specific stimulation levels may be related to consumer behaviour. So far, this research has linked high optimum stimulation leves (OSLs) with more willingness to take risks, to try new products, to be innovative, to seek purchase-related information and to accept new retail facilities.

OSL also seems to reflect a person's dessired level of lifestyle stimulation. For instance, if consumer's actual lifestyles are equivalent to their OSL scores, then they are likely to be quite satisfied. On the other and, if their lifestyles are understimulated (*i.e.,* their OSL is greater than current reality), they are likely to seek rest or relief. This suggests that the relationship between consumers lifestyles and their OSLs is likely to influence their choices of products or services and how they manage and spend their time. For instance, a person who feels bored (an understimulated consumer) is likely to be attracted to a vacation that offers much activity and an exciting time. In contrast, a person who feels overwhelmed (an overstimulated consumer) is likely to seek a quiet, isolated, relaxing and rejuvenating vacation.

Variety Novelty Seeking. Personality driven trait quite similar and related to OSL is variety or novelty seeking. There appears to be many different types of variety seeking; exploratory purchase behaviour (*e.g.* switching brands to experience new and possibly better alternatives), vicarious exploration (*e.g.*, where the consumer secures information about a new or different alternative and then contemplates or even day dreams about the option) and use innovativeness (*e.g.*, where the consumer uses an already adopted product in a new or novel way).

The third form of variety or novelty seeking use innovativeness is particularly relevant to technological products (such as home electronics products, where some models offer an abundance of features and functions, while others contain only a few essential features or functions. For example, consumers with higher variety seeking scores have been found to purchase calculators with more features than consumers with lower variety seeking scores.

The stream of research examined here indicates that the consumer innovator differs from the non-innovators in terms of personality orientation. A knowledge of such personality differences should help marketeers select target segments for new products and design distinctive promotional strategies for specific segments.

Visualizers Versus Verbalizers. One highly promising area of cognitive personality research classifies consumers as visualizers (Consumers who prefer visual information and products that stress the visual such as membership in a videotape casset club) or verbalizers (consumers who prefer written or verbal information and products, such as membership in book clubs or audiotape clubs). Some marketeers stress strong visual dimensions to attract visualizers",. Other features a detailed description or point-by-point explanation to attract verbalizers.

Consumer Susceptibility to Interpersonal Influence. Just as consumer researchers are interested in identifying characteristics of consumer innovators, they are also engaged in pinpointing the traits of consumer are likely to be responsive to the influence of others. To this end, consumer researchers have developed a twelve item scale (called "SUSCEP") designed to measure consumer's susceptibility to interpersonal influence. SUSCEP is assumed to be a general trait that reflects consumer differences in terms of response to social influence. According to the underlying theory upon which the scale was developed, there are three types of interpersonal influences: 1. informations influence, which is the tendency to accept information from others as evidence about reality; 2. value-expressive influence, which, captures consumers, desires to enhance their standing with others by being similar to them, and 3. utilitarian influence, where consumers conform with the wishes of others to obtain a reward or avoid punishment. The latter two types of influences (*i.e.,* value-expressive and utilitarian) are each normative and subjective in nature; that is, they reflect the consumer's own expectations of the objectives of others. Testing of the SUSCEP scale, shows that individuals who scored higher on susceptibility to interpersonal influence were less self-confident than consumers who scored lower on susceptibility to interpersonal influence. This was particularly true for the normative factor (a combination of value expressive and utilitarian influences).

Cognitive Personality Factors. In particular, two cognitive personality traits visualizers versus verbalizers and need for cognition have shown signs of being useful in understanding selected aspects of consumer behaviour.

Need for Cognition. Another promising cognitive personality characteristics is need for cognition (NC), which measures a person's craving for or enjoyment of thinking. Available research indicates that consumers who are high in NC are more likely to be responsive to the part of an ad that is rich in product-related information or description and unresponsive to the contextual or peripheral aspects of the ad, such as the presence of a celebrity endorser. In contrast, those consumers who are relatively low in NC are more likely to be attracted to the background or peripheral aspects of an ad such as an attractive model or well known celebrity.

One research suggests that consumers who are high in NC are more likely to be partial to cool colours (*e.g.* blue and green) than those who are low in NC and that individuals with a high need for cognition spend more time processing print advertisements, which results in superior brand and ad claim recall.

If substantiated by future research, such insights should provide advertisers with valuable guidelines for creating advertising messages and supporting are (including colour) that appeals to particular target consumers need for cognition.

From Consumer Materialism to Compulsive Consumption. Consumer researchers have become increasingly interested in exploring several interrelated consumption and possession traits. These traits range from consumer materialism to fixated consumption behaviour to consumer compulsive behaviour.

❑

12

Diffusion of Innovation

The diffusion process is concerned with four innovations spreadhow they are assimilated within a market. More precisely, diffusion is the process by which the acceptance of an innovation (a new product, new service, new idea, new practice) is spread by communication (mass media, sales people, informal conversation) to members of a social system (a target market) over a period of time.

This definition includes the four basic elements of the diffusion process: *(1)* the innovation, *(2)* the channels of communication, *(3)* the social system, and *(4)* time.

INNOVATION

The definition of innovation can be classified as firm oriented, product oriented, market oriented, and consumer oriented.

1. Firm Oriented Definitions. A firm oriented approach treats the newness of a product from the perspective of the company producing or marketing it. If the product is "new" to the company it is considered new. This definition ignores whether or not the product is actually new tp the market place. (*i.e.,* to competitors on to consumers while the definition has considerable merit if the objective is to examine the impact that a "new" product has on the firm. It is not very useful if the goal is to understand consumer adaptance of a new product.

Product Oriented Definitions. A product oriented approach focuses on the features inherent in the product itself and on the effects these features are likely to have on consumer's established usage patterns. One product oriented framework consider the extent to which a new product is likely to disrupt established behaviour patterns. It defines the following three types of product innovations:

(1) A Continuous Innovation has the least disruptive influence on established patterns. It involves the introduction of a modified product rather than a totally new product.

(2) A Dynamically Continuous Innovation is some what more disruptive than a continuous innovation, but still does not alter established behaviour patterns. It may involve the creation of a newproduct. For example, compact disc players, erasable-ink pens,

(3) A Discontinuous Innovation requires consumers to adopt new behaviour patterns. Examples include fax machines, home computers, video cassette recorders.

Television, a discontinuous innovation of major magnitude, has produced a variety of both dynamically continuous and continuous innovations and has even stimulated the development of other discontinuous innovations.

2. A product is considered new if it has been on the market for a relatively short period of time.

Consumer Oriented Definitions. Some researchers have suggested that a consumer oriented approach is the most appropriate way to define an innovation. In this context a "new" product is any product that a potential consumer judges to be new. In other words newness is based on the consumer's perception of the product, rather than on physical features or market realities. But the approach as received little systematic research attention.

PRODUCT CHARACTERISTICS THAT INFLUENCE DIFFUSION

All products that are "new" do not have equal potential for consumer acceptance. Some products seem to catch on almost overnight, while others take a very long time to gain acceptance.

Diffusion researchers have identified five product characteristics that seem to influence consumer acceptance of new products:

1. Relative Advantage. The degree to which potential customers, perceive a new product as superior to existing substitutes is its relative advantage. For example, Fax machine.

2. Compatibility (Suitableness). The degree to which potential consumers fuel a new product is consistent with their present needs, values and practices is a measure of its compatibility. A recent study of purchasers of CD players and high tech (such as computers, VCRs and telephone answering machines found that the key factors inhibiting product adoption was incompatibility with existing values and poor product quality.

3. Complexity. Any product difficult to use or understand affects product acceptance. The issue of complexity is especially instant when attempting to gain market acceptance for high-tech consumer products. Four types of technological fear act as barriers to new product acceptance *(1)* fear of technical complexity, *(2)* fear of rapid obsolescence, *(3)* fear of social rejection, and *(4)* fear of physical harm.

Trialability. It refers to the degree to which a new product is capable of being tried on a limited basis. The greater the opportunity to try a new product, the easier it is for consumers to evaluate if and ultimately adopt. In the case of products such as CD players, trialability was found to be the most salient to the potential consumers' overall decision process. In certain durable items it is difficult to try.

5. Observability or Communicability is the case with-which a product's benefit or attributes can be observed, imagined, or described to potential consumers. Products that have high degree of social visibility, such as fashion items, are more easily diffused than products that are used in home such as new type of toothbrush. Similarly, a tangible product is promoted more easily than intangible product.

The Channels of Communication. How quickly an innovation spreads depends to a great extent on communications between the marketeer and consumers, and communication among consumers.

(*e.g.*, word of mouth communication), More attention is paid to the transmission of product-related information through various communications channels, and to the impact of both the massages and the channels on the adoption or rejection of new products. Of central concern is the relative influence of impersonal sources (*e.g.* advertising and additional matter) and interpersonal sources (sales people and informal opinion leaders).

One result from diffusion research indicate that, relative to later adoption: early adoption:

— have more change agent contact (*e.g.* with sales people)

— have greater exposure to mass-media communications channels.

— Seek information about innovations more frequently.

— have greater knowledge of innovations; and

— have a higher degree of opinion leadership.

"A social system is a physical, so cultural environment to which people within which they function."

In other words, the social system boundary within which the diffusion of product is examined.

The orientation of a social system own special values or norms, is likely the acceptance or rejection of new product If the social system is modern in orientation the acceptance of innovations is likely to be high and vice-versa means if a social system is traditional in orientation, innovations are perceived as radical or as infringement established customs are likely to be avoided.

According to one authority, the characteristics typify a modern social system:

— a positive attitude towards change;

— an advanced technology and skilled lab force;

— a general respect for education and science;

— an emphasis on rational and ordered social relationship rather than on emotional ones;

— an outreach perspective, in which mernbers system frequently interact with outsiders facilitating the entrance of new ideas in social system; and

— the system's members can readily see then in quite different roles.

IMPORTANCE OF TIME IN THE DIFFUSION PROCESS

Time is the backbone of the diffusion process. It provides the study of diffusion in three ways: *(1)* purchase time, *(2)* the identification of adopter categories, and (3) the rate of adoption.

Purchase Time. Purchase time refers to the amount of time that elapses between consumer's initial awareness of a new product or service and the point at which they purchase or reject it.

Purchase time is an important concept because the average time a consumer takes to adopt a new product is a predictor of the overall length of time it will take for the new product to achieve widespread adoption. For example, when the individual's purchase time is short, a marketeer can expect that the overall rate of diffusion will be faster than when the individual's purchase time is long as is frequently the case in the purchase of a personal computer.

Adapter Categories. Five adapter categories are frequently cited in the diffusion literature. *(1)* innovators, *(2)* early adapters, *(3)* early majority, *(4)* late majority, *(5)* laggards.

Rate of Adoption. The rate of adoption is concerned with how long it takes for new product to be adopted by members of a social system. The general view that the rate of adoption for new products is increasing.

The diffusion of products worldwide is becoming a more rapid phenomenon. For example, it took black and white TVs about 12 years longer to reach the same level of penetration in Europe and

Japan as in the USA. For colour TVs, the lag time dropped to about five years for Japan and several more years for Europe. In contrast, for VCRs there was only a three or four-years spread, with the USA lagging behind Europe and Japan.

The objective in, marketing new products is usually to gain wide acceptance of the product as quickly as possible. Marketeer desires a rapid rate of product adoption in order to penetrate the market and quickly establish market leadership before, competition takes hold.

STAGES IN THE ADOPTION PROCESS

The consumer moves through five stages in arriving at a decision to purchase or reject a new ,product:

1. Awareness. During the first stage, consumers 'are exposed to the product innovation. This exposure is somewhat neutral, for they are not yet, sufficiently interested, to search for additional product information.

2. Interest. When the interest is developed in the product, they search for information about how the innovation can benefit them.

3. Evaluation. Based on their information, consumers draw conclusions about the innovationor determine whether further information is necessary. This stage represents a kind of "mental trial" of the product innovation. If the evaluation is satisfactory, the consumer will actually try the product innovation; if the mental trial is unsatisfactory; the product will be rejected.

4. Trial. At this stage consumers use the product on a limited basis. Their experience provide them with the critical information that they need to adopt or reject.

5. Adoption. Based on their trials and/or favourable evaluation, consumers decide to use the product on a full rather than limited basis or they decide to reject it.

A recent study of the consumer decision process for an energy-related innovation suggests that it may be appropriate to add two additional stages between trial and adoption-direct product experience (consequences) and product evaluation (confirmation).

— The adoption of some products and services may have minimal consequences, while the adoption of other innovations may lead to major behavioural and life style changes. Example of innovations with such major impact on society include the automobile, the television and refrigerator.

— The adoption process provides a framework for determining which types of information source consumers find most important at specific stages.

Limitations of the Adoption Process

1. It does not adequately acknowledge that a need or problem recognition stage may precedes the awareness stage.

2. It does not adequately provide for the rejection of a product after trial (*i.e.,* a consumer may reject the product after trial or never use the product on a continuous basis).

3. It does not adequately recognise that evaluation occurs throughout the decision making process and not solely at the evaluation stage.

4. It does not adequately account for the possibility that the five stages may not always occur in the specific order suggested. For example, trial may occur before evaluation.

THE INNOVATION DECISION PROCESS

To overcome the limitations traditional adoption process model has been updated into more general decision making model the innovation decision process.

1. Knowledge. Consumer is exposed to innovation's existence and gains some understanding of how it functions.

2. Persuasion (attitude formation). Consumers form favourable attitude towards the innovation.

3. Decision. Consumer engages in activities that lead to a choice to adopt or reject the innovation.

4. Implementation. Consumer puts the innovation into use.

5. Confirmation. Consumer seeks reinforcement for the innovation decision, but may reverse this decision if exposed to conflicting messages about the product.

The Consumer Innovator. It can be defined as the relatively small group of consumers who are the earliest purchasers of a new product.

In marketing diffusion studies, however; consumer researchers have desired the definition of the consumer innovator from the status of the new product under investigation. For example, if researchers define a new product as an innovation for the first three months of its availability than they define the consumers who purchase it during this period as "innovators" .

Other researchers have defined innovators in terms of their innovativeness that is, their purchase of some minimum number of new products from a selected group of new products. For instance, in the adoption of new fashion items, innovators can be defined as those consumers who purchase more than one fashion product from a group of ten new fashion products.

Non-innovators would be defined as those who purchase none or only one of the new fashion products.

Interest in the Product Category. Consumer innovators are much interested than either later adoptors or non adopters in the product category that they are among the first to purchase.

Consumer innovators are more likely than non-innovators to seek information concerning their specific interests from a variety of informal and mass-media sources. They are more likely to give greater deliberation to the purchase of new product or services in the areas of interest than are non innovators.

The Innovator is an Opinion Leader. There is strong tendency for consumer opinion leaders to be innovators. Consumer innovators provide other consumers with information and advice about new products, and these who receive such advice frequently follow it. Thus, in the role of opinion, leader, the consumer innovator often influences the acceptance, or rejection of new products.

Personality Traits. Researchers have learned about the personality of the consumer innovator.

1. Consumer Innovators generally are less dogmatic than non innovators. They tend to approach new or unfamiliar products with considerable operness and little anxiety. In contrast, non-innovators seem to find new products threatening they proper to delay the purchase.

2. Consumer innovators are also inter-directed, that is, they rely on their own values or standards when making a decision about a new product. In controct, non-innovators are other-directed relying on others for guidance.

To sum up consumer innovators seem to be more receptive to unfamiliar they are more willing to rely on their own values or, standards than the judgement of others.

They the are willing to run the risk of a poor product choice in order to increase their exposure to new products that will be satisfying.

For the marketeer; the personality traits that distinguish innovators from non-innovators suggest the need for separate promotional campaigns for innovators and for later adoptors.

Consumer innovators are more likely to react favourably to informative or fast oriented advertising the product category that appeals to their strong interest and to readily evaluate the men to a new product on the basis of their own personal standards.

Perceived Risk. It is another measure of a consumer's likelihood to try new product, or new brands. Perceived risk is the degree of uncertainty or fear about the consequences of a purchase that a consumer feels when considering the purchase of a new product.

Research indicates that the consumer innovator is a low-risk perceiver, that is, they experience little fear of trying new products or services.

Consumers who perceive little or no risk in the purchase of a new product are much more likely to make innovative purchases than consumers who perceive a great deal of risk. In other words, high-risk perception limits innovativeness.

Venturesomeness. This is a broad-based measure of a consumer's willingness to accept the risk of purchasing new products. A typical measurement scale might include such items as:

— I prefer to (try a new food product when it first comes out) (wait, and learn how good it is before trying it).

— When I am shopping and see a brand of heavy duty detergent I know about it but have never used, I am (very anxious or willing to try it), (hesitant about trying it), (very unwilling to try it).

— I like to be among the first people to buy and use new products that are in the market.

Therefore, venture someness seems to be an effective barometer of actual innovation behaviour.

Need for Uniqueness. There is a notion that innovative behaviour is an expression of a person's need for uniqueness. Research found that those new products, both branded and unbranded, that represent a greater change in person's consumption habits were viewed as superior when it came to satisfying the need for uniqueness. Therefore, to gain rapid acceptance of a new product, marketeers might consider appealing to consumers need for uniqueness.

❑

13

Opinion Leadership

Opinion Ledership is the process by which one person (the opinion leader) informally influences the actions or attitudes of others, who may be opinion seekers or merely opinion recipients. This influences the informal and usually verbal but it may take the form of non-verbal behaviour observed by others. The informal flow of consumption related influence between two people is sometimes referred to as product-related conversation, or word of mouth communication.

The key characteristic of word of mouth communication is that it is interpersonal and informal and takes place between two or more people, none of whom represents a commercial selling source. Word of mouth implies personal, or face-to-face, communication though it may also take place by telephone.

One of the parties is an informal product-related communication encounter usually offers advice or information about a specific product or product category. Such as which of several brands is best, or how a particular product may be used. This person, the "opinion leader", may become an opinion receiver when another product or product category is discussed.

Individuals who actively seek information and advice about products sometimes are called opinion seekers. For purposes of simplicity, the terms opinion receiver and opinion recipient will be used interchangeably in the following discussion to identify both those who actively seek information from others and those who receive unsolicited information. Simple examples of opinion leadership at work include the following:

(1) During lunch, one friend mentions the desire to purchase a large screen TV, and the other recommend a particular brand.

(2) A person shows a co-worker photographs of her recent European vacation, and the co-worker suggests that a different type of film might produce better flash pictures.

(3) A man who recently moved into a apartment building has leaky kitchen faucet and calls his neighgbbour for the name of "a good plumber".

DYNAMICS OF THE OPINION LEADERSHIP PROCESS

1. Opinion Leadership are Persuasive. As informal communication sources, opinion leaders are remarkably effective at influencing consumers in their product related decisions. Some of the reasons for the effectiveness of opinion leadership are discussed:

Credibility. Opinion leaders are highly credible sources of product-related information because they usually, are perceived as objective concerning the information or advice they dispense. Their intentions are perceived as being in the best interests of the opinion recipient, because they receive no compensation for the advice and apparently no "ax to grind". Because opinion leaders offen base their product comments on firsthand experience, their advice reduces for opinion receives the perceived risk or anxiety inherent in buying new products.

Positive Product Information. Information provided by marketeers is invariably favourable to the product. Thus, the very fact that opinion leadership provides both favourable and unfavourable information adds to their credibility. An example of an unfavourable or negative product comment is, "The problem with polyester shirts is that they don't breathe". Compared with positive or even neutral comment, negative comments are relatively uncommon. For this reason, consumers are especially not likely to such information and to avoid products or brands that receive negative evaluations.

Information and Advice. Opinion leaders are the source of both information and advice. They may simply take about their experiences with a product, relate what they know about a product, or more aggressively, advise others to buy or to avoid a specific product. The kinds of product related information that opinion leaders are likely to transmit during conservation including the following:

(i) which of several brands is best:

"In my opinion, lucas luggage is the most practicable luggage you can buy"

(ii) How to best use a specific product:

"In find that laser printers work best when you use high-quality paper".

(iii) Where to shop:

"When Dayton's has a sale, the values are terrific."

(iv) Who provides the best service:

"I've been taking.my cars to coach Auto Shop for tune-ups, breaks, and shocks for the past ten years, and, think their service can't be beat."

Opinion Leadership is Category-Specific. Opinion leadership tends to be categories about which they offer information and advice. When other product categories are discussed, however, they are just as likely to reserve their roles and become opinion receivers. A person who is considered particularly knowledgeable about automobiles may be an opinion leader in terms of this subject, yet when it comes to purchasing a camcorder, the same person may seek advice from someone else perheps even from someone who has sought his automotive advice.

Opinion Leadership is two-way Street. As the examples above suggests consumers who are opinion leaders in one product situation may become opinion receivers in another situation, even for the same product.

Consider the following example—Mary, a new homeowner contemplating the purchase of a show blower, may seek inf6rmation and advice from other people to reduce her indecision about which brand to subject. Once the snow blower has been bought, however, she may experience postpurchase dissonance and have a compelling need to talk favourably about the purchase to other people to confirm the correctness of her own choice. In the first instance, she is an opinion receiver, in the second, she assumes the role of opinion leader.

An opinion leader play also influenced by an opinion receiver as the result of a product-related conservation. For example a person may tell a friend about a favourite vocation campground in Minnesota and, in response to comments from the opinion receiver, came to realise that the campground is too small, too isolated, and offers vacationers fewer amenities than other campgrounds.

2. The Motivations Behind Opinion Leadership. To understand the phenomenon of opinion leadership, it is useful to examine the motivation of those who provide and those who receive product-related information.

The Needs of Opinion Leaders. What motivates a person to talk about a product or service" ? Motivation theory suggests that people may provide Information or advice to others in order to satisfy some basic needs of their own. However, opinion leaders may unwave of their own underlying motives. As suggested earlier, opinion leaders may simply be trying to reduce their own post-purchase dissonance. For instance, if Fred buys a new backyard barbecue and then is uncertain that he made the right choice, she may try to reassure himself by "taking up" the barbecue's advantage to others. In this way, he relieves his own psycholgical discomfort. Furthermore, if he can influence a friend or neighbour to also buy that brand, he confirms his own good judgement in selecting the product first. This, the opinion leader's true motivation may really be self-confirmation or self-involvement. Furthermore, the informtion or advice that an opinion leadership dispenses may provide all types of tengential personal benefits. It may confer attention, imply some type of status, grant superiority, demonstrate awareness and expertise, and give the feeling of possessing inside information and satisfaction of "converting" less adventurous souls.

In addition to self-involvement, the opinion leader may also be motivated by product involvement, other involvement, and message involvement. Opinion leaders who are motivated by product involvement may find themselves so pleased or so dissappointed with a product that they simply must tell others about it. For example; a study of opinion leadership for automobiles found that enduring involvement with autos appeared to give rise to opinion leadership.

Those who are motivated by involvement with others need to share product-related experience. In this type of situation, opinion leaders use their product-related conversations as expression of friendship, neighbourliness and love.

The pervasiveness of advertising in our society encourages message involvement. Individuals who are bombarded with advertising messages and slogans tend to discuss them and the products they are designed to sell. Such word of mouth conversation is typified by the popular use in everyday conversation of slogans such as Nike's "just do it", Godiva Chocolate's "How deep is your love" etc.

The Need of Opinion Receivers. Opinion receivers satisfy a variety of needs by engaging in product-related conversation. First, they obtain new product of new-usage information. Second, they reduce their perceived risk by receiving first hand knowledge from a user about a specific product or brand. Third, they reduce the search time involved in the indentification of a needed product or service. Moreover, opinion receivers can be certain of receiving the approval of the opinion leader when they follow that person's product endorsement or advice. For all these reasons people often look to friends, neighbours and other acquaintances for product information.

The type of person from whom opinion receivers tend to seek their information varies, depending on cultural background. Some researchers found that while American and British consumers tended to select close friends of similar age as sources of advice Chinese consumers preferred to seek advice from individuals who had acquired authority and respect. In contrast, African-Americans were drawn to individuals who had achieved a degree of notoriety, or who were hypcast by the press as charismatic. Finally, Asian-Indians were likely to select individuals recognized as possessing strong philosophical outlooks. These findings suggest that subculture and cross-culture factors are likely to influence the traits judged desirable in an opinion leader.

"As a final point, researchers have recently examined the influence of "purchase pals" as information sources who actually accompany consumers on shopping trips. While purchase pals were used only 9 per cent of the time for grocery items, they were used 25 per cent of the time for purchases of electronics equipment. Interestingly, male purchase pals are more likely to be used as sources of product category expertise, product, information and retail store and price information and retail store and price information. Female purchase pals are more often used for moral support and to increase confidence in the buyer's decisions.

METHODS OF MEASUREMENT OF OPINION LEADERSHIP

In measuring opinion leadership, the researchers has a choice of four basic measurement techniques: 1. the self designating method, 2. the sociometric method, 3. the key information method and 4. objective method.

Self-Designating Method. In self-designating method, responds are asked to evaluate the extent to which they have provided others with information about a product category or specific brand or have otherwise influenced the purchase decisions of others.

When researchers use the self-designating method, they usually divide consumer respondents into two categories: those who influence others and those who do not. While this two category classification scheme is simple and easy to use, it does not realistically reflect the extent to which an individual might function as an opinion leader. Some people classified as non-leaders may truly have no influence on others. While others so classified may actually influence the comsumption decision of other people to some degree. Therefore, it would be more appropriate to employ a classification scheme that explicitly considers a range of opinion-leading activity those who never or infrequently influence other, those who sometimes influence others and those who frequently influence others.

The self-designating technique is used more often than other methods for measuring opinion leadership because consumer researchers find it easy to include in market-research questionnaires. Because this method relies on the respondent's self-evaluation, however, it may be open to basic respondents perceive "opinion leadership" to be a desirable characteristic and thus overestimate their own roles as opinion leaders.

Consumer researchers have recently developed a companion instrument designed to provide consumers with an opportunity to reveal their susceptibility to influence others.

The socio-metric method measures the person-to-person informal communication of consumers concerning products or product categories. In this method respondents are asked to identify *(a)* the specific individuals (if any) to whom they provided advice or information about the product or brand under study and *(b)* the specific individuals (if any) who provided them with advice or information about the product or brand under study. In the first instance, if respondents identify one or more individuals to whom they have provided some form of product information, they are tentatively classified as opinion leaders. The researchers seek to validate this determination by interviewing the individuals named by the primary respondents and asking them to recall whether they did, in fact, receive such product information.

In the second instance, respondents are asked to identify the individuals (if any) who provided them with information about product under investigation. Individuals designated by the primary respondents are tentatively classified as opinion leaders. Again the researchers attempt to validate this determination by asking the individuals named whether they did, in fact, provide the relevant product information.

Thus, if Ravdi reports that information or advice concerning a specific product was received from Jack, Jack must confirm that such information or advice was given to Ravdi. In this way, the socio-metric method validly identifies the opinion leaders and opinion receivers in product-related conversations.

Consumer Behaviour Applications. The socio-metric approach to determining opinion leadership has useful application to the study of consumer behaviour.For example, consider the flow of opinion leadership among college students living in university housing. Each school year, dormitory students must select a long-distance telephone company. Wish this in mind, it would be useful for a long distance company to undertake a socio-metric study on a particular college campus to determine how word of mouth influence the selection of a long-distance telephone company. This information would provide the basis for subsequent promotional campaigns. On a more general level, any intact community provides an opportunity to measure and evaluate the flow of word-of-mouth communication concerning a new product and the subsequent impact on product trial.

Socio-metric Research Designs. In using the socio-metric method, researchers can study a study contained community or they can study a more widerspread respondent sample. In the first instance (such as a study of all the residents in a particular retirement community in: Scoitsdale, Arizona, or the student residents of a universing operated dormitory), it is relatively simple to verify consumers-related consversation. With a more widespread are pondent sample, researchers must be prepared to trace the web of word of mouth contracts by seeking out all individuals named by the primary respondent group, regardless of location because this research often is costly and difficult to manage, most sociometric consumer studies focus on intact self-containted communities.

Key Information Method. Opinion leadership can also be measured through the use of a key informant a person who is keen aware or knowledgeable about the nature of social communications among members of a specific group. The key informant is asked to identify those individuals in the group who are most likely to be opinion leaders.

The key informant does not have to be a member of the group under study, For example, a professor may serve as the key informant for a college class identifying those students who are most likely to be opined with regard to a particular issue. This research, method is relatively inexpensive, because it requires that only one individual or at most several individuals be intensivly interviewed, while the self-designating and socio-metric method require that a consumer sample or entire community be interviewed. However, the key informant method is generally not used by marketeers because of the difficult inherrent, in identifying an individual who can objectively identfy opinion leaders in relevant consumer group.

The key information method would seem to be of greatest potential use in the study of industrial or institutional opinion leadership. For example, a firm's salespeople might serve as key informants in the indentification of specific customers who are most likely to influence the purchase decisions of her potential customers. Similarly, the purchaing agent of a specific firm might serve as a key informant by providing a suppliers salesperson with the names of those persons in the firm who are most likely to influence the purchase decision. In the study of consumers, possible key informants include knowledgeable community members, such as the president of the women's club, the head of the local school board, or a prominent local business person.

Objective Method. The objective method of determining opinion leadership is much like a controlled experiment. It involves placing new product or new product information with selected individuals and then tracing the resulting "web" of interpersonal communication concerning the relevant products.

An intriguing classic study designed to measure the influence of opinion leaderships on household matters provides an unique example of the objective method. First the individual members of fifteen women's' friendship group living in a self-contained community were interviewed *via* the socio-metric method to assess their levels of opinion leadership in household management matters. The women who scored highest as opinion leaders in each of nine groups were chosen to serve as opinion leader "confederates". In each of the other six groups, the woman who scored lower in opinion leadership also were chosen to serve as opinion leader confederates. This research design enabled the researcher to compare the influence exerted by those identified as opinion leaders with the influence, exerted by those identified as non-leaders when all were placed in a "controlled" situation to serve as opinion leaders.

All fifteen participants selected to function as opinion leaders were provided with new freeze-dried food items and asked to serve them to their families. They also were asked to give sample of the new food products to all other members of their friendship groups and to suggest that they, in turn, serve the items to their families.

The results indicated that those individuals who received the new food items from "natural" opinion leaders tended to echo this leader's opinions concerning the new product. Conversely, these individuals who received samples of the new food items from artificially eveated opinion leaders shifted away from these "leaders" sentiments. These findings suggest that true opinion leaders are capable of altering group members opinions in the direction of their own opinions, while non-leaders may have an adverse effect on those they attempt to influence.

Profile Frequency and Overlap of Opinion Leadership

The generalised profile of opinion leadership is likely to be influenced by the context of specific product categories.

Knowledge and Interest. Opinion leaders tend to possess a high level of interest in the product or service category in which they provide advice or information. For this reason, they are likely to seek information about the product category and because of their knowledge, others may turn to them for product advice. Chief among the characteristics that distinguish opinion leaders from non-leaders in their degree of involvement with the subject. Compared with non-leaders in a particular product category, opinion leaders read more about related consumers issues, are more knowledgeable about related new-product developments, participate more often in related consumer activities and derive greater satisfaction from these product-related activities. For example, a study of financial opinion leadership found that opinion leaders are more involved in tracking their investments than non-leaders, and thus they are "media-omnivorous", that is, they make extensive use of print, electronic and subscription newsletter financial information sources.

Consumer Innovators. Opinion leaders tend to be consumer innovators consistent with their keen interest in a product category, they are likely to try new products in the category as soon as they are introduced. Thus, on the basis of first-hand knowledge, opinion leaders tend to speak with some authority when providing information or advice to others about new products and services.

Studies of consumer innovators for a variety of products and services (*e.g.*, stereo equipment, solar energy devices, car-care services, telephone equipment) have found that individuals identified as innovators also function as opinion leaders by recommending specific products or services based on 'their own experiences, or by showing the products to others. Consumer innovators often feel that others to whom they have spoken about new products or services have brought the specific products or services because of them.

Research conducted on behalf of the film industry confirms the close link between innovators and opinion leadership. For example, frequent movie goers who attend a movie within the first two weeks of its release tend to influence the attendance of their friends. This and other studies indicate that consumer innovators are likely to be opinion leaders in their areas of innovations.

Personal Characteristics. Although opinion leaders generally possess certain similar personality traits, other personal characteristics, such as social status and demographic characteristics, often are'linked to the product or service category in which they "specialize".

Personality Traits. Several personality characteristics of opinion leaders appear to bridge specific product-related contexts: Among these are self-confidence and gregariousness (*i.e.*, sociability). To advice others, individuals first must have confidence in themselves and their own opinions. Also opinion leaders must be socially inclined, have friendships, enjoy the company of others and be somewhat outspoken. These traits are not surprising for individual must be involved in social interaction to function as opinion leaders.

Researchers recently have linked yet another personality trait-public individuation (defined as a state in which a person feels differentiated from others and closes to act differently) with opinion leadership.

In a study among undergraduate students, public individuation scores helped distinguished between opinion leaders and non-leaders. Specifically, it appears that individuals who score higher on the public individuation scale are more likely to be opinion leaders.

Social Class. As with other personal characteristics the social status of the opinion leader appears to depend on the topic of interest. In most marketing studies, however, the opinion leaders were found to belong to the same socio-economic group as the opinion receiver. This is not surprising, it would be reasonable to expert an individual to turn for advice to person with whom he or she feels comfortable—someone within the same social class. Similarly, opinion leaders are most likely to give information or advice to those people with whom they regularly engage in informal communication, the people within their own social stratum.

Demographic Characteristics. Consumers tend to seek information and advice from people whom they perceive to be highly knowledgable. In the context of physician selection, for example, older people may be perceived as having more information and experience. In the context of women's fashions, younger people, those with higher incomes, and/or those with higher occupational status are often perceived as more knowledgeable.

Media Habits. Like consumer innovators, opinion leaders are likely to read special-interest publication devoted to the specific topic or product category in which they "specialize". For example computer opinion leaders read publication such as PC Magazine, PC World, and Byte. These special interest magazines serve not only to inform computer buffs about new computer hardware, and accessories that may be of personal interest, but also provide them with the specialised knowledge that enables them to make recommendations to relatives, friends and neighbour. Thus the opinion leaders tend to have greater exposure to media specifically relevant to his or her area of interest than the non-leader.

To take advantage of this point, mass and targeted (special interest) media like to point out the impact that their particular audience has on influencing the tastes and buying behaviour of others.

Frequency and Overlap of Leadership. Opinion leadership tend to overlap across certain combinations of interest areas. Overlap is likely to be highest among product categories that involve similar interests (*e.g.* large household appliances and small kitchen appliances; high-fashion clothing and hair-styles, cosmetics and other personal grooming aids, house hold cleansers and detergents, packaged food products). Thus, opinion leaders in one product area often are opinion leader in related areas in which they are also interested.

However, research does suggest the existence of a special category of opinion leader the market mover. These consumers possess a wide range of formation about many different types of products, retail outlets, and other dimensions of markets. They both initiate discussions with other consumers and respond to request for market information.

Market movers are distinguishable from opinion leaders because their influence stems not so much from product experience but from a more general knowledge or market expertise that leads to an early awareness of a wide array of new products and services. An initial investigation suggests that market movers play an important role in helping other consumers evaluate the differences among product brands and models. According to a recent study sponsored by popular mechanics, must know men are fascinated by electronics and computers, like to keep up with latest developments in science and technology, dream of travelling in space and want to know how cars work." Indeed, on examining 19 separate product/service categories, the study concluded that must know men influence 93.8 million people about motor oil, 85.1 million people about cars, 80.7 million people about building product, 78.8 million people about gasoline, 76 million people about hand tool, and 73.2 million people about home computers.

❐

14

Family Decision-Making

The family is a major influence in the consumer behaviour process. As the basic group to which an individual belongs, the family provides early childhood learning about products and product categories, provides the opportunity for product exposure and repetition, and sets the consumption norms for family members. As a major consumption unit, the family is a prime target for most products and product categories.

To understand how the family makes its purchase decisions and affects the future purchase behaviour of its young, it is useful to understand the functions provided and roles enacted by family members to fulfill their consumption needs. By way of background, we will first examine some basic family terminology then we will discuss family consumer decision-making and the marketing implications of the family life cycle.

Sociologists and consumer researchers have long been attracted to the concept of the family life cycle (FLC) as a means of depicting what was once a rather steady and predictable series of stages that most families, progressed through. However, with the advent of many diverse family and lifestyle arrangements what was the rule has been on the decline. This decline in the percentage of families that progress through traditional FLC (to be explored shortly) seems to be caused by a host of societal, factors, including an increasing divorce rate, the explosive number of out-ofwedlock births, and the 30-year (1950s to 1970s) decline in the number of extended families that transpired as many young families moved to advance their jobs and carrer opportunities.

Despite the decline in its perdictive precision, the FLC remains a useful marketing tool when one keeps in mind that there are family and lifestyle arrangements that are not fully accounted for by the traditional representation. FLC analysis enables marketeers to segment families in terms of a series of stage spanning the life course of a family unit. The FLC is a composite variable created by systematically combining such commonly used demographic variables as marital status, size of family, age of family members (focusing on the age of the oldest or youngest child), and employment status of the head of household. The ages of the parents and the relative amount of disposable income usually are inferred from the stages in the family life cycle.

To reflect the current realities of a wide range of family and lifestyle arrangements, our treatment of the FLC concept is divided into two sections. The first section considers the traditional FLC scheme. This depiction has dominated most of the thinking about the FLC, yet it is increasingly being challenged, because it fails to account for various important family living arrangements. To rectify these limitations, the second section focuses on alternative FLC stages, including increasingly important non-traditional family structures.

TRADITIONAL FAMILY LIFE CYCLE

The traditional FLC is a progression of stages through which many families pass, starting with bachelorhood, moving on to marrige (and the creation of the basic family unit), then to family growth (with the birth of children), to family contraction (as growth children leave the household), and ending with the dissolution of the basic unit (due to the death of one spouse). Although different researchers have expressed various preferences in terms of the number of FLC stages the traditional FLC models proposed over the years can be synthesized into just five basic stages as follows:

Stage I : Bachelorhood young single adult living apart from parents

Stage II : Honeymooners young married couple

Stage III : Parenthood married couple with at least one child living at home.

Stage IV : Post parenthood—An older married couple with no children living at home.

Stage V : Dissolution one surviving spouse

The following discussion examines the five stages in detail and shows how they lend themselves to market segmentation strategies.

Stage I. Bachelorhood, the first FLC stage consists of young single man and woman who have established households apart from their parents. Although most members of this FLC stage are fully employed. Many are colleges or graduate students who have left their parent's homes. Young single adults are apt to spend their incomes on rent, basic home furnishings, the purchase and maintenance of automobiles, travel and entertainment, and clothing and accessories. Members of the bachelorhood stage frequently' have sufficient disposable income to indulge themselves. Marketeers target singles for a wide variety of products and services.

In most large cities, there are travel agents, housing developments, health clubs, sports clubs, and other service and product marketeers that find this FLC stage a lucrative target niche. Meeting, dating, and mating are prominent concerns of many young adults who typically are beginning their working lines after recently completing college or some other form of career or job training. It is relatively easy to reach this segment, because many special-interest publications target singles for example, GQ and playboy and directed to a young, sophisticated, single male audience, whereas cosmopolitan and glamour are directed to young single females.

Marriage marks the transition from the bachelorhood stage to the honeymoon stage. Engaged and soon-to-be-married couples have a combined income of more than $48,000 (30 per cent greater than the average United States household) therefore, they are the target for many products and services (the bridal industry is a $32 billion-a-year market).

Stage II. Honeymooners, the honeymoon stage starts immediately after the marriage vows are taken and generally continues until the arrival of the couple's first child. This FLC stage serves as a period of adjustment to married life. Because many young husbands and wives both work, these couples have a available an combined income that often permits a lifestyle that provides them with the opportunites of more indulgent purchasing of possessions or allows them to save or invest their extra income.

Honeymooners than considerable start-up expenses when establishing a new home (major and minor appliances, bedroom and living room furniture, carpeting, drapes, dishes, and a host of utensils and accessory items). During this stage, the advice and experience of other married couples are likely to be important to newly weds. Also important as sources of new product information are the so-called shelter magazines, such as Better Homes and Gardens and Metropolitain Home.

Stage III. Parenthood, when a couple has its first child, the honeymoon is considered over. The parenthood stage (sometimes called the full-nest stage) usually extends over more than a 20 year period. Because of its long duration, this stage can be divided into shorter phases, the preschool phase, the elementary school phase, the high school phase and the college phase the elementary school phase, the high school phase and the college phase. Throughout these parenthood phase, the inter-relationaships of family members and the structure of the family gradually change. Furthermore, the financial resources of the family change signficantly, as one or both) parents progress in a career and as child rearing and educational responsibilities gradually increase and finally decrease as children become self-supporting.

An increase in the number of births among baby boomers (born between 1946 and 1964) has resulted in a "baby boomlet". These parents are older (34 to 52), better educated more affluent, and more socially aware. Many (44 per cent) also feel that they are better parents to their children than their parents were to them. Their children often become the focus of their lines, and they spend money accordingly. "Boomer" parents have become an important target for companies that serve the baby market. They also are an important market for many investment and insurance service.

Many magazines cater to the information and entertainment needs of parents and children. For example, there are many other special-interest publications, such as Humpty, Dumpty, designed for the young child just learning to read, scholastic Magazine, far the elementary school pupil; Boy's life, for young boys; and American girl, seventeen, glamour, and Mademoiselle, for teen and post-teen girls invested in fashion.

Stage IV. Post-parenthood, because parenthood extends over many years it is only natural to find that post-parenthood, when all the children have left home, is traumatic for some for many parents almost a "rebirth", a time far doing all the things. They could not do while the children were at home and they had to worry about soaring educational expenses. For the mother, it is a time to further her education, to enter or fe-enter the job market, to seek new interests. For the father, it is a time to indulge in new hobbies. For both, it is the time to travel, to entertain, perhaps to refurnish their home or to sell it in favour of a new home or condominium.

It tsduring this stage that married couples end to be most comfortable financially. Today's empty nesters have more leisure time. They travel more frequently, take extended vacations, and are likely to purchase a second home in a warmer climate. They have higher disposable incomes because of savings and investments and they have fewer expenses (no mortage or college tuition bills). For this reason, families in the post-parenthood stage are an important market for luxury-goods, new automobiles, expensive furniture, and vacations to faraway places.

Many empty nesters retire while they are still in good health. Retirement provides the opportunity to pursue new interests to travel, and to fulfil unsatisfied needs. Hotels, airlines, and car-leasing companies have responded to this market with discounts to consumers over 60; some airlines have established special travel clubs with unlimited mileage for a flat fee. Adult communities have sprung cup in many parts of the nation. Of course, for older retired couples who do not have adequate savings or income, retirement is far different and very restrictive.

Older consumers tend to use television as all important source of information and entertainment. They favour programmes that provide the opportunity to "keep up with what's haspening", especially news and pubiic affairs programmes. In addition a number of special interest magazines cater exclusively to this market, such as, Modern Maturity.

Stage V. Dissolution of the basic family unit occurs with the death of one spouse. When the surviving spouse is in good health, is working or has adequate savings, and has a supportive family and friends, the adjustment is easier. The surviving spouse (usually, the wife) often tends to follow a more economical lifestyle. Many surviving spouses seek each other out for companionship; others enter into second (or third and even fourth) marriages.

To complete the discussion of the traditional FLC stages. Maturing families are heavy consumer of many items, including cereals, fruit-drinks, and, potato chips, and older singles purchase a lot of frozen dinners.

Functions of the Family

Four basic functions provided by the family are particularly relevant to a discussion of consumer behaviour. These include economic well-being, emotional support, suitable lifestyles, and childhood socialization.

Economic Well-Being

Although the family in an affluent nation like the United States is no longer formed primarily for economic security, the provision of financial means to its dependents is unquestionably a basic family function. How the family divides its responsibilities for the provision of economic well-being has changed considerably during the past twenty years. No longer are the traditional roles of husband as economic provider and wife as homemaker and child rearer still valid; the majority of wives in this country are employed outside the home and their husbands share household responsibilities. The economic role of children also has changed. Today, despite the fact that many teenage children work, they rarely assist the family financially. Instead, they are expected to complete their formal educational training and prepare themselves to be financially independent.

Emotional Support

The provision of emotional and therapeutic support to its members is an important basic function of the contemporary family. In fulfilling this function, the family attempts to assist its members in coping with personal or social problems. If the family cannot provide adequate assistance when it is needed, it may turn to a professional counselor or psychologist as an alternative. In general terms, the selection of such professional services is similar to other types of consumption decisions made by the family.

Suitable Lifestyles

Another important family function in terms of consumer behaviour is the establishment of a suitable lifestyle for the family. Upbringing, experience, and the personal and jointly determined goals of the spouses determine the importance placed on education or career, on reading, on television viewing, on the frequency and quality of dining out, and the selection of other entertainment and recreational activities. Family lifestyle commitments, including the allocation of time, greatly influence consumption patterns. For example, the increase in married women working has reduced the time they have available for household chores and created a market for convenience products and fast-food restaurants.

Childhood Socialization

The socialization of young children is a central family function. In large part, this process consists of imparting to children the basic values and modes of behaviour consistent with the culture, which may include personality development, interpersonal competence, dress and grooming habits, appropriate manners and speech, and the selection of a suitable occupation or career. Socialization factors are imparted to the child directly through instruction, and indirectly through the behaviour of parents and older siblings.

The aspect of childhood socialization that is most relevant to the study of consumer behaviour is consumer socialization, which is defined as the process by which children acquire the skills, knowledge, and attitudes necessary to function as consumers. Several studies have focused on how children develop consumption skills. One researcher demonstrated that children's consumer behaviour norms are acquired through observation of their parents, who function as role models. While preadolescent children tend to rely on their parents and older siblings as the major source of cues for basic consumption learning, adolescents and teenagers are likely to look to outside friends for models of acceptable behaviour.

Consumer socialization fulfills a unique function as a tool by which parents influence other aspects of the socialization process. For instance, parents frequently use the promise or reward of material goods as a device to modify or control a child's behaviour. A mother may reward her child with a gift when the child does something to please her, or withhold or remove it if the child disobeys. One study showed that children's consumer knowledge structure becomes more sophisticated as they grow older. Thus younger children (ages 4 to 6) describe grocery shopping with their mothers in highly specific (episodic) terms ("Get a shopping cart...go get some pop, milk, fruit for my dad's lunch, pizza, spaghetti"). Older children (ages 7 to 10), on the other hand, tend to give very general (categorical) descriptions ("We go in the store, look around, find all the stuff you need come up to the counter and pay for it and then you can go home"). One study found that parents can teach children to apply economic reasoning. Children who were taught that they cannot have everything and must choose among realistic alternatives were found to be more satisfied with their choices. These findings were supported by a study which found that although children are generally satisfied with the presents they receive from their parents, children with high parent interaction experience somewhat more satisfaction. A study of black and white consumers suggests that observed differences in consumer behavior are attributable to different socialization patterns in each sub-culture.

Consumer socialization has two distinct components: those directly related to consumption, such as the acquisition of skills, knowledge, and attitudes concerned with budgeting, pricing, and brand attitudes; and those indirectly related to consumption, such as the underlying motivations that spur a young man to purchase his first razor or a young girl to want her first bra. While both are significant, the indirect component of consumer socialization is of most interest to marketing executives, who want to understand why people buy their products.

The socialization process is not confined to childhood it is an ongoing process. For example, when a newly married couple establishes a household, their adjustment to living and consuming together is part of that continuing process.

Although many marketeers recognize the family as the basic decision-making unit, they must fruquently examine the attitudes and behaviour of the other family member whom they believe to be the major decision-maker. In some cases, they also examine the attitudes and behaviour of the person most likely to be the primary user of the product or service. For instance, in the case of men's underwear, which is frequently purchased by women for their husbands and unmarried sons it is commonplace to seek the views of both the man who wear the underwear and the women who buy it. By considering both the likely user and the likely purchaser, the marketeer obtains a richer picture of the consumption process.

Family Roles. For a family to function as a cohesive unit, roles or tasks such as doing the laundry, preparing meals, setting the dinner table, taking out the garbage, and walking the dog must be carried out by one or more family members. In a dynamic society, family-related roles are constantly changing. For instance, give the substantial number of married women working outside the home, and the greater assumption of household tasks by men, marketeers must be particularly sensitive to how shifting family roles may affect the composition of their target markets. In addition, they must be careful to purchase their ads in ways that are appropriate and acceptable to their target markets.

Key Family Consumption Roles. There are eight distinct roles in the family decision-making process. A look at these roles provides further insight into how family members interact in their various consumption related roles.

— ***Influencers.*** Family members who provide information to other members about a product or service.

— ***Gatekeepers.*** Family member who, control the flow of information about a particular product or service into the family.

— ***Deciders.*** Family members with the power to determine unilaterally or jointly whether the shop for purchase, use, consumer, or dispose of a specific product or service.

— ***Buyers.*** Family members who transform the product into a form suitable for consumption by other family members.

— ***Users.*** Family members who use or consume a particular product so that it will provide continued satisfaction.

— **Disposers.** Family members who initiate or carry out the disposal or discontinuation of a particular product or service.

The number and identity of the family members who performs, these roles vary from family to family and from product to product. In some cases, a single family member will independently assume a number of roles, in other cases, a single role will be preformed jointly by two or more family members. In still other cases, one or more of these basic roles may not be required. For example, a family member may be walking down on the snack food aisle at a local supermarket when he picks out an interesting new chocolate candy. His selection does not directly involve the influence of other family members. He is the decider, the buyer and, in a sense the gatekeeper, however, he may or may not be the sole consumer (*i.e.* user) directly by two or more family members, or consumed indirectly by the entire family.

Influencing Spouses and Resolving Consumer Conflicts

When it comes to making purchasing decisions, husbands and wives frequently find themselves in disagreement about when to spend, or save, how much to spend on some item, what colour fits best, or where to, buy something. These are just a few of the many consumer behaviour decisions where there might be disagreement. To avoid or resolve potential disargreements, husbands and wives commonly attempt to influence each other to arrive at what they feel to be the best outcome. Six influence strategies for resolving husband wife consumption-related conflicts have been identified.

— **Expert.** An attempt by a spouse to use his or her superior information about decision alternatives to influence the other spouse.

— **Legitimacy.** An attempt by a spouse to influence the other spouse on the basis of position in the household.

— **Bargaining.** An attempt by a spouse to secure influence now that will be exchanged with the other spouse at some future date.

— **Emotional.** An attempt by a spouse to use an emotion lader reaction to influence the behaviour of the other spouse.

— **Reward.** An attempt by a spouse to influence the behaviour of the other spouse by differing a reward.

— **Impression.** Any persuasive attempts by one spouse to influence the behaviour of the other.

These influence strategies tend to be used by either husbands or wives when they find themselves in disagreement or in conflict with the other spouse regarding a specific consumer decision. For instance, we all have experienced occasion on which different family members want to eat at different types of restaurants, see different movies, or go on a different type of family vacation. These are only four examples of the almost end. Less possibilities of potential family consumption confliects that too might need to be resolved. Figure presents examples of other issues on which married couples tend to disagree.

How to spend money	24%
What TV programmes to watch	21%
Disciplining children	20%
How to spend weakends	16%
Housekeeping	13%
Which friends to see	9%
Spending money for kids	6%

Dynamics of Husband-Wife Decision-Making. Marketers are interested in the relative amount of influence that a husband and a wife have when it comes to family consumption choices. Most husband-wife influence studies classify family consumption decisions as husband dominated wife dominated joint and automatic.

Studies that have examined both the extent and nature of husband/wife influence in family decisions have found that such influence is fluid and likely to shift, depending on the specific product or service, the specific stage in the decision-making process, and the specific product features under consideration. All these factors are also mediated by changing lifestyles, particularly the increase in the number of working wives. A recent study found that families with modern sex-role norms showed less wife influence and greater joint and husband influence in areas traditionally assigned to the wife; conversely, there was less husband influence and greater joint and wife influence in areas traditionally handled by the husband.

Variations by Products or Service. The relative influence of a husband and wife on a particular consumer decision depends in part on the product and service category. For instance, during the 1950, the purchse of a new automobile was strong husband-dominated, while food and financial-banking decisions more often were wife-dominated. Forty years later, the purchase of the family's principal automobile is still often husband-dominated. However, in other contexts or situations (*e.g.* a second car or a car for a single or working woman), female car buyers are a repidly expanding segment of the automobile market, a segment to which many car manufacturers are currently paying separate marketing attention. Also in case of financial decision-making there has been a trend away from wife dominated decisions to joint decisions.

Variations by Family Role Structure Orentation. A family's orientation regarding sex roles is a key factor which it comes to consumption decisions. In families with a modern sex role oriented (*i.e.*, a commitment to husband-wife equality) consumption decisions like to be evenly distributed between the two spouses and there is less disagreement between husband and wife as to the purchase decision.

Role structure and decision-making within the family appear to be related to culture and sub-culture. Recent research comparing husband-wife decision-making pattenrs in the People's Republic of China and the United States reveals that among the Chinese there were substantially fewer "joint" decision and more "husband-dominated" decisions for many household purchases. However, when limited the comparison to urban and rural Chinse households (*i.e.*, within-China comparison), the research showed that in a larger city like Beijing, Married couples were most likely than rural couples to share equally in purchase decisions. Other research shows that Mexican-American families tend to be more husband-dominant than Anglo families and that Anglo familes engage in more joint purchase decisions. However, these findings may be influenced by the extent to which Hispanic-American couples have assimilated general American values and attitudes. Hispanic-American couples who are more assimilated with found to have husbands and wives who shared equally in decision-making whereas in more traditional households the husband more often dominated in arriving at a decision.

The sub-culutral factor of religion and the related dimension of religious orientation, also have been found to be associated with family decision-making. Specifically, in exploring the consumer related marital roles of catholic and Jewish families and pro-religious and non-religious families, research suggests that, in both catholic and pro-religious families, husband have the major influence on specific purchase. In contrast, in both Jewish and non-religious families, husbands and wives share equally in most decision making. For instance, In the majority of Danish families husbands and wives jointly decided how much to spend on an automobile, while in catholic families, husbands played a more dominant role in deciding how much to spend. Similarly, compared to the proreligious families, more of the non-religious families (regardless of which of the two religions was involved in the comparison) jointly decided what model automobile to purchase. In the case of proreligious families, husbands exercised more control.

Variations by Stage in the Decision-Making Process. The roles of husbands and wives may differ at various points throughout the decision-making process. A simple, three-stage, family decision-making model includes problem recognition search for information and final decision. The initial decision-making role pattern established in stage one (problem recognition) usually continues during the two remaining stages (search for information and final decision). However, for some decisions, there are stage-to-stage shifts. For instance, recognition of the need for a new washing machine may be wife-dominant, the search for information concerning the poential purchase might be largely autonomic (usually performed by the wife), and the final decision might be made jointly by both spouses.

ROLE OF CHILDREN

Children play an important role in family decision making. They not only are influenced by their families in terms of consumer socialization, they also exert influence on their families in terms of family purchase decisions. Young children attempt to influence family decisions as soon as they possess the basic communication skills needed to interact with other family members. ("Buy me a cookie." "1 want Sugar Loops." "Let's eat at McDonald's.") Older children are likely to participate more directly in family consumption activities. The study confirms the fact that children significantly influence family decisions. For each of the three major decision stages, there was a significant amount of child input into the decision. Children also played an influential role in the major dimensions of the decision, with the exception of how much to spend, which largely remained the province of the parents. Related research indicates that the age of a child and the type of restaurant being considered affects the extent of influence a child will have. Specifically, children over five are more likely to share in the family's decision to eat out, and parents tend to allow children more say when the choice is to be made among fast-food restaurants rather than conventional restaurants.

The parent-child relationship as it relates to consumer behaviour can be viewed as an influence versus yield situation. Specifically, children attempt to influence their parents to make a purchase (to yield). In-store observations of purchase behavior in supermarkets indicate that children not only attempt to influence their parents in areas of special interest to them (cereal, candy), but also with products of remote interest (laundry detergents). Several consumer behaviour studies report conflicting results on the nature of influence and yielding. One study that focused exclusively on breakfast cereals found that the more involved the mother was with her child, the more likely she was not to yield to the child's preference for sugar-coated breakfast cereals, presumably because she considered such cereals to be nutritionally unsound.

Another study, which examined child-parent interaction across a number of products (including cereals), found a significant positive relationship between the number of children's influence attempts and the yielding of their mothers. The study also found that children's attempts to influence tended to decrease somewhat with age, and mothers' yielding tended to increase with the child's age. These results seem to indicate that children become more discriminating in their requests as they get older, and that parents acknowledge their children's increased judgment by acceding more readily to their purchase requests.

Children and Television

A number of studies have investigated the impact of television viewing and advertising on children. One study found that older children and those with more media exposure tend to recall more advertising slogans. Another study showed that as children get older and acquire more education, they watch less television. However, a younger child in the family tends to expand the older child's TV use. Another provocative finding was that TV use tends to increase by some 15 minutes a day for each $10,000 of parental income.

Parents have expressed concern regarding the impact of TV advertising on their children. One study showed that parents with high socio-economic status were concerned with the nutrition and quality (especially the high sugar content) of foods advertised to children, while parents lower on the socio-economic scale were more concerned that such advertising would lead to family conflict with the child, and less concerned that it would promote bad eating habits.

The impact of TV advertising varies among children in different age groups. One study showed that preschoolers respond to perceptual cues and do not truly understand the difference between programmes and commercials. It was found that commercials targeted to adults have great influence on children. For example, TV commercials for lipstick favourably influenced nine and ten-year-old girls perceptions of the product and brand, because they associated the product with being an adult. A recent study showed that older children recognize more symbolism in advertising than younger children. Those who had experience with the product held strong consumption-based stereotypes, suggesting that personal experience is more important than media exposure.

There is some indication that children of parents who more strictly control their children's viewing behaviour (and who generally were found to be of a higher socio-economic level) exhibit a better understanding of the purpose and nature of advertising and make fewer purchase requests of their parents. Several studies point out the need to develop better measures of children's understanding of TV commercials. One study showed that traditional verbal measures usually underestimate the child's ability to understand TV ads, while non-verbal measures, such as asking the child to point at something, indicate that young children are capable of understanding TV commercials.

Teenage Children

A number of researchers have examined the influence of teenage children on family decision making. There is some evidence that girls with working mothers are somewhat more involved in homemaking activities than girls with non-working mothers. An ongoing survey sponsored by Co-ed (a magazine for teenage girls) indicates that an impressive number of high school girls plan or participate in the planning of family meals and shop for their family's food needs.

Although teenagers constitute a shrinking percentage of the American population, a significant number work, and most of their income is discretionary. Estimates of teen spending power range from $30 billion to over $40 billion a year. High school students in grades 7 through 12 are most interested in sports and fitness. Boys aged sixteen to nineteen spend most of their money on movies, dating, entertainment, car expenses, and clothing, while girls of that age spend most of their money on clothing, cosmetics, and fragrances. The income of both groups is about the same, and some 60 per cent of it is earned. Another study found that adolescents with earned income are more likely to save money than those who receive the money as a gift, but dual-income teenagers (allowance and earnings) are more inclined to spend the money on themselves. Teenagers are an important market segment not only because they influence family consumption decisions, but because the teenage years are formative ones in terms of later consumption patterns.

College students have also been shown to exert influence over the purchase decisions of their families. In one study, college students reported that they often attempted to influence family decisions concerning the purchase of television sets and automobiles, and they perceived that they often did in fact influence these decisions.

Despite the numbers of studies that have addressed the role children play in influencing family consumption decisions, the extent and specific nature of their influence (the range of products and the extent of their influence over such decisions) is still largely undocumented. Nevertheless, evidence makes it very clear that children wield important influence in family purchase decisions and thus constitute an important market segment.

ROLE OF FAMILY IN CONSUMER BEHAVIOUR

For a family to function as a cohesive unit, roles or taks such as doing the laundry, prepearing meals, setting the dinner table and walking the dog must be carried out by one or more family members. In a dynamic society family-related roles are constantly changing. For instance, given the substantial number of married working outside the home, and the greater assumption of household tasks by men, marketeers must be particularly sensitive to how shifiting family roles may affact the composition of their target markets. In addition, they must be careful to pharse their ads in ways that are appropriate and acceptable to their target markets.

By Family Consumption Roles. There are eight distinct roles in the family decision-making process. A look at these roles provides further insight into how family members intereact in there various consumption-related roles.

Influnces. Family members who provide informatin to other members about a product or service into the family.

Gatekeepers. Family members who control the flow of information about a product or service into the family.

Deciders. Family members with the power to determine unilaterally, or jointly whether to shop for purchase, use, consume, or dispose of a specific product or service.

Prepares. Family members who transform the product into a form suitable for consuption by other family members.

Buyers. Family members who make the actual purchaseof a particular product of service.

Users. Family members who use or consume a particular product or service.

Maintainers. Family members who service or repair the product so that it will provide continued satisfaction.

Disposals. Family members who initiate or carry out the disposal or discontinuation of a particular product or service.

The number and identification of the family members who fill these roles very from family to family and from product to product. In some cases, a single family member will independently assume a number of roles, in other cases, one or more of these basic roles may not be required for example, a family member may be walking down the sanck food aiste as a local supermarket when he wants an interesting new chocolate candy, his selection does not directly involve the influence of other family members. He is the decider, the buyer, and in a sense, the gatekeeper, however, he may or may not be sole consumer (*i.e.*, user). Products may be consumed by a single family member, consumed or used directly by two or more family members or consumed indirectly by the entire family.

Influencing Spouses and Resolving Consumer Conflicts. When it comes to making purchase decisions husbands and wives frequently find themselves in disagreement about what to spend or save, how much to spend on some item, what colour fits best or where to buy something. These are just a few of many consumer behaviour decisions where there might be disagreement. Husbands and wives commonly attempt to influence each other to arrive at what they feel to be the best outcome. Six ifluence strategies for resolving husband-wife consumption-related conflicts have been identified.

Export. An attempt by a spouse to use his or her superior information, about decision alternatives to influence the other spouse.

Leigtimacy. An attempt by a spouse to influence the other spouse on the basis of position in the household.

Bargaining. An attempt by a spouse to secure influence how that will the other spouse as some future date.

Reward. An attempt by a spouse to influence the behaviour of the other spouse by offering a reward.

Impression. Any persuasive attempts by one spouse to influence the behaviour the other.

Figure given below presents examples of other issues on which married couples tend to disagree.

How to spend money	24%
What TV Programmes to watch	21%
Disciplining Children	20%
How to spend weekends	10%
Housekeeping	13%
Which friends to see	11%

Dynamics of Husband-Wife Decision-Making. Marketeers are interested in the relative amount of influence that a husband and a wife have when it comes to family consumption choices. Most hubansd-wife influence studies classify family consumption deicisions as husband-dominated, wife-dominated joint and autonomic (*i.e.*, solemnly or unilateral).

Studies that have examined both the extent and nature of husband-wife influence in family decision have found that such influence is fluid and likely to shift; depending on the specific product or service, the family role structure orientation and the specific stage in the decision-making process. These factors also are influenced by changing lifestyles; particularly the changes in family lifestyle options associated with women working outside of the home and the increased occurrence of the income of households.

Variations by Product or Service. The relative influence of a husband and wife on a particular consumer decision depends in part on the product and service category. For instance, during the 1950s, the purchase of a new automobile was strongly husband dominated, while food and financial-bombing decisions more often were wife-dominated. Forty years later, the purchase of the family's principal automobile is still often husband-dominated. However, in other contexts or situations, female car buyers are a rapidly expanding segment of the automobile market, a segment to which many car manufacturers are currently paying sepearte marketing attention. Also, in case of financial decision-making, there has been a trend away from wife-dominated decisions to joint decisions.

Variatios by Family Role Structure Orientation. A family's orientation orgarding sex roles is a key factor when it comes to consumption decisions. In familes with a modern sex role orientation consumption decision are likely to be evenly distributed between the two spouses and there is less disagreement between husband and wife as to the purchase decision.

Role structure and decision-making within the family appear to be related to culture and sub-culture. Recent research company husband-wife decision-making patterns in the People's Republic of China and the United States reveals that among the Chinese there were substantially fewer "joins" decisions and more "husband-dominated" decisions for many household purchases. However, when limiting the comparison to urban and rural Chinese households, the research showed that in, a large city like Beijing married couples were more likely than rural couples to share equally in purchase decisions. Other research shows that Mexican-American families tend to be more husband-dominant than Anglo-families and that

Anglo families engage in more joint purchase decisions. However, these findings may be influenced by the extent to which Hispanic-American couples have assimilated general American values and attitudes. Hispanic-American couples who are more assimilated were found to share husbands and wives who shares equally in decision-making, whereas in more traditional households the husband more often dominated in arriving at a decision.

The sub-culture factor of religion and the related dimension of religious orientation also have been found to be associated with family decision making Specifically, in exploring the consumer-related mental roles of Catholic and Jewish families and proreligious and non-religious families, research suggests that in both Catholic and pro-religious families, husbands have the major influence on specific purchase decisions. In contact, in both Jewish and non-religions families, husbands and wives share equally in most decision making. For instance in that majority of Jewish families, husbands and wives jointly decide how much to spend on an automobile, while in. Catholic families, husbands played a more dominant role in deciding how much to spend. Similarly, compared to the pro-religious families jointly decided what model automobile to purchases. In the case of pro-religious families, husbands exercised more control.

❐

15

Consumer Attitudes and Purchasing Behaviour

Markets for consumer goods tend to become in increasingly competitive and saturated. In the fight for profitable survival the manufacturer is obliged to look outwards at his consumer rather than inwards at his production plant. What becomes important is not what can be made but what people wantand why? However, in studying consumers, one must take into account, not only the demographic characteristics and the economic circumstances of the individual, but also the more powerful influences of prejudices, feelings, attitudes, opinions and beliefs. This article sets out something of the progress made in consumer research in studying such psychological influences, from the qualitative approach of Motivation Research, through to the quantitative measurement of significant attitudes of consumer groups and the application of such studies to the mass-marketing problems of today. The emphasis throughout is upon cost benefit commercial utility, which is not necessarily at variance with the demands of a rigorous scientific discipline.

Evolution of Marketing Research

In the India of today, we are witnessing changes taking place (bo social and economic) at a staggering rate. The rapidity of these changes provides those interested in the modern science of marketing with a comprehensive canvas of economic activity. A quick look at this spectrum is an ideal means of demonstrating the need for marketing research in general and for consumer research in particular.

One can at the simplest level of trading, see straightforward barter taking place in the village, or the local craftsman selling his wares to a restricted clientele. From these, one sees cottage industries supplying a larger market through some form of retail distribution, though still at a restricted level. The escalation of scale goes on until one reaches the large manufacturer with production units far from the point of sale and a distribution system which, however efficient, still leaves him far removed from his customers.

The cot-maker in the village knows what product to make. He knows, also, what the local demand for his product is likely to be. He has all the marketing information he needs, without being aware of it in these terms.

As the evolution moves towards the large scale mass producer, one notices that the gap in communications between supplier and consumer becomes wider and wider. But, one may ask, does this matter?

The answer to this question depends very much upon the combination of economic, social and psychological factors operating in the particular market under consideration. Some of these influencing factors are shown in Figure 1, although not in any order of importance.

Now, it is to be admitted that markets can be classified in innumerable ways but using the simple dassification given above, it is obvious that manufacturers in certain market categories need considerably more feedback from the market than do others. One or two examples will sufice to make the point.

The fortunate manufacturer in market type I needs virtually no feedback, apart from the knowledge that his goods are getting to the retail outlets as fast as his production unit can manufacture. He is making a traditional product that everyone needs and has a monopoly. He therefore has no need of consumer research and little need of marketing research in the macro sense.

Fig. 1 : Types of Market

	T								I							
	E				D				E				D			
	M		C		M		C		M		C		M		C	
Market Type No.1	H	L	H	L	H	L	H	L	H	L	H	L	H	L	H	L
	1	2	3	4	5	6	7	8	9	10	11	12	13	14	15	16

Product Type	**Income Availability**
T = Traditional	E = Essential Expenditure
I = Innovation	D = Discretionary Expenditure
Type of Supply	**Demand**
M = Monopoly	H = Demands > Supply
C = Competition	L = Supply > Demand

At the other end of the spectrum we see the marketing man of type 14 who boldly hopes to sell something new, that is not essential, for which there is no demand. He would at least have some moral support if he had a competitor, thus transferring himself into market type.

This is the marketing man who may (or may not, as is often unfortunately the case) have a brilliant new product concept that will sweep the market in two years and guarantee his chairmanship of the company soon after. Now, this is the extreme case where the marketing man needs all the feed-back he can get about the potential for his new product, the form it should take, the likely target group, how this group should be approached through advertising and so on.

Whatever the market type, the small scale operator, or entrepreneur, may still be in a position to innovate on a local and experimental basis, cutting his losses if he finds the market unrewarding. The mass-marketeer is rarely in this position; his operation can only be profitable if the market is large enough. This brings with it the corollary that the financial risk involved can be very great. This applies particularly where heavy investment is required for new plant, if a start is to be made at all.

From this brief overview, one visualises a spectrum of conditions which call for less or more, marketing research of one type or another. The combinations of various intensities of the factors mentioned are inexhaustible but, in general, marketing research is not only desirable, but a necessity in any market where one or more of the following conditions prevail:

1. Competition.
2. High financial risk.
3. The need for high volume sales.
4. The need for diversification/innovation.
5. A lengthy communication chain between manufacturer and consumer.
6. Supply greater than demand (or no demand, in the case of new products.)

Now, much of the feed-back necessary to successful marketing in a competitive, mass-consumer field is gathered in what might be termed a 'desk research' manner. Any company will have access to certain government statistics, data from trade federations and, of course, information from its own production and distribution network. It may also, as is the case with Hindustan Lever, obtain feed-back on purchasing at the point of sale through the use of continuous retail audit data from a representative panel of outlets. However, in highly competitive fields, and particularly so in the case of new product areas, such information, though essential, is insufficient. Attention has to be paid to the ultimate consumer, for reasons which will become clear in the following sections.

Need for Consumer Research

The concept of 'mass-marketing' has been referred to in the previous section of this Chapter, without qualification. In the world of consumer goods, it can mean virtually all households in a country. For example, in most European countries, between 90 per cent and 100 per cent of all households buy some form of washing powder for fabric washing. Many of these markets are 'saturated' from the economic viewpoint. These products are truly 'mass-market'. However, other markets may be based upon only a minority segment of the population, for economic or other (perhaps more complex and interesting) reasons and these may well prove lucrative for the large manufacturer. This is particularly true in the India of today with its population of nearly 550 million. A target market of less than 1 per cent might be more than worthwhile.

Whether we are faced with a global or a minority market, whether it is saturated or not the same questions must be answered before successful commercial exploitation can take place:

1. What is the target group?
2. What differentiates them from others?
3. What needs (both physical and psychological) does the group have which could be met by a product or brand?
4. What physical characteristics must the product have to satisfy the physical consumer needs?
5. What media does one use to reach the target group and what should be said to appeal to them as people to persuade them to try it?
6. Who is buying the product after its launch?

If these questions need to be answered for marketing to be successful, the only recourse is to make a study of consumer to resolve them. In attempting to answer such questions, consumer researchers have brought to bear a large armoury of techniques and method in various areas, an armoury which is expanding constantly. It is beyond the scope of this Chapter to describe the various methods available for assessing consumer response to product ideas, products, packaging, promotions, price, advertising and so on. But having presented a brief case for the utility of consumer study, we shall now focus upon the importance of consumer feelings, beliefs and attitudes to the successful exploitation of a market. One such approach is that of 'Motivation Research' which is discussed in the following section.

Motivation Research

The swing away from macro-studies of markets to micro-studies of the consuming public was dramatic and extreme. It started, mainly in the USA and UK, many years back. It resulted largely from intense competition between brands offering similar physical results in saturated markets. Manufacturers (and their advertising agencies) became concerned-even desperate, in some cases-to establish what motivated people to buy their product or brand or, even more important still, what were the motives for buying the competitive product or brand.

The first approach to be used was, of course, to conduct consumer surveys in which respondents were asked 'why?' or 'why not?'. Unfortunately, such questions normally produce a rational, vague and superficial answers. Answers such as: 'it tastes better', 'It's good value', 'High quality', and so on are all too common. Such responses are clearly neither revealing nor actionable.

It was at this point that psychology offered its services through the use of techniques developed in the area of clinical psychology. In the study of human behaviour generally, it had become tacitly acknowledged that people are either unwilling, or unable, to reveal their true motives for behaviour. Most clinical study and treatment was based upon Freudian theories relating to the influence of the unconscious on behaviour. This principle was fairly naturally extended to the field of consumer behaviour. The individual, it was argued, is often unaware of the influences which lead him (or her) to select certain products. Only by means of unstructured and indirect interviewing procedures could personality characteristics, attitudes, prejudices, feelings, and the like be uncovered which would give the psychologist an insight into the personal an social influences which were determining buying behaviour.

This kind of research is normally confined to small samples of people, owing to the time involved in conducting such unstructured interviews and the difficulty of processing the mass of spontaneous information produced. The generalisation of findings to embrace a large population is, to say the least prone to large margins of error.

But, in certain markets, such research undoubtedly provided certain insights which were of value to marketing management. Everyone will doubtlessly agree that such a complicated and important decision as buying a new car will involve far more than technical considerations of power, braking ability, and so on. The decision will involve price of course, but even more important is the extent to which the model chosen projects the self image of the buyer to others. There must be significant psychological factors at work which drive the wealthy businessman in Delhi or Bombay to buy a large white Mercedes car, capable of cruising at 140 kms. per hour, when it can only be driven at 60 kms. per hour at maximum. The fact of his having a rather large joint family would be a plausible but insufficient explanation for most people.

Similarly, the classical and often quoted example of the launch of a new cake mix in the US illustrates thatpsychological factors can be important, even in buying decisions of an apparently mundane nature. This particular case was of a product that merely had to be mixed with water and placed in the oven for 20 minutes, or so. Result: a perfect cake. The problem was that it didn't sell. Motivation research provided the insight that (at that time) US housewives were highly resentful of any encroachment upon their role as family food providers. The cake mix denied them any credit for the final result. The marketing solution adopted was to remove the powdered egg from the mix and leave the housewife the task of beating in an egg before baking. Result: success. However in its early days, certain practitioners of motivation research indulged in such flights of fancy in their Freudian interpretation of buying motives that, to the distress of more responsible consumer researchers, the methods fell into disrepute. Marketing men, although always fascinated by the reports written by practitioners having overfertile imaginations, realised that the data was often not very actionable.

As an example one might give a typical case scathingly cited by Harry Henry in his excellent book 'Motivation Research':

"The ceremonial nature of smoking is usually explained as a continuation of, or regression to, infantile forms of auto-eroticism (such as thumb-sucking, masturbation, etc.). The nearest to such a case that I observed was Mrs. M. who smoked heavily at weekly meetings of some-Lesbians at which 'free-fights' took place between the women present."

To be fair, it may well be true that a market did exist for a cigarette appealing to such people, but one pities the advertising agency given the account.

Or yet another illustration, to make the point:

In a report on canned soup in the USA, the psychologist stated that:

> "Besides being a good food, stimulating to the appetite and easily assimilated into the bloodstream soup is consciously associated with man's deepest need for nourishment and reassurance. it takes us back to our earliest sensation of warmth, protection and feeding. Its deepest roots may lie in pre-natal sensations of being surrounded by the amniotic fluid in our mother's womb. No wonder people like soup and prefer it hot and in large quantities."

Again, this analysis may be fair, even if pursued to such psychological depths. The trouble is, it implies that everyone is in desperate need of soup, for very primaeval motives and the theory propounded gives no clue as to what kind of soup should be marketed to which target group and in what manner.

Much of the trouble in these early years was not so much the Freudian basis of explanation of human behaviour, but rather that psychologists were seeking parameters so deep and fundamental to the human organism, that one could hardly expect a relationship between them and the purchase of different brands of a fairly ordinary consumer product.

This was confirmed in a most thorough and systematic study carried out in the UK some years ago, in which various scales to measure certain personality characteristics (such as Neuroticism, Introversion/Extroversion, etc.), were applied to a large random sample. This survey, 'The Londoner', attempted to relate the scores of sub-groups on such scales to both purchasing of certain consumer goods and, also to media exposure (such as press, television, radio, etc.). The scales used certainly segmented the population but, again, the psychological characteristics measured were too fundamental to be closely related to either consumer buying or media habits.

A special report in 'Retail Business' in 1965 summed up the situation at that time in a fair way:

"Historically, motivational research passed through a period which reflected credit neither on itself nor on research in general, This was when psychologists' pet theories were substituted for sampling principles. At worst, the results were irrelevant to the marketing problem and at best they explained features of human behaviour being researched. Also there is still sometimes a feeling, possibly engendered by the actual title, that Motivational Research is 'not quite playing the game' and perhaps rather 'un-English'. Most important, though, there is usually a failure to appreciate what motivational research is attempting to do, and further, a lack of Understanding of its applications in marketing terms. Motivational Research is, in fact, an integral part of the total research operation, serving one set of functions in the same way that a retail audit serves. another."

For a violent diatribe expounding the view that such research is 'not playing the game', the reader is referred to the classic attack by Vance Packard in his book 'The Hidden Persuaders'. Nevertheless, the crucial point at issue is not whether 'Motivation Research' is 'fair', but whether it is action, able by marketing management. Since the earlier days, consumer researchers have realised that there are psychological parameters which are related to the purchase of consumer goods; parameters which are not just 'exploitable' by the marketing man but which enable him also to produce the goods that people want and to produce advertising which will appeal to them. Instead of talking about 'life in the womb' and so on, researchers are now concentrating upon less fundamental characteristics such as attitudes and beliefs. The utility of this approach, whilst still exploiting many of the techniques developed earlier, will be demonstrated in the final sections of this Chapter. Throughout, four criteria will be evident:

1. Psychological parameters used must be measurable with precision and reliability.
2. They must be applicable to quantitative surveys.
3. They must relate to purchasing or other important aspects of behaviour.
4. Results obtained from research of this type must be actionable by marketing management.

Relevance of Consumer Attitudes to Marketing Decisions

It is worth reiterating that a description of the consuming public in straightforward demographic terms is often inadequate for the needs of the mass-marketeer. Agreed, the price of an article in India (or any other country, for that matter) may rule out a significant proportion of the population from the potential target group. However, within the consuming group, one is still left with the nasty question of why some people buy one's own brand and why others buy other brands.

Competition tends towards price equality and also tends towards product similarity. It is true that certain cultural/socio economic groups will (or will not) buy certain things, but one finds that, in more and more markets in every country, product and brand purchasing can often not be related to such demographic characteristics. Even if a relationship is established, it rarely provides a causal explanation.

In the previous section, we have largely ruled out the use of fundamental psychological characteristics, so one may ask where do we go from here?

Figure 2 pictures the consumer in a schematic fashion, which will serve to define and classify certain concepts fundamental to the approach that follows. From a psychological viewpoint one can visualise the individual's basic personality structure stemming partly from inherited characteristics and partly from environmental circumstances surrounding the person both past and present. The total personaliry, in the adult at least, is fairly rigid and will very much determine general attitudes to life. At this latter level, we refer to such attitudes as : whether the individual is conservative or experimental;

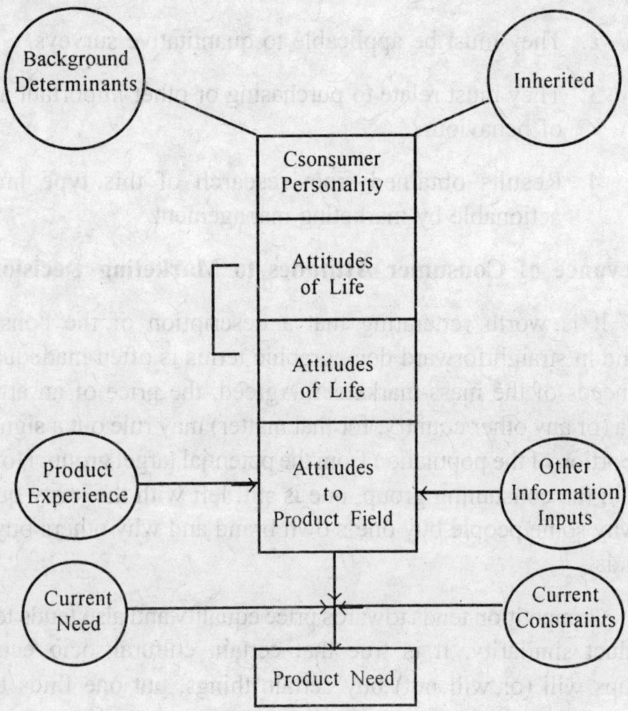

Fig 2.

whether he is passive or active; whether he is one who leads or one who follows; whether he is confident or timid and so on. These are relatively stable structures in the individual's mental make-up. Below this level, one may envisage attitudes which are, perhaps, a little more mundane. In the case of the housewife, one might study the extent to which she enjoys house work, or regards it as an unfortunate chore; the extent to which she is confident in her culinary ability; her attitudes to health, or her attitudes to oral hygiene, etc. Then, at the lowest (but not most insignificant) level in the hierarchy we may investigate how various products are regarded in relation to the task that has to be performed and in relation to all the factors mentioned so far. One might expect, for example, that a woman who basically regards cleaning as a chore would be less discriminating in judging the products available to her; that is, apart from whether they are easy and quick to use. In this figure, it has been implied that attitudes to products will not only be influenced by general personality and attitude characteristics, but also by experience of products and by other information inputs sucn as advertising and the expressed opinions of others. All this provides a background set of attitudes and feelings towards products which remain latent until triggered off by a current need, such as an empty packet! Even at this point, constraints (such as financial resources) will apply which influence the final decision of product need and its satisfaction through the act of purchasing.

Thus, one is faced with a dynamic interaction between people on the one hand, and products on the other. This is schematically illustrated in Figure 3. In this figure, two consumers (A and B) are illustrated. They may be very similar in many ways and yet different in others. Each of them is unique and (in part) as a result of the attitudinal influences outlined above, they perceive three brands in a product field (1, 2 and 3) slightly differently. They both have different product needs (NA and NB) which condition their perceptions. The important thing to remember is that the three products remain constant; it is the 'brand image' of the products that varies and the brand image is in the eye of the beholder. Also illustrated in this figure is that product 1 most closely approximates to consumer A's ideal and product 2 to that of consumer B. This situation can be demonstrated simply by placing identical product formulations within the context of different brand names, when the 'image' component will appear quite dramatically if different groups of consumers are asked to assess the product variants by giving preferences after use. It is fair to ask, at this point, whether all this theorising really works in practice?

An illustration is set out in Figure 4. It shows preferences, after use, for four different toothpaste formulations. The formulations

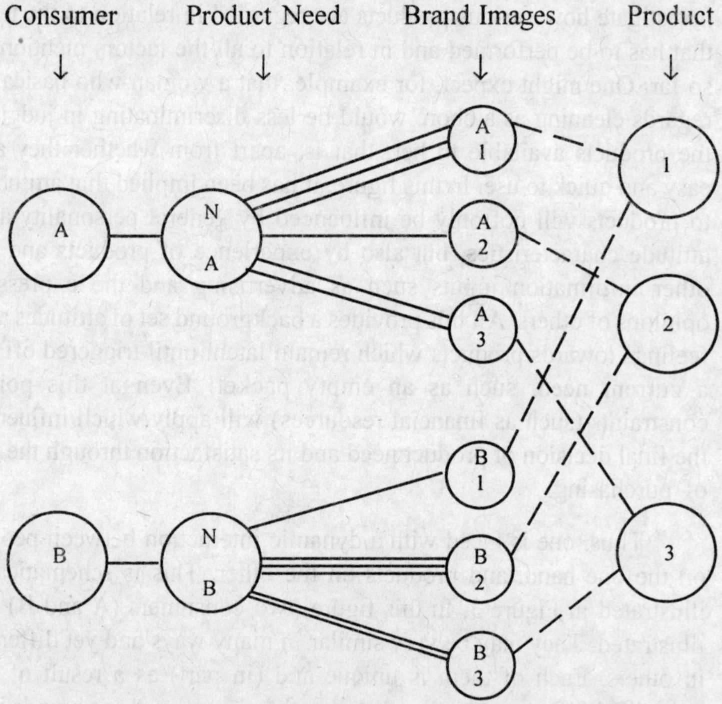

Fig. 3.

were packed in blank tubes and each respondent (a user of Signal Toothpaste in the UK) tested one pair out of the four. This method of testing is fairly common in consumer research and is referred to as a 'round robin' design. The analysis normally employed gives an effective net preference (in percentage terms) for each formulation. The analysis is such that all net preferences, positive and negative, seem to zero across products. In this figure one sees that, for the sample as a whole, differences in preference between any two of the formulations (A, B, C and) are not significant at the 5 per cent level of probability (2 Standard Errors of Difference). When the total sample is sub-divided according to two frequently used demographic breakdowns, socio-economic status and age, the differences between any two formulations are still below the 5 per cent probability level.

However, it is obvious from Figure 5 that when the data are re-analysed according to respondents' position on two attitude scales 'concern with bad breath' and 'belief in the importance of cleaning teeth' there are real preferences showing up. Now, it is quite true that, firstly, such differences would not always emerge in an analysis by attitudes and, secondly, such an illustration begs the question of marketing utility. One may ask whether the sub-groups having a low-medium position on the 'concern with bad breath' scale are really large' enough to warrant marketing formulation 'C'. This last comment is crucial in the tough world of consumer marketing. Clever consumer research is apt to be ignored if it is not commercially actionable-and rightly so. But, there we see a glimmer of hope that some psychological variables might be of relevance to marketing in cases where demography proves inappropriate or, better still, the possibility that the inter-relationship between demographic and attitudinal variables might offer even more fruitful information for the marketing man.

Fig. 4 : Signal Users, Overall Net Preferences (%)

Product	Total	Class		Age		
		ABC	DE	-34	35-49	50+
A	1	–11	8	1	–1	5
B	2	4	1	–3	6	3
C	–4	–3	–5	–7	–1	4
D	1	10	–5	–10	–3	–2
2 S.E.	14	22	16	22	20	28

All differences between flavours are non-significant at the 5 per cent level.

Fig. 5 Signal Users, Overall Net Preferences (%), Consumer Classification Scales

Product	Importance of not leaving bad breath			Importance of cleaning teeth		
	Low	Med.	High	Low	Med.	High
A	–7	–6	11	–17	–7	11
B	8	6	–4	9	14	–6
C	14	–11	–5	17	–16	–4
D	–17	12	–3	–6	13	–2
2 S.E.	30	20	20	32	26	18
Significant difference (5% level)	CvD	CvD	None	AvC	CvD BvC	None

Having presented some possibilities, it is now necessary to discuss the methodology of attitude measurement, in order that the reader may be convinced that a scientific procedure is possible in this area. This will be followed by a more exhaustive demonstration of the marketing possibilities than has been given so far.

Identification and Measurement of Attitudes

In one sense, everyone holds attitudes about most things. Therefore, the only firm foundation on which to build an attitude study is to start with a marketing problem. A typical problem is to establish what characterises a population segment using a certain type of product in order to study what approach might be made to those who do not use. A hypothetical example of such a problem will serve to illustrate the methodology used.

Let us, take the situation in India at the present time, regarding the use of toothpaste. The first thing to note is that a large section of the population will not use toothpaste in the foreseeable future because they cannot afford it. However, if our enquiry is confined to the upper/middle and upper income groups, it is apparent that all could afford the use of toothpaste, but many of them do not.

As we have said in an earlier section, the problem could be 'resolved simply' by asking representative samples of the user and non-user groups 'why?' and 'why not?' the result would not be very illuminating.

The Concept of an Attitude Scale

In using the term 'attitude scale' we merely refer to a means of measuring a mental state with something like the precision with which the scientist measures physical phenomena. We are seeking a ruler of some kind. As such, the goal is to produce an instrument which is stable (*i.e.*, reliable and reproducible), which is sensitive (*i.e.*, is able to discriminate between objects being measured) and which is valid (*i.e.*, it measures what it is supposed to).

A major difficulty is that, in the literal, physical science sense, attitudes (or any other mental process such as intelligence, for that matter) carmot be measured directly. Such measurement can be made only by inferences from observable reactions and from considerations of practicability, normally through the medium of words.

Nevertheless, it is easy enough to see the principles underlying the construction of verbal scales to measure attitudes by taking a simple example. Supposing one wished to classify individuals according to their interest in foreign affairs, then one could present a list of the countries of the world, together with the question: Who is the Head of State of each of these contries? Responses would then range from those who knew only the name of President Giri, to the very few who knew all the individuals concerned. It is more than probable that the distribution would be violently skewed towards the 'lack of knowledge' end of the continuum but the example is enough to make the point. One could also argue that such a measuring instrument measured only knowledge of heads of State. On this latter point, one would, of course, seek confirmation by measuring other aspects of interest in foreign affairs and correlating an individual's responses on all the alternative measures.

The Construction of Attitude Scales

Going back, now, to the users and non-users of toothpaste, the procedure adopted is illustrated in Figure 6.

In studying the mass of data from the original exploratory interviews; the researcher will note that many expressions of opinions, feelings or attitudes are common to both users and non-users of toothpaste. For example, all may feel strongly that to have healthy teeth is vital. Such common areas are unlikely to be of use in our attempt to discriminate between groups having different teeth care habits and who use different products. Therefore for this particular marketing problem, the researcher concentrates on differences between groups, He will select from the mass of transcript material, a large number of statements generally made by one group and not by the other, and vice-versa. These statement are, of course, chosen with some degree of subjectivity, to represent a range of viewpoints around a number of attitude areas he has hypothesised as possibly being relevant.

The next stage is to determine, to what extent certain statements seem to reflect an underlying attitude area. The principle involved is rather like the classical story of six blindfold men touching a different part of an elephant and, on being asked what it was, each one decided (from the evidence he had) that the object was a tree, a snake or something else. By pooling their perceptions, there would be a high probability of 'elephant' emerging as the true identity of the object being studied. In a normal attitude scale development phase, there will be about 100-120 statements which may (or may not) result in 12-18 attitude scales. About 200 respondents are adequate. Each respondent reacts to each statement on a verbal scale (usually of. 5 or 7 positions) ranging from 'I strongly agree' to 'I strongly disagree'. Examples of such statements in the field we have taken as our illustration might be:

1. Brushing teeth is unnatural.
2. Brushing teeth ruins the enamel.
3. Brushing teeth is no better than any other method.

4. Brushing teeth promotes healthy gums.
5. Brushing teeth is the only way to get them white.

In the way the imaginary statements have been set out, a fairly structured and graduated scale of beliefs is implied. It should be noted that all of the statements' presented in a real study will be in a random order and will certainly not take the 'neat and tidy' from given above.

The data obtained from this scale development study are subjected to mathematical treatment (usually some 'form of Factor Analysis) to determine whether any clear underlying attitude factors are present and, if so, to what extent responses to statements are mathematically correlated with a particular factor.

At this point, we have established a number of scales of attitude. Their reliability can be assessed by mathematical means; all that remains is to assess marketing utility.

For the toothpaste problem, the step that remains is to apply the scales to a large and representative sample of the target population (users and potential users of toothpaste). Only then can it be determined what attitudinal parameters distinguish between the users and non-users. This would give the manufacturer a dear lead, for example, as to the areas of resistance he faces in trying to crack open the non-user potential. Not only this, but the attitudinal data can be cross-tabulated against brand usership amongst the toothpaste using segment, thus enabling the marketing man to re-align his advertising campaign for an existing brand or, to pinpoint a consumer subgroup having clear characteristics but who are not buying one product significantly more frequently than another; for this group may well be the target for a new brand.

It should be noted that whilst we have briefly discussed the use of Factor Analysis and Mathematical tests of reliability, these have not been dealt with exhaustively. The interested reader is advised to consult the publications listed for more detailed mathematical and statistical information.

❐

16

Consumer Protection

Consumer protection in India is still in its infancy as here majority of the population are uneducated and live below the poverty line. Markets of developing countries are highly imperfect and the rural people are not integrated into the main stream of consumerism. Consumer is the forgotten and least organised man. In the recent years consumer awareness is increasingly felt both by the Government and the consumer himself. As there is a limit of cheating, adulteration, poor quality, variations in contents of the pack, lesser weight, misleading advertisement are some of the ways by which the consumer is exploited. In certain cases after-sale service and guarantee of the functioning of certain durable products such as fridge, T.V., air cooler, washing machines etc. in practice is a show on paper.

The traders never bother to keep their assurances and promises. Instead they always try to escape from the obligation, which they are supposed to fulfil towards the consumers. The consumer pays high fare for dirty raiiway compartments and dirty toilets. He pays rent for the telephone even when it does not serve him. He motors on roads that are dangerous. He has no pavement to walk on. The mail does not reach him on time. He eats food that is adulterated. He drinks water that is polluted and breathes in the air that is poisonous. The government is the largest supplier of goods and services enjoying monopoly right over most of them. Whether it is the supply of essential commodities or public services such as electricity, transport, communication and banking all the available evidence points out to a woeful lack of concern for the consumer."

The need for consumers' protection and satisfaction have been widely accepted all over the world. The USA has been pioneer in this respect. Britain has followed suit. India has taken up the concept of consumer protection more seriously and more vigorously.

Meaning of Consumer Protection. Consumer Protection means the protection of the consumers from their exploitation by the unfair practices of the producers. Producers exploit the consumers in several ways, such as:

1. false information regarding the quality of goods
2. adulteration
3. less weight or short measure
4. supply of inferior quality of goods
5. non-compliance of tenus of guarantee
6. not supplying goods on time even after taking the advance.

Consumer Exploitation or Problems. The consumers are generally exploited or have to face a number of problems every day and tolerate all this as their fate because of illiteracy, poverty, lack of education, lack of information, a traditional outlook of people to suffer in silence and ignorance of their legal rights against the remedy available in all such cases of exploitation are as:

1. Unfair Trade Practices. The traders adopt some of the trade practices for the purpose of promoting the sale, use or supply of any goods or for the provision of any services, any unfair or deceptive method including misleading and deceptive advertisement, promotional contests and free gift and lucky draw schemes etc. They falsely represent that the goods are of a particular standard, quality, quantity, grade, composition, style or model. Some of the unfair trade practices are discussed below:

(a) Misleading and Deceptive Advertisements. Business class spends huge amounts of money on advertising their products and services. Most of these advertisements are misleading, exaggerated and unprovable claims. Quality of their wares is poor and their claims unsustainable.

(b) **Offering Gifts and Prizes.** There are sometimes offers of "Free Gifts, sales discount schemes and Prizes Or Lucky draws" from various business firms in order to attract the customers. The impression given to the public is that something is being given 'Free of charge' whereas this may not be true. Sometimes, some manufacturers marginally reduce the quantity, size, colour, weight, length or breadth or reduce quality prior to the announcement of 'Gifts Scheme'.

2. Spiralling Prices. Producers unduly hike the prices of their products. These rising prices are generally followed by anti-social activities like hoarding, cornering, black marketing and artificial scarcity, thus leading to consumers exploitation and victimisation.

3. Poor Quality Products. Another ground of consumer exploitation is the poor quality or substandard products offered for sale. Mere declaration of manufacturers according to ISI, AGMARK, or FPO mark on the wrapper is not sufficient. There is no check on the manufacturers that the goods which are sold to consumers meet the specification of safety with the result that there are a large number of deaths and injuries on account of accidents as a result of substandard and unsafe domestic products like pressure cookers, electrical gadgets, cooking gas, kerosene stoves etc.

4. Adulteration. Another ground on which the consumers are exploited is the adulteration of goods which are sometimes dangerous to life or hazardous to health. The traders resort to many devices for making high profits. For example mixing animal fat with ghee, harmful seeds witll grams and pulses, mustard oil with mineral oil, chilli powder with saw dust, milk with dirty water: sale of synthetic milk in Kurukshetra and some other parts of Haryana etc.

5. Undenveight Supplies. Many manufacturers sell certain products in jars containing quantities not permitted by the Standards of Weight Rules, but consumers are exploited by giving them under weight products. For example, each LPG cylinder must contain

14.2 kg., of gas but sometimes underweight cylinders are supplied to the consumers.

6. Negligence in Service. Negligence in service is another cause of consumer exploitation. In Newspapers some cases of negligence in service are reported. For example, (i) By an oversight the wrong leg of a patient was amputated by a surgeon. (ii) About 2 dozen persons were operated in a government hospital or some nursing home. They lost their eye sight as a result of infection caught in the operation theatre.

7. Deceptive Packing. Many times packages are used by manufacturers as a camouflage to deceive customers by putting a smaller quantity of the product contained in the packet or sometimes some spellings of a reputed brand are changed a bit but the appearance of the wrapper is kept almost the same.

8. Deficiency in Services. Consumers are the sufferers a lot, because of poor or deficient service. For example *(i)* Undue delay by the courier services. *(ii)* Wrong billing by the electricity and telephone department. *(iii)* Over delay in setting insurance accident claims. *(iv)* Undue delay in handing over the possession of flats houses by Housing Boards/Development Authorities.

9. Monopolistic Trade Practices. Monopolist is the only producer or seller of a commodity. He exploits the consumer in various ways, *viz. (i)* unfair rise in price of the goods; *(ii)* unreasonable profits derived from the production, supply or distribution of goods and services *(iii)* undue reduction of competition in the market *(iv)* deterioration in the quality of goods and services *(v)* unreasonable reduction of or limitation on supply of goods to consumers.

Rights of Consumers

The consumer has the right to buy or not to buy a product that is offered for sale; to expect the product to be safe; to expect the product to be what it is claimed to be: to be adequately informed about the more important aspects of the product. He has a right to receive proper and efficient service and satisfaction. Under Section 6 of Consumer Protection Act, a consumer has following rights:

1. The Right to Safety. The right to be protected against the marketing of goods which are hazardous to health, life and property. There are various risks involved in the consumption and use of products such as pressure cookers, electrical appliances or drugs.

2. The Right to Choose. The right to choose has to be assured, wherever possible, access to variety of goods at competitive prices. He should not at all be made the victim of high pressure and aggressive salesmanship.

3. The Right to be Informed. The right to be informed about the quality, quantity, purity, potency, standard and price of goods, precaution, if any, to be taken etc.

4. The Right to be Heard. The right to be heard and to be assured that consumer interest will receive due consideration at appropriate Forum. This right includes the right to make protest and file complaints.

5. The Right to Consumer Education. The Consumer Education is an important determinant of consumer protection and satisfaction. This will help a consumer in protecting himself against fraudulent, deceptive and misleading advertisement and poor or negligent services.

6. The Right to Seek Redressal. The right to seek redressal against unfair trade practice or exploitation of the consumer. He has a right to get his claims and complains settled against the manufacturers and sellers.

NEED AND IMPORTANCE OF CONSUMER PROTECTION

The need and importance of consumer protection can be explained as:

1. Welfare State. India is a Welfare State, one of the Directive Principles enshrined in the Indian Constitution is that the State shall direct its policy towards securing that the operation of the economic system does not result in the concentration of wealth and means of production detrimental to common man. Keeping in view the consumers interest Government passed the monopolies and Restrictive Trade Practices Act, 1969. Later on, in 1984 provisions relating to Unfair Trade Practices were incorporated in the Act Wide powers have been granted to the MRTP Commission under the Act (more so after the recent amendments in 1991) to control and prohibit monopolistic, restrictive and unfair trade practices.

2. Economic Development. During 46 years of planning in India there is a spectacular change in the standards of living. The structural and institutional changes in the economy consequent upon Economic Reforms 1991 indicate clearly that there has been modernisation and globalisation of the economy. Wants of the consumers have multiplied. Hence the need for consumer interest has also grown and has become more important.

3. Role of Judicial System. Consumers Protection Act, 1986 (more so after amendments in 1993) has vested vast power upon the Supreme Court level for the protection of consumers rights, their safety and health. As a breakthrough the remedies for consumer protection are now simpler, more accessible quicker and less expensive.

4. Means of Transport & Communication. The rapid growth of means of transport and communication has brought the world consumers together. There is a strong 'demonstration effect' through mass media of T.V. Cable network that has made the consumers aware that they can no longer be exploited by the business community and kept isolated from other countries as far as their right to safety and health are concerned.

5. Lengthy Legal Process. The violation of the various Acts meant that an ordinary consumer had no other remedy but to initiate action by way of civil suit which involves lengthy legal process proving to be too expensive and time consuming. In fact, very often the time, cost and mental tension involved in the legal process is disproportionate to the compensation claimed and granted to an individual consumer. Therefore, it becomes necessary to evolve laws directed at protecting the consumers providing for remedies which are simpler. more accessible, quicker and less expensive.

6. Lok Adalats. The concept of Lok Adalats in India is catching up fast. Lok Adalts have become part of speedy, effective and economical redressal system. Interesting to note, lakhs of cases relating to motor accidents, complaints against postal circles, Delhi Development Authority and Mahanagar Telephone.

7. Unfair and Deceptive Trade Practices. Unfair and deceptive trade practices such as selling of defective or sub-standard goods, ignoring safety standards, charging exorbitant prices, misrepresenting the efficacy or usefulness of goods etc. have to make producers/ traders more accountable to consumers. It also becomes inevitable for consumers to unite at a common platform to deal with issues concerning consumer protection and having their grievances redressed satisfactorily.

8. Impact of Other Countries. In the United States of America. European Union, Australia, etc., have taken effective and strict measures to protect the interests of the consumers. Following these countries, India has also felt the necessity of consumer's protection. Nigam Ltd. Delhi Electric Supply Undertaking have been settled involving crores of rupees. The concept of Lok Adalats has been now extended to other areas.

9. Concept of Public Interest Litigation (PIL). For consumers protection a good number of petitions by way of PIL have been filed before High Courts and the Supreme Court. The concept of PIL is catching fast. Under PIL, it is not the aggrieved person, any person can move the Court in the interest of the weak or a group who or which may not be in a position to seek legal remedy on his own. Secondly, a complaint sent to the Supreme Court even on post card may be treated as a writ petition. PIL is virtually a consumer interest litigation and has helped a lot the cause of consumers protection.

10. Consumers Awareness. Spread of education, especially higher education has made people aware of their rights as consumers. The relief granted to the consumers and important judicial decisions regarding consumers protection of relief are often covered by newspapers. Rising incomes have increased the purchasing power of the people to spend more. The rise in prices of products has created in consumers an attitude to expect better quality or at least to expect the product to be worth their money. Consumers expect better services for their durables. Legislations leading to consumers protection have created an awareness among consumers about their rights and remedies available to them.

11. National Awards on Consumer Protection. The Ministry of Civil Supplies, Consumer Affairs and Public Distribution, government of India, has been conferring awards since 1988 on individuals as well as voluntary consumer organisations in recognition of their contribution to the cause of consumers.

12. Consumer Organisations. There are about 500 consumers organisations. These have contributed much to the spread and protect the consumers interests in the country. Some of these are worth mentioning: *(a)* Consumer Guidance Society of India, Mumbai. *(b)* Citizens Action Group, Mumbai. *(c)* Common Cause, New Delhi. *(d)* Consumers' Action Forum, Calcutta, Delhi and Chennai *(e)* The Citizens' Forum, Hubli. *(f)* Consumers' Forum, Udupi. *(g)* VOICE, New Delhi. *(h)* Mumbai Grahak Panchayat, Mumbai.

These consumers organisations are performing a number of functions such as bringing out brochure, journals, monographs; accelerating Consumer Awareness; collecting data on different products and testing them; arranging talks, seminars, workshops and conferences for the purpose of focusing the problems of consumers and finding solutions thereof filing suits, complaints and writ petitions on behalf of the consumers to resist price rigging, prevent adulteration, to prevent hoarding and black marketing to check under-weight selling to educate the consumers to help himself to help educational institutions to start consumer education and to set up voluntary complaint cells for consumers guidance and counselling etc.

THE CONSUMER PROTECTION ACT, 1986

A number of laws enacted and amended by the government to safeguard the interests of the consumers. One of them is the Consumer Protection Act, 1986 which is the landmark in the history of Consumerism in India wherein a big effort has been made to translate a saying "Consumer is the King" into reality. It is a small Act passed to provide for better protection of the interest of consumers and is unique in many respects.

Scope and Extent of the Act. The Indian Parliament enacted this legislation in December 1986. It came into force on April 15, 1987. Further various provisions of the Act have been amended *vide* the Consumer Protection (Amendment) Ordinance, 1993. The Act extends to whole of India except the state of J&K and applies to all goods and services unless otherwise notified by the central government.

Salient Features of the Act, 1986. Salient features of the Act are as follows:

1. Unique and Highly Progressive. It is a very unique and highly progressive piece of social welfare and is acclaimed as the 'Magna Carta' on consumer protection and a milestone in the history of socio-cconomic legislation in the country. This is they only law which directly pertains to market place and seeks to redress complaints arising from it.

2. Effective Protection. It provides more effective protection to the consumers than any corresponding legislation in force even in developed countries.

3. Effective Safeguards. It provides effective safeguards to the consumers against different types of exploitation such as defective goods, unsatisfactory or deficient service and unfair trade practices etc.

4. Three-Tier Grievances Redressal Machinery. For enforcement of the rights of the consumers, the Act has created

Consumer Courts. The provides for Three-Tier consumer grievance redressal machinery with Distt. Forum at the base; the State Commission at the middle level; and the National Commission at the apex level.

5. Simple and Inexpensive Redressal. The Act provides a simple, speedy and inexpensive redressal of consumer grievances relating to their complaints. It is not obligatory to engage any advocate. The complainant need only set out the grievance in the simplest form and furnish the name and address of the opposite party against whom the complaint is made.

6. Class Action. The Act allows filling of 'Class action' complaints or Public Interest Litigation (PIL) on behalf of group of consumers having common interest.

7. Excess Price. The Act also covers complaints relating to Unfair Trade Practices. Thus a consumer can directly protest against food adulteration, short weighing and over-charging directly to the District Forum.

8. Scope. All suppliers of goods and services both in the private and the public sector and cooperatives are covered by the Act. Hence the Act has a wider coverage.

9. Time Bound Redressal. The hallmark of the Act is that it has set a time limit for the disposal of cases.

10. Consumer Protection Councils. To promote the cause of consumer protection and educate the consumers, the Act provides for the formation of Consumer Protection Councils. However, these councils do not have any legal authority.

Redressal Machinery Under the Act 1986

The Act provides for Three-Tier quasi-judicial redressal machinery at District, State and National levels for redressal of consumer disputes and grievances. The District Forum has jurisdiction to entertain complaints where the value of goods/services complained against is less than Rs. 5 lakh the State Commission for claims between Rs. 5 lakh and Rs. 20 lakh; and the National Commission for claims exceeding Rs. 20 lakh.

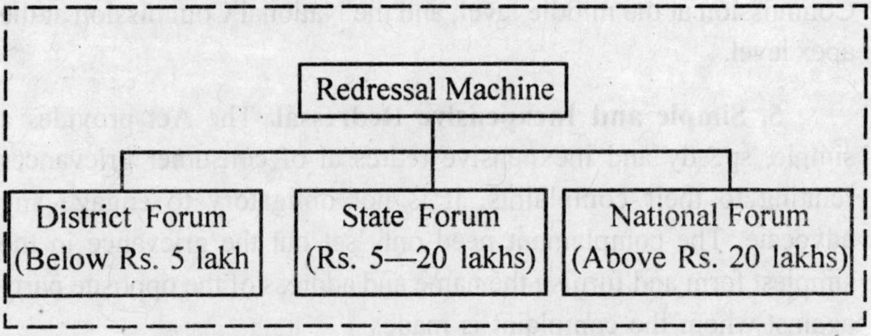

1. District Forum. Section 9 of the Act provides for the establishment of a District Forum by the State Government in each district of the State by notification. The State Government may establish more than one District Forum, if it deems fit to do so.

(i) Composition. A person who is or has been or has the qualifications of District Judge is appointed as its President along with two more members including at least one woman member, who are the persons of ability, integrity and standing. They are appointed by the State Government on the recommendations of the Selection Commit!ee on the terms and conditions, salary or honorarium and allowances whatsoever.

(ii) Jurisdiction. District Forum has *(a)* Pecuniary limits *(b)* territorial limits. Under the Pecuniary limits the District Forum can entertain complaints upto the dispute of Rs. 5 lakh only. Under the Territorial limits a complaint shall be constituted in the District Forum within the territorial jurisdiction wherein the opposite party resides or carries business or has a branch office or any cause of action arises wholly or in part. The District Forum passes orders against traders for any unfair trade practices or defects or deficiency in service whatsoever covered under the Act.

2. State Commission. The Act provides for the establishment of the State Consumer Disputes Redressal Commission by the State governmentin the State by notification.

(i) **Composition.** A person who is or has been or has the qualification of a High Court Judge is appointed by the State government in consultation with the Chief Justice of the High Court of the State, as its President along with two more members including at least a woman member who are the persons of ability, integrity and standing on the terms and conditions, salary or honorarium and allowances payable to them.

(ii) **Jurisdiction.** Section 17 of the Act provides the jurisdiction of the Commission as follows:

(a) the State Commission can entertain complaints where the value of the goods or services and the compensation as claimed does not exceed Rs. Twenty lakhs.

(b) the State Commission also has the power to call the records and pass appropriate orders.

(c) that State Commission also has the power to call the records and pass appropriate orders.

Thus, in short; the State Commission's jurisdiction may be original, appellant or revisional.

3. National Commission. Clause (c) of Section 9 provides for the establishment of the National Consumer Dispute Redressal Commission by the Central Government by notification in the Official Gazette.

(i) **Composition.** Section 20(1) provides that the National Commission shall consist of a person who is or has been a judge of the Supreme Court to be appointed by the Central Government (in consultation with the Chief Justice of India) who shall be its President.

Four other members who shall be persons of ability, integrity and standing and one of whom shall be a woman. Every appointment made under this clause by the Central

Government shall be made on the recommendations of a Selection Committee on the terms and conditions, salary or honorarium and allowances. Every member of the National Commission shall hold office for a term of five years or upto seventy years of age whichever is earlier, and shall not be reappointed.

(ii) **Jurisdiction.** Section 21 provides that the National Commission shall have jurisdiction

(a) to entertain complaints for the value exceeding Rs. 20 lakhs:

(b) to entertain appeals against the orders of any State Commission; and

(c) to call for the records and pass appropriate orders.

It is important to know that each hierarchy in the Act, is empowered to entertain a complaint by the consumer for value of the goods or services and compensation. The word 'compensation' in legal sense would constitute actual loss or expected loss and may extend to physical, mental or even emotional sufferings, insult or injury or loss. The act enables as consumer to claim and empowers the Commission to redress any injustice done to him.

Appeals. Under section 15 any person who is aggrieved by an order of the District Forum to the State Commission under Section 19 against the orders of State Commission to the National Commission; and under Section 23 against the orders of National Commission to the Supreme Court within a period of thirty days from the date of order by the Consumer Courts, may prefer an appeal.

Persons Who Can File a Complaint. The following categories of persons can file a complaint with the Consumer Court within two years from the date on which the cause of action has risen, under the Act: *(i)* a consumer, or *(ii)* any Voluntary Consumer Association, registered under the Companies Act, 1956 or under the Societies Registration Act 1960; or *(iii)* the Central Government or; *(iv)* any

State Government or *(v)* one or more consumers. However, a complaint must ensure that his complaint is not frivolours or vexatious. The Court has power to dismiss or impose punishment if the complaint is found to be frivolous of vexatious. Section 27 makes a provision for imprisonment or fine or both if orders of the Consumer Courts are not complied with.

Award of Compensation. The Consumer Forum/Commissions can order the relief for; *(i)* Removal of defects from the goods; *(ii)* Replacement of the goods; *(iii)* Refund of the price paid; *(iv)* Award of compensation for the loss or injury suffered.

Suggestion

In the history of consumer protection in India various large have been only a partially effective measure against the purchase, sale and store of spurious goods; unfair trade practices continue unabated; false advertisements are a common feature. There is an easy availability of spurious goods at temptingly cheap prices in the market, particularly in the electrical and automobile sectors. The problems of underweight and adulteration is more or less unchecked. These substandard and misbranded goods pose a grave danger to the life, health and safety of the public. It needs public awareness and change in the attitude of business as to serve the consumer. The following are the suggestions in this respect.

1. Emphasis on Consumer Education. To spread the awareness and consciousness among the consumers about their rights, there is need for consumer education. It can be done through posters, folk art, street plays, T.V. dramas, workshops, seminars, conferences, melas etc. because no law can become effective and forceful unless the consumer movement gains momentum and becomes a force to reckon with.

2. Integrated Approach. An integrated approach is necessary wherein the State, the consumer, the Consumers Associates and the business class have to participate to promote and protect the interest of the consumers. Above all it is the consumer who is exploited a lot. He should rise to occasion himself and play the predominant role.

3. Propaganda. The greatest weapon in the hands of the consumer organisation is the mass media. Newspapers, DD programmes should include something on consumer protection. CPA is the magna carta of consumer protection and a milestone in the history of socio-economic legislation in the country. The CPA may be enforced to achieve public co-operation and create moral fear among traders indulging in anti-social activities, unfair trade practices or restrictive trade practices.

4. Emphasis on Rural Sector. Rural sector needs specific emphasis where the consumer is exploited because of illiteracy, poverty, lack of information and suffers in silence and ignorance of his legal rights and redressal machinery available to him which is now simpler, quicker and inexpensive. The state and the mass media can play supportive role. Government controls need be more strictly enforced and efficiently administered. The Government should launch a massive training programme on consumer protection.

5. National Awards. With a view to encouraging the participation of consumer organisations and youth in the field of consumer protection, the ministry has instituted three awards *(i)* National Award on Consumers Protection *(ii)* National Youth Award on Consumer Protection *(iii)* National Women Award for Consumer Protection. These awards are given every year.

6. Standardisation and Quality Control. With a view to making available quality of goods to th consumers, provisions have been made for standardization and quality control of goods. This function is performed in India by the Bureau of Indian Standards (BIS). This Bureau is engaged in protecting the interests of the consumers through Quality Certificate Scheme. The Bureau issues certificates for those goods whose quality is properly assessed by it. Goods bearing ISI or AGMARK are considered to be of high quality and their use does not involve exploitation of the consumer.

It is essential to educate the consumer if their interests are to be protected. To achieve this objective every year Consumer's Day is observed throughout the country from 15th to 21st March. Emphasis is laid on making consumers aware of their rights. Exhibitions, seminars and public meetings are held. They are made aware of the legal remedies available to them against adulteration, short measure and under weight, etc. Since March 1991, a quarterly "Consumers Awareness" has been published. 15th March is observed as Consumers Rights Day allover the world.

7. Consumer Welfare Fund. Of the amount from Central Excise Duty and Customs Duties which is not refunded to the manufacturers and importers a corpus has been created in the form of Consumer Welfare Fund. It will be used to encourage welfare of the consumers.

❐

17

Consumer Behaviour Studies in India

In this Chapter will study the different behaviours of social class, groups, culture, cross-culture and other Service Marketings for Consumer behaviour in India.

Social class is defined as the division of members of a society into a hierarchy of distinct status classes, so that members of each class have relatively the same status and members of all other classes have either more or less status.

SOCIAL CLASS AND SOCIAL STATUS

Researchers measure social class in terms of social status, that is, they define each social class by the amount of status the member of that class have in comparison with members of other social class.

Status includes, wealth, power (the degree of personal choice or influence over others) and prestige.

In consumer behaviour and marketing research, status is most often defined in terms of one or more of the demographic (socio-economic) variables-family income, occupational status and educational attainment. These variables as expression of status are used by marketing practitioners on a daily basis to measure social class.

FEATURES OF SOCIAL CLASS

Social Class is Hierarchical. Social class categories usually are ranked in hierarchy ranging from low to high status.

Thus, members of a specific social class perceive members of other social classes as having either more or less status then they do. To many people, therefore, social class categories suggest that others are neither equal to them (about the same social class); superior to them (higher social class), or inferior to them (lower social class).

This hierarchical aspect of social class is important to marketers. Consumers may purchase certain products because those products arc favoured by members of their own or higher social class; and consumer may avoid other products because they perceive the products to the "lowerclass" products.

Social Class and Market Segmentation. The various social class strata provide a natural basis for market segmentation for many products and services. In many instances, consumer researchers have been able to relate product usage to social class membership.

Social Class Hand Behavioural Factors. The classification of society's members into a small number of social classes had enabled researchers to note the existence of shared values, attitude and behaviour, patterns among members within each social classes and differing values, attitudes and behaviour between social classes. Consumer researchers have been able to relate social-class standing to consumer attitudes concerning specific products, and to examine social-class influence on the actual consumption of products.

Social Classes. Social classes have several characteristics:

1. persons within each social class tend to behave more alike than persons from two different social classes.

2. persons are perceived as occupying inferior or superior positions according to their social class.

3. a person's social class is indicated by a number of variables, such as occupation, income, wealth, education and value orientation, rather than by any single variable.

4. individuals can move from one social class to another—up or down during their life time.

Social classes show distinct product and brand preferences in such areas as clothing, home furnishings, leisure activities and automobiles.

Classification of Social Class

1. Upper Uppers (1%)
2. Lower Uppers (2%)
3. Upper Middle Class (12%)
4. Middle Class (32%)
5. Working Class (38%)
6. Upper Lowers (9%) (just above poverty)
7. Lower Lowers (7%).

SOCIAL CLASS CATEGORY

Variations in number and types of Social Class Categories—Two Category Social Class

— Blue collar, white collar

— Lower, upper

— Lower, middle

Three Category Social Class

— Blue collar, grey collar, white collar

— Lower, middle, upper

Four Category Social Class

— Lower, lower-middle, white collar, upper.

Five Category Social Class

— Lower, working Class, lower-middle upper-middle, upper.

— Lower, lower-middle, middle, upper-middle, upper

Six Category Social Class

Lower-lower, Upper-lower, lower-middle, upper-middle, lower-upper, upper-upper:

Seven Category Social Class

—Real-lower, a lower Class of people but not the lowest, working class, middle Class, upper-middle, lower-upper, upper-upper.

Nine Category Social Class

—Lower-lower, middle-lower, upper-lower, lower-middle, middle-middle, upper-middle, lower-upper, middle upper, upper-upper.

Selected Social Class Distribution in Population

Name of Classes	% of Population
Five Category	11.4%
Upper	12.7%
Upper-middle	20.6%
Middle	16.6%
Lower-middle	28.0%
Lower	
	89.3%
Six Category	
Upper-upper	0.9%
Lower-upper	—
Upper-middle	7.2%
Lower-middle	28.4%
Upper-lower	44.0%

Lower-lower	19.5%
	100.0%

Seven Catagory

Upper-upper	0.3%
Lower-upper	1.2%
Upper-middle	12.5%
Middle	32.0%
Working Class	38.0%
A lower group but not the lowest	9.0%
Real lower-lower	7.0%
	100.0%

PROFILE OF SOCIAL CLASS

The Upper-Upper Class—Country Club Establishment

* Small number of well-established families
* Belong to best country clubs and sponsor major charity events
* Serve as trustees for local colleges and hospitals
* Prominent physicians and lawyers
* May be heads of major financial institutions, owners of major long established firms
* Accustomed to wealth, so do not spend money conspicuously

The Lower-Upper Class-New Wealth

* Not quite accepted by the opper crust of society
* Represent "new money"

* Successful business executives
* Conspicuous users of their new wealth

The Upper-middle class-Achieving Professionals

* Have neither family status not unusual wealth
* Career-oriented
* Young successful professionals, corporate managers, and business owners.
* Most are college graduates, many with advanced degrees
* Active in professional, community and social activities
* Have a keen interest in obtaining the "better things in life"
* Their homes serve as symbols of their achievements
* Consumption is often conspicuous
* Very child-oriented.

The Lower-middle class—Faithful Followers

* Primarily non-managerial white-collar workers and highly paid
* blue collar Workers
* Want to achieve "respectability" and be accepted as good citizens
* Want their children to be well-behaved
* Tend to be churchgoers and are often involved in church-sponsored activities
* Prefer a neat and clea appearance and tend to avoid faddish or mghly-styled clothing
* Constitute a major market for do-it-yourself products

The Upper-lower class-Security-Minded Majority

* The largest social-class segment
* Solidly blue collar
* Strive for security (sometimes gained from union membership)
* View work as a means to "buy" enjoyment
* Want children to behave properly
* High wage earners in this group may spend impulsively
* Interested in items that enhance their leisure time (*e g.*, TV sets; hunting equipment)
* Husbands typically have a strong "macho" self-image
* Males are sports fans: heavy smokers, beer drinkers

The Lower-lower class—Rock Bottom

* Poorly educated, unskilled labourers
* Often out of work
* Children are often poorly treated
* Tend to live a day-to-day existence

MEASUREMENT OF SOCIAL CLASS

1. Subjective measure, 2. Reputational measure, 3. Objective measure

Under this approach individuals are asked to estimate their own social-classposition.

Which one of the following four categories best describes your social class the lower class, the lower-middle class; the upper-middle class or the upper class?

		Reputational Measure
Lowee class	( )	Objective measures fall into two
Lower-meddle class	( )	basic categories
Upper-middle class	( )	(a) Single variable index
Upper class	( )	(b) Composite variable index,
Do not know/refuse to answer	( )	Single variable Index (a) Occupation, (b) Education.

Composite-Variable Indexes. Composite indexes systematically combine a number of socio-economic factors to form one over all measure of social-class standing. More important composite indexes are—*(l)* Index of Status Characteristics, *(2)* Socio-economic Status Score.

The SC is a measure of the following socio-economic variables: occupation source of income, house type and the dwelling area (quality of neighbourhood).

Socio-economic Status Score (SES). Combines three basic socio-economic variables: Occupation, family income and educational attainment.

Composite Measure of Social Class

Composite Index	**Variables**
Index of Status Characteristics (ISC)	Occupation Source of Income House type Dwelling area
Socio-economic Status Scores (SES)	Occupation Family income Education

SOCIAL MOBILITY CHARACTERISTICS

While individuals can move either up or down in social class standing from the class position held by their parents, we primarily think in terms of upward mobility.

—Since upward mobility has always been attainable, the higher social classes often become reference groups for ambitious men and women of lower social status.

—Recognizing that individuals often aspire to membership in higher social classes, marketeers frequently incorporate the symbols of higherclass membership both as products and props in advertisements targeted to a lower-social class audiences.

—That products and services traditionally within the realm of one social class may filter down to lower social classes: For instance, plastic surgery was once affordable by only movie-stars and other wealthy consumers. Today, however, consumers of all economic strata uses cosmetic procedures.

Signs of Downward Mobility. There are some strong signs of downward mobility in terms of better house, jobs, more disposable incomes, more savings and in terms of education.

Selected Consumer Behaviour Application of Social Class

1. Clothing, Fashion and Shopping. 2. The pursuit of Leisure. 3. Saving, Spending and Credit.

Role of Social Factors

Social Factors. A consumer behaviour is also influenced by such social factors as reference groups, family and social roles and status.

Reference Groups. A person's reference groups consists of all the groups that have a direct (face to face) or indirect influence on the person's attitudes or behaviour.

Groups having a direct influence on a person are called membership groups. These are the groups to which the person belongs and interacts.

Some are primary groups, such as family, friends and neighbours with which the person interacts.

A person also belongs to secondary groups such as religious, professionals and trade-union groups, which tend to be more formal and require less continuous interaction.

Marketeers try to identify the reference groups of their target customers.

People are significantly influenced by their reference groups in three ways:

1. They expose an individual to new behaviours and life styles.
2. They also influence the person's attitudes and self-concept because he or she normally desires to "fit in."
3. And they create pressures of conformity that may affect the person's actual product and brand choice.

Family. We can distinguish between two families in the buyer's life.

The family of orientation consists of one's parents. From parents a person acquires orientation towards religion, politics-and economies and sense of personal ambition.

—Family of procreation, namely, one's spouse and children.

The family is the most important consumer buying organisation in society. Marketeers are interested in the roles and relative influence of the husband, wife and children in the purchase of large variety of products and services.

The marketeer needs to determin which member normally has the greater influence in choosing various. products. Often it is a matter of who has more power or expertise. For example:

Husband dominant—Life Insurance, automobiles, T.V.

Wife dominant. Washing machine, carpeting, furniture, kitchen ware.

Equal. Vacation, housing, outside entertainment.

4. Family member's influence can vary with different sub-decisions made within a product category. For example:

"When to buyan automobile" is influenced primarily by the husband in 68% of the cases; primarily by the wife in 3% of the cases, and eqaually in 29% of the cases.

The decision on "What colour automobile to buy" was influenced primarily by the husband in 25% of the cases, by the wife in 25% of the cases, and equally in SO% of the cases.

An automobile company would need to research the varying decision roles in designing and promoting its cars.

Role and Status.

— A person participates in many groups throughout life-family, club, organizations.

— The person's position in each group can be defined as role and status.

— A role consists of the activities that a person is expected to perform. Each of a person's rules will influence some of hislher buying behaviour.

— Each role carries a Status *e.g.*, people choose products that communicate their role and status in the society.

Marketeers are aware of the status symbol potential of products and brands.

Personal Factors. A buyer's decisions are also influenced by personal characteristics such as the buyer's age and life cycle stage, occupation, economic circumstances, life style and personality and self concept.

Age and Life-Cycle Stage. People buy different goods and services over their life-time. Fot example, different types of food.

People's taste inclothes, furnitute and recreation is also age related.

—Consumption is also shaped by thet tage of the family life-cyck Nine stages of the family life cycle are listed' below:

Stages in family life cycle	Buying or behavioural pattern
1. Bachelor stage, young, single people not living at home.	Few financial burdens, fashion opinion leaders, Recreation oriented. Buy: - basic kitchen equipment, basic furniture, vacations.
2. Newly married couples, young, no children.	Better off financially, higher purchase rate. Buy; cars, refrigerators etc.
3. Full nest I: Youngest child under six.	Home purchasing at peak. interest in new products. Buy: washers, T.V., baby food, vitamins, dolls etc.
4. Full nest II: youngest child six or over.	Buy larger-size packages. Buy: many foods, cleaning materials, bicycles, music lessons.
5. Full nest III: older married couples with dependent children.	Financial position still better. High average purchase of durables. Buy: new, more tasteful furniture, auto travel, magazines.
6. Empty nest I: older married couples, no children living with thein, head in lab. force.	Home ownership at peak. Most satisfied with financial position and money saved. Not interested in new products. Buy: luxuries, home improvements.
7. Empty nest II: older married. No children living at home, head retired.	Drastic cut in income. Buy: medical appliances, medical care products, sleep and digestion.
8. Solitary survivor, in lab force.	Income still good.
9. Solitary survivor, retired. for	Drastic cut in income, special need affection and security.

Occupation. This also influences consumption pattern. For example—a blue-collar worker and a company president.

Marketeers try to identify the occupational groups that have above average interest in'their products and services. A company can specialise their products for certain occupational group such as brand managers, engineers, lawyers and physicians.

Economic Circumstances. People's economic circumstances consist of their spendable income, savings and assets, debts, borrowing power and attitude toward spending versus saving.

Marketeers of income-sensitive goods keep constant attention to trends in personal income, savings and interest rates.

If economic indicators point to a recession, marketeers can take steps to redesign reposition and reprice their products.

Life Style. A person's life-style is the person's pattern of living in the world as expressed in the person's activities, interests and opinions.

Marketeers will search for relationship betgween their products and life style groups.

With the exception of those very few people who are classified as hermits, most individuals interact with other people on a daily basis. Like almost all human behaviour, an individual's social behaviour and social relationships often are motivated by expectations of satisfying specific needs. For example, a person might become a Boy Scout or Girl Scout leader to satisfy a need for community service and recognition. Another person might risk a beat dance club to meet compatible people and satisfy social needs. A third person might join a warehouse membership club to obtain the benefits of group buying power. Thosc are just a few of the most infinite number of reasons why people interact with others.

A group may be defined as two or more people who interact to accomplish either individual or mutual goals.

TYPES OF GROUPS

Primary versus Secondary Groups—If a person interacts on a regular basis with other individuals (with members of his family, with neighbours or with co-workers whose opinion are valued) then these individuals can be called a primary group.

If a person interacts only occasionally with others, or does not consider their opinions particularly important are called a secondary group.

Thus, the critical distinctions between primary and secondary groups are the perceived importance of the groups to the individual and the frequency or consistency with the individual interacts with them.

Formal Vs. Informal Groups. If a group has a highly defined structure, specific roles and authority levels and specific goals, then it would be classified as a formal group.

If a group is more loosely defined it is considered to be informal group.

Informal social or friendship groups are generally more important to the marketeer because their less clearly defined structures provide a more conducive environment for the exchange of information and influence about consumption-related topics.

Membership Vs. Symbolic Groups. A group to which a person either belongs or would qualify for membership is called a membership group. For example, college alumni association, India in Medical Association.

A group in which an individual is not likely to receive membership, despite acting like a member by adopting the group's values, attitudes, and behaviour is considered a symoblic group.

In short, small, informal, primary membership groups are of the greatest interest to marketeers because they exert the greatest potential influence on consumption decisions.

Consumer-Relevant Groups

1. The Family. An individual's family often is in 'the best position to influence his or her consumption decision.

2. Friendship Groups. Friendship fulfils a wide range of needs: they provide companionship, security and opportunities to discuss problems that an individual may be reluctant to discuss with family members.

The opinions and preferences of friends are an important influence in determining the products or brands a consumer ultimately selects. Recognizing the power of poor group influence, marketeers of products such as brand-name, clothing, fine jewellery, and alcoholic, beverages depict friendship situations in their advertisements.

Forinal Social Groups. Membership in a formal social group may influence a consumer behaviour in several ways. For example, members of such groups have frequent opportunities to informally discuss products, services or stores. Some members may copy the consumption behaviour of other members whom they admire.

Shopping Groups. Two or more people who shop together-whether for food, for clothing or simply to pass time can be called a shopping group.

A special type of shopping group is the in-home shopping group, which typically consists of a group who gathers together in the home' of a friend to attend a "party" devoted to demonstrating and evaluating a specific line of proqucts.

The in-home party approach provides marketeers with an opportunity to demonstrate line features of their products simultaneously to a group of potential customers.

Consumer-Action Groups. This group can be divided into two categories. *(i)* those that organise to correct a specific consumer abuse and then disband and *(ii)* those that organise to address broader, more pervasive problem areas and operate over an extended or indefinite period of time.

Work Groups. Both formal work group and the informal friendship/work group can influence consumer behaviour.

A reference group is any person or group that serves as a point of comparison (or reference) for an individual in framing either general or specific values attitudes, or behaviour. This basic concept provides a valuable perspective for understanding the impact of other people on an individual's consumption beliefs, attitudes, and behaviour. It also provides some insight into the methods marketcers sometimes use to effect desired changes in consumer behaviour.

WHAT IS A REFERENCE GROUP?

From a marketing perspective, reference groups are groups that serve as frames of reference for individuals in their purchase on consumption decisions. The usefulness of this concept is enhanced by the fact that it places no restrictions on group size or membership, nor does it requires that consumers identify with a tangible group (*i.e.*, the group can be symbolic, prosperous business people, rock stars, sports heroes).

Reference groups that influence general or broadly defined values or behaviour are called normative reference groups. An example of a child's normative reference group is the immediate family which is likley to play an important role in moulding the child's general consumer values and behaviour (*e.g.*, which foods to select for good nutrition appropriate ways to dress for specific occasions, how arid where to shop, what constitutes "good" value).

Reference groups that serve as benchmarks for specific or narrowly defined attitudes or behaviour are called comparative reference groups. A comparative reference group might be a neighbouring family whose lifestyle appears to be admirable and worthy imitation (the way they maintain their home, their choice of home furnishings and cars, the number and types of vacations. they take).

Both normative and comparative reference groups are important. Normative reference groups influence the development of a basic code of behaviour; comparative. It is likely that the specific influences of comparative reference groups to some measure depend on the basic values and behaviour pattern established early in a person's development by normative reference groups.

Broadening the reference group concept like many other concepts borrowed from the behavioural sciences, the meaning of "reference group" has changed over the years. As originally employed reference groups were narrowly defined to include only these groups with which a person interacted on a direct basis (*e.g.*, family and close friends). However the concept gradually has broadened to include both direct and indirect individual or group influences. Indirect reference groups consists of those individuals or groups with whom a person does not have direct face-to-face contact, such as movie stars, sports heroes, political leaders, or TV personalities.

Referents who a person might use in evaluating his or her own general or specific attitudes or behaviour vary from one individual, to several family members, to a broader kinship from a voluntary association to a social class, a profession, an ethnic group; a community, or even a nation or culture.

APPLICATIONS OF THE REFERENCE GROUP CONCEPT

Reference group appeals are used very effectively by some advertisers to communicate with their markets. People or group situations with whom a target audience can identify are used to promote goods and services by subtly inducing the prospective consumer to identify with the pictured user of the product or service. This identification may be based on admiration (*e.g.*, of an athlete), on aspiration (of a celebrity or a way of life), on empathy (with a person or a situation), or on recognition (of a person—real or stereotypical or of a situation). In some cases, the prospective consumer may think, "If she uses it, it must be good: If use it, I'll be like her." In other cases, the prospective consumer says to liimself, "he has the same' problems that I have. What worked for him will work for me."

Four major types of reference group appeals in common marketing usage are celebrity appeals, expert appeals, commonman 'appeals, and executive appeals. These appeals as well as less frequently employed appeals, are often operationalized in the form of testimonials or endorsements. In the case of the commonman, they may be presented as slice-of-life commercials.

Celebrities. Celebrities, particularly movie stars, TV personalities, and sports heroes, provide a popular type of reference group appeal to their loyal followers and to much of the general public, celebrities represent an idealization of life that most people would love to live. Advertisers spend enormous sums of money to have celebrities promote their products, with the expcctation that the reading or viewing audience will react positively to the celebrity's association with their product.

Research comparing the impact of advertisement with and without celebrity endorsers found that those featuring celebrities were rated more positively. This was especially there among teenagers, who were most likely to project the celebrity's ability to the advertising inessage and the endorsed product.

How celebrities are used? A firm that decides to employ a celebrity to promote its product or service has a choice of using the celebrity to give a testimonial, to give an endorsement, as an actor in a commercial or as a company spokesperson. These promotional roles differ as follows:

1. Testimonials. If the celebrity has personally used the product or service' and is in a position to attest to its quality, he or she may give a testimonial citing its benefits. In an ad for Miracle-Gro plant food, actor Richard Dysart (perhaps best known for his role on the hit TV show L.A. Law) states that his father introduced him to Miracle-Gro and he has been "using it ever since".

2. Endorsement. Celebrities often are asked to lend their names to ads for products or services with which they may or may not be experts. For example, Chuck Daly, coach of the New York Nets basketball team, has endorsed sharp photocopying equipment.

3. Actor. A celebrity may be asked to present a product or service as part of a character enactment, rather than as a personal testimonial or endorsement. For instance, Jerry Stiller and Ann Meara are a husband-and . wife comedy team who have acted in commercials for a host of products and services.

4. Spokesperson. A celebrity who represents a brand or company over an extended period of time, often in print and television ads, and in personal appearances, is usually called a company spokesperson. Eventually, the celebrity's appearance becomes closely associated with the brand or company. For the past several years, for example, Linda Rvans served as a spokesperson for Clarial Ultress Hair Colouring.

Credibility of the Celebrity. Of all the positive charateristics that a celebrity might contribute to afirm's advertising programme-fame, talent, credibility, charisma-credibility with the consumer audience is the most important. By credibility we mean the audience's perception of both the celebrity's expertise (how much the celebrity knows about the prpduct area) and trustworthiness (how honest the celebrity is about what he or she says about the product). To illustrate, when a celebrity endorses only the product, consumers are likely to perceive the product in a highly favourable light and indicate a greater intention to purchase it. In contrast, when a celebrity endorses a variety of products, his, or her perceived credibility is reduced because of the apparent economic motivation underlying the celebrity's efforts.

The Expert. A second type of reference group appeal used by marketeers is the expert a person who, because of his or her occution, special training, or experience, is in a unique position to help the perspective consumer evaluate the product or service the advertisement promotes. For example, an advertisement for a quality frying pan may feature the endorsement of a chef, an ad for fishing tackle may contain the endorsement of a professional fishing guide.

The "Commonman". A reference group appeal that employs the testimonials of satisfied customers is known as the common-man approach. The advantage of the commonman appeal is that it demonstrates to prospective customers that someone just like them uses and is statisfied with the product or service being advertised. The commonman appeal is especially effective in public-health announcements (*e.g.*, antismoking or high-blood pressure messages),' for most people seem to identify with peoplc like themselves when it comes to such messages.

The saturn corporation consistently has used avariation of the commonman approach, when it tells of the interesting experiences of satisfied saturn customers. In one example, Darline and Tom Robison were "run off the highway, rolled their car", and yet were able to walk away from the accident. The ad makes a strong case for the inherent safety and crashworthiness of saturn automobiles.

The Executive Spokesperson. During the past two decades an increasing number of firms have used their top executives as spokesperson in consumer ads. The popularity of this type of advertising probably is due to the success and publicity received by a number of innovative executive spokespersons. For instance, lee la cocca was highly effective in persuading consumers that Chryster automobiles were worthy of their purchase consideration. Similarly, Frank Perdue spoke about the superiority of his Perdue Chickens; Victor Kiam, the president of Remington Products, about the benefits of his made-in-America shavers; and Bill Marriott, the president of the Marriott corporating, promotes the chain's hotels.

Like the celebrity spokesperson, executive spokespersons seem to be admired by the general population because of their achievements and the status implicity conferred on business leaders in the United States. The appearance of a company's chief executive in its advertising seems to imply that someone at the top is watching over the consumers' best interests, and encourages consumers to have more confidence in the firm's products or services.

A variation on the executive spokesperson is the frontline employee who speaks to the consuming public. This type of spokesperson may be a factory worker who tells the consumer how he or she is working to build the best products, or even an engineer or scientist who was responsible for creating, discovering, or developing a particular product. The power of such advertising is that it appears to be "eye-to-eye" the employee talking directly to the consumer.

TYPES OF REFERENCE GROUPS

Reference groups can be classified in terms of a person's membership or degree of involvement with the group, and in terms of the positive or negative influences they have on his or her values, attitudes, and behaviour.

The four types of reference groups that emerge from a cross-classification of these factors contractual group, aspirational group, disclaimant group, and avoidance group.

A contractual group is one in which a person holds membership or has regular face-fo-face contact and of whose values, attitudes, and standards he or she approves. Thus, a contractual group is likely to have a congruent influence on an individual's attitude or behaviour.

An aspirational group is a group in which a person does not hold membership and does pot have face-to-face contact, but wants to be a member. Thus, it often serves as a positive influence on that person's attitudes or behaviour. An ad for Gatorade appearing in sports illustrated for kids and starving retired basketball great Michael Jordan applies the aspirational group concept when it says "Be like Mike!"

A disclaimant group is a group in which aperson holds membership or has face-to face contact but dissapproves of the groups values, attitudes, and behaviour. Thus, the person tends to adopt attitudes and behaviour that are in opposition to the norms of the group.

A avoidance group is a group in which a person does not hold membership and does not have face-to-face contact and of whose values, attitudes, and behaviour he or she disapproves. Thus, the person tends to adopt attitudes and behaviour that are in opposition of those of the group.

To illustrate, consider David Glenn; a senior Majoring in Marketing at large state university in the Midwest. The School's Marketing Club, of which he is Vice-President, serves as one of

David's contractual groups. David believes that continuing his education to obtain an MBA will ennance his career opportunities. It is clear that individuals who hold MBA degrees serve as an aspirational group for him. Furthermore, although he enjoys his position as a photographer in the university's newspaper, recent editorials (endorsed by most of the staff) urging students to adopt a more liberal political philosophy run counter to his own views. Thus, the newspaper staff is currently a disclaimant group. Finally, David personally knows a number of students who have quit college during their final year. These former students serve as an avoidance group.

Factors that Effect Reference Group. The degree of influence that affect, reference exerts on an individual's behaviour usually depends on the nature of the individual and the product, and on specific social factors. This section discusses how and why some of these factors influence consumer behaviour.

Information and Experience. An individual who has firsthand experience with a product or service, or an easily have full information about it, is less likely to be influenced by the advice or example orothers. On the other hand, a person who has little or no experience with the product or service, and does not expect to have access to objective information about it is more likely to seek out the advice or example of others. For instance if a Law school student wants to impress his new girlfriend, he may take her to a restaurant that he knows from his experience to be good, or to one that has been high recommended by the local newspapers Dining out Guide. If he has neither personal experience nor information, he regard as valid, he may seek the advice of friends or imitate that behave of others by taking her to a restaurant he knows is frequently by attorney's whom he admires.

Credibility Attractiveness, and Power of Referring Group. A reference group that is preceived as credible, attractive, or powerful can induce consumer attitude and behaviour change. For example, when consumers are concerned with obtaining accurate information about the performance or quality of a product or service, they are likely to be persuaded by those they consider trustworthy and knowledgeable. That is, they are more likely to be persuaded by source with high credibility.

When consumers are primarily concerned with the acceptance or approval of others they like, with whom they identify, or who offer them status or other benefits, they are likely to adopt their product, brand, or other behaviour characteristics. When consumers are primarily concerned with the power that a person or group can exert over them, they might choose product or services that conform to the norms of that person or group in order to avoid ridicule or punishment. However, unlike other reference groups that consumers follow because they are credible or because they are attractive, power groups are not as likely to cause attitude change. Individuals may conform to the behaviour of a powerful person or group, but are not as likely to experience a change in their own attitudes.

Different reference groups may influence the beliefs, attitudes, and behaviour of an individual at different points in time different circumstances. For example, the dress habits of young male executives may very, depending on his place and role. He may confirm to the dress code of his office by wearing white shirts and conservatives business suits by day and drastically alter his mode of dress after work by wearing more trendy, flamboyants styles.

Conspicuousness of the Product. The potential influence of a reference group on a purchase decision varies according to how visually or verbally conspicuous the product is to others. A visually conspicuous product is one that will stand out and be noticed (*e.g.* a luxury item or novelty product); a verbally conspicuous product may be highly interesting or it may be easily described to others. Products that are espeically conspicuous and status revealing (a new automobile, fashion clothing, home furniture) are most likely to be purchased with an eye to the reactions of relevant others. Products that are less conspicuous (canned fruits, laundry soaps) are less likely to be purchased with a reference group in mind.

The success of status sport shoes such as Head, Cole-Haan, or Bally is aided by the facts that it is relatively easy to spot a person wearing them given the distinctive logos strategically placed on the shoes themselves (*e.g.* on the tongue on the shoe, the heel, or even the sole). In a somewhat similar fashion, the success of the nicotine patch is aided by the fact that it is potentially conspicuous product about which a current smoker may ask questions This, in turn lead the smoker to consider trying the patch.

Reference Groups and Consumer Conformity. Marketeers are particularly interested in the ability of reference group to change consumer attitude and behaviour (*i.e.*, to encourag"e conformity). To be capable of such, influence, a reference group must:

1. Inform or make the individual aware or a specific product or brand;
2. Provide the individual with the opportunity to compare his or her own thinking with the attitudes and behaviour of the group.
3. Influence the individual to adopt attitude and behaviour that are consistent with the norms of the group; and
4. Legitimize an individual's decision to use the same product as the group.

How group Membership affects brand choice often depends on the specific product (*e.g.* pizza verses toothpaste), the type of social relationship (roommates, friends, dates), and the social structure of the group (extent of personal ties between group members). For example, research conducted among members of a college concluded that members of close-knit groups were likely to reveal a preference for the same brimds. The findings also suggest that product conspicuousness is unnecessary for similarity of brand choice to occur. Specifically, the evidence indicates that even for relatively "Private" products (*e.g.* shampoo and toethpasate), strong brand congruence may occur when the particular social setting provides an opportunity fot such products to be observed (*e.g.* when sisters happen to share the same bathroom). This evidence underscores the fact that a consumers selection of a product category, brand, style, or type of product often is influenced by the preferences and actions of others.

The sum of learned beliefs, values and customs that serve to direct the consumer behaviour of members of a particular society is known as culture.

The beliefs and value components of our definition refer to the accumulated feelings and priorities that individuals have about "things" and possessions. More precisely, beliefs consist of the very large number of mental or verbal statement that reflect a person's particular knowledge and assessment of something. Values also are beliefs. Values differ from other beliefs, however, because they meet the following criteria:

1. they are relatively few in number, 2. they serve as a guide for culturally appropriate behaviour, 3. they are enduing of difficult to change 4. they are not tied to specific objectives or situations and 5. they are widely accepted by the members of society.

Therefore, in a broad sense, both values and beliefs are mental images that affect a wide range of specific attitudes, which, in turn, influence the way a person is likely to respond in a specific situation. For example, the criteria a person uses to evaluale alternative in product category or his or her eventual decisions regarding these brands, are influenced by both the person's general values and specific beliefs (*e.g.*, particular preceptions about the quality, workmanship, staffs, design and esthetics of the cameras.

In contrast to beliefs and values, custom are overt modes of behaviour that consitute culturally approved or acceptable ways of behaving in specific situations. Customs consist of everyday or routine behaviour. For example, a customers routine behaviour, such as adding sugar and milk to coffee, or going out to dinner with family after religious services are customs. Thus, while beliefs and values are guides for behaviour, customs are usual and acceptable ways of behaving.

Hence, it is easy to understand that various cultures of a society helps marketeers product consumer acceptance of their products.

CHARACTERISTICS OF CULTURE

The Invisible hand of Culture. The impac of culture is so natural and automatic that its influence of behaviour is usually taken for granted. For instance, when consumer researchers ask people why they do certain things, they frequently answer, "because it's the right thing to do". This seemingly superficial response partially reflects the ingrained influence of culture on our behaviour. Offen, it is only when we are exposed to peeple with different cultural values or customs (*e.g.*, when visting a different region or a different country) that we become aware of how culture has moulded our own behaviour. Thus, a true appreciation of the influence culture has on our daily life requires some knowledge of at least one other society with different cultural characteristics. For example, to understand that brushing our teeth twice a day with flavoured toothpaste is a cultural phenomenon requires some, awareness that members of another society either do not brush their teeth at all or do so in manner distinctly different from our own.

Culture Satisfies Needs. Culture exists to satisfy needs of the people within a society. It offers order, direction and guidance in all phases of human problem solving by providing "tried-and-true" methods of satisfying physiological, personal and social needs. For example, culture provides standards and "rules" about when to eat, where to eat, and what is appropriate to eat for breakfast, lunch, dinner and snacks and what to, serve to guests at a dinner party, a picnic, or a wedding. Soft drink companies would prefer that consumers received their morning "jolt" of caffeine from one of their products, rather than from coffee. Because most Americans do not consider soda a suitable breakfast beverage, the real challenge for soft drink companies is to overcome culture, not competition. In fact, according to industry estimates, coffee accounts for 47 per cent of the morning' beverage market, followed by juice with 21 per cent, milk at 1 per cent, tea at 17 per cent and soft drinks at only 4 per cent.

Cultural beliefs, values and customs continue to be followed so long as they yield satisfaction. When a specific standard no longer satisfies the members of society, however, it is modified or replaced so that the resulting standard is more in line with current needs and desires. Thus, culture gradually but coninually evolves to meet the needs of society.

In a cultural context, it firm's products and services can be viewed as offering appropriate or acceptable for individual or societal needs. If a product no longer is acceptable because a value or custom that is related to its use does not adequately satisfy human needs, then the firm producing the product must be ready to revise its product offering. Marketeers also must be alert to newly embraced customs and values. For example, as Americans have to become more health and fitness conscious, there has been an increase in the number of walkers, joggers and runners on the nations's streets and roads. Astute who manufacturers who responded by offering an increased variety (If appropriate footwear have been able to improve their market positions.

Culture is Learned. Anthropologists have identified, three distinct forms of cultural learning formal learning in which adults and older sibilngs teach a young family member "how to behave", informal learning, in which a child learns primary by imitating the, behaviour of selected others family, friends, TV heroes and technical learning in which teachers instruct the chiid. In an educational enviornment about what should be done, how, it should be done and why it should be done.

A young girl who is told by her mother to stop climbing trees because "girls don't do that" is formally learning a value that her mother feels is right. If she watches her mother preparing food; she is informally learning certain cooking habits. And if she takes ballet lessons, she is experiencing technical learning. Although a film's advertising can influence all three types of cultural learning, it is likely that many product advertisements enhance inform cultural learning by providing the audiance with a model of behaviour to intimate.

The repetition of advertising message creates and reinforces cultural beliefs and values. For example, many advertisers continually stress the same selected benefits a integral features of their product or brands. Ads for telephone answering machines often stress features such as beeperless remote message retrieval, unlimited message length, remote outgoing message change capability, call screening and a toll saver device. It is difficult to say where product owners after several years of cumulative exposure to such potent advertising appeals, inherently desire these benefits from their telephone answering machines or have been taught by marketeers to desire them. In a sense, although specific product advertising may reinforce the benefits that consumers want from the product, such advertising also "teaches" future generation of consumers to expect the same benefits from the product category.

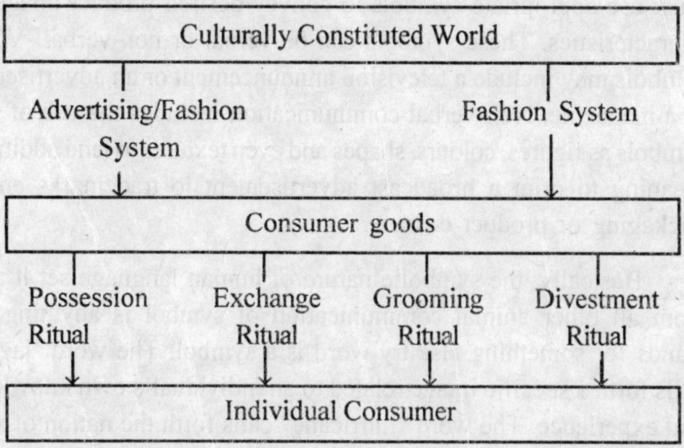

The above figure shows that cultural meaning moves from the cultural constituted world to consumer goods, and from there to the individual consumer by means of various consumption-related vehicles.

Enculturation and Acculturation. When discussing the acquisition of culture, anthropologists often distinguishes between the learning of one's own, or native culture and the learning of some other culture, The learning of one's own culture is known as enculturation. The learning of a new or foreign culture is known as acculturation. In acculturation, it is an important concept for marketeers who plan to sell their products in foreign or multinational market. In such cases, marketeers must study the specific culture of their potential target markets to determine whether their product will be acceptable to its members, and if so, how they can best communicate the characteristics of their products to persuade the target market to buy.

Language and Symbols. To acquire a common culture, the members of society must be able to communicate with each other through a common language. Without a' common language, shaved meaning could not exist and true communication would not take place.

To communicate effectively with their audience, marketeers must use appropriate symbols to convey desired product images or characteristics. These symbols can be verbal or non-verbal. Verbal symbols may include a television announcement or an advertisement in a magazine. Non-verbal communication includes the use of such symbols as figures, colours, shapes and even textures to lend additional meaning to print a broadcast advertisement to trademarks and to packaging or product designs.

Basically, the symbolic nature of human language set it apart from all other animal communication of symbol is anything that stands for something else try word is a symbol. The word 'jaguar" calls forth a specific image related to an individual's own knowledge and experience. The word "hurricane" calls forth the nation of wind and rain and also has the power to stir us emotionally, arousing feeling of danger and the need for protection and safety. Similarly, the word "jaguar" has symbolic meaning.

Because the human mind can process symbols, it is possible for person to "experience the advertisement for lane's recliners by implicity understanding that the illustration of an antique bathtub visually reinforces the notion that lane's recliners reduce stress and aid relaxation. The capacity to learn symbolically primarily a human phenomenon; most oiher animals learn by direct experience. Clearly, the ability of humans to understand symbolically how a product service, or idea can satisfy their needs makes it easier for marketeers to "sell;' the features and benefits of their offerings. Though a shaved language and culture, individuals already know what the image means; thus, an association can be made without activity thinking about it. Table A illustrates how beer advertisers use common "symbols" drawn from our shaved culture to evoke particular meanings in consumers.

A symbol may have several, even contradictory, meaning so the advertisers must ascertain exactly what the symbol is communicating to its intended auidence. For example the advertiser who uses a trademark depiciting an old craftsman to symbolise careful workmanship may instead be communicating an image of outmoded methods and lack of style. The marketeer who uses a slang in an advertising to attract a teenage audience must do so with great care. Slang that is misused or outdated will symbolically date the marketeer's firm and product.

Table A

Brand	Symbol	Meaning
Busch	Cowboy	Applies the myth of the frontier as pure free from the corruption of civilisation, yet full of sudden danger. The cowboy demonstrates mystery over nature; the cowboy is the archetypical man's man.
Busch Rolling Rock, Heileman's old style, Molson's Golden	Stream water	Stress that beer is a form of bottled nature, that drinking beer is a safe way to face the challenge of nature.
Busch	Wild horses	Implies untamed nature drinking beer is a substitute for taming wild horses.
Old Milwankee	Wildness	Special place untouched by civilization; allows men to engage in recreational activities not possible in the city of suburbs; drinking beer acts as a substitute for actually visiting the place.
Busch, Old Milwankee Budweiser	Labourers and athletes	Depicts physical challenge; beer presented as a reward for hard work or play, drinking beer is a way to symoolically re-enact the feat.

Price and channels of distribution also are significant symbols of the marketeer and the marketeer's product. For example, price often implies quality to potential buyers. For certain products (*e.g.* clothing), the type of store in which the product is sold also is an important symbol of quality. In fact, all the elements of the marketing mix the product, its promotion, price and the stores at which it is available are symbols that communicate ranges of quality to potential buyers.

Ritual. Inaddition to language and symbols, culture includes various ritualised experiences and behaviours that until recently have neglected by consumer researchers. A ritual is a type of symbolic activity consisting of a series of steps occurring in a fixed sequence and repeated over time.

In practice, rituals extend over the human life cycle from birth to death, including a host of intermediate events. These rituals can be very public, elaborate, religious, or civil ceremonies; or they can be as mundane as an individual's grooming behaviour. Ritualized behaviour is typically rather formal, and often is scripted behaviour. It is also likely to occur repeatedly over time (*e.g.* singing the national anthem before a base ball game).

Most important from the standpoint of marketeers is the fact that rituals tend to be replete with ritual artifacts (product) that are associated with or somehow enhance the performance of the ritual. For instance, free ornaments, stocking and various food items are linked to the ritual of Christmas celebr'!tion; other rituals have their own specific artifacts associated with them for special occasions, such as wedding anniversaries, some types of artifacts are preceived as more appropriate and appreciated than others such as jewellery versus household goods.

Culture is Shared. To be considered a cultural characteristic, a particular belief, value, or practice must be shared by a significant portion of the society. Thus, culture frequently is viewed as group customs that link together the member of society. Of course, common language is the critical cultural component that makes it possible for people to share values, experiences, and customs.

Various social institutions within a socicty transmit the elements of culture and make. the sharing of culture a reality. Chief among such institutions is the family, which serves as the primary agent for enculturation the passing alone of basic cultural beliefs, values, and customs to society's newest members, a vital part of the enculturation of the young. This includes teaching such basic consumer-related values and skills as the meaning of money, the relationship between price and quality, the establishment of product tastes, preferences and habits and apptopriate methods of response to various promotional messages.

In addition to the family, two other institutions traditionally share much of the responsibility for the transfer of selected aspects of culture educational institutional and houses of worship.

Educational institutionals specifically are changes with imparting basic learning skill, history, patriotism, citizenship and the technical training needed to prepare people for significant roles within society. Religious institutions provide a perpetuate religious consciousness, spiritual guidance, and moral training. Although the young receive much of their consumer training within the family setting, the educational and religious systems reinforce this training by teaching economic and ethical concepts.

A fourth frequently overlooked, social instiutions that plays a major role in the transfer of culture throughout society is the: mass media. Given the extensive exposure of the American population to both print and broadcast media and the easily ingested, entertaining format in which the contents of such media usually are presented, it is not surprising that the mass media are powerful vehicles for imparting a wide range of cultural values.

We are exposed daily to advertising, an important component of the media. Advertising not only underwrites or makes economically feasible, the editorial or programming, contents of the media, but also transmits much about our culture. Without advertising it would be almost impossible to disseminate information about products, ideas and causes. A leading historian noted that advertising now compares with such long-standing institutions as the schools and the church in the magnitude of its social influence.

Consumers receive important cultural information from advertising. For example, it has been hypothesized that one of the roles of advertising in sophisticated magazines such as vanity fair is to instruct readers how to dress, how to decorate their homes, and hat food and wines to serve guests. In other words, what types of behaviour are most appropriate to their particular social class.

Culture is Dynamic. To fulfil its need-gratifying role, culture continually must evolve if it is to function in the best interest of a society. For this reason, the marketecrs must carefully monitor the society cultural environment in order to market an existing product more effectively, or to develop promising new product.

This is not an easy task, because many factors are likely to produce cultural changes within a given society. For example, a major cultural hange in our society is the expanding role choices of American women.

Today, most women work outside the home, frequently in careers that were con idered exclusive male. Also women are increasingly active in social and athletic activities outside the home. All this adds up to a blurring of traditional male-female sex roles. These changes mean that marketers have had to reconsider who are purchasers and the users of their products, when they do their shopping, how and where they can be reached by the media and what new product and service needs are emerging.

Marketeers who monitor cultural changes often find new opportunities to increase corporate profitability. For example, not too long ago beer advertising was almost exclusively directed at men. Yet a recent advertisement for Coors Light Beer proclaimed; "You don't have to be a man to appreciate a great beer." The recent cultural changes in the role of woman have justified such changes in marketing focus. Marketeers of such products as life insurance, leisure wear, toy electric trains and small cigars are among those who have attempted to exploit the dramatically shifting sense of what is feminine.

To illustrate, recent Virginia Slims ads reposition smoking as a feminine way for women to assert their independence. One example feature a woman on a motorcycle, saying, "I don't necessarily want to run the world but I wouldn't mind taking it for a little ride". This differs from the "You've come a long way, baby" ads that depicted 19th century women hiding to smoke because it was not feminine. This sex role shift has also had an impact on traditional male roles. Today, for instance, cosmetic firms market skin care and other cosmetic products to men.

CONTENT ANALYSIS

Content analysis, as the flame implies, focuses on the content of verbal, written and pictorial communications. Content analysis can be used as a relatively objective means for determining what social and cultural changes have occurred in a specific society. For instance, researchers use content analysis to examine how African-Americans, women, and the elderly have been depicted in mass media. Content analysis is also used to explore trends in the style and layout of various types of advertising. For example, a small California fragrance company recently used content analysis to determine the most effective way to appeal to sophisticated urban adults through magazine advertising. Their searchers revelaed that the product, together with a person and the logo, was the most frequently used advertising format by competing perfume makers. Yearning for the product was created through visual association with a person Who has value to the consumer. Another study, a content analysis of Ms. Magazine advertising during its first 15 yrs. of publication found that the portrayal of women as subordinate to men or as merely decorative had decreased over time.

Consumer Fieldwork. When examining a specific-society, anthropology frequently immerse temselves in the enviornment under study. As trained researchers, they are likely to select a small sample of people from a particular society and carefully observe their behaviour. Based on their observations, researchers draw conclusions about the values, beliefs and customs of the society under investigation. For example, if researchers were interested in how people select compact discs (CDs), they might position trained observed in record stores and note how specific types of CDs selected. The researchers also might be interested in the degree of search that accompanies the choice that is, how often consumers tend to take a CD off the display, read the description and place it back again before selecting the CD they finally purchase.

The distinct characteristics of field observation are that—*(l)* it takes place within a natural environment, *(2)* it is performed sometimes without the subjects awareness, and *(3)* it focuses on observation of behaviour. Because the emphasis is on a natural environment and observation behaviour, field observation concerned with consumer behaviour often focuses on instore shopping behaviour and less frequently on in have preparation and consumption. In some cases, instead of just observing behaviour, researchers become participant observers. For example, if a researcher is interested in examining how men selected their shoes, he or she might take a sale position in a men's shoe department to observe directly and even to interact with customers in the transaction process.

Both field observation and participant observer research require highly skilled researchers who can seperate their own emotions from what they actually observe in their professional roles. Both techniques provide. valuable insights that might not easily be obtained through survey research that simply asks consumers, questions about their behaviour.

In addition to fieldwork methods, depths interviews and focus group sessions are also often employed by marketeers to get, a "first look" at an emerging social" or cultural change. In the relatively informal atmosphere offocus-group discussions, consumers are apt to reveal attitude of behaviour that may signal a shift in value that, in turn, may affect he long-run market acceptance of a product or service. For instance, one of the authors has been involved in a series of focus group studies concerned with indentified mrketing programmes that reinforce established customer loyalty and goodwill. A common thread running throughout these studies showed that established customers, especially of services, wish to have their loyality acknowledgement in the form of personalised services. These observations have led various services and product companies to refine or establish loyalty programmes that are more personalised in the way that they treat, their established customers. This is just one of numerous example showing how focus groups and depts interviews are used to spot social trends.

Value Measurement Survey Instruments. Anthropologists have traditionally oberved the behaviour of members of a specific society and inferred from such behaviour the dominant or underlying values of the society. In recent years, however, there has been a gradual shift to measuring values directly by means of survey research. Researchers use data collection instrument called value instrument to ask people how they feel about basic personal and social concepts as freedom, comform national security and peace.

Research into the relationship between people's value and their actions as consumers still is in its infancy. This is an area that is destined to receive increased attention, however, for its taps a broad dimension of human behaviour that could not be explored effectively before the availability of standardised value instrument.

A popular value instrument that has employed in consumer behaviour studies is the Rokeach Value Survey. This self-administered value inventing is divided into two parts with each part measuring different but complementary types of personal values. The first part consists of 18 terminal value items, which are designed to measure the relative importance of end states of existence. The second part consists of 18 instrumental value items, which measures basic approaches an individual might take to reach end state values. Thus, the first half of the measurement instrument deals, with ends, while the second half considers means.

SUB-CULTURE

Culture has a potent influence CD all consumer behaviours. Individuals are brought up to follow the beliefs, values and customs of their society and to avoid behaviour that is frowned upon or considered taboo. In addition to cultural segmentation, marketeers segment larger societies into smaller sub-groups (sub-cultures) that consists of people who are similar terms of their ethnic origin, their customs, and or the ways they behave. These sub-cultures provide important marketing opportunities for astute marketing strategists.

The discussion of sub-cultures, therefore, has a narrower focus than the discussion of culture. Sub-cultural divisions are based on a variety of socio-cultural and demographic variables, such as nationality, religion, geographic locality, race, age, sex, even working status.

Meaning of Sub-culture. The members of a specific sub-culture possess beliefs, values, and customs, that set them apart from other members of the same society, In addition, they adhere to most of the dominant cultural beliefs, values and behaviourial patterns of the larger society. We define sub-culture, then, as a distinct cultural group that exists as an identifiable segment within a larger, more complex society.

Thus the cultural profile of a society or nation is a composite of two distinct elements—*1.* the unique beliefs; values and customs sub-scribed to by members, of specific sub-cultures, and *2.* the central or care cultural themes that are shared by most of the population, regardless of specific sub-cultural membership. The figure 'presents a simple model of relationship between two sub-cultural has its own. unique traits, yet both groups share the dominant traits of the overall American culture.

We can define it in another way: Each American is, in large part, a product of the "American way of life." Each American, however, is at the same time a member of various sub-cultures. For example, a 14 year-old boy may simultaneously be Hispanic, Catholic, a teenager and a New Yorker. We would expect that membership in each different sub-culture would provide its own set of specific beliefs, values, attitudes and customs. The table lists the typical sub-cultural categories and corresponding examples of specific sub-cultural groups. This list is by no means exhaustive. College graduates feminists, girl scouts, and single parents in fact; any group that shares common beliefs and customs may be classified as a sub-culture.

Relationship between Culture and Sub-culture

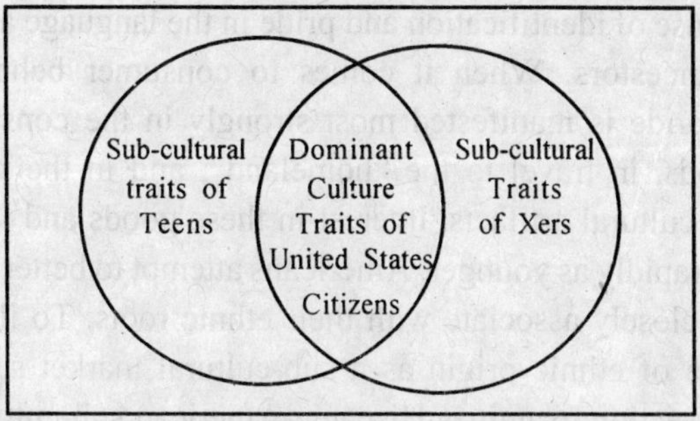

Examples of Major Sub-cultural Categories

Categories	Examples
Nationality (*i.e.* birthplace of ancestors)	French, Puerto Rigan, Korean
Religion	Catholic, Hindu, Jew
Geographic region	South eastern, midwestern, eastern
Race	African, American, Canadian, Asian
Age	American
Gender	Teens, Xers, middle age, elderly femal, male
Occupation	engineer, cook, plumber
Social class	Lower, middle, upper

Subculural analysis enables the marketing manager to focus on sizeable and "natural" market segments. When carrying out such analyses the marketeer must determine whether the beliefs, values and customs shared by members of specific sub-group make them desirable candidates for special marketing attention. Sub-cultures, therefore, are relevant units of analysis for market research.

Some Important Subcultural Categories

Nationality Sub-cultures. Most U.S. citizens especially those born in the United States, see themselves as Americans, they frequently retain a sense of identification and pride in the language and customs of their ancestors. When it comes to consumer behaviour, this ancestral pride is manifested most strongly in the consumption of ethnic foods, in travel to the "homeland", and in the purchase of numerous cultural artifacts. Interest in these goods and services has expanded rapidly as younger. Americans attempt to better understand and more closely associate with their ethnic roots. To illustrate the importance of ethnic origin as a sub-cultural market segment, the following section examines Hispanic-American sub-culture.

Hispanic Sub-culture. This represents about 9 per cent of the United States population (more than 25 million people, with buying power of $ 205 billion). In contrast to other American population segments, Hispanic-Americans are younger (the median age of Hispanics is about 7 years younger than the median age of non-Hispanics), they are members of larger families, and they are more likely to live in an "extendal family" household, with members consisting of several generations.

With a 53 per cent populat on increase during the decade from 1980 to 1990 (and a 27 per-cent growlh rate expected for the decade 1990 (to 2000) Hispanic-Americans are projected to supplant African Americans within 20 years as the largest American minority group. Indeed, Hispanic have alrea y become the dominant minority in New York, Los Angeles, San Diego, Phoenix, San Francisco and Denner and they represent majority in San Antonio, Texas.

This sub-cultural group can be considered as a single market, based on common language and culture, or as a separate sub-cultural markets that correspond to different Hispanic countries of origin. There are twelve Hispanic sub-groups now identified in the United States. The three largest Hispanic sub-cultural groups consists of Mexican Americans (about 60 per cent of total Hispauic-Americans), Puerto Ricans (approx. 12 per cent of the total), and Cubans (almost

5 per cent of the total). These sub-cultures are heavily concentrated geographical, with more than 70 per cent of their members residing in California, Texas, New York and Florida.

Understanding Hispanic Consumer Behaviour. Available evidence indicates that Hispanic and Anglo consumers differ in terms of a variety, of important buyer behaviour variables.

While mindful of their tradition, Hispanic-Americans, like other major sub-cultural groups, are a dynamic and evolving portion of the overall society. For this reason, growing number of Hispanic consumers are food shopping in nonethnic large American style supermarkets. They appear to be engaged a process of acculturation, that is, they are gradually adopting the consumption patterns of the majority of United States consumers. Similarly, other research indicates that when it comes to clothes shopping. Hispanic youths are more fashion-conscious and are more likely to seek out and be loyal to well-known brands and to generally like the act of shopping more than their non-Hispanic counterparts.

Defining and Segmenting the Hispanic Market. Marketeers who are targeting the verse Hispanic sub-cultural groupings are concerned with finding the best ways to define segment this market. Research shows that those who strongly identify with being Hispanic (*i.e.* strong Hispanic identifiers) are more frequent users of Spanish language media, are more brand loyal are more likely to buy prestige brands, are more likely to seek the advice of another and to more often be influenced by friends or family and are more likely. to buy advertised to Hispanic than weak Hispanic identifiers. This pattern suggests that the degree of Hispanic identification is a useful segmentation variable when one is targeting the Hispanic Market.

SEX AS A SUB-CULTURE

In Relation to Consumer Behaviour. All societies tend to assign certain traits and roles to males and others to females. In American society, for instance, aggressiveness, competitiveness, independence, and self confidence often were considered traditional masculine 'Traits' neatness, tactfulness, gentleness and talkativeness were considered traditional feminine traits. In terms of role differences, women have historically been cast as homemakers with responsibility for child care and men as the providers or bread winners. Although such traits and roles are no longer relevant, or so strongly associated with members of a specific sex, sonre advertisers continue to appeal to such sex linked roles.

Consumer Products and Sex Roles. Within every society it is quite common to find products that are either exclusively or strongly associated with the members of one sex. In the United States, for example, shaving equipment, cigars, pants, ties and work clothing were historically male products; bracelets, hair spray, hair dryer and sweet-smelling colognes generally were considered feminine products. For most of these products; the sex link has either diminished or disappeared; for others, the prohibition still lingers. An interesting product category with regard to the blurring of a gender appeal is men's fragrances. Although men are increasingly wearing fragrances, it is estimated that 30 per cent of men's fragrances are worn by women. Also; although women have historically been the major market for vitamins men are increasingly being targeted for vitamins exclusively formulated for men.

Despite the fact that the line between "male only" and "female only" products has become blurred in recent years, consumers tend to imput a sex, or gender, to products. For this reason, advertising executives should consider not only the sex of their target market but also the perceived sex of the product category in the development of their advertising campaigns.

The Working Woman. Marketeers and consumer researchers have been increasingly interested in the working woman, especially the married working woman. They recognize that married women who work outside of the'home are a large and growing market segment one whose needs differ from those of women who do not work outside the home. It is the size of the working woman market that makes it so attractive. Approx 72 per cent of American women work full time and only 3.5 percent of American families consist of the traditional-arrangement of a bread winning husband and a homemaking wife. Young women, with young children, have been the fastest-growing segment in the female work force. The number of workings, wives with children under the age of six has risen by more than 400 per cent since 1948 and among those ith children 6 to 17 years of age, the increase has been more than 200 per cent.

Segmenting the Working Woman Market. To provide a richer framework for segmentation, marketeers have develop categories that differentiate the motivations of working and non-working women. For instance, a number of studies have divided the female population into four segments; stay at home house-wives; plan to work housewives, "just a job" and "career oriented" working women is primarily by a sense that the family requires the additional income, whereas "career oriented" working women, who tend to be in a managerial or professional position, are driven more by a need to achieve and success in their chosen careers.

Shoping Patterns of Warking, Women. Working wome speed 'less time in shopping than non-working women. They accomplish this "time economy" by shopping less often and by being brand and store loyal. Not surprisingly, working women also are likely to shop during evening hours and on weekend, as well as to buy through direct mail catalogues.

Reaching the Working Woman. An examination of magazine advertisement appearirig in general audience magazines concludes that the proportion of males shown as workers and, co-workers remained almost constant from 1970-1988, whereas the proportion of women shown as workers or co-workers (as opposed to homemakers and/or mothers) nearly doubled. A study examining, advertising respoose to financial services concluded that the use of a "modern" positionirig strategy (with a focus on career and family) proved more effective with women than a more traditional positioning strategy (which focused an nurturing and family). However,' there is a danger in positioning a married working woman as a "Super Woman" (*e.g.* who perfectly "balances" per career; advertisements that portray a "balance" between work and home obligations are likely to be appreciated.

Sub-cultural Interaction. All consumers are simultaneously members of more than one sub-cultural segment (for example, a consumer may be an elderly African-American Baptist working wife living in the Pacific Northwest). For this reason, marketeers should strive to understand how multiple sub-cultural membership, interact. to influence target consumers relevant consumption bepaviour promotional strategy should not be limited to target a single sub-cultural membership.

Sub-cultural analysis enables marketeers to segment their markets to meet the specific needs, motivations, perceptions and attitudes shared by members of a specific sub-cultural group. A sub-culture is a distinct cultural group that exists as an ident fiable segment within a larger, more complex society. Its members possess beliefs, values and customs that set them apart from other members of the same society, at the same time they hold to the dominant beliefs of the overall society. Major sub-cultural categories in this country include nationality, religion; geographic location, race, age and sex. Each of these can be broken down into smaller segments that can be reached through special copy appeals and selective media choices: In some cases, (*e.g.* the eldest consumer) product characteristics can be tailored to the specialized needs of the market segment. Because all consumers simultaneously are members of several subcultural groups, the marketeer must determine for the product category how specific sub-cultural memberships interect to influence the consumer's purchase decisions.

CROSS-CULTURE

While world-wide consumers may be similar in many ways, any differences in attitudes or behilviour can be crucial in determining the satisfaction and may provide an opportunity for segmenting consumers in terms of cultural differences. For example, while more than 50 per cent of Japanese and American women work outside of the home, Japanese women have been slower to embrace the liberated attitudes of their counterpart. Working women in the United States, seen in this light, the determination as to whether or not to market time-saving clearing device as a world brand is a critical strategic decision. Some firms might attempt to establish a global branding strategy, one that treats Japanese and American working women differently. One marketing authority aptly stunned up the issue as follows; "The only ultimate truth possible is that humans are both deeply the same and obviously different.

Global psychographic research often reveals cultural differences of great importance to marketeers. For example, Rober Starch World-wide, a major multinational marketing research company, recently completed a 40 country cross-cultural psychographic segmentation study consisting of some 37,743 consumer interviews that are projectable to 1.97 billion adults world-wide. The results revealed that the following four major shopping styles dominate world-wide consumers: Local makers, "Price seakers", "Brand Loyalists", and "Luxury innovators". The Gallup Organisation, another leading marketing research company, has also recently completed a regional multinational segmentation study of the metropolitan areas of the following five Latin-American countries: Argentina, Brazil, Chile, Colombia and Mexico. This segmentation model identified the following eight segments: "Emerging professional Elite", "Traditional Elite", "Progressive Upper Middle Class", 'Self-Made, Middle Class," "Skilled Middle Class", "Self-Skilled Lower Middle Class", "Industrial Working Class", and "Struggling Working Class".

Marketing Mistakes a Failure to Understand Differences. In most cases, the gamble for Marketeers in International Marketing is not knowing whether the product, the professional appeal, the pricing policy, or the retail channels that are effective in one country will work in others countries and trying to determine what specific changes should be made to ensure a ceptance in each foreign market. The following examples of some international marketing blunders illustrate that failure to adopt Marketing Strategy to target Market's distinctive traits can lead to costly mistakes.

Product Problems. International marketeers frequently neglect to modify their products to meet local customs and tastes. American Marketers, selling food products in Japan, frequently learn and hard way (through poor sales performance) that they must alter traditional product characteristics. For example, recently Snapple failed to sustain sales momentum in Japan because consumers preferred clear, less sweet iced tea. It appears that Snapple was unwilling or too slow to alter its ingredients to conform to local Japanese taste. Kellogg's, the giant cereal company, in pursuing international expansion, has attempted to avoid the numerous "cultural traps" that are associated with cross-cultural Marketing offood stuff. It has learned to draw careful distinctions between the Irish, who consume 17 pounds of cereal per person per year (the highest rate in the world), and French, Italians, and Greeks, whose meager breakfast tend not to include cereal. Still another example showed that, when Oreos were introduced in Japan, Nabisco reduced the amount of sugar in the cookie batter (the box promoted them as having a "bitter twist") to meet Japanese tastes. However, some Japanese consumers still considered too sweet and told the company that they "just wanted to eat the base" without the cream. Nabisco belatedly introduced new Petit Oreo Non-cream cookies that consisted of single wafers without the cream. To avoid such problems, marketeers must ascertain in advance whether the physical characteristics of their products will be acceptable to the new market.

Mc Donald's, which has been very successful in its ongoing efforts to bring fast-food to the world, has reached a point at which its international operations now bring in more than half of its operating income. Its international expansion plans are ambitious it currently anticipated opening more than 600 outlets in China and just finished developing a vegetable and-fish burger that is designed to be culturally acceptable to India's 800 Million non meat-eating Hindus.

Colour is also critical variable in international Marketing, because th same colour often has different meaning in different cultures. For example, consider the colour blue. In Holland, it stands for warmth; in Iran, it represents death. In Sweden, it connotes coldness in India, it means purity. Furthermore, bellow which represents, warmth in the United States, connotes infidelity in France. Pepsodent erred when it tried to sell its toothpaste in southeast Asia by promising white teeth. In that part of the world, chewing betel nuts is considered an elite habit and consequently, brownish red teeth are viewed as a status symbol. Thus, Pepsodent's slogan. "You'll wonder where the yellow want" did not help to sell the product. It is critical that the colour of products and packages convey the proper meaning in the contries in which they are marketed.

Promotional Problems. When communicating with consumers in different parts of the world, the promotional message must be consistent with the language and customs of the particular target society. International Marketeers have faced various problems in communications with widely differ nt customs groups. For example, the Seven Up company's high successful "Uncola" theme, developed for the United States Market, was considered inappropriate for many foreign. Markets because it did not translate well into other languages. Similarly, something got lost, when IBM had translated from English to Japanese, its global theme. "Solutions for a small planet". It came out as "Answers that make people smaller" not a very pleasant portrayal. Learning from earlier mistakes, Multinational firm like P&G and Ford now work harder to be responsive to particular tastes an values of local markets. For instance they recently withdraw their sponsorship of television programming in some countries when the sex and violence of the shows were judged to be too strong.

Product names and promotiopal phrases can also cause considerable problem for international marketeers. The word "clock" in Chinese sounds like the word "death". The Chevarled Nova did not sell well in Latin America because in Spanish the word "nova" means "If doesn't run". GM also blundered with its "body by Fisher" fag line, which in Flemish translate into "corpse by Fisher". The United States government made a miscalculation recently when it moved to drop the word "North" from Nmth American Free Trade Agreement (*i.e.* to Move from NAFTA to AFTA) so as to make it more inclusive. The trouble began when Brazil pointed out that Portuguese "AFTA sound like the words that mean "an Open Mouth Sore".

International Direct Marketing has increased in recent years. For example, the framed British retailer Harrods invited consumers to participate in a transatlantic shopping space by means of a toll free

800 number. American direct marketeers who now enter overseas markets are likely to have a competitive edge over those who follow in future years. These firms, however, must be aware of the differences in doing business in other countries.

Pricing and Distribution Problems. International Marketeers must adjust their pricing distribution policies to meet local economical conditions and customs. For instance, in many developing nations, small-sized product packages offer are a necessity because consumers cannot afford the outlay required for the larger size popular in the United States and other affluents countries. Even in developed nations, important differences do exist. For example, supermarkets are very popular in Switzerland, but in France, which is just across the border, consumers prefer smaller and more intimate stores for grocery shopping.

Japan's traditional distribution system from the United States in that a close, complex relationship exist among the larger Japanse Manufacturers and their distributors and retailers, For example, it took 24 years from the time Japan allowed the introductions of United States apples, until they actually reached the marketplace where Japanese customers could buy them. Thus, Marketeers must vary their distribution channels by nations.

POLITICAL MARKETING

Political marketing has become a very sophisticated, consumer-oriented marketing process in which the creation of a party's political platform is based on extensive consumer research. All major political parties conduct consumer (*i.e.* voter) research. They use the findings of quantitative surveys (*e.g.* polls) to segment voters according to their specific and interests and to identify, quantify and qualify voters opinions, and values on a variety of issues. They use the findings of qualitative research (*i.e.* focus group) to focus campaign themes more precisely to reflect voter attitudes and interests.

Voter Research. Political research has long been in the forefront of consumer research, using sophisticated sampling methods and computer analyses with great skill and creativity. Voter surveys (*i.e.*

political polling) became a major force in the 1972 presidential elections in USA. Since that time all candidates and even elected officials, employ polling experts to help them determine voter reactions to issue on a day-to-day basis Polls help politicians gain insight into the minds of the American public and enable them to forecast where public opinion is heading; Political researchers conduct demographic and psychog'raphic surveys to segment the voter population by various criteria (*e.g.* age, sex, race, family income and party affiliation) in order to tailor appropriate issues to each segment.

Polling is designed to yield findings that can be projected to the entire population. For example, a random of 1200 people can be statistically representative of the total American, population. One way that pollsters obtain sample is by using at list of all telephone prefixes; then a randomly generates the last four digits, so that theoretically everyone in the country has a chance of being called. Well-conducted surveys make an effort to all back anyone who has not answered the, first time to avoid skewing the results. Overnight surveys (conducted over one evening) do not permit call backs to unanswered phones, and thus do not adequately represent the population.

Special interest groups sometims use questionable polling methods to achieve "findings" that support their own positions. Selections of a non-random sample, or defect in selecting a random sample, and the use or "leading" survey questions can all bias survey results. For example, professional pollsters identified two major flaws in a mail-in-survey used by Presidential Candidates Ross Perot; a skewed sample (based on the self-selection process of TV Guide readers to a mail-in-survey published in a magazine) and biased (*i.e.* leading) questions. The same questions were posted to a nation-wise random sample and a more, neutrally worded version was given to still another nation-wide random sample, each version yielded dramatically different findings from Perot's Survey.

Focus groups enable campaign, consultants to elicit detailed opinions from voters that help them shape their candidate's image, and issues. Although focus groups are not representative of the voter population, they provide important insights into the thought process and attitudes behind voter decision making. Focus group participants are chosen by independent research agencies that do not identify campaign sponsorship which in itself might big response. In some instances, participants are paid to watch videos of the candidates and to answer questions Rosed by moderator about, everything from choice of issues to the candidates clothing, to use of words and jargon. The sessions are frequently observed behind one-way mirrors and are video-taped for further analysis.

Issue Positioning. One of the purpose of political research is to determine which issues are most important in the voter's mind. Fot example the Republican's contract with America, was thoroughly tested in focus group beore it was introduced to the public in 1993. Political advisors tested different versions of the "contract" on different voters to be determine the relative importance of various positions. This led to the decision to put "balanced budget" (ostensibly themost popular issue) at the top of the list and "term limits" (the second most popular issue) at the bottom of the list, so that voters scanning the "contract" would see things they liked.

From 1952 to 1992, foreign policy was perceived by voters as more critical than domestic issues. The cold war and nuclear proliferation were at the forefront and voters were most concerned with selecting a president that they felt they could trust in handling foreign affairs. Presidents—Eisen Hower, Kennedy, Johnson, Nixon, Carter and Bush—were all seen as able foreign policy expor.

Although President Reagan was viewed as having limited foreign policy experience, his cogenial personality, combined with strong support of the military gave voters confidence that he could be "trusted".

The dissolution of the Soviet Union led to change in the political climate of the 1990s with domestic policy issues taking precedence over foreign policy. Political researchers discovered through focus groups that the general public was concerned about the domestic economy, the loss of jobs, the depletion of savings and the high cost of health care. It was in this atmospher ,that then Governor Cinton, who had no foreign policy experience whatever to and a record of avoiding military service during the Vietnam War, was able to become president. Clinton emphasized domestic issues in his campaign platform, while the incumbent President Bush, flush with victory of the Persian Gulf War, would not even acknowledge the deepening economic recession. President Bush's failure to achieve re-election has been attributed to his apparent lack of empathy or even recognition of voter concerns about the domestic economy. Although foreign issues commanded headline attention in the 1996 election campaign, domestic concerns continued to dominate the minds of the American public during this period. This imagery invoked In campaign rhetoric is most impprtant. For example, the 1996 campaign debate had democrats accusing the Republicans of wanting to "cut Medicare Spending" while the Republicans claimed they just wanted to "increase spending at a slower rate." Republicans talked about "balancing the budget to protect future generations" while Democ rats decla red that balancing the budget would "hurt ordinary people, while the wealthy get tax breaks.

Although actual debate over conflicting issues is complex, most voters make up their minds based on a few key words or phrases. The relative importance of the issues and responses to specific wording are tested in focus groups. For example, during 1996 elections in USA, both President Clinton and Senator Dole used the word "values" in many of vice to connect to the American community and claimed that Republicans were "outside the mainstream" or "too extreme". These phrases were carefully selected and frequently used, until it was believed that the terms had become cliches.

The immediacy of major issues affects voter turnout, especially with the young. Almost 90% of youths aged 18 to 29 yrs. old (some 21% of the electorate) voted in 1992 election. This young group was motivated by the issues of abortion, gay rights, and the environment. The issue of social security, welfare, and taxation, which dominated the 1994 election, however did not foster a sense of urgency in the young, their percent of the voting electorate dropped to only 14%.

Political Imagery. Imagery and positioning play increasingly pivotal roles in the "packaging" of political candidates. Ever since 1960, when the televised Kennedy-Nixon debates gave voters a sense of personal access to the candidates, charisma, charm and good looks have tended to overshadow substantive issues. Since then, politicians have recognized that packaging of candidates is all important.

In 1984 Presidential contest, Ronald Reagan's television commercial showed beautiful sunsets, parades of high school bands, pretty girls and waving flags, challenger Walter Mondale's commercials painted images of nuclear destruction starvation and poverty. Reagan's theme was nostalgia, patriotism and the opportunities America offers its young citizens; Mondale talked about raising taxes. Reagan—a former actor and professional communicator, projected a warm, likeable, sincere manner oil television. Mondale appeared lifeless and uncomfortable. Reagan's vettal imagery included words like prosperity, opportunity, respect and growth, Mondale used words like debt unfairness and fear. After the political frustration of 1960s and 1970s, voters welcomed a candidate who reflected the notions of nostalgia, love of country; self improvement, hope and pride, Reagan's Campaign advisers demonstrated a solid understanding of the demographic and psychographic trends in the nation.

The importance of imagery was even more apparent in the 1998 Presidential election. Republican strategists repackaged an awkward, stilled George Bush to appear relaxed, confident, genial, likeable and engaging. The Democratic candidate, Michael Dukakis, with the emphasis on competence and administration, appeared serious, solemn, taciturn and unapproachable. As one pollster said "...competence is only a part of image. A President has to be open and caring, as well as tough and hard. He must project a comfortable image. The 1998 Presidential campaign was totally dominated by television imagery and television ads. It was also the first time in American history that Presidential candidates used at least as much" negative advertising to slander their opponents as I they used positive advertising to promote themselves. It was estimated that more than half of the ads for both camps were negative.

Many voters were outraged at the lack of substantive discussion of issues by either side in the 1988 campaign. They recognized that the candidates appeared in staged events solely for the television cameras, avoided probing questions, and relied on "spin-doctors" (glorified public relations people) to interpret the impact of ther remarks and debates for public consumption. The timing and substance of televised debates were carefully negotiated between the parties, questions and questioners were prescreened and preapproved and politically correct answers were rehearsed. No opportunities were made available for extemporaneous discussions or spontaneous question and answer sessions.

The 1992 Presidential race changed all that. Ross Perot, the Texas billionaire who established his own political party, began appearing on popular talk shows and made himself accessible to questions from the public through electronic "town halls" that he initiated. Soon candidate Clinton also appeared on late right talk shows and even played his saxophone on television to show that he was a man of the people. President Bush was forced to become some that more accessible, but still maintained his slightly patrician air. On a campaign visit to a supermarket, his absolute amazement at seeing the products scanners at the checkout counters caused voter at how out of touch he was with everyday living.

To the American public, a candidate's family just as important as the candidate. Hillary Clinton has constantly redefined her image. Early in the 1992 election process, her image evoked intelligence, competence, and a partnership with her husband. Then to appeal to a broader spectrum of women and to make herself seem less imposing to men. Mrs .Clinton emphasized her interest in children and family, and even revealed a favourite cookie recipe. On her husband was elected President and placed her in charge of developing a new national health care plan, Mrs. Clinton ignored the softer image and again ,stressed her intelligence and competence. After health care plan failed, 'Hillary Clinton was once again repositioned with a softened image that made her appear more likeable, with a renewed interest in women's and children's issues.

The dominant issues in political advertising research have been the impact of advertising on voter beliefs, affect and behaviour (*i.e.* the three components of attitudes) and the ways that voters cognitively process political ads.

Positive advertisement often feature photo opportunities of the candidates and their families, indicate patriotism and are "warm and furry". Rarely do these ads present substantive issues and they have little effect on voters. On the other hand, negative advertisements that attack the opponent seem to elicit is more vigorous viewer response. Some tracking polls have shown that people who? see a negative ad at least eight times begin to shift away from the attacked candidate. Positive ads increase voters attempt turnout negative ads are known to discourage potential voters of all parties from voting at all. In fact, negative ads have been used by some campaign strategists as a way of ensuring low turnout when they believe high turnout would be to their condidate's disadvantage.

Researh on the use of comparaive political advertisements (sponsor-positive and opponent-negative or simple opponent-negative) found that, negative ads produced negative reactions from voters, reflected negatively on the ad sponsor, and had less impact on the opposing candidate than , sponsor-positive ads. Widespread negative advertising has been found to reduce all candidates in the eyes of the public, as well as their believability across all issues.

Political Persuasion. Political strategists are masters of the art of persuasion. Researchers who have studied political persuasion techniques have noted that many political advertisements are really unfair appeals to bias-and emotion. Of course, that description also applies to much non-political advertisement, but unfortunately, none, of the restrictions on deceptive product advertising apply to political advertising, leaving the opportunity open for great abuse.

An attack ad makes a strong negative claim about an opponent, especially in the last days of a campaign when there is little time for the attack target to refute it. The main impact of attack ads is, among undecided voters. They tend to discourage these voters from voting altogether.

With one-sided arguments, the candidate argues in generalities that a particular course of action is the correct one, but gives no details with which the audience can analyse, discuss or or rebut the argument. In two-sided arguments the candidate says something favourable as to the reasonableness of an opponent's position before at tacking it. This technique boosts the credibility of those who use it, because it suggests to the audience that the candidate is objective, open-minded, and fair in examining the issues.

In agenda setting, candidates or political parties proclaim the one issue. They are interested in as crucial and all others as irrelevant. This technique establishes the candidates as the "champion" of a specific popular issue and downgrades the issues supported by the opposing party.

Political marketing is by far the most controversial area in which behavioural research is conducted. The potential for manipulation of the voter by politicians or special interest groups is undeniable. On the other hand, like other areas of consumer behaviour research, voter behaviour studies offer the promise of a deeper understanding of voter needs and the development of improved voter communications programmes.

HEALTH CARE MARKETING

The provision of health care services is a major component of the non-profit sector with annual expenditures for health care skyrocketing in 1993 to almost $ 885 billion dollars. Until recently, hospitals and physicians (the traditional health care providers) knew little, if anything; about marketing and they thought it unprofessional to market their services. However, the incidence of third party payers (insurance companies, employers and government programmes such as Medicare and Medicaid) increased and medical costs soared, the health care environment changed dramatically. The insurance companies targeted physicians; hospitals, pharmaceutical companies and, other health care providers and intermediaries to persuade them to join managed care networks on as salary, fixed fee, or volume basis recorder to put together a comprehensive service that in turn they could market to employers and individuals. Pressures were placed on hospitals to reduce impatient care and on network doctors to reduce costly medical testing and specialist referrals.

Despite the fact that managed care has begun to limit the costs of health care, there is a growing concern that the quality of care is being compromised when patients are denied access to specialists by gate keepers or denied coverage for certain experimental or expensive procedures. Further, complicating the issue is the fact that managed care plans are often privately owned by investor groups, whose profit making goals may conflict with patients feeds for medically necessary services. A national debate is under way, making the marketing of health care in this competitive atmosphere enormously challenging.

Market Segmentation. To position themselves to best meet consumer demands in a highly competitive market place health care providers are marketing to end-users (*i.e.* patients) as well as to other health care intermediaries; Hospitals are conducting denynpilc analyses, compiling physician profiles and establishing affiliation agreements with other organisations. Independent community hospitals are conducting surveys of local community health needs (community health assessments) to assist in their decisions making as to which services to add, cut, or expand to best maximize revenues.

Health care organisations are looking for niches to satisfy consumer demand for services. Consumers are segmentd by their unique needs and their programmes and services are created to best satisfy those needs. For example the needs of certain patient groups (*e.g.* drugs addicts; alcohols, AIDS patients, pregnant teenagers) have led to specially tailored programmes. The growing needs of the aging population have led to increased provisions of getriatric services and long-term care facilities. The' managed care emphasis on preventive care and outpatient treatments has led to hospitals offering health education programmes to the community and expanding their outpatient clinics. The finanial disincentive of high-cost hospitalizations and recognition that many medical treatments can be given in patients home have led to the development and expansion of home care services.

Marketing to Intermediaries. The ultimate consumer of the health care.delivery system is the patient. However, intermediaries play a major role in influencing the usage of medical services: physicians who order tests, admit patients and who may be part of a managed care network. Insurers and managed care networks, who may direct their enrolles to use specific physicians or facilities; the government, which may control where Medicare and medicaid patients and government employees seek treatment and employers, who offer health care plans to their employees and retires. Health care organizations have dramatically increased their marketing efforts to appeal to all of these groups in order to increase patient volume at a time when admission rates and length of stay are declining.

Health Care Organizations. Both hospitals and managed care network are marketing to physicians, especially primary care physicians, in order to establish referral sources for their specialized services and impatient care. They provide the doctors with resources to assist them in caring for patients, such as high-technology equipment and access to specialist. To attract both doctors and patients many hospitals advertisers. "physician referral centres," which direct inquiring consumers to associated physicians in adjacent medical office buildings at which office management and group purchasing services are available.

Large medical centers are actively "counting" physician group practices and regional hospitals in order to generate patient referrals to -their hightechnology services and specialists. Use of innovative marketing media, such as the Internet and the world wide Web has allowed hospitals to extend their geographic reach to physicians in outlaying areas.

Hospitals are cutting costs and marketing themselves as "low cost providers" to insurers and managed a care networks. They are reducing overhead by methods such as reorganizing their management structures and reducing staff, by streamlining admissions and billing processes, and by purchasing supplies in bulk to achieve economies of scale. Critics have raised concerns that some cost-cutting measures are compromising the quality of patient care, so administrators must weigh the trade-offs involved in balancing the needs of both patients and intermediaries.

Insurers and managed care networks are actively marketing the federal and state governments to provide low-cost managed care to government employees and people on government assistance. In fact there is a rapid increase in the number of Medicare and Medicaid managed care plans designed for this population group an a growing number of individuals are enrolling in such programmes.

Because employees influence the selection of managed health care plans offered to their employees, managed care networks and hospitals are targeting these employers directly with information about their medical services. One hospital distributes a quarterly "Employer Newsletter", this newsletter is sent to the President/CEO, Vice President of Human Resources and Benefits Administrator of more than 5000 regional companies meeting certain criteria.

Marketing to Patients. Many hospitals conduct patient satisfaction surveys to assist them in improving patient care and the perception of patients about the quality of their care. The surveys aim to identify the parts of the services delivery system that matter most to the patients; the hospitals then try to improve efficiency in these areas to achieve a corresponding increase in patient's satisfaction. These surveys are usually taken after the patient is discharged from the hospital. It has been shown that selfadministered questionnaires, rather than telephone surveys, yield the most constructive comments and are less costly to administer.

In addition to actual teatment received, perceptions of care are ultimately responsible for whether a patient is willing to return to that hospital or to reler other people. Improved communication with patients while they are in the hospital, both through staff education and a responsive complaint process, can positively improve the hospital experience. Family and friends of the patients may be harder to satisfy than the patient and, addressing the concerns of these individuals can positively influence future dcisions to use the hospital's services again."

As a by product of patient satisfaction surveys, hospitals are emphasizing customer service. Seminars are being held for employees to teach empathy, thoughtfulness, politeness and basic etiquettes. New positions are programmes being created to reinforce this patient-focused approach. By satisfying both patients and their insurers hospitals hope to generate an expanded patient base.

A number of marketing techniques are practiced by innovative hospitals to increase and/or impress their patient population. Physician referral centres, health information hot lines, and health fairs have become popular methods of developing bonds with potential patients. Some hospitals are providing "hotel acommodations" for family members of patients. Others have Improved their food service and have even added ethnic food to satisfy certain patient market segments.

Marketing on the Internet is proving to be a cost-effective way to educate, inform and communicate with both patients and intermediaries. For example, to develop closer bonds with potential patients (and their doctors), the Mayo Clinic developed "The Mayo Clinic family Health Book" in book form and on CD-ROM, sales have been a good revenue source and image builder among consumers.

Employers are eager to switch their employees and retirees from fee for service insurance to managed care networks in order to control the costs of providing health care benefits. To provide incentives, both the employers and networks are emphasizing features of the managed care plans which surveys indicate are most likely to appeal to these individuals.

Demarketing Versus Remarketing Health Care Services. A marketing strategy called de-marketing was introduced in 1987 for the purpose of reducing the utilization of health care services. It was based on the assumption that health care providers could discourage the consumption of some services by such methods as increasing prices and reducing their availability and convenien. The purpose of selecting demarketing is to reduce demand by "Parts of the market which are less profitable or less in need of service." Critics believe this marketing approach is both ethically questionable and professionally risky and causes more problems than it solves.

In another approach, called remarketing, health care providers seek to lower demand for certain services by offering and promoting better alternatives than the services they wish to discourage. Examples include encouraging preventive care (exercise, dieting and other wellness programmes), promoting the cessation of smoking and alocohal, consumption, advising, consultation with pharmacists to answer drug questions and recommend over the counter medicines and promoting the use of bicycle and motorcycle helmets to reduce head injuries.

Health Care Advertising. Hospitals have increased their advertising budgets to promote their medical staff credentials, their specialised diagnostic and treatment services, their affiliation agreements with other organizations and their caring approach. Critics, questions whether such consumer-oriented advertising campaigns are ethical and whether such dollars are being wasted. Since managed care networks have greater influence than patients over the selection of facilities. Proponents claim that advertising is justified because consumers often select a managed care network based on which hospitals and physicians are associated with it, thus "educating" consumers helps them make an informed choice. Health care providers target advertising to special consumer markets, such as woman and promote, specialized services to patients requiring such treatment as orthopedics, cosmetic surgery, or laser eye surgery.

Providers have found that they can increase their advertising effectivehess by reducing the perceived risk of making a health care purchase decision. Elements that reduce patients preceived disk include assurance (trust and confidence in the staff), reliability (ability to provide the service as promised), empathy, (personal attention), responsiveness (promptress and ability to another questions thoroughly), and tangibles such as the physical appearance of the facility and state-of-the act equipment.

Pharmaceutical companies have created advertising campaigns that have dual goals, to market certain products and to improve their image among consumers by describing their research and development efforts and their community involvement. These manufacturers attempt to persuade consumers that they are getting more by paying more for the advertised trademark brands than for generic products.

Non-Profit Organizations also conduct blood donation drives in an attempt to contribute age consumers to "contribute to the community's well-being" by adding to the nation's blood supply. Organ donation is marketed as a way to "ease the emotional trauna of losing a loved one' and to foster, the healing process.

Special interest groups conduct advocacy advertising to influence consumer opinion and impact legislative action. Often, the public is unware of who is funding these groups, because the special interests use a "front group" with an innocuous name.

Advocacy advertising is being practiced by groups opposed to the proliferation of managed care. Health care unions are trying to strengthen their members image and medical importance by appealing directly to the public through advocacy advertising. For example, a nurses association advertised directly to consumers that registered nurses are critical to good quality care and advised them to avoid hospitals that use low-cost labour alternatives.

❑

18

Consumer Orientation

Marketing research is the inclusive term which embraces all research activities carried on in connection with the management of marketing work. It includes various subsidiary types of research, such as *(1)* Market Analysis which is a study of the size, location, nature, and characteristics of markets, *(2)* Sales Analysis which is largely an analysis of sales data, *(3)* Consumer Research, of which Motivation Research is a type, which is concerned chiefly with the discovery and analysis of consumer attitudes, reactions, and preferences, and *(4)* Advertising Research, which is carried on chiefly as an aid to the management of advertising work. Although no single definition has yet been accepted as delineating the exact scope of marketing research, as it is continuously expanding, marketing research can be taken as the term applied to any critical and searching study and investigation of a problem hypothesis or proposed course of action conducted systematically and objectively to uncover facts useful in the field of marketing.

Marketing research activity probably began around 1960 and developed as more companies began to be interested in regional and then national markets. The field was expanded markedly by the development of sampling techniques in the 1930, and the application of psychological interviewing and measurement techniques.

In advanced countries, marketing research is considered no longer in its pioneering stages although in India very few companies are in fact doing marketing research and particularly on scientific lines. Even in India in some companies, enlightened business managers do look upon it as an indispensable tool for profitable customer-oriented marketing. For example, the author's survey of 200 executives in Western India, indicated market research as a very important function of marketing management. They realize the importance of basing marketing policies and decisions on solid facts resulting in top management demanding more fact, particularly in connection with decisions on forecasting, planning and budgeting.

As in other countries, in India also advertising agencies saw the need for organized research operations much earlier than manufactures. In fact, except for a few large companies which can afford a separate department the others who need research generally rely on advertising agencies and marketing research agencies for conducting research on their behalf in India.

Acceptance of the marketing concept necessitates a thorough knowledge of the consumers' preferences, attitudes and motivations. These also change over a period of time. Marketing Research can help management in its desire to remain consumer oriented in its decisions. Take the example of the need for consumer-orientation in the cotton textile industry. Mills desiring to sell their products abroad must realize that habits and preferences of people in different countries differ. Persons in Venezuela for instance have an aversion for yellow colour as this colour is immediately identified with the uniform of the conservancy staff in the towns of that country. Similarly, a superstitious dislike for blue exist in the Arabian countries.

Export decisions based on inadequate information about the consumer can result in unsuitable products being offered at unsuitable prices with the help of ineffective promotional strategies. Besides, there has already taken place an almost imperceptible revolution in the dressing habits of people in India. May conventional modes of dressing have largely gone out of fashion. For example, the pyjama, the pants and the bush shirt have almost driven the dhotie, the long coat and the turban from the urban areas such as the Bombay city. Even the villager wants switch from wearing grey cloth and asks the local dealer stock goods to suit his new and refined tastes. Urban dwells mostly prefer processed sarees, printed, dyed and coloured. Great care is now taken in the selection of blouses and per coats.

Women are insisting on new designs, colours and shade. Increase in education has resulted in people insisting on qualify and the customer can no longer be taken for granted to a large extent. All these changes require adequate consumer-orientation on the part of management of the cotton textile mills. This equally applied in many other industries.

Despite this need, the majority of our mills do not conduct any market research. As in many other industries, production is dictated by management on the basis of their own views on the consumers' tastes which often result in unwanted cloth lying in the market and unsold stocks at the mills. In view of this, the Millowners' Association felt that research should be undertaken in marketing. For example, consumer's taste changed from season to season. The Association was of the view that a State-wise survey for different income groups in representative towns and villages should be made regarding *(a)* composition of the consumer's demand for different seasons of the year; *(b)* consumer's preference between mill cloth, handloom cloth and powerloom cloth, cotton piecegoods and man-made fabrics; *(c)* consumer's keeness to buy and capacity to pay higher prices for durability, novel designs, special processes such as shrinkproof, water-repellant, dip and dry, wash and wear, etc.; *(d)* specific occasions of the year when purchase of cloth were made; *(e)* the size of purchase effected at a time and *(f)* the methods of purchases, *i.e.*, whether on cash basis or on credit. This also indicates the wide scope of marketing research activities.

Apart from the need for consumer-orientation being assist by research, marketing research can considerably reduce the risks involved in marketing decisions. Facts resulting from marketing research can form the basis of planning, selling, sales promotion, advertising, etc. For example, the marketing manager responsible for the introduction of new products can make better decision if he has relevant information such as consumer's preference, the performance of alternative packing materials, prevailing prices of competitors' products and dealing reaction to various types of sales promotion.

In such situation the information needed may be readily available by direct observation or the marketing manager's past experience may provide a basis for arriving at a decision. In many cases, observation and experience are not enough. In the majority of cases, the decision-making authority is far away from the point of sale to observe customers' reactions directly. Such observations can be misleading even when they can be made.

The main limitation of experience is that conditions change and policies that work at one time may not be effective at a later stage. Moreover, is possible to learn completely erroneous facts. Since direct observation and experience are insufficient guides to marketing managers, formal research becomes necessary to obtain to details required for selecting from intelligent alternatives. The unproductive use of research is often caused by lack of confidence in the research and a lack of knowledge concerning research on the part of marketing management.

Market research assists in minimizing the risks involved in marketing decisions in two ways, namely, by providing:

(1) current information necessary for the marketing manager to take decisions; and

(2) generalized knowledge or theory about the marketing process.

Specialized knowledge and experience are required for planning marketing research and executing it effectively. Therefore the actual conduct of marketing research activities is entrusted to staff specialists or outside professional agencies. However, the marketing manager should porsess enough knowledge and appreciation of research problems and methods to:

(1) determine when such specialized assistance is required;

(2) assist the specialist in planning the research investigations;

(3) decide whether the results of a proposed marketing research are likely to be beneficial to the company when compared with the cost involved in conducting the research; and

(4) apply the research findings to decision-marketing vvith due attention to the shortcomings of various types of information.

Marketing research is an aid to decision-making. Sometimes marketing research gets out of touch with decision-making. The best way to make full use of research is that both the marketing executive and research specialists should relate their problems to a common framework in which a direct connection is made between decision problems and research problems. For instance, a firm considering introduction of a new product may think that it will be profitable to market the product provided the sales so generated exceed some minimum level.

A market test may be instituted to estimate what sales can be expected if the product is marketed in a particular way. Thus the best way to look at marketing researchers is to think of them as helping in marketing problem-solving. They should not be viewed as merely persons supplying some information. Even in countries like U.S.A. where the art and science of marketing research has progressed considerably and advanced techniques have been introduced, it is not being used to its full potential. It is often used for resolving short-term tactical decisions, where undoubtedly it is useful. However, it should be used for deciding on major strategic issues, such as:

> Should the company enter into a particular type of business? Should it spend Rs. 5 lakhs on a new plant for a new product? Should it spend Rs. 2 lakhs for advertising a particular brand?

How far it will be used for such purposes often depends upon the place of research in the organization. Where the research function becomes a part of the top management team full participation by marketing research is more likely, and this type of major questions would be sought to be answered with the help of the research section. If, however, it is only used is a service arm of brand management, as is often done, it with only result in tactical type research accounting.

Many consumer goods' companies have adopted the brand manager type of organization. However, most of these brand managers have the minimum profit authority and, therefore are merely concerned with tactical decisions, such as:

> Should a new package design be introduced? Or what sale promotion gimmick should be used?

Crisp divides the range of marketing research activities into three groups, namely: *(a)* Research on Product or Services *(b)* Research on Markets and *(c)* Research on Sales Methods and Policies.

Research on Products or Services. Research on products may relate to existing products or new products. It may include study of the competitive standing of a company's products in its industry and economic research showing the trend in industry volume and the affinity between the company or industry sales and economic indicators.

For example, the level of consumer incomes would have its effect on future sales' prospects in case of most consumer products. The Research may seek to company the consumer or customer acceptance of the company's products or services with that of competitors' similar products or services. It may show the dissatisfaction (and its reasons) with the company's products among its present and post customers volume of a product has been declining. Studies can also show the present and new uses for the company's products. Such new uses indicated by research can be utilized in advertising and the promotional campaign to extend the volume of sales of the product. When a new product is developed by a competitor, it becomes necessary to identify the product innovations which are significant. For example, when Lever Brothers introduced Chlorodent toothpaste with the ingredient chlorophyll promoting it with a breath-deodorizing story all dentifrice manufacturers has to appraise this development and many introduced the innovation. Similarly in India, the use of detergents for washing clothes posed a problem to producers of soap used for this purpose. When introducing new products it is necessary to estimate its possible demand, to determine the consumer acceptance and continuously to appraise its progress after the product has been launched.

Research on Markets. It is useful to analyse the size of the total market, or the industry volume. This would help in forecasting the sales and ascertaining what share of the total market the company concerned should attempt to secure. An analysis of the potential sales in a particular territory may help determine whether to expand into a particular geographical area. It would also aid the division of the whole market sought to be covered into its territorial smaller units.

Research on Sales Methods & Policies. Research on sales methods and policies may require an assessment of territorial variations in sales yield and sales effectiveness. In this way strong territories can be separated from the weak ones so that remedial measures can be adopted where required. This may result in a revision of sales territories. It is also necessary to evaluate the effectiveness of individual salesmen and ascertain the extent of their contribution to the progress of the company. It can also include studies of the effectiveness of the company's distribution channels and the availability of the company's products as compared with competing products. Thus the scope of marketing research activities is ever expanding into new fields. However, before it is introduced by an organization the question of cost is extremely relevant. It is necessary to assess the probable results against the possible costs of marketing research as this would form a part of the total marketing cost.

It should however be remembered that this cost is more in the nature of an investment than an expense and the question is whether it would ultimately payoff in dividends. Thus although in certain cases the immediate benefit is derived in the form of net profits (*i.e.*, after covering the cost one may generally have to provide for the pay off period and not expect it to be immediately self-liquidating. Let us now consider the type of marketing research under-taken by an industrial products company. The Metal Box Company of India Ltd. undertakes three main type of marketing research work, namely:

(a) Industry Research,

(b) Retailer Research, and

(c) Consumer Research

Its Industry Research is concerned with the immediate market for the company's products (*i.e.* customers—present and market for existing and new products. This is both quantitative (*e.g.* size of the total market, brand shares, etc.) and qualitative *e.g.* seasonal factors, factors governing pack preferences, etc. Industrial Research includes:

(i) Intelligence Work which consists primary of desk research and also a small amount of interviewing and is devoted to answering small buy very important queries, and

(ii) Major Surveys which involve large-scale interviewing and are aimed at studying a specific problem in depth.

The Company's Retailer Research a aimed at providing information on product acceptability, brand preference, shelf life, the effect of price variations on sales and stock build-up and connected matters. Retailer Research includes:

(i) Retail Audit which is concerned with movements in the volume of retail sales;

(ii) Retail Intelligence on new packages, new application of existing packages, significant promotional activities, etc., and

(iii) Retail Surveys which involves sampling and interviewing and are aimed at studying a specific problem in depth.

The Company's Consumer Research is concerned with ascertaining the behaviour, attitudes and experience of the general public as purchasers of consumer goods. A limited amount of consumer research facilities are also offered to the company's customers. Now let us deal with the research procedure. The following are generally the steps involved in handling a marketing problem through marketing research, namely:

Step 1 Crystallize the marketing problem;

Step 2 Identify the marketing research problems involved;

Step 3 Determine information needed and sources;

Step 4 Secure the relevant facts;

Step 5 Analyse and interpret the facts with reference to the problem; and

Step 6 Prepare research report incorporating and findings.

In order to avoid waste in time and money it is necessary, as the first step, to define the marketing problem in specific terms. The emphasis at the commencement is one the marketing and not the marketing research problem, which is really an accent on clarifying the objective. In solving a complex marketing problem, such as an unexplained decline in sales, Crisp suggests as an aid in the early efforts at defining the problem the establishment of a general framework of major marketing elements, such as the *(1)* industry elements; *(2)* competitive elements; *(3)* market elements; and *(4)* company elements. With regard to the "industry element", the question of the size of the industry's volume, its trend and the economic climate as affecting such value may be considered.

The "competitive elements" may include the ascertainment of the company's major competitors, their market shares, changes in such shares, the emergence of new competitors, competitive product innovation and price changes. In connection with "market elements", the characteristics of the market for products of the industry and the major changes, it any, in such characteristics may be the subjects for research, study of "company elements" may cover the characteristics of the company's products and how they compare with the major competitors with regard to customer acceptance, pricing practices, quality of the sales organization and distribution channels. Such a comparison may indicate that the decline in sales merely a reflection of similar decline in the entire industry or that the company's product is poor as compared with that of competitors, thus crystallizing the reason for the decline.

An early and necessary step in the marketing research process is a "situation analysis" or a survey of available data regarding the company, its products, the market, the industry, its advertising, dealer situation, etc., which can be gleaned from discussions with executives, available published materials, and internal records. Here the researcher tries to obtain all the information he can regarding the problems of the company and the environment in which the analysis has to be made. In this way the research man arrives at a hypothesis or a tentative theory or presumption arrived at provisionally, which may form the basis or guide as to the reasons why certain things have happened so that further investigation may be proceeded with along those lines. For example, if it is ascertained that the important question relates to the quality of the product as compared with that of leading competitors, "product research" may be indicated. If the problem indicated is the question of the size of consumer franchise, a "consumer survey" may be the right answer. If the important questions suggested were regarding the efficiency of the sales organization and distribution may be necessary with the help of a small number of skilled persons. After the situation analysis, the analyst continues to formulate his hypothesis and refine his problem definition by going outside the company and talking informally with informed people such as intelligent and efficient retailers, wholesalers, consumers and key men in the industry to get their point of view and thus get the feel of the problem.

In this way, he tries to crystallize, through information interviews, the central problem. By this time the problem should be considerably narrowed down so that mere specific questions can be asked of informed people. Sometimes such an informal investigation may make further research unnecessary. In any case it should provide the foundation for the subsequent research. A single marketing problem might involve a number of different problems of marketing research. In such a case separate plans may have to be prepared for each problem, here a single plan cannot cover all the problem. A plan may be prepared for each problem and a master plan should combine all the plans as far as possible.

In determining the type of information required, the objectives of the research must be kept in mind as the information must both he necessary and relevant to those objectives. Collecting information merely on the basis of its being interesting would result in a waste of time, effort and money. After a problem has been defined in clear terms, management is in a position to determine what information is required to take a decision. Sometimes decisions can be made on the basis of experience and judgement without assembling the facts. At other times the required information is available and it has to be assembled and organized. Occasionally it is necessary to collect and analyse fresh information by a formal research.

Facts which constitute the raw material for the marketing research man are derived from various sources. These are generally divided into two classifications, namely: (1) Primary Data and (2) Secondary Data. The information gathered by .an investigator for solving his problem are described as primary data. Information collected by other organization or individuals which might be relevant to the study are described as secondary data or data from secondary sources. It is necessary to consider both these sources.

Primary Sources. Primary sources may consistent *(1)* company's own records; *(2)* consumers; *(3)* buyers and *(4)* dealers. Research should generally start with the internal fact, that is facts secured from the organization's own records. Often it is found that a major problem can be solved by a intensive analysis of sales data already available in the files to the organization. In smaller organizations, sales analysis often the only source of such information. As these facts ftre already available, the cost involved is low.

Besides, a careful sales analysis helps in pinpointing the type of problem, thus reducing the scope of the external research required and the cost involved. Consumers and Buyers constitute generally the source of information in respect of most researches. The distinction between buyer and user should however be noted. A buyer may not be the user of the product, although in some cases the buyer and the user might be the same person. For example, in case of products consumed within the home, the housewife may be the buyer for the family. However, in case of industrial products there are a number of persons who might influences decision to buy. Besides the purchasing agent, the top executive often exercises control. In addition, maintenance men and factory workers may have an important influence on the buying policy and may constitute a valuable source of information in marketing research. Again, dealers, *i.e.* both wholesalers and retailers are an important source of marketing research information. These are buyers although not consumers and can give valuable indications regarding the consumers.

Secondary Sources. There are innumerable sources for which data can be obtained externally, and only a few can be mentioned here. The information may be obtained from Government sources or private sources. There are many useful Government publications of both the Centre and the States. The Central Statistical Organization and the National Council of Apply Economic Research are important sources of valuable data India 1974 gives valuable information inter alia on the physical background, power and mineral resources, demographic background, the social pattern, educational statistics, mass communication (including broadcasting, the press and films), the economic structure including the national and per capita incomes, livelihood patterns, working force, principal industries, unemployment, prices, planning, finance, agriculture including agricultural marketing, irrigation and power industry including information on industrial production in principal industries, plantation industries, small-scale and cottage industries, pattern of trade, transport, communication, labour and housing. The Times of India Directory and Year Books is another valuable source of information. Indian Industries gives information on the economic and industrial set-up of India, Indian exporters, Chambers of Commerce, Associations, etc., and has sections of textile, chemical engineering, food, mining, plantation, and miscellaneous industries as well as for transport. The Report on Currency and Finance gives valuable information and statistics. Thompson's Urban Market Index 1973, would also be useful. By giving adequate weightage, Thompson's Index provide guidance as to the marketing possibilities of various towns. It has used economic-indicators which include *(1)* population as a basic factor; *(2)* employment in urban occupations such as small and large industry, construction and transport as they have more discretionary spending power; *(3)* increase in population, as faster growth indicates increased buying abilities; *(4)* number of literates, as higher ratios show better markets; *(5)* number of radio sets; *(6)* number of private cars; *(7)* bank deposits and advances as the former indicates discretionary spending potential and the latter is a measure of the economic activity in the area; *(8)* number of doctors; *(9)* number of chemists and druggists; *(10)* number of cinema seats; *(11)* domestic consumption of electricity; *(12)* Sales tax and entertainment tax as a measure of relative economic activity and greater spending ability respectively; *(13)* number of households being an indicator of greater potential for the consumption of domestic durables and other household goods; and *(14)* number of telephones as indicator, at relative economically advanced nature of the area.

The Thompson Rural Market Index, issued in 1972; is an equally comprehensive compilation of data but for the rural market. This type of indexes would be very valuable to those who are considering territory to be covered by distribution, advertising or salesmen Besides, Trade associations and Chambers of Commerce in India can supply certain type of information.

Once a decision is taken that secondary sources are insufficient, in the process of planning, a selection will have to be made of the method to be adopted for the research. There are three basic types of methods which can be used, namely *(1)* the observational method; *(2)* the experimental method; and *(3)* the survey method including *(4)* the panel research.

The Observational Method. This method relies have direct observation of the physical phenomena in gathering data and avoids talking directly, with people thus recognizing in defects inherent in direct questioning. Thus, instead of asking persons what they use, the analyst can make a physical inventory of the products actually in the home or kept in stock by retailers. This type of observation is focussed on a well defined problem and not merely on a broad activity. For example, the object is to consider the question of locality for a retail shop, a person may be stationed to count the traffic flowing by this location with a view to measure the potential.

This method is said to be more objective and accurate as it eliminates human element which is present in the other methods but in course restricted to measurement of the physical elements overt behaviours. It is suitable for a wide range of situation and can also be used in conjunction with other techniques as an effective supplementary tool. The use of mechanical recorders in American and in England connected to television or radio set is a form of observational research. These show exactly when the set was turned on, to what station or channel it was tuned and so on and gives more accurate information that could be secured by making calls on members of the family.

The Experimental Method. This method is based on the premise that a small-scale experiment is useful to indicate what can be expected in a large-scale experiment. For example, it is believed that if an article is put in the front position it increases its sales. An experiment can be conducted here by having the article placed in different positions in different shops and thereafter the importance of the position can easily be checked. This method can be used for various purposes even by retailers such as for testing, packaging, pricing, display, promotional plans and new products.

A person desiring to test whether a black and white or a coloured advertisement in a newspaper would be more effective may select three areas in one of which a black and white advertisement would be inserted, in another a coloured advertisement and in the third no advertising would be indulged in. Then in terms of the sales produced the effectiveness of the two advertisements would be considered as it would give an indication of the sales trend under normal and no advertising circumstances. This method however is not very commonly used because it involves more time and is costly.

The Survey Method. This method involves talking directly to consumers. There are three types of surveys namely: *(1)* the Telephone, *(2)* Mail, and *(3)* Personal Interview. This method is referred to at times as the "questionnaire technique" and involves the furnishing of data by an individual through a conscious effort to answer questions. It is the most widely used technique. Again the survey may be a factual survey, an opinion survey or an interpretive survey. The "factual survey" requires factual information. An example of such a survey is where the consumer is asked "Do you use a Motor-car? The answer is generally recorded in one of two boxes provided against the question on the questionnaire, one of which is labelled "yes" and the other "No". In an "opinion survey", the personal opinion of the person interrogated is required. He is required to make an evaluation or appraisal or report his judgement on a particular matter. An example would be illustrated by the question "What are the important things you would requirement a motor-car"? it is considered that the existence of a specific opinion strongly held is tantamount to a fact and, in the opinion of some, more important than a fact. In the "interpret survey" the person interviewed is required to do more the reporting merely a fact or an opinion, and acts as an interpreter.

The Panel Research. The difference between the survey and the panel techniques lies in the number of contacts with the respondent. In the panel research the same group of respondents gives information on two or more occasions. Thus basically there is very little difference in the two approaches. For example, in the matter of sampling, the methods used are the same. Of course, in a panel research the respondent must operate more as he is required to do so on more than one occasion. Thus in view of the refusal rates being higher, the sampling problem becomes difficult. This technique is very useful in the experimental approach.

As already indicated there are three types of surveys namely *(1)* Personal Interview, *(2)* Mail Questionnaire and *(3)* Telephone Interview.

The Personal Interview Survey. Here the questions are asked by face to face interviewing. The amount of information which can be secured in such a single interview is much greater than through any other method. A relatively long questionnaires can be used. The skill of the interviewer can result in maintenance of interest and co-operation of the person inverviewed. Besides, it is possible for the interviewer to observe characteristics of the neighbourhood, home, etc., and more accurately classify the respondent. Again, exhibits and advertisements, can be shown to the respondent with view to eliciting his opinions, attitudes and views.

The Mail Survey. In this method the questionnaire is sent with a covering letter, the letter explaining the purpose of the study. A gift or incentive is often offered. A stamped or post prepaid envelope or reply card is included to ensure reply being sent. This method is an economical one. However cost comparison should be on the basis of the number of questionnaires sent out. For example, if a mail survey costs fifteen paise per mailing and the return secured is 10 per cent, the actual cost per return is Rs 1.50. The other advantage is the distribution of interviews covering a wider geographic area within a limited amount of money.

This method eliminates the interviewer bias as it eliminates the personal element. The data secured is likely to be more accurate as the tendency for the person conducting the interview to suggest answers is remote. It is also possible to reach certain types of people who are hard to get for interviews. The respondents get as much time as they wish to answer the questions and therefore the answers may be more thoughtful.

Distortion of replies is remote because the answers are sent anonymously and therefore there is no desire to please the interviewer or to give a more acceptable rather than accurate answer. As against this, it is difficult to get a suitable list to cover the universe sought to be sampled. This is because, however carefully one distributes and theoretical sample, the sample is represented by the actual returns. There will be a difference in the percentage of replies received from different localities as certain people are more ready to reply. For example in general the middle class groups respond more readily than the high income or low income groups. There is no flexibility as ambiguity cannot be removed as it can be done in a personal interview. There is no scope for an observational survey. The mail questionnaire has to be very brief.

The Telephone Survey. This method resembles the personal interview, except that here the interviewer is stationed a telephone. This saves time and travelling. Here the into viewer can reach quickly the respondents widely separated go graphically. It can result in more interviews per day than case of personal interviews. There is greater flexibility than case of the mail survey. People difficult to reach can be interviewed by this method.

As the respondents have to reply immediately, the influence of other individuals is eliminated. At against this, it is not possible to get a representative section of the public and the survey is therefore restricted to a highly selective and relatively small proportion of the total population, namely, telephone subscribers. This distorts the sample. These is no possibility of obtaining information through observations which would enable adequate classification of the respondent such as by occupation, age and economic condition.It is possible to combine these techniques. For example, the mail questionnaire before it is used may be pre-tested by personal interviews. Again the mail questionnaire can be used to cover territories which cannot be adequately covered by personal interviews. Often the failure in research does not lie in its technique but in management's inability to implement it research department's finding.

It is at this stage necessary to determine the number and kinds of persons sought to be covered. It is not possible to cover the entire population. For example, in case an investigation is to be made for products used by men only, all men is India who can afford to buy the products would form the universe or population. As it is not advisable or possible to cover all such persons, a smaller representative group has to be fixed and is called the sample. The fundamental concept as given in Crisp is:

> If a small number of items or parts (called a sample) are chosen at random from a larger number of items or a whole (called a universe, or population) the sample will tend to have the same characteristics, and to have them in approximately the same proportion, as the universe. It is necessary to take a moderately large number of cases to ensure statistical stability or reliability. The items must be taken at random. The different constituents should be represented in the sample in the same proportion as in the universe. The sample must be large enough to overcome chance sampling errors. For example, the sample in a particular crowded area may be taken by interviewing every tenth person passing by. With regard to how big the sample should be, the general rule is that the more diverse the population, the more differences that exist among its members, the larger should be the sample. Thus the size of the sample is not dependent upon the size of the total population or the universe. A large universe which is homogeneous can be sampled through a few cases chosen at random.

There are many major sampling approaches used in marketing research. The approach may consist of sample random sampling, or more sophisticated techniques such as stratified random sampling.

Simple Random Sampling. Simple random sampling involves the selection of sampling units from a predetermined universe in such a way that every elementary sampling unit has a full and equal chance of being selected and included in the sample. This is sometimes called random sampling. This is the easiest probability sampling method to understand. Every unit in the sample has an equal chance or probability, of being selected.

Stratified Random Sampling. In a proportional random sample, any given value in the sample varies in the same proportion as in the full universe. Thus the proportion of men of any given age group in a proportional random sample approximates the proportion which each such group or segment represent the total population. Thus if carefully executed, each group (*e.g.* age group), will tend to be approximately in the same portion of the sample as it is of the whole population. However in a simple random sample the proportionality might vary rather widely through natural processes of the laws of chance. To vide against this and to eliminate some of the difficulties in to careful designing and execution of the simple random samples another approach known as the stratified sampling was introduced. A stratified sample is explained by Crisp as follows:

> In a stratified sample, the whole population is first divided into two or more parts (called Strata), and then a sample (technically, a sub-sample) is taken from each of the strata. The resulting stratified sample is a combination of two more samples from different parts or strata of the population.

For example, if we were conducting a survey of individuals is a city like Bombay, and we knew from a recently completed centre that the division of the total population was 60 per cent females and 40 per cent males, in our survey we must control the sample in such a way that it is divided in the same proportion. This would result in a stratified sample of male and female respondents. The sample would be proportional in terms of the variable. When a stratum of a sample is further sub-divided into two or more sub-divisions of the sample having common characteristics they are known an sample cells. The sample must then be to planned as the number respondents in each cell is large enough to provide the desired precision.

When proportional is also maintained it is called "proportionate stratified random sample". Thus in stratified random sampling, the universe is the sub-divided (or stratified) into groups that are mutually exclusive but together include all items in the universe. Then a simple random sample is selected from each such group (or stratum) Thus a designated number of items is selected at random for each stratum. This method therefore results in greater reliability. Besides it enables deductions being made with regard to component parts of a universe.

Cluster Sampling. In this method, groups or clusters of observations are selected at random. It consists of sampling from a universe of groups or clusters of items instead of sampling from a universe of individual items.

Systematic Random Sampling. In this method for example, from a list of 1,000 retail stores, say every fifth store in the list is selected after starting at an item in the list at random. The main advantage of this method is its simplicity. It is also faster than the simple random sampling method.

Area Sampling. This is another variation of the cluster sampling technique. Here it is first necessary to define a universe of areas (*e.g.* city blocks) and then a sample selected of a few of such areas for detailed investigation.

Non-Probability Sampling. All the above methods were probability sampling techniques as every element in the universe had a known chance or probability of being selected. There are methods used in practice which do not meet this requirement and are therefore often referred to as "non-probability sampling" methods. The most important of these are *(i)* Convenience Sampling; *(ii)* Judgement sampling and *(iii)* Quota Sampling.

In case of Convenience Sampling, as the expression itself suggests, the sample is chosen on the basis purely of convenience.

This type of sampling is useful in the pre-test phase of research. In Judgment Sampling, items in the universe are selected for the sample on the basis of "expert judgement". For example, a sales manager may himself select the sample stores which he feels are representative of the universe. Quota Sampling is similar to the stratified random sampling method.

The data now collected requires analysis and interpretation. In order to assist the step of interpretation, the tabulated that has to be manipulated into the best form of statistical summarization. Whether it be percentages, averages, etc., the form of statistical summarization must be so selected as to fix the to give the greatest value in the interpretive work which is to follow. It may be necessary to find out the negative or positive correlation between product usage and income levels.

In example, in case of an expensive article such as motorcycle ownership is expected to be relatively higher among the upper than the lower income respondents. The statistical conclusions must then be converted into recommendations on marketing policies. Some research do not make any recommendation and merely draw statistical conclusions. It is only when statistical conclusions are translated into specific recommendations useful for the company that the interpretive aspects of marketing research come into play. At this stage each statistical generalization has to be analysed in terms of what it means for the company. This requires the use of sound logical reasoning from the facts to the recommendations and constructing recommendations so that they may be carried into practice. The desire to be spectacular should be avoided. There is a tendency overemphasize the revolutionary nature of certain discoveries and recommendations which might result in reading into the statistical findings interpretations unwarranted being merely the wishful thinking of the researcher. The desire for complete solution should also be curbed as many business problems not admit of such solutions. The interpretation must be supported by evidence balanced against crucial exceptions to the proposed interpretation observed in the evidence.

The relationship between the facts and the recommendations must be real.

A purely theoretical interpretation may be modified by practice considerations, such as the condition of the company and market and the probable opposition of executives. If possible recommendations can and should be interpreted into concern gains which would follow the proposed course of action.

After the interpretation stage, the marketing research man knows what the research has disclosed. This information has now to be translated into a form so that others can understand it. Research reports are generally prepared in written form although sometimes they are presented orally. The report should be properly presented, that is, it should neither be too long nor too short. It should not be dull but should be interesting as well as convincing. It is not only necessary to hold the interest of the reader but to convince him by presenting him proof and evidence. The choice of words, adequate emphasis, correct statistical presentation, avoidance of flowery language and ability to express ideas directly and simply in an organized framework are essential. Thus in addition to having the sentences short and simple, using words which are clear, and writing is grammatically sound language, the report must present an organized arrangement. It should not be necessary for the reader to compare one section with another and constantly to back track.

The difficulty in marketing research analyst may face is that he may have to satisfy two distinct type of persons, namely, *(1)* General executives and *(2)* Research men. It was therefore the practice in the earlier days to have two reports called *(1)* the technical report and *(2)* Research men. It was therefore the practice in the earlier days to have two reports called *(1)* the technical report and *(2)* the popular report. The technical report was for people who were fully informed and had to be complete, logical, accurate, impersonal and had to contain only pertinent matter. It was also chocked full of details regarding the methods employed, statistical tables, bibliography and so on.

The popular report consisted of selecting the most significant materials from this technical report and making it a dramatic presentation for the genera) business executive who was very busy and had very little time and considered research merely as a Ispecial issue. Today it is only necessary to have one report. The "technical details such as methodological innovations, questionnaires, other forms used, instructions, etc. are included in the appendix to the research report. The attention is primarily fixed on what the research discloses and what it means to the company.

With regard to the framework of the report, it generally starts with the title page. The title may seek to reflect the objectives of the research or attempt to be provocative besides giving the name of the organization or client for whom the research was conducted. A brief introductory material is generally given at the beginning mentioning the objectives of purposes of the research and the methodology used.

An overall organization plan of the report may also be briefly mentioned. A table of contents would generally be useful for future reference as it is desirable that research reports should also be used subsequently. The body of the research report also contains the findings, which should be presented as a unified whole showing dearly the relationships of the various parts to each other. The appendix may contain questionnaires, forms used in research, a more lengthy technical discussion on methodology. Sample designs as well as illustrative material.

Use may be made of diagram, charts, bar charts, pie charts, pictorial charts and so on. Bar charts are useful to show the relative values between two or more factors. Circle or Pie charts should be confined to the showing of component parts which are not many in number. Any descriptive matter should be readable without turning to the chart. Whether visual material of this nature should be used, should be decided against the cost factor. Preparing such visual presentation is relatively expensive although it makes the report more attractive.

It is controversial whether the research report should include recommendations. It is felt by some that marketing research being a staff advisory function should merely supply useful information to the line executives who will arrive at sound decisions. Besides, marketing research generally provides only part of the answer to a major marketing problem. As against this, the other view is that a marketing research person secures intimate understanding of the problem through extensive work and the value of the report is substantially reduced if he does not include his considered judgement regarding the desirability of alternative future course of action. With the growing acknowledgment of the importance of the marketing concept, the report should be customer-oriented to facilitate its easy acceptance. It should be written from the customer's point of view and given a management rather than a research slant. Instead of using professional research jargon, management language and emphasis on the meaning of the findings for managerial action should be used. It is better to talk the management language using words such as profits, cost and sales, recommend specific steps, present, results on a rupee or monetary basis and sell and reports indispensably. Let us now take the example of an actual company in India. The objective of research at Bata is to ascertain as far as possible the customer's demands regarding the Product as well as to assess the efficiency of the company's organization both with regard to production and distribution. The following are the company's sources of information, namely:

(a) its own employees;

(b) the statistical evidences of sale and stock from its Distribution Units; and

(c) its customers.

Besides, from periodical conferences of the sales people and the field officers the company also tries to find answers to questions such as:

(a) customers' opinion of the quality and the style;

(b) customers comparison of prices and value of Bata shoes as against competitors;

(c) what customers think of the company's products as against competition in Men's, Women's and Children shoes; and

Marketing, research activities increase business success in may ways. It keeps the business in constant touch with the markets. By interpreting markets, the pulse of the demand in the market is constantly felt and the business policies are geared to profitable avenues. Through the discovery of new uses for established products, new markets, and the introduction of new products, new sources of profits are developed. Waste in marketing methods can be reduced as the effectiveness of such methods can be measured.

Changes in the market can be anticipated or forecast. Marketing research constitutes an insurances against such risks. The research findings can help to motivate the consumer and develop sales. Finally enthusiasm is infused in the executives in the form of confidence which flows from the knowledge that they are operating on the basis of knowledge of the markets and customers and not rushing into a blind alley.

Emerging from elementary sales-record keeping analysis, marketing research has widened its horizons to include not only getting facts in each function of the marketing activity but also to help solve general management problems. It has been found to be a great aid to decision-making although it is not a substitute for sound judgement. In India it has still to gain greater acceptance due to the prevalence of the seller's market in most products.

As selling becomes more difficult, as customers increase in sophistication through increased education, as competition gets strengthened, a greater need will be felt for consumer-orientation. This is bound to result in more since use of research. Even in America, researching foreign markets is of recent origin and was stimulated after the Second World War by increased competition in international markets and greater use of overseas manufacturing facilities.

There are many factors that generate resistance to great acceptance of marketing research. The basic impediment is the lack of understanding on the part of executives of the value such research. It is not so easy to measure quantitatively the results of marketing research. Again marketing research cannot predict future behaviour which is often expected by the executives. It is time marketing research was taken out of its ivory tower.

The marketing research manager himself can make a contribution in this direction. He should devote more time to learning about problems of marketing management than on worrying about techniques. He cannot be successful unless he thinks in terms of such problems. He should also work on problems of importance to management instead of devoting most of his time to the collection of statistics and preparation of routine reports. He should concentrate on matters which have an important effect on profits. Finally he should spend more time in the marketplace instead of remaining in his office. He must know his company's customers, scales force and channels of distributing. He will gain greater respect if his management knows that the research manager is aware of what really happens in the marketplace.

❐

